ASP.NET Core and Angular 2

Learn how to connect ASP.NET Core and Angular 2 to build a powerful and dynamic applications from scratch with this guide to cutting-edge web development

Valerio De Sanctis

BIRMINGHAM - MUMBAI

ASP.NET Core and Angular 2

First published: October 2016

Production reference: 2061016

Published by Packt Publishing Ltd.
Livery Place
35 Livery Street
Birmingham
B3 2PB, UK.
ISBN 978-1-78646-568-9

www.packtpub.com

Credits

Author	**Copy Editor**
Valerio De Sanctis	Safis Editing
Reviewer	**Project Coordinator**
Vincent Maverick Durano	Ulhas Kambali
Commissioning Editor	**Proofreader**
Edward Gordon	Safis Editing
Acquisition Editor	**Indexer**
Reshma Raman	Mariammal Chettiyar
Content Development Editor	**Production Coordinator**
Onkar Wani	Arvindkumar Gupta
Technical Editor	**Cover Work**
Shivani K. Mistry	Arvindkumar Gupta

About the Author

Valerio De Sanctis is a skilled IT professional with more than 12 years of experience in lead programming, web-based development, and project management using ASP.NET, PHP, and Java. He previously held senior positions at a range of financial and insurance companies, most recently serving as Chief Technology Officer and Chief Operating Officer at a leading after-sales and IT service provider for many top-tier life and non-life insurance groups.

During the course of his career Valerio De Sanctis helped many private organizations to implement and maintain .NET based solutions, working side by side with many IT industry experts and leading several frontend, backend and UX development teams. He designed the architecture and actively oversaw the development of a wide number of corporate-level web application projects for high-profile clients, customers and partners including London Stock Exchange Group, Zurich Insurance Group, Allianz, Generali, Harmonie Mutuelle, Honda Motor, FCA Group, Luxottica, ANSA, Saipem, ENI, Enel, Terna, Banzai Media, Virgilio.it, Repubblica.it, and Corriere.it.

He is an active member of the Stack Exchange Network, providing advices and tips for .NET, JavaScript, HTML5 and Web related topics on the StackOverflow, ServerFault, and SuperUser communities. Most of his projects and code samples are available under open-source licenses on GitHub, BitBucket, NPM, CocoaPods, JQuery Plugin Registry, and WordPress Plugin Repository.

He also runs an IT-oriented, web-focused blog at www.ryadel.com featuring news, reviews, code samples and guides to help developers and enthusiasts worldwide.

I would like to thank those who supported me in writing this book: my beloved and beautiful wife for her awesome encouragement and invaluable support; my children Viola and Daniele; my parents and my sister for always being there in times of need; my IT colleagues and partners in Ryadel, Teleborsa and Assirecre Group for their enduring friendship. A special thanks to Vincent Maverick Durano for helping me to work through software and UI issues to determine if they were bugs or user errors, and to all Packt Publishing folks who worked hard to bring this book to life.

About the Reviewer

Vincent Maverick Durano works as a Technical Lead Developer in a research and development company, focusing mainly on web and mobile technologies. His exploration into programming began at the age of 15; Turbo PASCAL, C, C++, JAVA, VB6, Action Scripts and a variety of other equally obscure acronyms, mainly as a hobby. After several detours, he is now on the VB.NET to C# channel. He now works on ASP.NET, C#, MSSQL, EF, LINQ, AJAX, JavaScript, JQuery, Angular, HTML5, and CSS which go together like coffee crumble ice cream. He's an eight-time Microsoft MVP, two-time C# Corner MVP, Microsoft Influencer, Dzone MVB, and a regular contributor at CodeASP.net in which he also moderate, CodeProject, C# Corner, AspSnippets, and Xamarin but more often at the official Microsoft ASP.NET community site where he became one of the All-Time Top Answerer with ALL-STAR recognition level (the highest attainable level with 100,000+ points). He authored a few e-books for C# Corner: GridView Control Pocket Guide, ASP.NET MVC5: Beginner's Guide and is now working on a new e-book entitled ASP.NET Core and Angular 2 Code Venture. He runs a blog at http://proudmonkey.azurewebsites.net/ and created a few open-source projects that is hosted in Codeplex and GitHub.

www.PacktPub.com

For support files and downloads related to your book, please visit www.PacktPub.com.

Did you know that Packt offers eBook versions of every book published, with PDF and ePub files available? You can upgrade to the eBook version at www.PacktPub.com and as a print book customer, you are entitled to a discount on the eBook copy. Get in touch with us at service@packtpub.com for more details.

At www.PacktPub.com, you can also read a collection of free technical articles, sign up for a range of free newsletters and receive exclusive discounts and offers on Packt books and eBooks.

https://www.packtpub.com/mapt

Get the most in-demand software skills with Mapt. Mapt gives you full access to all Packt books and video courses, as well as industry-leading tools to help you plan your personal development and advance your career.

Why subscribe?

- Fully searchable across every book published by Packt
- Copy and paste, print, and bookmark content
- On demand and accessible via a web browser

Table of Contents

Preface

It is common knowledge among many seasoned web developers that building a website from scratch 15 years ago was a rather simple task. To begin with, we didn't have to deal with the insane amount of screen resolutions brought by big-size monitors, ultra-high resolutions, and mobile devices; we could avoid the urge of learning a lot of (back then) "experimental" stuff such as AJAX, JSON, and XMLHttpRequest, as the established DHTML-based techniques we already knew were more than enough to get the job done; our simple, quick 'n' dirty JavaScript hacks could easily shine among friends and colleagues without being embarrassed by cross-platform JS libraries such as jQuery (2006); we didn't have to implement time-consuming and/or knowledge-demanding features such as login with Facebook, Sharing buttons, SEO meta tags, Twitter Cards and RSS feeds because they were either not there yet or not so important. On top of all that, there still weren't that many fully-featured, great-looking, award-winning CMS solutions such as Drupal (2001), Wordpress (2003), and Joomla (2005) to compare our results with.

Sounds pretty reasonable, right? Except it's not. The Web is always changing, just like the rest of the world: the complexity level of the average website is constantly increasing because the usage is more diversified, widespread and intense, however, such growing excitement was also a great thing for those who wanted to make a living out on building web applications, assuming they had the guts to keep studying, communicating, and living the blowing storm of new technologies behind these winds of change. As seasoned developers, we should be able to cope with such simple, yet inevitable truth, adapting ourselves before and better than our customers instead of being trampled by their increasing demands.

The main purpose of this book is to demonstrate that is still possible to develop great web applications from scratch, providing that we use the proper tools and have the patience to understand how we can blend them together to achieve what we want. Luckily enough, the insane amount of additional work required nowadays can be mitigated by a lot of powerful frameworks that make their way through the development scene: we're talking of server-side runtime environments like ASP.NET and Node.js and also of many client-side frameworks such as Bootstrap, jQuery, React, AngularJS and Angular 2. We chose to focus on two of them – ASP.NET Core to cover the server-side aspects, Angular 2 to deal with the client-side not only for their stunning set of features and elegant design, but also because they happen to have something revolutionary in common: they are both a complete rewrite of their massively-popular previous installments, who played a leading role in their respective field.

Why a development team should do that? What's the purpose of reinvent their own widely-acknowledged wheel despite it still rocks? The answer most likely lies in what we said earlier: in an ever-changing world such as the one we're living in we need to be humble and wise enough to keep moving forward, embracing – sometimes even enforcing – the iterative processes required to forge better tools for building a more complex, yet also more enticing World Wide Web.

The guys behind ASP.NET and Angular were brave enough to accept the challenge: after a few months of unstable releases and breaking interface changes it definitely seems that their choice was worth the effort, as they're about to hit a decisive score.

What about you?

What this book covers

Chapter 1, *Getting Ready*, introduces the ASP.NET Core and Angular 2 frameworks, explaining how they can effectively be used to build a feature-rich, modern SPA. It then enumerates the core aspects of a common SPA project, which will be addressed throughout the following chapters. The last part covers the required steps for setting up a .NET Core Web Application project, together with its required packages and components, up to a buildable and running app skeleton.

Chapter 2, *ASP.NET Controllers and Server-Side Routes*, explains how we can interchange Json data between a server-side .NET Controller and a client-side Angular 2 Component. The reader will learn how to handle the HTTP request-response cycle and also how to configure the improved routing logic built upon the .NET Core pipeline.

Chapter 3, *Angular 2 Components and Client-Side Routing*, focuses about the client-side aspects of our SPA: the reader will learn how to fetch JSON objects with Angular 2 core classes and show the retrieved data on screen using the Angular 2 Template Syntax. We will also explain how the client-side routing works in a SPA and what we need do to implement a viable routing pattern for our project using the PathLocationStrategy.

Chapter 4, *The Data Model*, is dedicated to the building of a proper, DBMS-based Data Model using Entity Framework Core. The reader will learn how to install and properly configure the required EF Core packages: we will also explain how to properly implement them to build a list of Entities and persist them into a stable Database structure using the Code-First approach.

Chapter 5, *Persisting Changes*, will explain how to update the application code to make full usage of the EF Core entities defined in Chapter 4, *The Data Model*. The reader will learn how to fetch and persist the application data by using the Database instead of the sample mocking methods.

Chapter 6, *Applying Styles*, will introduce LESS, a powerful dynamic stylesheet language that can be compiled into CSS. After a brief overview of the LESS language syntax, the reader will learn how to add, implement and compile LESS scripts within the application project to greatly improve the front-end UI.

Chapter 7, *Authentication and Authorization*, will guide the reader through the most relevant auth-related concepts for building a web application. The reader will learn how to implement a sample Token-based authentication provider and also how to properly add and configure it throughout the existing Entity Framework entities, .NET core services and HTTP middleware list.

Chapter 8, *Third-Party Authentication and External Providers*, further expands the authentication and authorization topics introducing OpenIddict, an open-source .NET library based upon the AspNet OpenID Connect Server (ASOS) that can be used to handle internal and external auth providers. The reader will learn how to install OpenIddict and configure it to support Facebook, Google and Twitter authentication.

Chapter 9, *User Registration and Account Edit*, is dedicated to account-related features such as user registration and edit account mechanism. The reader will learn how to properly handle such requests by implementing a dedicated .NET Core Controller together with a versatile Angular 2 Model-Driven form.

Chapter 10, *Finalization and Deployment*, describes the most common tasks to publish a potentially shippable web application onto a production server. The reader will learn how to replace its localDb instance with an external SQL Server, create FTP and FileSystem publishing profiles, upload their compiled application to an external server and configure it to run under IIS using the .NET Core Windows Server Hosting bundle; he will also learn how to deal with the most common issues with the help of some .NET Core specific troubleshooting techniques.

What you need for this book

- Windows 7 SP1 or newer, up to and including Windows 10.
- Visual Studio 2015 with Update 3 (or newer): any version will work, including the freely available Community Edition.
- Microsoft SQL Server 2014 (o newer) for Chapter 10, *Finalization and Deployment* only: any version will work, including the freely available Express Edition.
- Windows Server 2008 R2 (or newer) for Chapter 10, *Finalization and Deployment* only.
- All ASP.NET, Angular 2, JavaScript and CSS packages used throughout the book are open-source and freely available for download using Visual Studio package managers such as NuGet, MyGet, NPM and Bower.

Who this book is for

This book is for seasoned ASP.NET developers who already know about ASP.NET Core and Angular 2, but want to blend them together to craft a production-ready SPA.

Conventions

In this book, you will find a number of text styles that distinguish between different kinds of information. Here are some examples of these styles and an explanation of their meaning.

Code words in text, database table names, folder names, filenames, file extensions, pathnames, dummy URLs, user input, and Twitter handles are shown as follows: "We can include other contexts through the use of the include directive."

A block of code is set as follows:

```
<%@ taglib prefix="c"
    uri="http://java.sun.com/jsp/jstl/core"%>

    <!DOCTYPE html>
    <html lang="en">
        <head>
            <meta charset="utf-8">
            <meta http-equiv="X-UA-Compatible"
             content="IE=edge">
            <meta name="viewport" content="width=device-width,
             initial-scale=1">
```

When we wish to draw your attention to a particular part of a code block, the relevant lines or items are set in bold:

```
<dependency>
    <groupId>org.springframework</groupId>
    <artifactId>spring-webmvc</artifactId>
    <version>4.2.2.RELEASE</version>
</dependency>
```

Any command-line input or output is written as follows:

```
Java(TM) SE Runtime Environment (build 1.8.0_91-b15)
Java HotSpot(TM) 64-Bit Server VM (build 25.91-b15, mixed mode)
```

New terms and **important words** are shown in bold. Words that you see on the screen, for example, in menus or dialog boxes, appear in the text like this: "Click on the **Java Platform (JDK) 8u91/8u92** download link"

Warnings or important notes appear in a box like this.

Tips and tricks appear like this.

Reader feedback

Feedback from our readers is always welcome. Let us know what you think about this book—what you liked or disliked. Reader feedback is important for us as it helps us develop titles that you will really get the most out of.

To send us general feedback, simply e-mail feedback@packtpub.com, and mention the book's title in the subject of your message.

If there is a topic that you have expertise in and you are interested in either writing or contributing to a book, see our author guide at www.packtpub.com/authors.

Customer support

Now that you are the proud owner of a Packt book, we have a number of things to help you to get the most from your purchase.

Downloading the example code

You can download the example code files for this book from your account at http://www.packtpub.com. If you purchased this book elsewhere, you can visit http://www.packtpub.com/support and register to have the files e-mailed directly to you.

You can download the code files by following these steps:

1. Log in or register to our website using your e-mail address and password.
2. Hover the mouse pointer on the **SUPPORT** tab at the top.
3. Click on **Code Downloads & Errata**.
4. Enter the name of the book in the **Search** box.
5. Select the book for which you're looking to download the code files.
6. Choose from the drop-down menu where you purchased this book from.
7. Click on **Code Download**.

You can also download the code files by clicking on the **Code Files** button on the book's webpage at the Packt Publishing website. This page can be accessed by entering the book's name in the **Search** box. Please note that you need to be logged in to your Packt account.

Once the file is downloaded, please make sure that you unzip or extract the folder using the latest version of:

- WinRAR / 7-Zip for Windows
- Zipeg / iZip / UnRarX for Mac
- 7-Zip / PeaZip for Linux

The code bundle for the book is also hosted on GitHub at https://github.com/PacktPublishing/ASPdotNET-Core-and-Angular-2. We also have other code bundles from our rich catalog of books and videos available at https://github.com/PacktPublishing/. Check them out!

Downloading the color images of this book

We also provide you with a PDF file that has color images of the screenshots/diagrams used in this book. The color images will help you better understand the changes in the output. You can download this file from `https://www.packtpub.com/sites/default/files/downloads/ASPdotNETCoreAndAngular2_ColorImages.pdf`.

Errata

Although we have taken every care to ensure the accuracy of our content, mistakes do happen. If you find a mistake in one of our books—maybe a mistake in the text or the code—we would be grateful if you could report this to us. By doing so, you can save other readers from frustration and help us improve subsequent versions of this book. If you find any errata, please report them by visiting `http://www.packtpub.com/submit-errata`, selecting your book, clicking on the **Errata Submission Form** link, and entering the details of your errata. Once your errata are verified, your submission will be accepted and the errata will be uploaded to our website or added to any list of existing errata under the Errata section of that title.

To view the previously submitted errata, go to `https://www.packtpub.com/books/content/support` and enter the name of the book in the search field. The required information will appear under the **Errata** section.

Piracy

Piracy of copyrighted material on the Internet is an ongoing problem across all media. At Packt, we take the protection of our copyright and licenses very seriously. If you come across any illegal copies of our works in any form on the Internet, please provide us with the location address or website name immediately so that we can pursue a remedy.

Please contact us at `copyright@packtpub.com` with a link to the suspected pirated material.

We appreciate your help in protecting our authors and our ability to bring you valuable content.

Questions

If you have a problem with any aspect of this book, you can contact us at `questions@packtpub.com`, and we will do our best to address the problem.

1
Getting Ready

ASP.NET Core MVC is a web framework, built on top of the core .NET framework, specifically made for building efficient web applications and APIs that will be able to be reached by a massive range of clients including web browsers, mobile devices, smart TVs, web-based home automation tools, and more.

Angular 2 is the second major installment of AngularJS, a world-renowned development framework born with the idea of giving the coder the toolbox needed to build reactive, cross-platform web-based apps, which are optimized for desktop and mobile: it features a structure-rich templating approach which is based upon a natural, easy-to-write, and readable syntax.

These two frameworks were put together with the same assumption in mind: the HTTP protocol is not limited to serving web pages, it can be also used as a viable platform to build web-based APIs to effectively send and receive data. This theory has slowly made its way through the first 20 years of the World Wide Web and is now an undeniable, widely acknowledged statement, and also a fundamental pillar of almost every modern web development approach.

As for the reasons behind this perspective switch, there are plenty of good reasons for it, the most important of them being related to the intrinsic characteristics of the HTTP protocol. It is simple to use, flexible enough to match most development needs in the always-changing environment which the World Wide Web happens to be, not to mention how universal it has become nowadays, almost any platform that you can think of has an HTTP library, so HTTP services can reach a broad range of clients, including browsers, mobile devices, and traditional desktop applications.

Two players one goal

From the perspective of a fully-functional web-based application, we could say that the Web API interface provided with the ASP.NET Core framework is a programmatic set of server-side handlers used by the server to expose a number of hooks and/or endpoints to a defined request-response message system, typically expressed in structured markup languages such as JSON or XML. This "exposition" is provided using the HTTP protocol thanks to a publicly available web server (typically IIS). Similarly, Angular can be described as a modern, feature-rich client-side library that gives the browser the ability to bind input and/or output parts of an HTML web page to a flexible, reusable, and easily testable JavaScript model.

These assumptions allow us to answer a simple, yet inevitable question: can we put together the server-side strengths of ASP.NET Core's Web API capabilities with the frontend capabilities of the Angular library in order to build a modern, feature-rich, and production-ready web application?

The answer, in short, is yes. In the following chapters, we'll see how we can do that by analyzing all the fundamental aspects of a well-written, properly designed web-based product and how ASP.NET Core and/or Angular can be used to handle each one of them.

What's new in Angular 2?

The new major version of Angular is a complete rewrite of the previous one, entirely based upon TypeScript and ECMAScript 6 specifications. The choice of not making it backward compatible with the previous installment clearly demonstrates the intention of the authors to adopt a completely new approach, any developer who already knows AngularJS will undoubtedly face a huge number of breaking changes, not only in the code syntax but also in the way of thinking and designing your client app. Angular 2 is highly modular, entirely component-based, features a new and improved dependency injection model and has the main goal of being able to easily integrate with other server-side and client-side frameworks.

However, the most important reason why we're picking Angular 2 over other excellent JS libraries such as `ReactJS` and `EmberJS` is the fact that it arrives with a huge stack of features out of the box, making it way simpler to use than the aforementioned competitors. If we combine that with the consistency given by TypeScript language we could very well say that, despite being the youngster, Angular 2 has embraced the framework approach more convincingly than the others. That's a great reason to invest in it, hoping it will keep up with these compelling promises.

The ASP.NET Core revolution

Summarizing what has happened in the ASP.NET world within the last year is not an easy task, in short, we could say that we're undoubtedly facing the most important series of changes in the .NET Framework since the year it came to life. ASP.NET Core is a complete re-implementation of ASP.NET, which unites all the previous web application technologies such as MVC, Web API and Web Pages into a single programming module, formerly known as MVC6. The new framework introduces a fully featured cross-platform component, also known as .NET Core, shipped with a brand new open source **.NET Compiler Platform** (currently known as **Roslyn**), a cross-platform runtime (known as **CoreCLR**), and an improved x64 Just-In-Time compiler (**RyuJIT**).

You might be wondering what happened to ASP.NET 5 and Web API 2, as these used to be quite popular names until mid-2016.

ASP.NET 5 was the original name of ASP.NET Core, before the developers chose to rename it to emphasize the fact that it is a complete rewrite. The reasons for that, together with the Microsoft vision about the new product, are further explained in the following blog post from Scott Hanselman that anticipated the changes on January 16, 2016:

`http://www.hanselman.com/blog/ASPNET5IsDeadIntroducingASPNETCore1AndNETCore1.aspx`

For those who don't know, Scott Hanselman has been the outreach and community manager for .NET/ASP.NET/IIS/Azure and Visual Studio since 2007.

Additional information regarding the perspective switch is also available in the following article by the senior Microsoft developer (and NuGet Program Manager) Jeffrey T. Fritz:

`https://blogs.msdn.microsoft.com/webdev/216/2/1/an-update-on-asp-net-core-and-net-core/`

As for Web API 2, it was a dedicated framework for building HTTP services returning pure JSON or XML data instead of web pages. Initially born as an alternative to the MVC platform, it has been merged with the latter into the new, general-purpose web application framework known as MVC6, which is now shipped as a separate module of ASP.NET Core.

The field of choice – single-page application

In order to demonstrate how ASP.NET Core and Angular 2 can work together to their full extent, we couldn't think of anything better than building a single-page application project. The reason for that is quite obvious: although neither ASP.NET Core nor Angular came into being with the specific purpose of building a SPA, there is no better approach for showcasing some of the best features they have to offer nowadays: we're talking about HTML5 pushState API, webhooks, data transport-based requests, dynamic web components, UI data bindings, and a stateless, AJAX-driven architecture capable of flawlessly encompassing all of these.

Common features of a competitive SPA

If you have never worked on building single-page applications, you need to know what you'll be facing. If you already have, feel free to skip to the following paragraph, unless you don't mind taking another look at the key features provided by any competitive SPA:

- **No server-side round-trips**: A competitive SPA is able to redraw any part of the client UI without requiring a full server-side round-trip to retrieve a full HTML page. This is mostly achieved by implementing a separation of concerns design principle, meaning that the data will be separated from the presentation of data by using a model layer that will handle the former, and a view layer that reads from the latter.

- **Efficient routing**: A competitive SPA is able to keep track of the user current state and location during his whole navigation experience using organized, JavaScript-based routers. This is usually accomplished in one of two ways: the **Hashbang** technique and HTML5 **History API** usage. We'll talk about both of them in Chapter 2, *ASP.NET Controllers and Server-side Routes*.

- **Performance and flexibility**: A competitive SPA usually transfers all of its UI to the client thanks to its JavaScript SDK of choice (Angular, JQuery, Bootstrap, and so on). This is often good for network performance, as increasing client-side rendering and offline processing reduces the UI impact over the network. But the real deal brought about by this approach is the flexibility granted to the UI, as the developer will be able to completely rewrite the application's frontend with little to no impact on the server, aside from a few static resource files.

The list could easily grow, as these are only some of the major advantages of a properly designed, competitive SPA. These aspects play a major role nowadays, as many business websites and services are switching from their traditional multi-page application (also known as **MPA**) mindset to fully committed or hybrid single-page application based approaches. The latter have become increasingly popular since 2015 and are commonly called **Native Web Applications** (**NWAs**) because they tend to implement a number of small-scale, single-page modules bound together upon a multi-page skeleton rather than building a single, monolithic SPA.

Furthermore, there are also a lot of enterprise level single-page applications and NWAs flawlessly serving thousands of users everyday, examples include WhatsApp Web, Teleport Web, and Flickr, plus a wide amount of Google web services including Gmail, Contacts, Spreadsheet, Maps, and more. Most of these services are not there, thanks to the heat of the moment; they were intentionally built that way years ago, and they are meant to stay.

Product owner expectations

One the most interesting, yet underrated, concepts brought out by many modern agile software development frameworks such as SCRUM is the importance given to the meanings and definitions of roles. Among these, there's nothing as important as the product owner, also known as the customer in **Extreme Programming** methodology, or customer representative elsewhere. In case you don't know, he's the guy that brings the expectations you'll struggle to satisfy to the development table. He will tell you what's most important to deliver and when; he will prioritize your work based on its manifest business value rather than its underlying architectural value; he'll be entitled by the management to take decisions and make tough calls, sometimes these are great, sometimes not so, that will often have a significant impact on your development schedule. In short, he's the one in charge of the project, that's why, in order to deliver a web application matching his expectancies, you'll need to understand his vision and feel it as if it were yours.

This is always true, even if your project's product owner is your dad, wife, or best friend; even if he happens to be you.

Now that we've made that clear, let's take a look to some of the most common product owner's expectations for a typical web-based single-page application project, we ought to see if the choice of using ASP.NET Core and Angular is good enough to fulfill each one of them:

- **Early release(s)**: No matter whether you're selling a bunch of salad or web-based services, the customer will always want to see what he's buying. If you're using SCRUM, you'll have to release a potentially-shippable product at the end of each sprint; in a Waterfall-based approach you'll have Milestones, and so on. One thing is for sure, the best thing you can do in order to efficiently organize your development is to adopt an iterative and/or modular-oriented approach. ASP.NET Core and Angular, along with the strong separation of concerns granted by their underlying**MVC** or **MVVM** based patterns, will gracefully push you into the mindset needed to do just that.
- **GUI over backend**: You'll often be asked to work on the GUI and frontend functionalities because they will be the only real viewable and measurable thing for the customer. This basically means that you'll have to mock up the data model and start to work on the frontend as soon as possible, delaying everything that goes on under the hood, even if that means leaving it empty, we could say that the hood is what you need the most. Please notice that this kind of approach is not necessarily bad, by all means, we're not tying up the donkey where the (product) owner wants. On the other hand, the choice of using ASP.NET Core together with Angular will grant you the chance of easily decoupling the presentation layer and the data layer implementing the first and mocking the latter, which is a great thing to do. You'll be able to see where you're going before wasting valuable time or being forced to make potentially wrong decisions. ASP.NET Core's Web API interface will provide the proper tools to do that by allowing you to create a sample web application skeleton in a matter of seconds using **Visual Studio** Controller templates and in-memory data contexts powered by the**Entity Framework 6**, which you will be able to access using entity models and code-first. As soon as you do that, you'll be able to switch to the GUI design using the Angular 2 presentation layer toolbox as often as you want until you reach the desired results. Once you are satisfied, you'll just need to properly implement the web API controller interfaces and hook up the actual data.
- **Fast completion**: None of them will work unless you also manage to get everything done in a reasonable time span. This is one of the key reasons for choosing to adopt a server-side framework and a client-side framework working together with ease. ASP.NET Core and Angular 2 are the tools of choice not only because they're both built on solid, consistent ground, but also because they're meant to do precisely that: get the job done on their respective side and provide a usable interface to the other partner.

- **Adaptability**: As stated by the Agile manifesto, being able to respond to change requests is more important than following a plan. This is especially true in software development, where we could even claim that anything that cannot handle change is a failed project. That's another great reason to embrace the separation of concerns enforced by our two frameworks of choice, as this grants the developer the ability to manage, and even welcome, to some extent, most of the layout or structural changes that will be expected during the development phase.

That's about it. Notice that we didn't cover everything here, as it would be impossible without undertaking an actual assignment. We just tried to give an extensive answer to the following general questions. If we were to build SPA, would ASP.NET Core and Angular 2 be an appropriate choice? The answer is undoubtedly yes, especially when used together. Does it mean that we're done already? Not a chance, as we have no intention of taking this assumption for granted. Conversely, it's time for us to demonstrate it by ceasing to speak in general terms and starting to put things in motion.

A sample single-page application project

What we need now is to conceive a suitable test-case scenario similar to the ones we will eventually have to deal with: a fully featured, production-ready single-page application project complete with all the core aspects you would expect from a potentially shippable product.

In order to do this, the first thing we need to do is to become our own customer for a minute and come up with an idea, a vision to share with our own other self. We'll then be able to put our developer shoes back on and split our abstract plan into a list of items we'll need to implement: these will be the core requirements of our own project. Finally, we'll set up our workstation by getting the required packages, adding the resource files, and configuring both the ASP.NET Core and Angular 2 frameworks into the Visual Studio 2015 IDE.

The vision

If we're going to demonstrate the key features of ASP.NET Core and Angular we can't really take into consideration the number of presentation-oriented websites such as demos, product galleries, corporate or marketing showcases, photo/video/media reels, and so on, as we need something that can show the asynchronous and parallel request processing capabilities of both frameworks to their full extent. In order to fulfill these expectations, we would instead need something similar to a blog engine, a content-management system, and/or a groupware platform such as a community forum or a wiki.

The latter seems to be the most appropriate, as it will mean going through a number of implementation challenges including account management, login/session handling, search-based navigation, full-text search queries, titles and contents indexing, multi-language support, markup syntax rendering, dynamic media handling and a not-so-trivial data model on top of an ever-growing, potentially huge amount of data.

The application we are going to build won't be just a shallow demonstration; we won't throw some working code here and there and expect the reader to connect the dots. Our objective is to create a solid, realistic application using our frameworks of choice while following the current development best practices. Each chapter will be dedicated to a single core aspect and if you feel like you already know your way there, feel free to skip to the next one. Conversely, if you're willing to follow us through the whole loop, you'll have a great journey through the most useful aspects of ASP.NET Core and Angular 2 and how they can work together to deliver the most common and useful web development tasks, from the most trivial ones to the more complex beasts. It's an investment that will pay dividends, as it will leave you with a maintainable, extensible, and well-structured project, plus the knowledge needed to build your own.

To avoid making things too boring, we'll pick an enjoyable, enticing theme from the entertainment industry: a collaborative, wiki-enabled database of open-source video games, where registered users will be able to add/modify entries.

We'll call it **OpenGameList**, also known as `opengamelist.com`. Luckily enough, the domain was still available at the time of writing this book. If you go there now, you'll be able to see what we're going to build from scratch (don't do that if you don't like spoilers, as it could ruin some of your fun).

Core requirements

Our application will follow a rather classic approach: our users will be able to browse the latest entries and navigate through the wiki using internal wiki links or via simple or complex search queries. If they're authenticated, they'll also be allowed to switch to edit mode to modify an item or add a new one, otherwise, they'll be prompted to enter their credentials via a classic login or registration form. On top of all that, we'll also add an administration area where we can do our management stuff such as deleting entries, editing/disabling/deleting users, running maintenance tasks, and so on.

Let's break down these requirements to a list of development topics:

- **Routing**: The app will be able to properly respond to client requests, that is to say, routing them accordingly to what they're up to.
- **Data model**: We'll definitely adopt a database engine to store our entries and the proper tools to access it in a modern, fashionable way. In order do so, we need to define our data architecture by setting up Data Repositories and Domain Entities that will be handled by the server and hooked to Angular 2 through ASP.NET Core's Web API controller interfaces.
- **Web API controllers**: From an MVC-based architectural perspective, one of the main differences between multi-page and single-page applications is that the former's controllers are designed to return views, while the latter ones, also known as API controllers, return serialized data. These are what we will need to implement to put Angular 2 components in charge of the presentation layer.
- **Angular components**: Switching to client-side, we will need to define a set of components to handle UI elements and state changes. As you probably already know, components are the most fundamental elements in Angular 2, replacing Angular 1's controllers and scopes. We'll get to know more about them soon enough.
- **Authentication**: Soon enough we'll have the need to empower our application with a membership context, that way we'll be able to restrict CRUD operations to authenticated users only, keep track of each user actions, prepare the administration layer, and so on.

These will be our main development challenges: if we don't know how to properly handle them, we won't be able to succeed.

The following chapters will address each one of them: we'll also cover other important aspects such as SEO, security, and deployment, as they will be very important when you are ready to publish your application.

Preparing the workspace

The first thing we have to do is to set up our workstation: it won't be difficult because we only need a small set of essential tools. These include Visual Studio 2015, the web platform installer, .NET Framework 4.5 or higher, a web server such as IIS or IIS Express, and a decent source code control system such as Git, Mercurial, or Team Foundation, which we will take for granted as you most likely already have them in place. Just make sure you're all set with these before going further.

IMPORTANT

If you haven't already, be sure to download and install **Visual Studio 2015 Update 3** and the **.NET Core for Visual Studio Tools Preview 2**. These are the latest updates at the time of writing, but will be updated in the near future.

These updates will address some important issues for web development tools, as well as adding improved support for **TypeScript**, **NPM**, and other components that we'll be using later on:

- **Visual Studio 2015 Update 3**: `http://go.microsoft.com/fwlink/?LinkId=691129`

- **.NET Core for Visual Studio Tools Preview 2.0.1**: `https://go.microsoft.com/fwlink/?LinkID=824849`

Setting up the project

The first thing we need to do is to create a new **ASP.NET Core web application project**:

1. Fire up Visual Studio 2015 and, from the **File** menu, expand **New** and select **Project** to open a new project modal window.

2. From the **Templates** tree, expand the **Visual C#** node and select the **Web** subfolder: the right section of the modal window will be populated by a number of available project templates. Among these, there are two choices for creating an ASP.NET Core web application project: the first one, optimized for cross-platform deployment, entirely relies upon the new .NET Core Framework; the other one, ideal for a Windows environment, is based upon the latest .NET Framework version (4.6.1 at the time of writing).

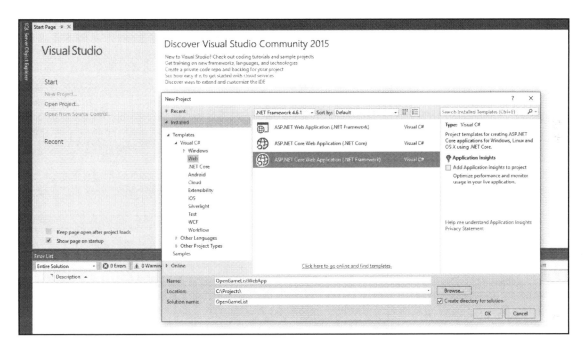

3. The good thing here is that, thanks to the ASP.NET Core versatility, we are free to choose the approach we like the most, as both frameworks are mature enough to support almost everything we will use within this book. The only relevant downside of the .NET Core choice is the lack of compatibility with some NuGet packages that haven't been ported there yet: that's why, at least for our example, we'll be choosing to stick with the full-scale .NET Framework. In order to do that, select the **ASP.NET Core Web Application (.NET Framework)** template and fill in the relevant **Name**, **Location**, and **Solution name** fields. We'll name the solution **OpenGameList**, while the project will be called**OpenGameListWebApp**, as shown in the previous screenshot. Once done, click **OK** to continue.

4. In the next modal window, we can further customize our template by choosing the default contents to include in our project (Empty, Web API, or Web Application) and the authentication mechanism, should we want to use one. Choose **Web API** and **No authentication**, then click the **OK** button to create the project.

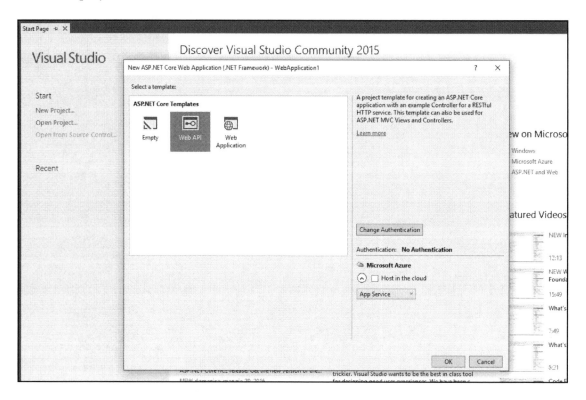

5. If you're used to the Visual Studio Web Application Project templates from previous ASP.NET versions you may be tempted to choose **Empty** instead, thus avoiding the insane amount of sample classes, folders, and components, including a number of potentially outdated versions of various client-side frameworks such as **Bootstrap**, **KnockoutJS**, **JQuery**, and more. Luckily, these new ASP.NET Core project templates are extremely lightweight – the one we did choose comes with nothing more than a /Controller/ folder, a ValuesController.cs sample, and some useful references in the Startup.cs file.

Package and resource managers

Now that our project has been created, it's time to add the resources we're going to use. As we already mentioned, the layout of a standard ASP.NET Core solution is quite different from what it used to be. The main differences are:

- The solution's projects are now created in a `/src/` folder by default. This is just a convention, though, as they can be placed anywhere.
- There is a brand-new `wwwroot` folder, which will contain the compiled, ready-to-publish contents of our application, while everything else will be the project source code.

Other things worth noting are a `Controller` folder, containing a sample `ValueController.cs` class, a `Startup.cs` file containing the application class and a couple of other files we'll address in a while.

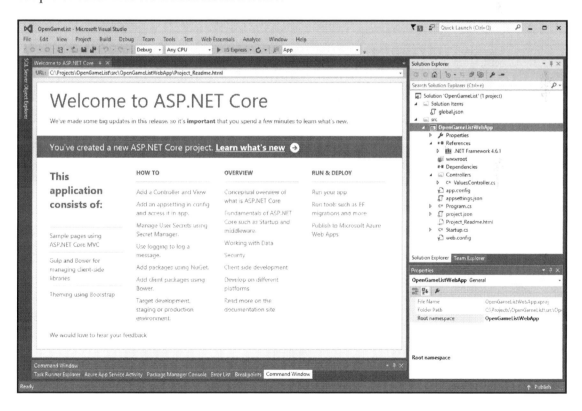

The first thing we need to do is to add a folder called `Scripts` to the root of our project. We'll use this folder to place all of our JavaScript files, and then we'll combine and minify these using a **JavaScript Task Runner** such as Gulp, this way we'll make sure that the resulting file will be added to the `wwwroot` folder automatically after each build.

Installing the packages

Now it's time to make a good use of the three package managers natively supported by ASP.NET, namely **NuGet**, **NPM**, and **Bower**. These tools will allow you to gather all the resources you need to build your application: they will download all the resources and their dependencies automatically, so you needn't do it manually, thus saving a lot of time. In case you're wondering why we need three of them, it can be useful to briefly recap their scope:

- **NuGet**: This will take care of all the .NET native and third-party packages such as Entity Framework, ASP.NET MVC, and so on. The full package list is stored in the `project.json` file so they can be retrieved and/or checked for updates at any time.
- **NPM**: This was the default package manager for the JavaScript runtime environment known as **Node.js**. Over the last few years, though, it has also been used to host a number of projects, libraries, and frameworks of any kind, including **Angular 2**. The package list is stored in the `package.json` file.
- **Bower**: Another package management system for client-side programming, created by Twitter and maintained on GitHub, specifically designed for frontend development such as **jQuery**, **Bootstrap**, and **AngularJS**. It depends on Node.js and NPM and works under `git`. Its configuration file is called `bower.json`. Notice that, since the Angular 2 team is pushing their code using NPM rather than Bower, we won't be using it in our project.

NuGet and ASP.NET

ASP.NET Core gives us at least four different ways to add NuGet packages to our project:

- Using the Visual Studio powered GUI, accessible by right-clicking the project and choosing **Manage NuGet Packages**.
- Using the Package Manager Console, with the well-renowned `Install-Package` command followed by the package name and build version.

- Using the on-screen helper tools provided by Intellisense, limited to the native .NET modules/libraries.
- Directly adding the package reference to the project's NPM configuration file, also known as `project.json`.

The first three methods, although being absolutely viable, are basically shortcuts for populating the fourth one; the latter has the advantage of being the less opaque one, so we'll just use it.

Project.json

Open the `project.json` file, find the `dependencies` section and add the following packages to the list (new lines are highlighted):

```
"dependencies": {
  "Microsoft.AspNetCore.Mvc": "1.0.0",
  "Microsoft.AspNetCore.Server.IISIntegration": "1.0.0",
  "Microsoft.AspNetCore.Server.Kestrel": "1.0.0",
  "Microsoft.Extensions.Configuration.EnvironmentVariables": "1.0.0",
  "Microsoft.Extensions.Configuration.FileExtensions": "1.0.0",
  "Microsoft.Extensions.Configuration.Json": "1.0.0",
  "Microsoft.Extensions.Logging": "1.0.0",
  "Microsoft.Extensions.Logging.Console": "1.0.0",
  "Microsoft.Extensions.Logging.Debug": "1.0.0",
  "Microsoft.Extensions.Options.ConfigurationExtensions": "1.0.0",
  "Microsoft.AspNetCore.Diagnostics": "1.0.0",
  "Microsoft.AspNetCore.Routing": "1.0.0",
  "Microsoft.AspNetCore.Authentication.JwtBearer": "1.0.0",
  "Microsoft.AspNetCore.StaticFiles": "1.0.0",
  "Microsoft.VisualStudio.Web.BrowserLink.Loader": "14.0.0"  }
```

We have added a space to visually separate the default dependencies required by all ASP.NET Core projects from our newly added ones.

The listed builds are the latest at the time of writing, but they won't last forever: as soon as ASP.NET Core passes its initial release (1.0.0 at the time of writing), these numbers will gradually increase over time, whenever a new version comes out. To check the latest version of each package, just place the cursor between the quotes and delete the version number, a dynamic drop-down list will be shown containing all the latest versions for that given module.

While we're here, it can be useful to check which version of the .NET Framework we are targeting by looking at the `frameworks` key. Since we choose the .NET Framework template, we should find something like this:

```
"frameworks": {
  "net461": { }
},
```

This will most likely change in the future, so be sure to target a version compatible with the packages you want to use. For the purpose of this book, the **.NET Framework 4.6.1** will do the job.

As soon as we save the `project.json` file, Visual Studio will start to retrieve the missing packages from the web. Wait for it to finish, then proceed with opening the `Startup.cs` file, which is also in the project root.

Startup.cs

If you're a seasoned .NET developer you might already be familiar with the `Startup.cs` file, introduced in OWIN-based applications to replace most of the tasks previously handled by the good old `Global.asax` file. In ASP.NET Core, the `Startup.cs` file serves the same purpose as the `OWIN` startup class, being nothing less than the application main entry point, it is the place where we can add services, choose which application modules and middleware functions to load, handle dependency injection tasks, and configure the pipeline.

However, the similarities end here, the class has been completely rewritten to be as pluggable and lightweight as possible, meaning that it will include and load only what's strictly necessary to fulfill our application's tasks.

To better understand this, let's take a look at the following lines taken from the `Startup.cs` source code shipped with the ASP.NET Core Web API project template we chose:

```
// This method gets called by the runtime. Use this method to configure the
HTTP request pipeline.
public void Configure(IApplicationBuilder app, IHostingEnvironment env,
ILoggerFactory loggerFactory)
{
    loggerFactory.AddConsole(Configuration.GetSection("Logging"));
    loggerFactory.AddDebug();

    app.UseMvc();
}
```

Notice how empty our application's HTTP request pipeline is, it won't ever serve static files, since there is nothing telling it to do so. To better understand it, let's perform a quick test before proceeding.

Testing the HTTP request pipeline

In order to check that the ASP.NET pipeline is properly working, click on the **Start** Debugging option in the **Debug** menu, or just hit the *F5* hotkey. If everything is OK, your default web browser will open pointing to the following URL: `http://localhost:14600/api/values`.

The page content will show the following:

If we're seeing the preceding screenshot, it means that the request pipeline is working fine, the MVC module has been added within the `Startup.cs` file and it's working as expected. That's because there's a sample `ValueController.cs` class in the `/Controllers/` folder, conveniently added by the Web API project template we chose a while ago, that behaves exactly like this.

Now let's try to request the static `Project_Readme.html` file, also added by our chosen template in the project root. In order to reach it, we need to move it inside the `/wwwroot/` folder. Once done, it should be reachable by pointing at the following URL: `http://localhost:14600/Project_Readme.html`.

However, if we try to do that, and then issue that request using the same browser we used before, we would get the following response:

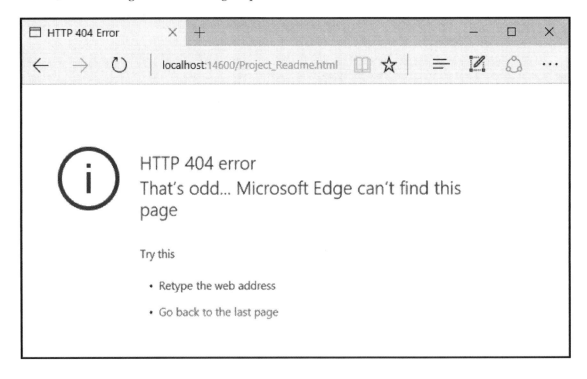

This HTTP 404 error clearly demonstrates what we've just said, the HTTP request pipeline won't serve static files, simply because we didn't tell it to. However, we can easily fix that behavior by adding them to the pipeline within the `Startup.cs` file (new lines highlighted):

```
// This method gets called by the runtime. Use this method to configure the
HTTP request pipeline.
public void Configure(IApplicationBuilder app, IHostingEnvironment env,
ILoggerFactory loggerFactory)
{
    loggerFactory.AddConsole(Configuration.GetSection("Logging"));
    loggerFactory.AddDebug();

    // Configure a rewrite rule to auto-lookup for standard default files
such as index.html.     app.UseDefaultFiles();
    // Serve static files (html, css, js, images & more). See also the
following URL:
    // https://docs.asp.net/en/latest/fundamentals/static-files.html for
further reference.
    app.UseStaticFiles();
    // Add MVC to the pipeline
    app.UseMvc();
}
```

While we are here, we also added the following:

- A rewrite rule to enable support for the most common default files (such as `index.htm`, `index.html`, and so on), which will be automatically served without the user having to fully qualify the URI.
- A series of comments to better clarify the meaning of each module, including a reference link to the official ASP.NET Core documentation.

If we run our application again, we should now be welcomed with the following:

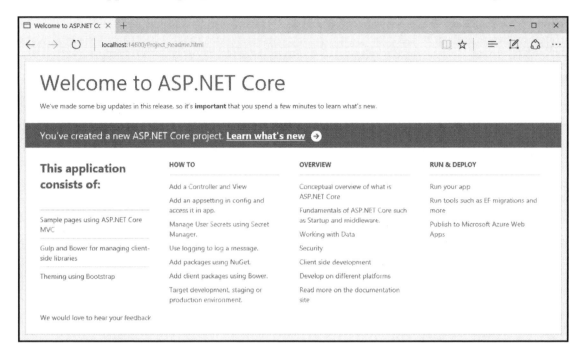

That's it. We have enabled static file support, so that we'll be able to serve not only HTML but also CSS, JS files, and so on. Delete the `Project_Readme.html` and get ready to install an important third-party NuGet package that we'll be using a lot in the following chapters.

Newtonsoft.Json

If you're working with ASP.NET and you've never heard about **Newtonsoft.Json** (formerly **Json.NET**), you've almost certainly missed something that could've eased your job, big time. We're talking about one of the finest libraries – and most useful tools, ever developed for .NET, at least for the writer. It's a very efficient (and thus very popular), high-performance JSON serializer, deserializer, and all-around framework for .NET, which also happens to be completely open source.

We won't dig into it anymore here, as we'll be using it soon enough. For now, let's just install it by right-clicking on our solution's node in the **Solution Explorer**, then choosing **Manage NuGet Packages for this Solution...** to open up the following panel:

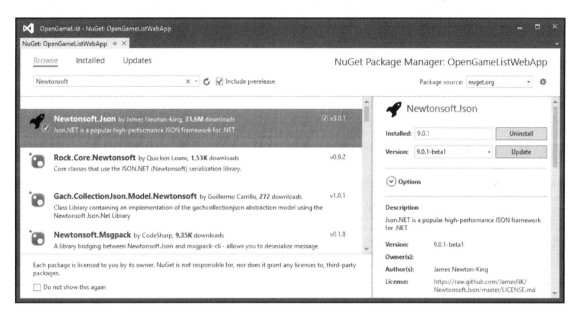

Search for `Newtonsoft.Json` to make it appear if it isn't there already, then left-click to select it. Ensure to select the latest stable version (9.0.1 at the time of writing), click on **Install**, and then wait for the installer to complete its job.

That's it for now: if we open the `project.json` file now, we can see that the `Newtonsoft.Json` package reference has been added at the end of the `dependencies` section, together with the other project-specific dependencies we've manually added before. We'll be installing other packages using the GUI in the following chapters, as soon as we need them, now that we know how easy it is to do that.

JavaScript, TypeScript, or Dart?

Now it's time to choose the client programming language to adopt. Given the fact we're planning to use Angular 2, our choices are basically the following three: good old JavaScript, its Microsoft superset known as **TypeScript**, or the Google growing beast known as **Dart**.

In this project, we're going to use TypeScript for a number of good reasons, the most important of them are as follows:

- TypeScript has a number of features that JavaScript doesn't, such as static typing, classes, and interfaces. Using it in Visual Studio also gives us the chance to benefit from the built-in IntelliSense, which, together with its distinctive features, will allow us to spot most programming errors as we type the code, potentially saving a great amount of time.

- For a large client-side project, TypeScript will allow us to produce a more robust code, which will also be fully deployable anywhere a plain JavaScript file would run. As a matter of fact, since TypeScript is a superset of JavaScript it can be used alongside any JavaScript code without problems.

- Dart is a wonderful newcomer, and it will probably surpass its ECMA script-rivals soon. Currently though, it is still quite immature in terms of available third-party libraries, documentation, development support, and overall community knowledge.

We're not the only ones praising TypeScript: it's something acknowledged by the Angular team itself, considering the fact that the Angular 2 source code has been written using TypeScript, as proudly announced by Microsoft in the following MDSN blog post: `https:/ /blogs.msdn.microsoft.com/typescript/215/3/5/angular-2-built-on-typescript/`.

Adding the tsconfig.json file

The first thing we hav to do to set up TypeScript is to add a `tsconfig.json` file to our root project.

In the **e to do to set up TypeScript is to add a tsconfig.json file to our root project. In the Solution Explorer**, right-click on the root project node and select **Add**, then **New Item**; switch to the **client-side** from the top left tree view, then select **TypeScript Configuration File,** and add the `tsconfig.json` file to the project root.

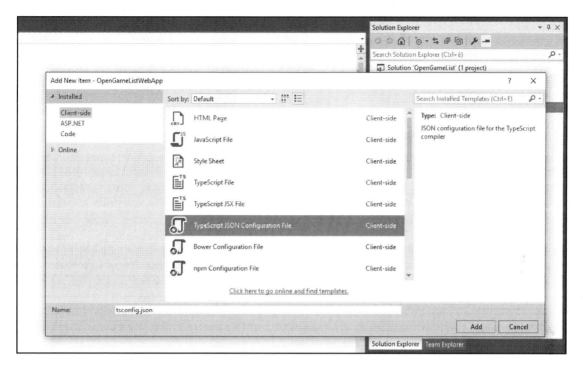

The `tsconfig.json` file will be generated with its default set of options, which are good for most scenarios but not ideal for what we're going to do. That's why we need to add/change some settings until it will look like the following:

```json
{
  "compileOnSave": false,
  "compilerOptions": {
    "emitDecoratorMetadata": true,
    "experimentalDecorators": true,
    "module": "system",
    "moduleResolution": "node",
    "noImplicitAny": false,
    "noEmitOnError": false,
    "removeComments": false,
    "target": "es5"
  },
  "exclude": [
    "node_modules",
    "wwwroot"
  ]
}
```

These instructions will influence how Intellisense and our external TypeScript compiler will work; two things that will help us, big time.

Wait a minute, did we just say external TypeScript compiler? What about the built-in, integrated TypeScript compile feature provided by the Visual Studio IDE?

Well, we just said that one of TypeScript's biggest advantages is that we can use it anywhere a plain JavaScript file would run, that's because any .ts file can be compiled into a .js file without any problem. The compile task is handled by the TypeScript compiler itself, also known as **tsc**, which can be run directly from the Visual Studio IDE with the help of the tsconfig.json we added in the preceding paragraph. That file, as we've just seen, contains a wide set of compiling options such as creating source maps, creating definition files, concatenating everything into a single output file, and so on. Looking great, isn't it?

Unfortunately, not so much. Although Visual Studio 2015 does a pretty decent job of acting as a bridge between our TypeScript sources and **tsc**, it still lacks an important key feature, it doesn't give the option to minify/uglify the resulting JS files, thus leaving them uncompressed after the compile task.

Such feature can be trivial during development, yet it happens to be quite important in production because we'll definitely want to cloak our source code before publishing it. That's why the best thing we can do is to stop the Visual Studio IDE from compiling TypeScript files and implement a custom alternative that does support minify/uglify.

 In case you're wondering about what the terms minify and/or uglify actually mean, we strongly suggest that you read the following Wikipedia page: https://en.wikipedia.org/wiki/Minification_(programming).

Luckily, we're going to use something we would need anyway, a dedicated, streamlined, and modern task runner that goes by the name of **Gulp**. In order to install it, though, we need to set up the appropriate package manager.

Introducing NPM

NPM is the tool we will use to add some important packages to our project, the most relevant ones being **Gulp** and **Angular 2**. To install it, do the following:

1. Go to the **Solution Explorer.**
2. Right-click on the root project node.
3. Select **Add**, then **New Item.**
4. Switch to **Client-side** from the top left tree view, then select **NPM Configuration File**, and add the package.json file to the project root.

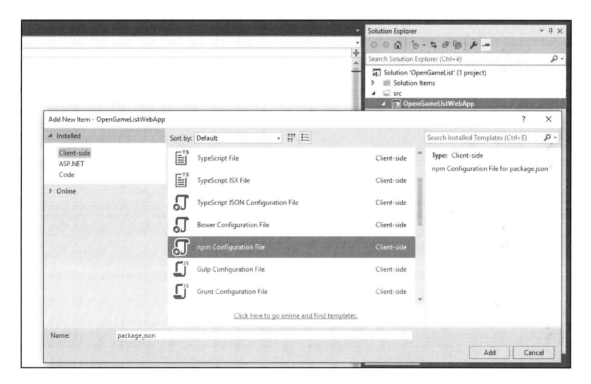

Change the contents of the automatically-generated `package.json` file to match the following:

```
{
    "version": "1.0.0",
    "name": "opengamelistwebapp",
    "private": true,
    "dependencies": {
    },
    "devDependencies": {
        "gulp": "^3.9.1",
        "gulp-clean": "^0.3.2",
        "gulp-concat": "^2.6.0",
        "gulp-sourcemaps": "^1.6.0",
        "gulp-typescript": "^2.13.6",
        "gulp-uglify": "^2.0.0",
        "typescript": "^1.8.10"
    }
}
```

Please notice that, at the time of writing, Gulp 3.9.1 is the latest version. You can check the most recent build by checking the Visual Studio **Intellisense**, which is able to perform impressive real-time update checks upon each package's latest build just like it does within the `project.json` file:

As an alternative, you can always visit the Gulp project NPM page at `https://www.npmjs.com/package/gulp` and change the build version numbers accordingly.

Notice that you aren't forced to input precise build numbers, as you can also use the standard **npmjs** syntax to specify auto-update rules bound to custom version ranges using the supported prefixes, such as the following:

- **The Tilde (~)**: ~1.1.4 will match all 1.1.x versions, excluding 1.2.0, 1.0.x and so on.
- **The Caret (^)**: ^1.1.4 will match everything above 1.1.4, excluding 2.0.0 and above.

This is another scenario where Intellisense will come in handy, as it will also suggest how to do it.

 For an extensive list of available `npmjs` commands and prefixes, you can also check out the official npmjs documentation at `https://docs.npmjs.com/files/package.json`.

Working with Gulp

As you most likely already know, Gulp is a powerful task runner toolkit that we will use to automate some time-consuming tasks in our development workflow. If you never worked with a task runner, think of it as a batch file or, even better, a PowerShell script powered with some useful web development tools such as file concatenation, js/css shrinking, and more.

You will notice that, together with Gulp, we're also installing some Gulp-related plugins:

- `gulp-clean`: This deletes the contents of the destination folders
- `gulp-concat`: This merges multiple files into one
- `gulp-sourcemaps`: This generates the Source Maps
- `gulp-typescript`: This compiles TypeScript files into JS
- `gulp-uglify`: This minifies JavaScript files

Configuring Gulp is as simple as adding the **Gulp Configuration** file to your project. You can do that just like you did with the **NPM Configuration** file, right-click on the root project node in the **Solution Explorer** and select **Add**, then **New Item**. From the **client-side** tree panel, locate and select the **Gulp Configuration** file and add a `gulpfile.js` file to the project root.

The Gulp configuration file, generally known as **Gulpfile**, is basically a list of tasks and commands that Gulp will execute, written using a mostly readable JavaScript syntax. Working with it can be tricky at first, especially if you want to use it to handle complex tasks. Digging too much into it would take us out of the scope of this book, so we'll just see how we can tell it to do a rather simple set of jobs, merge all the JavaScript files in the /Scripts/ folder, minus those in a directory for third-party scripts/libraries, into a single, minified all.min.js file which will be generated into the wwwroot folder. This can be obtained with the following code:

```
var gulp = require('gulp'),
    gp_clean = require('gulp-clean'),
    gp_concat = require('gulp-concat'),
    gp_sourcemaps = require('gulp-sourcemaps'),
    gp_typescript = require('gulp-typescript'),
    gp_uglify = require('gulp-uglify');

/// Define paths
var srcPaths = {
    app: ['Scripts/app/main.ts', 'Scripts/app/**/*.ts'],
    js: ['Scripts/js/**/*.js']
};

var destPaths = {
    app: 'wwwroot/app/',
    js: 'wwwroot/js/'
};
// Compile, minify and create sourcemaps all TypeScript files and place
them to wwwroot/app, together with their js.map files.
gulp.task('app', function () {
    return gulp.src(srcPaths.app)
        .pipe(gp_sourcemaps.init())
        .pipe(gp_typescript(require('./tsconfig.json').compilerOptions))
        .pipe(gp_uglify({ mangle: false }))
        .pipe(gp_sourcemaps.write('/'))
        .pipe(gulp.dest(destPaths.app));
});

// Delete wwwroot/app contents
gulp.task('app_clean', function () {
    return gulp.src(destPaths.app + "*", { read: false })
        .pipe(gp_clean({ force: true }));
});

// Copy all JS files from external libraries to wwwroot/js
gulp.task('js', function () {
    return gulp.src(srcPaths.js)
        // .pipe(gp_uglify({ mangle: false })) // disable uglify
```

```
        // .pipe(gp_concat('all-js.min.js')) // disable concat
        .pipe(gulp.dest(destPaths.js));
});

// Delete wwwroot/js contents
gulp.task('js_clean', function () {
    return gulp.src(destPaths.js + "*", { read: false })
    .pipe(gp_clean({ force: true }));
});

// Watch specified files and define what to do upon file changes
gulp.task('watch', function () {
    gulp.watch([srcPaths.app, srcPaths.js], ['app', 'js']);
});
// Global cleanup task
gulp.task('cleanup', ['app_clean', 'js_clean']);

// Define the default task so it will launch all other tasks
gulp.task('default', ['app', 'js', 'watch']);
```

Here's a brief explanation of what these commands actually do:

- In lines 1-6, we set up Gulp and the required plugins. Notice that every one of them will be initialized into a variable, as that's the way Gulp works.

- In lines 8-17,we define the file paths we will use. Doing that here will allow us to write them only once, thus making the Gulp file easier to maintain. Notice that we're splitting the source and the destination paths into two distinct objects, this will mentally help us to keep the development environment separated from the production one.

- In lines 19-27, we have the app task, which is the most important and complex one. This task makes use of three different plugins: sourcemaps, typescript, and uglify. Notice how each line is bound to a specific plugin action, which takes care of a single job, following the *"It should do one thing"* paradigm Gulp is all about. Line 21 defines the source files, line 22 initializes the sourcemaps plugin, line 23 instructs the plugin to fetch the TypeScript compiler options from the tsconfig.json file, and so on.

- In lines 29-33, we have the app_clean task, which will erase every file and subfolder within the wwwroot/app target path.

- In lines 35-39, we define the `js` task, which is meant to publish external JavaScript libraries manually added to the project. This is a rather simple task, as it performs a mere copy of the `.js` files from a source folder into its production counterpart. Notice how we could easily choose to also minify and/or concatenate the source files into a single one by uncommenting a few lines of code. However, since this task is meant to handle third-party JavaScript libraries, it would be wise not to manipulate their code.

- In lines 43-47, there's the `js_clean` task that will erase everything within the `wwwroot/js` target path.

- In lines 49-52, we have the `watch` task. This is basically a file watcher/monitoring task that will execute the `app` and `js` tasks if one or more of their source files will change.

- In lines 54-55, we created a `cleanup` task that will erase the content of all destination paths by launching the `app_clean` and `js_clean` tasks. It can be useful to reset these folders to their initial state.

- Last but not least, in lines 57-58, we define the `default` task that will execute all the other tasks, including `watch`, within a single call. This is the one we will launch.

 It's worth noting that the **uglify** plugin requires the `mangle` option to be set to `false`: this is a workaround for a bug in the Angular 2 RC5 that will hopefully be fixed in future releases. For more info regarding this topic, check out the following URL from the official Angular 2 GitHub repository: `https://github.com/angular/angular/issues/1618`.

To execute the Gulp file, right-click on it from the **Solution Explorer** and choose **Task Runner Explorer**, or open it manually by selecting it from **File**, **Other Windows** in the Visual Studio 2015 main menu bar. Once opened, click the refresh button, then right-click the `default` task and select **Run** to activate it.

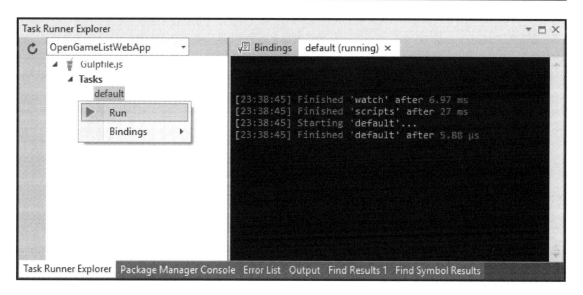

Once you do that, the `watch` task we just created will silently run in background, keeping tracks of our changes and act accordingly. Notice the **default (running)** word within the tab label, which will remind us that there is still an ongoing task: closing that console window will immediately shut it down.

That's everything we'll ever need from Gulp for this project; there's no need for us to go further. If you want to learn more about Gulp and its configuration file syntax, you will find a lot of resources and documentation, together with a lot of useful samples, in the official website at the following address: `http://gulpjs.com/`.

Dependent tasks

Since we're going to do a lot of modifications to the files contained in the `/Scripts/app/` folder within the following chapters, it would be great if the `app_clean` task could run automatically before the `app` task: such behavior would ensure that we'll always get rid of outdated and orphaned files without having to manually perform the `cleanup`. Luckily enough, Gulp allows us to easily do that by passing an optional array of dependent tasks that will be launched before the main one.

Let's go back to the line where we defined the `app` task and add the following (updated code are highlighted):

```
gulp.task('app', ['app_clean'], function () {
```

That's it. From now on the `app` task will launch the `app_clean` dependent task and wait for its completion before executing itself, meaning that the `/wwwroot/app/` folder contents will be erased before the arrival of the new file, this is precisely what we wanted.

 It's worth noting that the synchronous behavior of the `app_clean` task is guaranteed by its `return` value, whenever a dependent task is returning itself, the main task will wait for its completion before running.

Using Grunt instead of Gulp

Before Gulp was widely welcomed by the web application development community, **Grunt** used to be the king of the hill. Does that mean the former killed the latter? Well, most certainly not. Grunt is still an excellent tool and can be a great alternative to Gulp, especially if you already know how to use it. Unless you do, though, we suggest starting with Gulp because we think that it has a fair edge on code flexibility, and also a more streamlined approach. However, if you don't feel like using it, sticking to Grunt and its renowned plugins is just as good, you won't ever get fired for such a choice.

Using Grunt instead of Gulp is as easy as doing the following:

1. In **NPM's** `package.json` file, replace the Gulp references – together with the relevant plugins, with the Grunt packages.
2. In the **Solution Explorer**, add a `gruntfile.js` file instead of a `gulpfile.js`.
3. In the `gruntfile.js`, rewrite the same tasks defined previously using the Grunt syntax.

This is a good example of the Grunt-powered `package.json`:

```
{
  "version": "1.0.0",
  "name": "opengamelistwebapp",
  "private": true,
  "dependencies": {
  },
  "devDependencies": {
    "grunt": "^0.4.5",
    "grunt-contrib-clean": "^1.0.0",
    "grunt-contrib-copy": "^1.0.0",
```

```
    "grunt-contrib-uglify": "^1.0.0",
    "grunt-contrib-watch": "^0.6.1",
    "grunt-ts": "^5.3.2",
  }
}
```

And this is how the `gruntfile.js` would look after porting all the Gulp tasks defined previously to Grunt syntax:

```
module.exports = function (grunt) {
    grunt.loadNpmTasks('grunt-contrib-clean');
    grunt.loadNpmTasks('grunt-contrib-copy');
    grunt.loadNpmTasks('grunt-contrib-uglify');
    grunt.loadNpmTasks('grunt-contrib-watch');
    grunt.loadNpmTasks('grunt-ts');

    grunt.initConfig({
        clean: [
            'Scripts/app/*',
            'Scripts/js/*'
        ],
        ts: {
            base: {
                src: [
                    'Scripts/app/main.ts',
                    'Scripts/app/**/*.ts'
                    ],
                outDir: 'wwwroot/ app',
                tsconfig: './tsconfig.json'
            }
        },
        uglify: {
            my_target: {
                files: [{
                    expand: true,
                    cwd: 'wwwroot/ app',
                    src: ['**/*.js'],
                    dest: 'wwwroot/ app'
                }]
            },
            options: {
                sourceMap: true
            }
        },

        // Copy all JS files from external libraries and required NPM
packages to wwwroot/js
        copy: {
```

```
        main: {
            files: [{
                expand: true,
                flatten: true,
                src: [
                    'Scripts/js/**/*.js'
                ],
                dest: 'wwwroot/js/',
                filter: 'isFile'
            }]
        }
    },

    // Watch specified files and define what to do upon file changes
    watch: {
        scripts: {
            files: [
                'Scripts/**/*.ts',
                'Scripts/**/*.js',
                ],
            tasks: ['clean', 'ts', 'uglify', 'copy']
        }
    }
});

// Global cleanup task
grunt.registerTask('cleanup', ['clean']);

// Define the default task so it will launch all other tasks
grunt.registerTask('default', ['clean', 'ts', 'uglify', 'copy',
'watch']);
};
```

As we can see, the syntax is very different but the underlying logic and features are quite similar, we still have a bunch of dedicated tasks to handle TypeScript files, minify actions, copy operations, and monitor content change, and then the default one to wrap everything up. Notice how, just like we did with Gulp, the TypeScript compiler options are fetched from the `tsconfig.json` file so we don't have to write them a second time.

 To learn more about Grunt and its configuration file syntax you can visit the official website at the following address: http://gruntjs.com/.

That's basically all we need to know about task runners. Too bad we don't yet have any TS and/or JS files to properly test what we just did! Don't worry, though, we'll get there soon enough. Before that, let's finish our **NPM** journey by bringing the last (but not least) of our players into the loop.

Adding Angular 2

There are basically two ways to get Angular 2, both with their pros and cons, using NPM, which implies fetching the latest build and hosting the code within our project, or by a dedicated set of links to a suitable CDN.

Using NPM

To install Angular 2 using NPM we need to open the `package.json` file and add a bunch of packages under the `dependencies` node. This is how the file should look like at the end (Angular lines are highlighted):

```json
{
  "version": "1.0.0",
  "name": "OpenGameListWebApp",
  "private": true,
  "dependencies": {
    "@angular/common": "2.0.0-rc.5",
    "@angular/compiler": "2.0.0-rc.5",
    "@angular/core": "2.0.0-rc.5",
    "@angular/http": "2.0.0-rc.5",
    "@angular/platform-browser": "2.0.0-rc.5",
    "@angular/platform-browser-dynamic": "2.0.0-rc.5",
    "@angular/upgrade": "2.0.0-rc.5",
    "core-js": "^2.4.1",
    "reflect-metadata": "^0.1.3",
    "rxjs": "5.0.0-beta.6",
    "systemjs": "^0.19.37",
    "zone.js": "^0.6.12"
  },
  "devDependencies": {
    "gulp": "^3.9.1",
    "gulp-clean": "^0.3.2",
    "gulp-concat": "^2.6.0",
    "gulp-sourcemaps": "^1.6.0",
    "gulp-typescript": "^2.13.6",
    "gulp-uglify": "^2.0.0",
    "typescript": "^1.8.10"
  }
}
```

The packages starting with the @ symbol are part of the Angular 2 bundle, which, at the time of writing, reached its **Release Candidate 5** (**RC5**) development stage. The other ones are a set of ES6 shims (`core-js`), polyfills (`reflect-metadata`), loading libraries (`systemjs`), dependencies (`rxjs`), and helper tools (`zone.js`).

All of these packages are required for a number of good reasons:

- They ensure backward-compatibility between the new **ECMAScript v6** (**ES6**) language features – used by most Angular 2 packages, and **ECMAScript v5** (**ES5**), which will be our compilation target.
- They make our code compatible with the most common/used web browsers, including older ones.
- They adopt a modern, module-based loading API to handle the required JS dependencies in an efficient way.
- They use Angular 2 features to their full extent.

 All this information can be quite confusing, especially for old-school JavaScript developers, but don't worry, we're going to come back to these topics later on.

As usual, all of these packages will be downloaded in the background by the IDE as soon as you **Save** the file. Eventually, you will have a local instance of Angular 2 available under the following folder:

```
<project_root>/node_modules/@angular/
```

It's worth noting that we have also added a new `script` node that will execute a post-install command against the `typings` package we just added.

Now we need to move these files to the `wwwroot` folder. We can achieve this by adding a dedicated task to our Gulp configuration file as follows (new lines are highlighted):

```
/*
This file in the main entry point for defining Gulp tasks and using Gulp
plugins.
Click here to learn more. http://go.microsoft.com/fwlink/?LinkId=518007
*/
var gulp = require('gulp'),
    gp_clean = require('gulp-clean),
    gp_concat = require('gulp-concat'),
    gp_sourcemaps = require('gulp-sourcemaps'),
    gp_typescript = require('gulp-typescript'),
    gp_uglify = require('gulp-uglify');
```

```
/// Define paths
var srcPaths = {
    app: ['Scripts/app/main.ts', 'Scripts/app/**/*.ts'],
    js: [
        'Scripts/js/**/*.js',
        'node_modules/core-js/client/shim.min.js',
        'node_modules/zone.js/dist/zone.js',
        'node_modules/reflect-metadata/Reflect.js',
        'node_modules/systemjs/dist/system.src.js',
        'node_modules/typescript/lib/typescript.js'
    ],
    js_angular: [
        'node_modules/@angular/**'
    ],
    js_rxjs: [
        'node_modules/rxjs/**'
    ]
};

var destPaths = {
    app: 'wwwroot/app/',
    js: 'wwwroot/js/',
    js_angular: 'wwwroot/js/@angular/',
    js_rxjs: 'wwwroot/js/rxjs/'
};

// Compile, minify and create sourcemaps all TypeScript files and place
them to wwwroot/app, together with their js.map files.
gulp.task('app', ['app_clean'], function () {
    return gulp.src(srcPaths.app)
        .pipe(gp_sourcemaps.init())
        .pipe(gp_typescript(require('./tsconfig.json').compilerOptions))
        .pipe(gp_uglify({ mangle: false }))
         .pipe(gp_sourcemaps.write('/'))
        .pipe(gulp.dest(destPaths.app));
});

// Delete wwwroot/app contents
gulp.task('app_clean', function () {
    return gulp.src(destPaths.app + "*", { read: false })
        .pipe(gp_clean({ force: true }));
});

// Copy all JS files from external libraries to wwwroot/js
gulp.task('js', function () {
    gulp.src(srcPaths.js_angular)
        .pipe(gulp.dest(destPaths.js_angular));
    gulp.src(srcPaths.js_rxjs)
```

```
        .pipe(gulp.dest(destPaths.js_rxjs));
    return gulp.src(srcPaths.js)
        // .pipe(gp_uglify({ mangle: false })) // disable uglify
        // .pipe(gp_concat('all-js.min.js')) // disable concat
        .pipe(gulp.dest(destPaths.js));
});

// Delete wwwroot/js contents
gulp.task('js_clean', function () {
    return gulp.src(destPaths.js + "*", { read: false })
    .pipe(gp_clean({ force: true }));
});

// Watch specified files and define what to do upon file changes
gulp.task('watch', function () {
    gulp.watch([srcPaths.app, srcPaths.js], ['app', 'js']);
});

// Global cleanup task
gulp.task('cleanup', ['app_clean', 'js_clean']);

// Define the default task so it will launch all other tasks
gulp.task('default', ['app', 'js', 'watch']);
```

As you can see, it hasn't changed much, we just added a bunch of JS files that we need to copy from the /node_modules/ folder into the wwwroot/js/ folder, the same one we were already using to host third-party libraries. There's nothing odd there, NPM package files are external libraries, after all. For this very reason, it is also preferable to restrain ourselves from uglifying and/or concatenating them. It's also worth noting that we defined a separate, dedicated folder for **Angular 2** and **Rxjs** packages, since both of them are spanned into multiple files.

Adding Typings

Before moving forward, there is another thing we need to take care of. Since we plan to transpile our TypeScript code into ECMAScript5, we have added the core-js NPM module into our package.json file. In case you've never heard of it, let's just say that it happens to be a standard JavaScript library providing a great set of polyfills for ES6, which is precisely what we need.

If you would like to know more about the core-js, here's the URL to the project's official GitHub repository: https://github.com/zloirock/core-js.

The only problem is that it doesn't come with a proper TypeScript definition file, meaning that both of our TypeScript compilers, either Visual Studio's or Gulp's, won't be aware of its existence, thus throwing a fair amount of TS2304 (type not found) exceptions upon each build attempt.

The best thing we can do in order to fix that is to add the proper type definitions to our project. To do that, open the `package.json` file again and add the following (new lines are highlighted):

```
{
  "version": "1.0.0",
  "name": "opengamelistwebapp",
  "private": true,
  "dependencies": {
    "@angular/common": "2.0.0-rc.5",
    "@angular/compiler": "2.0.0-rc.5",
    "@angular/core": "2.0.0-rc.5",
    "@angular/http": "2.0.0-rc.5",
    "@angular/platform-browser": "2.0.0-rc.5",
    "@angular/platform-browser-dynamic": "2.0.0-rc.5",
    "@angular/upgrade": "2.0.0-rc.5",

    "core-js": "^2.4.1",
    "reflect-metadata": "^0.1.8",
    "rxjs": "5.0.0-beta.6",
    "systemjs": "^0.19.37",
    "typings": "^1.3.2",
    "zone.js": "^0.6.12"
  },
  "devDependencies": {
    "gulp": "^3.9.1",
    "gulp-concat": "^2.6.0",
    "gulp-sourcemaps": "^1.6.0",
    "gulp-typescript": "^2.13.6",
    "gulp-uglify": "^2.0.0",
    "typescript": "^1.8.10"
  },
  "scripts": {
    "postinstall": "typings install dt~core-js --global"
  }
}
```

We can see that there are two new things here:

- A new NPM package called `typings`, which is a TypeScript type definition manager. In other words, a tool we can use to retrieve type definitions from the web.
- A whole new `script` key containing a small command that will be executed during the post-install phase. This basically means that the script will trigger every time we change something within the `package.json` file, right after all the NPM modules are retrieved and installed (or removed).

As soon as we **Save** our `package.json` file, a new `typings` folder will be added to our **OpenGameListWebApp** project's root, containing the type definition file we need.

If typings didn't install successfully during the **Save**, try to use the **Restore Package** option by right-clicking on the project's **Dependencies** node. Another way is to use the command line to install the typings explicitly. To do this, navigate to the root folder of your app and press CTRL+SHIFT, then select **Open command window here**. In the command line, type the following command:

> npm run typings install

That should do the trick.

Using a CDN

At the time of writing, the only valid CDN hosting Angular 2 updated builds is npmcdn.com. If we want to use it, we can avoid updating our `gulpfile.js` file and wait until we are working on the `index.html` and `systemjs.config.js` files. Keep reading, as we'll get there shortly.

Upgrading the typescriptServices.js file

At the time of writing, adding Angular 2 via NPM would produce the following TypeScript compilation error:

Invalid module name in augmentation, module '../../Observable' cannot be found.

This is due to a known bug in the TypeScript version currently shipped with Visual Studio 2015. The most effective way to fix that is to replace this local VS2015 file: `C:\Program Files (x86)\Microsoft Visual Studio 14.0\Common7\IDE\CommonExtensions \Microsoft\TypeScript\typescriptServices.js`.

With the following remote file:
`https://raw.githubusercontent.com/Microsoft/TypeScript/Fix8518/lib/type scriptServices.js`.

Doing that will also fix a couple more errors we will most likely get in `Chapter 3`, *Angular 2 Components and Client-Side Routing*. Needless to say, it's highly advisable to make a backup of the original file before replacing it.

Additional information regarding the bug is available through the following URLs: `https://github.com/Microsoft/TypeScript/issues/8518` and `https://github.com/Microsoft /TypeScript/pull/757`.

Setting up the client code

It's time to lay down the first bricks of our app, a working skeleton, used as a starting point for what we're going to do in the next chapters. It will consist of:

- An Angular 2 component file: `Scripts/app/app.component.ts`
- An Angular 2 module file: `Scripts/app/app.module.ts`
- An Angular 2 bootstrap file: `Scripts/app/main.ts`
- A module loader configuration file: `wwwroot/systemjs.config.js`
- An HTML file to wrap everything up: `wwwroot/index.html`

The component file

The component is the most basic and fundamental concept in Angular 2. Think of it like a class that controls a specific piece of a web page where we can either display some data to each user and/or respond to their feedbacks. We can say that our Angular 2 app will be almost entirely built upon multiple **Components** serving specific purposes-most of them will be reusable, others will be only used once. They can also either be as small as a few lines or they can result in a ridiculously long piece of code.

Luckily, our first component is quite simple. In the **Solution Explorer**, right-click on the `/Scripts/app/` folder and add a new `app.component.ts` file:

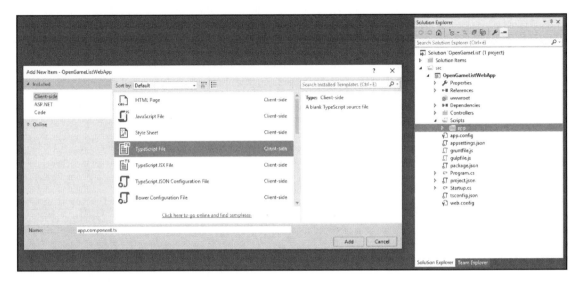

Once created, feed it with the following code:

```
import {Component} from "@angular/core";

@Component({
    selector: "opengamelist",
    template: `<h1>OpenGameList</h1><div>Work in progress...</div>`
})

export class AppComponent { }
```

That's it. Let's see what we just did here in detail:

- In line 1, we're importing the Component function from the Angular 2 main library, which is `@angular/core`. The Component function is what we need to define a Component's metadata for a class, which basically means being able to make Components, this is a required step for what we'll do next.
- In line 3-6, we're creating our first Component by applying the Component function to the class. In TypeScript, we do that by prefixing it with the `@` symbol and invoking it just above the component class. In other words, the `@Component` instruction tells Angular that this class is an Angular component. Notice that the `selector` and `template` fields are passed as a configuration object, as we will analyze them soon enough.

- In line 8, we're defining the `AppComponent` class. Notice the `export` keyword, which will allow us to `import` it from other components. The act of exporting makes our `app.component.js` file a module.

A word on components and modules

Angular 2 is a modular framework: this means that Angular 2 apps are also modular, as they consist of many files dedicated to a specific purpose. Typically, most application files export a single `Component` class, which is a class bundled with component metadata. Our `app.component.js` file, for example, exports the `AppComponent` class decorated with its component metadata, thus being a Module file exporting a Component class. We could also say that the Component is the content, while the Module is the file itself. We'll see how to import Components in the next chapter.

The module file

Angular Modules, also known as `NgModules`, have been introduced in **Angular 2 RC5**, which is the latest version at the time of writing, and are a great and powerful way to organize and bootstrap any Angular 2 application. They help developers to consolidate their own set of components, directives, and pipes into reusable blocks.

 If you've already played with previous versions of Angular 2, you will find the following URL useful to understand the transition by checking out the following URL:

`https://angular.io/docs/ts/latest/cookbook/rc4-to-rc5.html`.

Every Angular 2 application since RC5 must have at least one module, which is conventionally called the root module and given the `AppModule` class name.

From the **Solution Explorer**, right-click on the `/Scripts/app/` folder, add a new `app.module.ts` file, and fill it with the following code:

```
///<reference path="../../typings/index.d.ts"/>
import {NgModule} from "@angular/core";
import {BrowserModule} from "@angular/platform-browser";
import {HttpModule} from "@angular/http";
import "rxjs/Rx";

import {AppComponent} from "./app.component";

@NgModule({
    // directives, components, and pipes
    declarations: [
```

```
        AppComponent
    ],
    // modules
    imports: [
        BrowserModule,
        HttpModule
    ],
    // providers
    providers: [
    ],
    bootstrap: [
        AppComponent
    ]
})
export class AppModule { }
```

Again, let's take a look at what we just wrote:

- In line 1, we added a reference to the type definitions we fetched during the previous section to ensure our TypeScript compiler(s) could find it. Notice that, if we're using a CDN or a pre-compiled version of Angular 2, we could (and should) definitely remove this line.
- In lines 2-4, we import the basic Angular 2 modules that we will need right from the start.
- In line 5, we import the `rxjs` library definition file(s), which will be useful to compile the Angular 2 libraries.
- In line 7, right after the first empty line, we import the application root component that we just wrote.
- In line 9, we declare our root `NgModule`. As we can see it consists in an array of named arrays, each one containing a set of Angular 2 objects that serves a common purpose: directives, components, pipes, modules, and providers. The last one of them contains the component(s) we want to bootstrap, which in our case is the `AppComponent` one.

Working with the root module only is a very viable approach until the Angular 2 app grows to a certain size. When it becomes bigger, it will be more practical to refactor it into a number of feature modules, each one of them grouping together a set of related tasks.

The bootstrap file

Now that we have our root module, we need to bootstrap it. From the **Solution Explorer**, right-click on the /Scripts/app/ folder and add a new main.ts file, then fill it with the following code:

```
import {platformBrowserDynamic} from "@angular/platform-browser-dynamic";
import {AppModule} from "./app.module";

platformBrowserDynamic().bootstrapModule(AppModule);
```

Now we're just missing an entry point to load with the browser. Let's add it right now.

The module loader configuration file

In this application, we're going to use the **SystemJS** module loader library to load our application and all the required Angular 2 modules and dependencies. In order to do that, we have to add a systemjs.config.js file to the wwwroot folder and define a number of configuration rules within it, as follows:

```
(function (global) {
    // map tells the System loader where to look for things
    var map = {
        'app': 'app', // our application files
        '@angular': 'js/@angular', // angular2 packages
        'rxjs': 'js/rxjs' // Rxjs package
    };

    // packages tells the System loader which filename and/or extensions to
look for by default (when none are specified)
    var packages = {
        'app': { main: 'main.js', defaultExtension: 'js' },
        'rxjs': { defaultExtension: 'js' }
    };

    // configure @angular packages
    var ngPackageNames = [
      'common',
      'compiler',
      'core',
      'http',
      'platform-browser',
      'platform-browser-dynamic',
      'upgrade',
    ];
```

```
    function packIndex(pkgName) {
        packages['@angular/' + pkgName] = { main: 'index.js',
defaultExtension: 'js' };
    }

    function packUmd(pkgName) {
        packages['@angular/' + pkgName] = { main: '/bundles/' + pkgName +
'.umd.js', defaultExtension: 'js' };
    };

    var setPackageConfig = System.packageWithIndex ? packIndex : packUmd;
    ngPackageNames.forEach(setPackageConfig);
    var config = {
        map: map,
        packages: packages
    }
    System.config(config);
})(this);
```

The code is pretty much self-documented with inline comments, yet it could be useful to highlight the most relevant tasks:

- The map variable will host the three dynamic packages we're using SystemJS for, all of them relative to /wwwroot/: app for our application; js/@angular for Angular 2 and js/rxjs for Rxjs.
- The packages variable will set the default filename and/or extension values for each package. These will be used whenever we define an import statement without specifying them.
- The rest of the file is dedicated to dynamically loading the Angular 2 built-in packages.

If we want to use a CDN instead of relying upon the local JS folder, we only need to perform a minor update within the previous code, in the map section, as follows:

```
    var map = {
        'app': 'app', // our application files
        '@angular': 'js/@angular', // angular2 packages
        'rxjs': 'https://npmcdn.com/rxjs@5.0.0-beta.6' // Rxjs package
(CDN)
    };
```

And also within the two module loader functions:

```
function packIndex(pkgName) {
    packages['https://npmcdn.com/' + pkgName] = { main: 'index.js',
defaultExtension: 'js' };
}

function packUmd(pkgName) {
    packages['https://npmcdn.com/' + pkgName] = { main: '/bundles/' +
pkgName + '.umd.js', defaultExtension: 'js' };
};
```

 For further info regarding SystemJS and its Configuration API, including advanced options, we strongly suggest reading the official documentation on the project's GitHub page:
https://github.com/systemjs/systemjs and https://github.com/syst emjs/systemjs/blob/master/docs/config-api.md.

Why use a dynamic module loader?

Before going further, it might be useful to explain why we worked so hard with a module loader instead of adding all the relevant JS files into the index.html file right from the start.

To keep it simple, we did it because it's the only way to efficiently handle any modern JavaScript modular system such as Angular 2, Rxjs and also all applications based upon them, including the one we're working on right now.

What's a modular system exactly? It's nothing more than a package, library, or application split into a series of smaller files which depend on each other using reference statements such as import, require, and so on. ASP.NET, Java, Python, and most compilation-based languages have it. That's not the case with script-based languages such as PHP and JavaScript: they that are doomed to pre-load everything in the memory before being able to determine whether they'll be using it or not. All of these changes, with the introduction of **ECMAScript 6 (ES6)**, bring a fully-featured module and dependency management solution for JavaScript. **SystemJS** basically acts as an ES6-polyfill for browsers that don't support it already, allowing us to get that module system working in modern browsers. Since both Angular 2 and Rxjs leverage that dynamic-loading approach, implementing it within our project will result in a huge performance gain.

Keep in mind that **SystemJS** is not the only choice we have to load Angular 2 packages: there are other good choices out there, for example the popular module bundler known as **webpack**. Should we want to use that instead, here's a great guide for doing that: `https://angular.io/doc`
`s/ts/latest/guide/webpack.html`.

The index.html file

The HTML file serves two main purposes: being an entry point for the browser so it can load the client-script files and execute the application, and laying out the DOM structure used by Angular 2 to display it. In the **Solution Explorer**, right-click on the `wwwroot` folder and add a new `index.html` file, then fill it with the following code:

```
<!DOCTYPE html>
<html>
<head>
    <base href="/">
    <title>OpenGameList</title>
    <meta name="viewport" content="width=device-width, initial-scale=1">

    <!-- Step 1. Load libraries -->
    <!-- Polyfill(s) for older browsers -->
    <script src="js/shim.min.js"></script>
    <script src="js/zone.js"></script>
    <script src="js/Reflect.js"></script>
    <script src="js/system.src.js"></script>

    <!-- Step 2. Configure SystemJS -->
    <script src="systemjs.config.js"></script>
    <script>
      System.import('app').catch(function(err){ console.error(err); });
    </script>
</head>

<!-- Step 3. Display the application -->
<body>
    <!-- Application PlaceHolder -->
    <opengamelist>Loading...</opengamelist>
</body>
</html>
```

After adding the `index.html` file, we need to set it as the main entry point when executing our app in the Debug mode. In the **Solution Explorer**, right-click on the project node and select **Properties**, then switch to the **Debug** tab and change the **Launch URL** parameter accordingly.

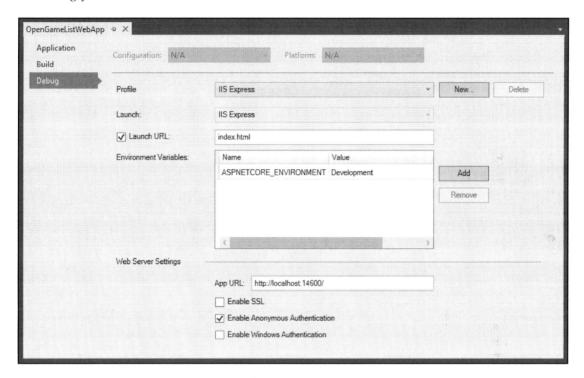

 While we're here, we might also take the chance to set the HTTP port that will be used by the local web server during development by changing the numeric part of the **App URL** textbox value. As we can see in the preceding screenshot, we're going to use **14600** throughout the whole book.

If we want to use a CDN instead of local JS files, we can replace the `<script>` elements right below the Step 1 comment with the following:

```
    <script
src="https://cdnjs.cloudflare.com/ajax/libs/core-js/2.4.1/shim.min.js"></sc
ript>
    <script src="https://npmcdn.com/zone.js@0.6.12"></script>
    <script src="https://npmcdn.com/reflect-metadata@0.1.3"></script>
    <script src="https://cdnjs.cloudflare.com/ajax/
libs/systemjs/0.19.37/system.js"></script>
```

These are the latest versions at the time of writing. Be sure to replace them with the most recent Angular 2-compatible versions.

First run

Now that we've set everything up, it's time to take a look at where we're doing. The first thing we should do is to turn our task runner on:

1. Expand the root node, right-click to the **default** task, and hit **Run**.
2. From the **Solution Explorer**, right-click on your `gulpfile.js` file and select **Task Runner Explorer**.
3. If you did everything correctly, the Task Runner will silently execute its tasks, keeping the one named `watch` active in background.

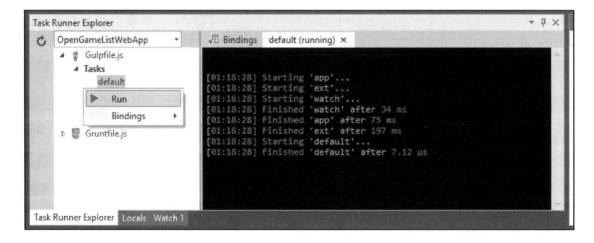

4. Right after that we can hit *F5* (or left-click the **Start Debugging** button) and test our still rather minimalistic, yet fully functional, home screen.

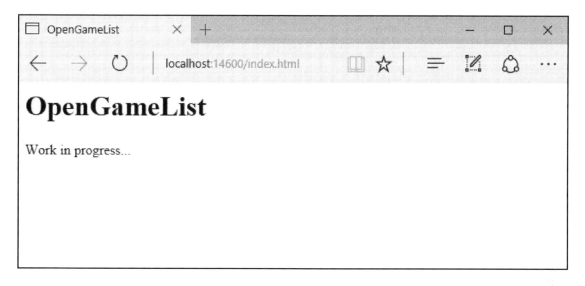

If things are working as they should, we will see something very close to the preceding image. That's pretty good. Before going further, let's check if our task runner and its plugins are also working as they should.

Back in Visual Studio, open the /Scripts/app/app.component.ts file and change the <div> content with the highlighted text as follows:

```
import {Component} from "@angular/core";

@Component({
    selector: "opengamelist",
    template: `<h1>OpenGameList</h1><div>...the best is yet to come!</div>`
})

export class AppComponent { }
```

After you're done, hit *CTRL + S* or **Save**, then move back to the browser and issue a page refresh by hitting *F5* to see if the task runner did its job. If it did, you should see something like the following:

So far so good, we have just set up a working skeleton of what's about to come.

Caching issues

If you're not seeing this, and the page is still showing the Work in progress…, phrase, chances are that you have caching issues. This is quite a common issue, since our client code relies upon static files (such as `index.html`) which are served by default with a set of `cache-control` HTTP headers to ensure a proper client-side cache. This is usually great for production, but it can be quite annoying while our app is in the development stage. If we want to fix it, we need to change the default caching behavior for static files.

If we were developing an ASP.NET 4 web application, we could do that by adding some lines to our main application's `web.config` file such as the following:

```
<caching enabled="false" />
<staticContent>
  <clientCache cacheControlMode="DisableCache" />
</staticContent>
<httpProtocol>
  <customHeaders>
    <add name="Cache-Control" value="no-cache, no-store" />
```

```
            <add name="Pragma" value="no-cache" />
            <add name="Expires" value="-1" />
        </customHeaders>
    </httpProtocol>
```

And that should be it.

However, that's not the case. The new ASP.NET Core's configuration system has been re-architected from scratch and is now quite different from the previous versions. The most important consequence of this is that XML configuration files such as web.config, together with the whole System.Configuration namespace, are not part of the new pattern and shouldn't be used anymore.

The new ASP.NET Core configuration pattern

The new configuration model is based upon key/value settings that can be retrieved from a wide variety of sources, including, and mostly being, Json files. Once retrieved, they can be accessed within our code in a strongly-typed fashion. We can take a look at the new pattern by watching a couple of lines contained within the Startup class constructor, which is contained in the Startup.cs file (relevant lines are highlighted):

```
public Startup(IHostingEnvironment env)
{
    var builder = new ConfigurationBuilder()
        .SetBasePath(env.ContentRootPath)
        .AddJsonFile("appsettings.json", optional: true, reloadOnChange:
true)
        .AddJsonFile($"appsettings.{env.EnvironmentName}.json", optional:
true)
        .AddEnvironmentVariables();
    Configuration = builder.Build();
}
```

And also the appsettings.json file they refer to:

```
{
  "Logging": {
    "IncludeScopes": false,
    "LogLevel": {
      "Default": "Debug",
      "System": "Information",
      "Microsoft": "Information"
    }
  }
}
```

Now that we understand the basics, let's see how we can solve that caching issue by taking advantage of the new configuration model.

The first thing to do is to understand how we can modify the default HTTP headers for static files. As a matter of fact, we can do that by adding a custom set of options to the `app.UseDefaultFiles()` method we added to the `Startup` class earlier. In order to do that, open the `Startup.cs` and change that part of code in the following way (new/modified lines are highlighted):

```
// Configure a rewrite rule to auto-lookup for standard default files such
as index.html.
app.UseDefaultFiles();

// Serve static files (html, css, js, images & more). See also the
following URL:
// https://docs.asp.net/en/latest/fundamentals/static-files.html for
further reference.
app.UseStaticFiles(new StaticFileOptions(){
    OnPrepareResponse = (context) =>
    {
        // Disable caching for all static files.
        context.Context.Response.Headers["Cache-Control"] = "no-cache, no-
store";
        context.Context.Response.Headers["Pragma"] = "no-cache";
        context.Context.Response.Headers["Expires"] = "-1";
    }});
```

That wasn't hard at all. However, we're not done yet, now that we've learned how to change the default behavior, we just need to change these static values with some convenient references pointing to the `appsettings.json` file.

To do that, we can add the following key/value section to the `appsettings.json` file in the following way (new lines are highlighted):

```
{
  "Logging": {
    "IncludeScopes": false,
    "LogLevel": {
      "Default": "Debug",
      "System": "Information",
      "Microsoft": "Information"
    }
  },
  "StaticFiles": {
    "Headers": {
      "Cache-Control": "no-cache, no-store",
      "Pragma": "no-cache",
```

```
        "Expires": "-1"
      }
    }
  }
```

And then change the preceding `Startup.cs` code accordingly (modified lines are highlighted):

```
// Configure a rewrite rule to auto-lookup for standard default files such
as index.html.
app.UseDefaultFiles();

// Serve static files (html, css, js, images & more). See also the
following URL:
// https://docs.asp.net/en/latest/fundamentals/static-files.html for
further reference.
app.UseStaticFiles(new StaticFileOptions(){
    OnPrepareResponse = (context) =>
    {
        // Disable caching for all static files.
        context.Context.Response.Headers["Cache-Control"] =
        Configuration["StaticFiles:Headers:Cache-Control"];
        context.Context.Response.Headers["Pragma"] =
        Configuration["StaticFiles:Headers:Pragma"];
        context.Context.Response.Headers["Expires"] =
        Configuration["StaticFiles:Headers:Expires"];
}});
```

That's about it. Learning how to use this pattern is strongly advisable, as it's a great and effective way to properly configure our application's settings.

A faster alternative using scaffolding tools

In the latest few paragraphs, we basically built our very own server-side and client-side environment by configuring everything manually. Truth be told, what we just did is neither the quickest nor the most effective way to start a project involving a client-side framework such as Angular 2, as a matter of fact, we could achieve the same results in a fraction of the time we just spent by using the ASP.NET Core project scaffolding tools such as **Yeoman**, which are available through NPM, together with a proper generator template such as `aspnetcore-spa`.

Not only will these tools generate a fully-functional ASP.NET Core and Angular 2 boilerplate, much like the one we just made, they'll also take care of a number of issues beforehand that we would otherwise have to manually set up later. These include server-side pre-rendering, efficient cache management, optimized production builds, and much more. On top of that, they can be easily enhanced with other helper packages such as **WebPack** and **JavaScriptServices**, a great set of tools and middlewares for building SPA projects with ASP.NET Core and Angular 2.

The reasons to say no (not yet)

All of this sounds so exciting that we may well ask ourselves why in the world didn't we go for that?

The reason is simple, what we just made, together with a lot of things we'll assemble during the course of the following chapters, is also part of our learning process. In other words, this is why we're reading this book instead of just copying some working samples from a bunch of web pages, or GitHub projects, and putting them together. This doesn't mean we don't have to use **Yeoman**, as a matter of fact, we will be using it, together with a lot of other great tools that will speed up our development and help us to write better code. Eventually, just not on our first run, that's for sure. We don't want our journey to be spoiled, do we?

A quick scaffolding sample

However, it's also true that taking a look at these tools, and eventually being able to properly use them, can easily be seen as part of our learning process. If you want to do that, you need to have Node.js installed, unless you prefer to use what's bundled with Visual Studio 2015.

Open a command prompt with administrative rights and navigate through theNode.js installation folder. If you're using the one shipped with VS2015 it should be something like the following: `C:\Program Files (x86)\Microsoft Visual Studio 14.0\Web\External`.

If you went for a new install, it should be the following (for x64 architectures): `C:\Program Files\Nodejs`.

Once there, type the following command and execute it to update NPM to the latest version:

```
npm install npm -g
```

Then type and execute the following to install **Yeoman** together with the `aspnetcore-spa` generator:

```
npm install -g yo generator-aspnetcore-spa
```

Finally, type and execute the following commands to create your application's entry point:

```
cd C:\Projects\Your-SPA-folder\
yo aspnetcore-spa
```

That's about it. For further reference regarding how to use **Yeoman**, it's strongly advisable to take a look at the official documentation at the following URL: `http://yeoman.io/learning/`.

If you're bold enough to also install WebPack and JavaScriptServices, you should definitely read the ASP.NET Core JavaScript Services official documentation, written by *Steve Sanderson*, who is the author of the JavaScriptServices project and the **KnockoutJs** library, as well as being a Microsoft employee: `https://github.com/aspnet/JavaScriptServices#javascriptservices`.

 Before moving forward, it's very important to understand the fact that we will not cover these packages throughout the book. We will take it for granted that we don't have these features available, so we will often spend some time designing and building our own implementation. That's why we don't suggest that you do that during the first reading.

References

- *Native Web Apps*, Henrik Joreteg, 2015.
- *Manifesto for Agile Software Development*, Kent Beck, Mike Beedle and many others, 2001

Suggested topics

SCRUM, Extreme Programming, MVC and MVVM architectural patterns, ASP.NET Core, .NET Core, Roslyn, CoreCLR, RyuJIT, task runner, Gulp, Grunt, NuGet, NPM, ECMAScript 6, Bower, SystemJS, Rxjs, Cache-Control, HTTP Headers.

Summary

So far, so good, we have just set up a working skeleton of what's about to come. Before moving further, let's quickly recap what we just did in this first chapter.

We briefly described our platforms of choice, ASP.NET Core and Angular 2, and acknowledged their combined potential in the process of building a modern web application. Then we chose a NWA with a single-page application approach as the ideal field of choice for testing what our frameworks are able to do (and how to do it).

In an attempt to reproduce a realistic production-case scenario, we also went through the most common SPA features: first from a technical point of view, then by putting us in the shoes of a typical product owner and trying to enumerate his expectations. We also made a quick list of everything we need to put together a potentially shippable product featuring all the expected goodies.

Eventually, we spent an appropriate amount of time setting up our development environment. This included installing package managers, choosing a suitable client-side framework, introducing task runners and configuring both ASP.NET Core and Angular 2.

Finally, we performed a quick test to see that all the bricks we'd lain were in place and ready to hold their ground against what's coming next, setting up a request-response cycle, building our very first controller, defining efficient routing strategies, and more.

2
ASP.NET Controllers and Server-Side Routes

Now that we have our skeleton up and running, it's time to explore the client-server interaction capabilities of our frameworks. To put it in other words, we need to understand how Angular 2 will be able to fetch data from ASP.NET Core using its brand new Core Web API structure. We won't be worrying about how will ASP.NET Core retrieve these data, be it from session objects, data stores, DBMS, or any possible data source. All of that will come later on. For now, we'll just put together some sample static data in order to understand how to pass them back and forth by using a well-structured, highly configurable, and viable interface.

Data flow

As you might already know, a Native Web App following the single-page application approach will roughly handle the client-server communication in the following way:

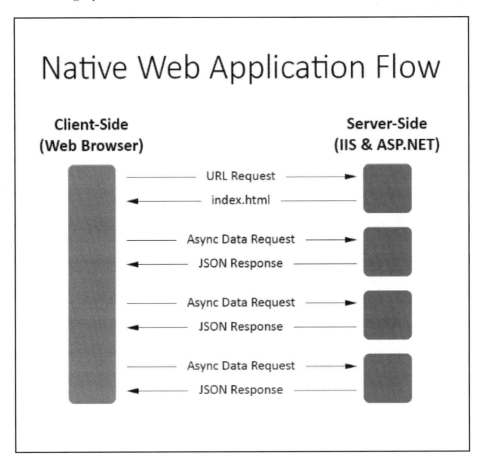

In case you're wondering about what these **Async Data Requests** actually are, the answer is simple: everything, as long as it needs to retrieve data from the server, which is something that most of the common user interactions will normally do, including (yet not limited to): *pressing a button* to show more data or to edit/delete something, *following a link* to another app view, *submitting a form*, and so on.

In other words, unless the task is so trivial, or it involves a minimal amount of data, that the client can entirely handle it, meaning that it already has everything that they need. Examples of such tasks are as follows: show/hide element toggles, in-page navigation elements (such as internal anchors), and any temporary job requiring a *confirmation* or *save* button to be pressed before actually being processed.

The preceding diagram shows, in a nutshell, what we're going to do: define and implement a pattern to serve these JSON-based, server-side responses that our application will need to handle the upcoming requests. Since we've chosen a strong, data-driven application pattern such as a Wiki, we'll surely need to put together a bunch of common CRUD-based requests revolving around a defined object which will represent our entries. For the sake of simplicity, we'll call it "item" from now on.

These requests will address some common CMS-inspired tasks such as displaying a list of items, viewing/editing the selected item's details, handling filters and text-based search queries, and also deleting an item.

Before going further, let's have a more detailed look at what happens between any of these**Data Requests** issued by the client and **JSON Responses** sent out by the server, that is, what's usually called the request/response flow:

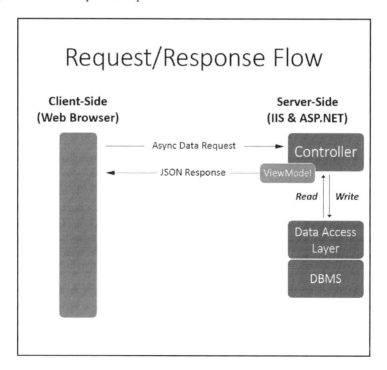

As we can see, in order to respond to any client-issued **Data Request** we need to build a *server-side* Core Web API **Controller** featuring the following capabilities:

- **Read** and/or **Write** data using the **Data Access Layer**
- Organize this data in a suitable JSON-serializable **ViewModel**
- Serialize the **ViewModel** and send it to the client as a **Response**

Based on these points, we could easily conclude that the **ViewModel** is the key item here. That's not always correct: it could or couldn't be the case, depending on the project we're building. To better clarify that, before going further, it could be useful to spend a couple of words on the **ViewModel** object itself.

The role of the ViewModel

We all know that a **ViewModel** is a container-type class, which represents only the data we want to display on our web page. In any standard MVC-based ASP.NET application, the **ViewModel** is instantiated by the **Controller** in response to a GET request using the data fetched from the model. Once built, the **ViewModel** is passed to the **View**, where it's used to populate the page contents/input fields.

The main reason for building a **ViewModel** instead of directly passing the model entities is that it only represents the data that we want to use and nothing else. All the unnecessary properties that are in the model domain object will be left out, keeping the data transfer as lightweight as possible. Another advantage is the additional security it gives since we can protect any field from being serialized and passed through the HTTP channel.

In a standard Web API context, where the data is passed using RESTful conventions via serialized formats such as JSON or XML, the **ViewModel** could be easily replaced by a JSON-serializable dynamic object created on the fly, such as this:

```
var response = new {
    Id = "1",
    Title = "The title",
    Description = "The description"
};
```

This approach is often viable for small or sample projects, where creating one (or many) **ViewModel** classes could be a waste of time. However, that's not our case. Conversely, our project will greatly benefit from having a well-defined, strongly typed **ViewModel** structure, even if they will all be eventually converted into JSON strings.

Our first Controller

Now that we have a clear vision of the request/response flow and its main actors, we can start building something up. Let's start with the *Welcome View*, which is the first page that any user will see upon connecting to our Native Web App. This is something that in a standard web application would be called *Home Page*, but since we are following a single-page application approach, that name isn't appropriate. After all, we're not going to have more than one page.

In most wikis, the *Welcome View/Home Page* contains a brief text explaining the context/topic of the project and then one or more lists of items ordered and/or filtered in various ways, such as:

- The last inserted ones (most recent first)
- The most relevant/visited ones (most viewed first)
- Some random items (in random order)

Let's try to do something like that. This will be our master plan for a suitable *Welcome View*:

In order to do that, we're going to need the following set of API calls:

- `api/items/GetLatest` (to fetch the last inserted items)
- `api/items/GetMostViewed` (to fetch the last inserted items)
- `api/items/GetRandom` (to fetch the last inserted items)

As we can see, all of them will be returning a list of items ordered by a well-defined logic. That's why, before working on them, we should provide ourselves with a suitable **ViewModel**.

The ItemViewModel

One of the biggest advantages in building a Native Web App using ASP.NET and Angular 2 is that we can start writing our code without worrying too much about data sources because they will come later and only after we're sure about what we really need. This is not a requirement either. You are also free to start with your data source for a number of the following good reasons:

- You already have a clear idea of what you'll need
- You already have your entity set(s) and/or a defined/populated data structure to work with
- You're used to starting with the data and subsequently moving to the GUI

All the preceding reasons are perfectly fine. You won't ever get fired for doing that. Yet, the chance to start with the frontend might help you a lot if you're still unsure about what your application will look like, either in terms of GUI and/or data. In building this Native Web App, we'll take advantage of that. Hence, why we'll start defining our `ItemViewModel` instead of creating its data source and entity class?

From **Solution Explorer**, right-click to the project root node and **Add** a **New Folder** named `ViewModels`. Once created, right-click on it and **Add** a **New Item**. From the server-side elements, pick a standard **Class**, name it `ItemViewModel.cs`, and hit the **Add** button. Then, type in the following code:

```
using System;
using System.Collections.Generic;
using System.ComponentModel;
using System.Linq;
using System.Threading.Tasks;
using Newtonsoft.Json;

namespace OpenGameListWebApp.ViewModels
{
    [JsonObject(MemberSerialization.OptOut)]
    public class ItemViewModel
    {
        #region Constructor
        public ItemViewModel()
```

```
    {

    }
    #endregion Constructor

    #region Properties
    public int Id { get; set; }
    public string Title { get; set; }
    public string Description { get; set; }
    public string Text { get; set; }
    public string Notes { get; set; }
    [DefaultValue(0)]
    public int Type { get; set; }
    [DefaultValue(0)]
    public int Flags { get; set; }
    public string UserId { get; set; }
    [JsonIgnore]
    public int ViewCount { get; set; }
    public DateTime CreatedDate { get; set; }
    public DateTime LastModifiedDate { get; set; }
    #endregion Properties
  }
}
```

As we can see, we're defining a rather complex class. This isn't something we could easily handle using a dynamic object created on the fly; hence why we're using a `ViewModel` instead?

Remember the Newtonsoft's `Json.NET`package we installed in `Chapter 1`, *Getting Ready*, using NuGet? We'll start using it in this class by including its namespace in line 6 and decorating our newly created `Item` class with a `JsonObject` attribute in line 10. That attribute can be used to set a list of behaviors of the `JsonSerializer`/`JsonDeserializer` methods, overriding the default ones. Notice that we used `MemberSerialization.OptOut`, meaning that any field will be serialized into JSON unless being decorated by an explicit `JsonIgnoreAttribute` or `NonSerializedAttribute`. We're making this choice because we're going to need most of our ViewModel's properties serialized, as we'll be seeing soon enough.

The ItemsController

Now that we have our `ItemViewModel` class, let's use it to return some server-side data. From your project's root node, open the `/Controllers/` folder, right-click on it, select **Add | New Item**, then create a **Web API Controller Class**, name it `ItemsController.cs`, and click on the **Add** button to create it.

The controller will be created with a bunch of sample methods, they are identical to those present in the default ValuesController.cs, which we already tested in Chapter 1, *Getting Ready*, and hence, we don't need to keep them. Delete the entire file content and replace it with the following code:

```
using System;
using System.Collections.Generic;
using System.Linq;
using System.Threading.Tasks;
using Microsoft.AspNetCore.Mvc;
using OpenGameListWebApp.ViewModels;
using Newtonsoft.Json;

namespace OpenGameListWebApp.Controllers
{
    [Route("api/[controller]")]
    public class ItemsController : Controller
    {
        // GET api/items/GetLatest/5
        [HttpGet("GetLatest/{num}")]
        public JsonResult GetLatest(int num)
        {
            var arr = new List<ItemViewModel>();
            for (int i = 1; i <= num; i++) arr.Add(new ItemViewModel() {
                Id = i,
                Title = String.Format("Item {0} Title", i),
                Description = String.Format("Item {0} Description", i)
            });
            var settings = new JsonSerializerSettings() {
                Formatting = Formatting.Indented
            };
            return new JsonResult(arr, settings);
        }
    }
}
```

This controller will be in charge of all item-related operations within our app.

As we can see, we started defining a `GetLatest` method accepting a single integer parameter value. The method accepts any GET request using the custom routing rules configured via the `HttpGetAttribute`, this approach is called **attribute routing**, and we'll be digging more into it later in this chapter. For now, let's stick to the code inside the method itself.

The behavior is really simple since we don't have a data source we're basically mocking a bunch of `ItemViewModel` objects. Notice that, although it's just a fake response, we're doing it in a structured and credible way, respecting the number of items issued by the request and also providing different content for each one of them.

It's also worth noticing that we're using a `JsonResult` return type, which is the best thing we can do as long as we're working with `ViewModel` classes featuring the `JsonObject` attribute provided by the `Json.NET` framework. That's definitely better than returning plain `string` or `IEnumerable<string>` types, as it will automatically take care of serializing the outcome and setting the appropriate response headers (`Content-Type`, `charset`, and so on).

Let's try our controller by running our app in the debug mode: select **Debug** | **Start Debugging** from the main menu or press *F5*. The default browser should open, pointing to the `index.html` page because we set it as the `Launch URL` in our project's debug properties. To test our brand new API Controller, we need to manually replace the URL with the following:

```
/api/items/GetLatest/5
```

If we have done everything correctly, it will show something like the following:

```
localhost                    ×   +                               —   □   ×

←   →   ⟳   |   localhost:14600/api/items/GetLatest   □  ☆  |   ≡  ✍  ⟁  ⋯

[
  {
    "ID": 1,
    "Title": "Item 1 Title",
    "Description": "Item 1 Description",
    "Text": null,
    "Notes": null,
    "Type": 0,
    "Flags": 0,
    "AuthorID": 0,
    "CreatedDate": "0001-01-01T00:00:00",
    "LastModifiedDate": "0001-01-01T00:00:00"
  },
  {
    "ID": 2,
    "Title": "Item 2 Title",
    "Description": "Item 2 Description",
    "Text": null,
    "Notes": null,
    "Type": 0,
    "Flags": 0,
    "AuthorID": 0,
    "CreatedDate": "0001-01-01T00:00:00",
    "LastModifiedDate": "0001-01-01T00:00:00"
  },
  {
    "ID": 3,
    "Title": "Item 3 Title",
    "Description": "Item 3 Description",
```

Our first controller is up and running. As you can see, the `ViewCount` property is not present in the JSON-serialized output: that's by design since it has been flagged with the `JsonIgnore` attribute, meaning that we're explicitly opting it out.

Now that we've seen that it works, we can come back to the routing aspect of what we just did: since it is a major topic, it's well worth some of our time.

Understanding routes

In `Chapter 1`, *Getting Ready*, we acknowledged the fact that the ASP.NET Core pipeline has been completely rewritten in order to merge the MVC and WebAPI modules into a single, lightweight framework to handle both worlds. Although this certainly is a good thing, it comes with the usual downside that we need to learn a lot of new stuff. Handling routes is a perfect example of this, as the new approach defines some major breaking changes from the past.

Defining routing

The first thing we should do is give out a proper definition of what routing actually is.

To cut it simple, we could say that URL routing is the server-side feature that allows a web developer to handle HTTP requests pointing to URIs not mapping to physical files. Such techniques could be used for a number of different reasons, including the following:

- Giving dynamic pages semantic, meaningful, and human-readable names in order to advantage readability and/or search-engine optimization (SEO)
- Renaming or moving one or more physical files within your project's folder tree without being forced to change their URLs
- Setup aliases and redirects

Routing through the ages

In earlier times, when ASP.NET was just Web Forms, URL routing was strictly bound to physical files. To implement viable URL convention patterns the developers were forced to install/configure a dedicated URL rewriting tool using either an external ISAPI filter such as Helicontech's SAPI Rewrite or start with IIS7-the IIS URL Rewrite Module.

When ASP.NET MVC was released, the routing pattern was completely rewritten: the developers could set up their own convention-based routes in a dedicated file (RouteConfig.cs and Global.asax, depending on the template) using the Routes.MapRoute method. If you've played along with MVC 1-5 or WebAPI 1 and/or 2, snippets like this should be quite familiar to you:

```
routes.MapRoute(
    name: "Default",
    url: "{controller}/{action}/{id}",
    defaults: new { controller = "Home", action = "Index", id =
UrlParameter.Optional }
);
```

This method of defining routes, strictly based upon pattern matching techniques used to relate any given URL requests to specific controller actions, went by the name of convention-based routing.

ASP.NET MVC5 brought something new, as it was the first version supporting the so-called attribute-based routing. This approach was designed as an effort to give developers a more versatile approach. If you used it at least once you'll probably agree that it was a great addition to the framework, as it allowed the developers to define routes within the controller file. Even those who chose to keep the convention-based approach could find it useful for one-time overrides such as the following, without having to sort it out using some regular expressions:

```
[RoutePrefix("v2Products")]
public class ProductsController : Controller
{
    [Route("v2Index")]
    public ActionResult Index()
    {
        return View();
    }
}
```

In ASP.NET Core MVC (MVC 6), with the routing pipeline being completely rewritten, attribute-based routing is quickly becoming a de facto standard, replacing the convention, based approach in most boilerplates and code samples. Setting routing conventions using the Routes.MapRoute() method is still possible, yet it ceased to be the preferred way of work. You won't be finding anything like that in the new Startup.cs file, which contains a very small amount of code and (apparently) nothing about routes.

Handling routes in ASP.NET Core

We could say that the reason behind the `Routes.MapRoute` method disappearance in the application's main configuration file is due to the fact that there's no need to set up default routes anymore. Routing is handled by the two brand new `services.AddMvc()` and `services.UseMvc()` methods called within the `Startup.cs` file, which respectively register MVC using the dependency injection framework built into ASP.NET Core and add a set of default routes to our app.

We can take a look at what happens under the hood looking at the current implementation of the `services.UseMvc()` method in the framework code (relevant lines are highlighted):

```
public static IApplicationBuilder UseMvc(
    [NotNull] this IApplicationBuilder app,
    [NotNull] Action<IRouteBuilder> configureRoutes)
{
    // Verify if AddMvc was done before calling UseMvc
    // We use the MvcMarkerService to make sure if all the services were
added.
    MvcServicesHelper.ThrowIfMvcNotRegistered(app.ApplicationServices);

    var routes = new RouteBuilder
    {
        DefaultHandler = new MvcRouteHandler(),
        ServiceProvider = app.ApplicationServices .
    };

    configureRoutes(routes);

    // Adding the attribute route comes after running the user-code because
    // we want to respect any changes to the DefaultHandler.
    routes.Routes.Insert(0,
    AttributeRouting.CreateAttributeMegaRoute(
        routes.DefaultHandler,
        app.ApplicationServices));

    return app.UseRouter(routes.Build());
}
```

The good thing about this is the fact that the framework now handles all the hard work, iterating through all the controller's actions and setting up their default routes, thereby saving us some work. It is worth noticing that the default ruleset follows the standard RESTful conventions, meaning that it will be restricted to the following action names: Get, Post, Put, and Delete. We could say here that ASP.NET Core is enforcing a strict WebAPI-oriented approach, which is to be expected, since it incorporates the whole ASP.NET Core framework.

Following the RESTful convention is generally a great thing to do, especially if we aim to create a set of pragmatic, RESTful-based public APIs to be used by other developers. Conversely, if we're developing our own app and want to keep our API accessible only to our eyes, going for custom routing standards is just as viable. As a matter of fact, it could even be a better choice to shield our controllers against most trivial forms of request flood and/or DDoS-based attacks. Luckily enough, both the convention-based routing and the attribute-based routing are still alive and well, allowing you to set up your own standards.

Convention-based routing

If we feel like using the most classic routing approach, we can easily resurrect our beloved MapRoute() method by enhancing the app.UseMvc() call within the Startup.cs file in the following way:

```
app.UseMvc(routes =>
{
    // Route Sample A
    routes.MapRoute(
        name: "RouteSampleA",
        template: "MyOwnGet",
        defaults: new {
            controller = "Items",
            action = "Get"
        }
    );
    // Route Sample B
    routes.MapRoute(
        name: "RouteSampleB",
        template: "MyOwnPost",
        defaults: new {
            controller = "Items",
            action = "Post"
        }
    );
});
```

Attribute-based routing

The previously shown `ItemsController.cs` makes good use of the attribute-based routing approach, featuring it either at the controller level:

```
[Route("api/[controller]")]
public class ItemsController : Controller
```

And also featuring it at the action method level:

```
[HttpGet("GetLatest")]
public JsonResult GetLatest()
```

Three choices to route them all

Long story short, ASP.NET Core is giving us three different choices for handling routes: enforcing the standard RESTful conventions, reverting back to the good old convention-based routing, or decorating the controller files with the attribute-based routing.

It's also worth noticing that attribute-based routes, if/when defined, would override any matching convention-based pattern. Both of them if/when defined, would override the default RESTful conventions created by the built-in `UseMvc()` method.

In this chapter, we're going to use all of these approaches in order to learn when, where, and how to properly make use of either of them.

Adding more routes

Let's get back to our `ItemsController`. Now that we're aware of the routing patterns we can use, we can use that knowledge to implement the API calls we're still missing.

Open the `ItemsController.cs` file and add the following code (new lines are highlighted):

```
using System;
using System.Collections.Generic;
using System.Linq;
using System.Threading.Tasks;
using Microsoft.AspNetCore.Mvc;
using OpenGameListWebApp.ViewModels;
using Newtonsoft.Json;

namespace OpenGameListWebApp.Controllers
{
    [Route("api/[controller]")]
```

```csharp
public class ItemsController : Controller
{
    #region Attribute-based Routing
    /// <summary>
    /// GET: api/items/GetLatest/{n}
    /// ROUTING TYPE: attribute-based
    /// </summary>
    /// <returns>An array of {n} Json-serialized objects representing
the last inserted items.</returns>
    [HttpGet("GetLatest/{n}")]
    public IActionResult GetLatest(int n)
    {
        var items = GetSampleItems().OrderByDescending(i =>
        i.CreatedDate).Take(n);
        return new JsonResult(items, DefaultJsonSettings);
    }
    /// <summary>
    /// GET: api/items/GetMostViewed/{n}
    /// ROUTING TYPE: attribute-based
    /// </summary>
    /// <returns>An array of {n} Json-serialized objects representing
the items with most user views.</returns>
    [HttpGet("GetMostViewed/{n}")]
    public IActionResult GetMostViewed(int n)
    {
        var items = GetSampleItems().OrderByDescending(i =>
        i.ViewCount).Take(n);
        return new JsonResult(items, DefaultJsonSettings);
    }
    /// <summary>
    /// GET: api/items/GetRandom/{n}
    /// ROUTING TYPE: attribute-based
    /// </summary>
    /// <returns>An array of {n} Json-serialized objects representing
some randomly-picked items.</returns>
    [HttpGet("GetRandom/{n}")]
    public IActionResult GetRandom(int n)
    {
        var items = GetSampleItems().OrderBy(i =>
Guid.NewGuid()).Take(n);
        return new JsonResult(items, DefaultJsonSettings);
    }
    #endregion
    #region Private Members
    /// <summary>
    /// Generate a sample array of source Items to emulate a database
        (for testing purposes only).
    /// </summary>
```

```
/// <param name="num">The number of items to generate:
    default is 999</param>
/// <returns>a defined number of mock items (for testing purpose
only)
</returns>
private List<ItemViewModel> GetSampleItems(int num = 999)
{
    List<ItemViewModel> lst = new List<ItemViewModel>();
    DateTime date = new DateTime(2015, 12, 31).AddDays(-num);
    for (int id = 1; id <= num; id++)
    {
        lst.Add(new ItemViewModel()
        {
            Id = id,
            Title = String.Format("Item {0} Title", id),
            Description = String.Format("This is a sample
description
            for item {0}: Lorem ipsum dolor sit amet.", id),
            CreatedDate = date.AddDays(id),
            LastModifiedDate = date.AddDays(id),
            ViewCount = num - id
        });
    }
    return lst;
}
/// <summary>
/// Returns a suitable JsonSerializerSettings object that can
be used to generate the JsonResult return value for this
Controller's
methods.
/// </summary>
private JsonSerializerSettings DefaultJsonSettings
{
    get
    {
        return new JsonSerializerSettings()
        {
            Formatting = Formatting.Indented
        };
    }
}
#endregion
    }
}
```

We did a lot of things there, that's for sure. Let's see what's new:

- We added the `GetMostViewed(n)` and `GetRandom(n)` methods, which are built upon the same mocking logic used for `GetLatest(n)`. Either one requires a single parameter of integer type to specify the (maximum) number of items to retrieve.
- We added some new private members:
  - The `GetLatestItems()` method to generate some sample `Item` objects when we need them. This method is an improved version of the dummy item generator loop we had inside the previous `GetLatest()` method implementation, as it acts more like a dummy data provider. We'll discuss this in more detail later on.
  - The `DefaultJsonSettings` property, so we won't have to manually instantiate a `JsonSerializerSetting` object every time.
- We also decorated each class member with a dedicated `<summary>` documentation tag explaining what it does and its return value. These tags will be used by IntelliSense to show real-time information about the type within the Visual Studio GUI. They will also come in handy when we want to generate an autogenerated XML documentation for our project by using industry-standard documentation tools such as Sandcastle.
- Finally, we added some `#region/#endregion` pre-processor directives to separate our code into blocks. We'll do this a lot from now on, as this will greatly increase our source code readability and usability, allowing us to expand or collapse different sections/parts when we don't need them, thus focusing more on what we're working on.

For more info regarding documentation tags, take a look at the following MSDN official documentation page: `https://msdn.microsoft.com/library/2d6dt3kf.aspx`.
If you want to know more about C# pre-processor directives, this is the one to check out instead: `https://msdn.microsoft.com/library/9a1ybwek.aspx`.

The dummy data provider

Our new `GetLatestItems()` method deserves a couple more words. As we can easily see, it emulates the role of a data provider, returning a list of items in a credible fashion. Notice that we built it in a way that it will always return identical items, as long as the `num` parameter value remains the same:

- The generated items `Id` will follow a linear sequence, from 1 to `num`.
- Any generated item will have incremental `CreatedDate` and `LastModifiedDate` values based upon their `Id`: the higher the `Id` is, the most recent the two dates will be, up to 31 December, 2015. This follows the assumption that most recent items will have a higher `Id`, as it normally is for DBMS records featuring numeric, auto-incremental keys.
- Any generated item will have a decreasing `ViewCount` value based upon their `Id`: the higher the `Id` is, the less it will be. This follows the assumption that newer items will generally get fewer views than older ones.

While it obviously lacks any insert/update/delete features, this dummy data provider is viable enough to serve our purposes until we'll replace it with an actual, persistence-based data source.

 Technically speaking, we could do something better than we did by using one of the many Mocking Frameworks available through NuGet: Moq, NMock3, NSubstitute, or Rhino, just to name a few.
These frameworks are the ideal choice when using a test-driven development (TDD) approach, which is not the case in this book. In this specific scenario, our dummy data provider is still a viable way to get what we need while keeping the focus on our main topic: ASP.NET Core and Angular 2 interaction.

Dealing with single items

Our updated `ItemsController` class has everything we need to build our *Welcome View*: as soon as we learn how to call it from our client code, we'll be able to fetch the required data to populate all the item lists we expect to have within our GUI.

However, we don't have anything yet to handle any kind of user interaction. When our users click an item, they will surely expect to read something more about it; ideally, they will want to see something similar to a detail page.

To put it in other words: since our *Welcome View* features a list of clickable items, sooner or later we'll have to give our users the chance to select one of them, ideally with a left mouse click and display the selected item's details: something like a master/detail navigation pattern of any sort.

We're not dealing with the client-side code yet, so we don't know how we'll present such a scenario to the user. However, we already know what we'll eventually need: an API call to retrieve a single `Item` by passing its unique `Id`. To do that we need to provide our controller with the appropriate API method, which could be something like this:

```
/api/items/Get/{id}
```

This means that we need to add something more to our `ItemsController` source code. While we're at it, let's take the chance to make some more improvements:

- A sample method based upon the standard RESTful conventions, just to demonstrate how we can handle that
- A parameterless overload for each method, to make their usage easier
- A couple more private properties to define:
    - The default number of items to retrieve using the parameterless overload
    - The maximum number of items to retrieve within a single API call

The resulting code can be seen as follows (new lines are highlighted):

```
using System;
using System.Collections.Generic;
using System.Linq;
using System.Threading.Tasks;
using Microsoft.AspNetCore.Mvc;
using OpenGameListWebApp.ViewModels;
using Newtonsoft.Json;

namespace OpenGameListWebApp.Controllers
{
    [Route("api/[controller]")]
    public class ItemsController : Controller
    {
        #region RESTful Conventions
        /// <summary>
        /// GET: api/items
        /// </summary>
        /// <returns>Nothing: this method will raise a HttpNotFound HTTP
         exception, since we're not supporting this API call.</returns>
        [HttpGet()]
```

```
public IActionResult Get()
{
    return NotFound(new { Error = "not found" });
}
/// <summary>
/// GET: api/items/{id}
/// ROUTING TYPE: attribute-based
/// </summary>
/// <returns>A Json-serialized object representing a single item.
</returns>
[HttpGet("{id}")]
public IActionResult Get(int id)
{
    return new JsonResult(GetSampleItems()
        .Where(i => i.Id == id)
        .FirstOrDefault(),
        DefaultJsonSettings);
}
#endregion
#region Attribute-based Routing
/// <summary>
/// GET: api/items/GetLatest
/// ROUTING TYPE: attribute-based
/// </summary>
/// <returns>An array of a default number of Json-serialized
    objects representing the last inserted items.</returns>
[HttpGet("GetLatest")]
public IActionResult GetLatest()
{
    return GetLatest(DefaultNumberOfItems);
}


/// <summary>
/// GET: api/items/GetLatest/{n}
/// ROUTING TYPE: attribute-based
/// </summary>
/// <returns>An array of {n} Json-serialized objects representing
the last inserted items.</returns>
[HttpGet("GetLatest/{n}")]
public IActionResult GetLatest(int n)
{
    if (n > MaxNumberOfItems) n = MaxNumberOfItems;
    var items = GetSampleItems().OrderByDescending(i =>
i.CreatedDate).Take(n);
    return new JsonResult(items, DefaultJsonSettings);
}


/// <summary>
```

```
        /// GET: api/items/GetMostViewed
        /// ROUTING TYPE: attribute-based
        /// </summary>
        /// <returns>An array of a default number of Json-serialized
         objects representing the items with most user views.</returns>
        [HttpGet("GetMostViewed")]
        public IActionResult GetMostViewed()
        {
            return GetMostViewed(DefaultNumberOfItems);
        }


        /// <summary>
        /// GET: api/items/GetMostViewed/{n}
        /// ROUTING TYPE: attribute-based
        /// </summary>
        /// <returns>An array of {n} Json-serialized objects representing
the items with most user views.</returns>
        [HttpGet("GetMostViewed/{n}")]
        public IActionResult GetMostViewed(int n)
        {
            if (n > MaxNumberOfItems) n = MaxNumberOfItems;
            var items = GetSampleItems().OrderByDescending(i =>
i.ViewCount).Take(n);
            return new JsonResult(items, DefaultJsonSettings);
        }


        /// <summary>
        /// GET: api/items/GetRandom
        /// ROUTING TYPE: attribute-based
        /// </summary>
        /// <returns>An array of a default number of
        Json-serialized objects representing some randomly-picked items.
         </returns>
        [HttpGet("GetRandom")]
        public IActionResult GetRandom()
        {
            return GetRandom(DefaultNumberOfItems);
        }


        /// <summary>
        /// GET: api/items/GetRandom/{n}
        /// ROUTING TYPE: attribute-based
        /// </summary>
        /// <returns>An array of {n} Json-serialized objects representing
some randomly-picked items.</returns>
        [HttpGet("GetRandom/{n}")]
        public IActionResult GetRandom(int n)
        {
```

```
            if (n > MaxNumberOfItems) n = MaxNumberOfItems;
        var items = GetSampleItems().OrderBy(i =>
Guid.NewGuid()).Take(n);
        return new JsonResult(items, DefaultJsonSettings);
    }
    #endregion

    #region Private Members
    /// <summary>
    /// Generate a sample array of source Items to emulate a database
(for testing purposes only).
    /// </summary>
    /// <param name="num">The number of items to generate: default is
999</param>
    /// <returns>a defined number of mock items (for testing purpose
only)</returns>
    private List<ItemViewModel> GetSampleItems(int num = 999)
    {
        List<ItemViewModel> lst = new List<ItemViewModel>();
        DateTime date = new DateTime(2015, 12, 31).AddDays(-num);
        for (int id = 1; id <= num; id++)
        {
            date = date.AddDays(1);
            lst.Add(new ItemViewModel()
            {
                Id = id,
                Title = String.Format("Item {0} Title", id),
                Description = String.Format("This is a sample
description for item {0}: Lorem ipsum dolor sit amet.", id),
                CreatedDate = date,
                LastModifiedDate = date,
                ViewCount = num - id
            });
        }
        return lst;
    }

    /// <summary>
    /// Returns a suitable JsonSerializerSettings object that can be
used to generate the JsonResult return value for this Controller's methods.
    /// </summary>
    private JsonSerializerSettings DefaultJsonSettings
    {
        get
        {
            return new JsonSerializerSettings()
            {
                Formatting = Formatting.Indented
```

```
            };
        }
    }

    /// <summary>
    /// Returns the default number of items to retrieve when using the
     parameterless overloads of the API methods retrieving item lists.
    /// </summary>
    private int DefaultNumberOfItems
    {
        get
        {
            return 5;
        }
    }
    /// <summary>
    /// Returns the maximum number of items to retrieve when using the
        API methods retrieving item lists.
    /// </summary>
    private int MaxNumberOfItems
    {
        get
        {
            return 100;
        }
    }
    #endregion
    }
}
```

We've already explained the new goodies out there, yet it can be useful to focus on a couple of them:

- Our brand new `Get()` method won't do anything more than return a `404 HTTP Error` with a custom error string. We added it to grant an explicit response to that RESTful default call and also to demonstrate how we can choose between handling them or not.

- The `DefaultNumberOfItems` and `MaxNumberOfItems` have been added to store their values in a centralized way, so we can avoid repeating them multiple times. We made them as properties, but they could also be defined as constants or private variables as well since they are meant to be for internal use only; we won't reference them outside this class or anywhere else.

Let's test our new methods: select **Debug** | **Start Debugging** from the main menu (or hit *F5*) and type the following URLs in the browser's address bar:

```
/api/items
```

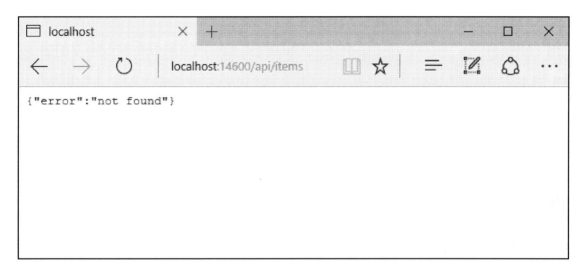

```
/api/items/5
```

As we've already said, the **404 Page Not Found** error in response to the first HTTP request is perfectly fine; we did it on purpose to demonstrate how we can handle these kinds of errors. This is also good practice when dealing with ASP.NET Core API interfaces; since we chose to not accept any /api/items get call without parameters, we want the client to be aware of that.

So far, so good; we've got ourselves a number of server-side APIs to retrieve JSON arrays filled by a client-defined (or default) number of latest items, and an additional one to retrieve a single item from its unique ID. All of these calls will be very handy in the following chapter, where we'll start developing client-side components using Angular 2.

Suggested topics

HTTP request, HTTP response, convention-based routing, attribute-based routing, RESTful conventions, mock objects, test-driven development, XML documentation tags, and C# preprocessor directives.

Summary

We spent some time putting the standard application data flow under our lens: a two-way communication pattern between the server and their clients, built upon the HTTP protocol. We acknowledged the fact that we'll be mostly dealing with JSON-serializable object such as **Items**, so we chose to equip ourselves with an ItemViewModel server-side class, together with an ItemsController that will actively use it to expose the data to the client.

We started building our MVC6-based Web API interface by implementing a number of methods required to create the client-side UI we chose for our *Welcome View*, consisting of three item listings to show to our users: last inserted ones, most viewed ones, and some random picks. We routed the requests to them by using a custom set of attribute-based routing rules, which seemed to be the best choice for our specific scenario.

While we were there, we also took the chance to add a dedicated method to retrieve a single Item from its unique Id, assuming that we were going to need it for sure.

In the next chapter, we will see how we can consume the ASP.NET Core Web API using Angular 2 in order to build an interactive user interface for our application.

3
Angular 2 Components and Client-Side Routing

Our server-side Web API is working fine; however, the `ItemsController` is still missing parts that we're going to need eventually, such as the POST-based methods to insert, update, and delete items. There's no sense in adding them now since we're still mocking up our objects. We'll implement these soon enough when we switch to a real data model.

For the time being, let's see how we can make good use of what we just did by implementing a basic master-detail navigation pattern using Angular 2, which is our application client framework of choice.

Let's summarize what we're going to do in this chapter:

- Greet our users with a **Welcome View** with three different lists of items: latest, most viewed, and random. We'll populate these by fetching the relevant data using the `ItemsController` API methods built in Chapter 2, *ASP.NET Controllers and Server-Side Routes*.
- Let our users navigate to an **Item Detail View** upon clicking on any item.
- Allow our users to go back from the **Item Detail View** to the **Welcome View** upon clicking on a back link.

This isn't anything different from a standard, straightforward master-detail pattern. When we're done, users will be able to perform a basic navigation loop like the following:

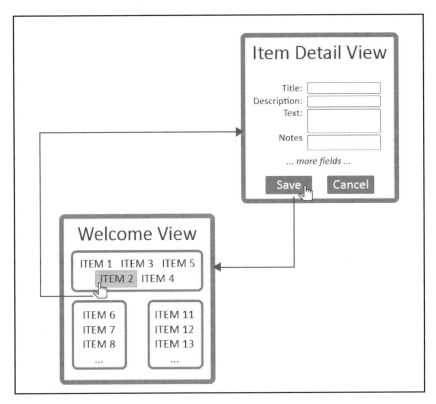

Notice that we will also give the user the chance to modify some item fields, reflecting these changes in the underlying client-side data model. Doing this in Angular 2 is a rather seamless task due to the framework's built-in two-way data binding features.

Persisting these changes to the application's data source is a whole different story though, as it requires us to implement a couple more features:

1. A dedicated server-side API that will receive the updated data from the client model and sync it to the server model.
2. A client-side update command pattern, such as a button, a focus event, or something like that, that will trigger the aforementioned update API call.

This is something we'll do in the next chapter by implementing a persistent data source and replacing our dummy data provider sample with a working one. We won't be able to properly handle any persisting update command until then.

Master-detail binding

Our main focus now is to implement a master-detail navigation pattern. We'll do that in two steps:

1. Putting together a temporary, component-based master-detail relationship based upon the Angular 2 data-binding feature.
2. Replacing the preceding with a view-based navigation pattern with full client-side routing support.

Truth be told, step *1* isn't mandatory. We could just implement step *2* and get the task over with. However, by choosing to do that, we would skip some really important concepts regarding Angular 2 and its interactions with the Web API structure we just built. This stuff will come in very handy later on; therefore, it's highly recommended that we restrain ourselves from rushing things.

The Item class

The first thing we need to do is to add the `Item` class to our Angular-enabled client. Wait a minute… should we really do that? Can't we just use the raw JSON data sent by the controller's `Get` and `GetLatest` methods defined earlier, consuming them as anonymous JavaScript objects?

Theoretically speaking, we could try as much as we could output raw JSON from the controller instead of creating our `ItemViewModel` class. In a well-written app, though, we should always restrain ourselves from the temptation to handle raw JSON data and/or to use anonymous objects for a number of good reasons:

- We're using TypeScript because we want to work with type definitions: anonymous objects and undefined properties are the exact opposite and lead into the JavaScript way of doing things, which is something we wanted to avoid in the first place.
- Anonymous objects are not easy to validate. We don't want our data items to be error prone, being forced to deal with missing properties or anything like that.
- Anonymous objects are hardly reusable and won't benefit from many Angular 2 handy features, such as the object mapping, which will require our objects to be actual instances of an interface and/or a type.

The first two points are very important, especially if we're aiming for a production-ready application. However, point 3 is also crucial as long as we want to use Angular 2 to its full extent. If that's still the case, using an undefined array of properties like raw JSON data basically would be out of the question. We're going to use objects, i.e., actual instances of classes.

That's why we need a client-side, TypeScript `Item` class to properly map our JSON-serialized `ItemViewModel` class.

From the **Solution Explorer**, add a new **TypeScript File** in the `/Scripts/app/` folder, call it `item.ts`, and fill it with the following code:

```
export class Item {
    constructor(
        public Id: number,
        public Title: string,
        public Description: string
    ) { }
}
```

Notice that we're not adding all the properties present in the `ItemViewModel` class. As a general rule of thumb, we'll be keeping these classes as lightweight as possible, defining only what we know we're going to use for sure. We can always add more properties later, as soon as we need them.

The ItemService class

Now that we can properly handle JSON-serialized `Item` objects, we need to set up a service to fetch the required data from the Web API. We'll do that by issuing a request to the `ItemsController` we built in the first part of this chapter.

We will do that using HTTP, which is the primary protocol for browser/server communication. Notice that thanks to the features introduced with HTML5, this is not our only option anymore. We could use the WebSocket protocol as well. We won't cover it in this chapter, though, as the HTTP request pattern is still viable enough to do what we need to do: fetch a JSON array of `Item` objects.

To be more specific, we're going to use the Angular HTTP client to communicate via XMLHttpRequest (**XHR**), which is a rather complex HTTP-based API that provides client functionality for transferring data between a client and a server. We won't have to dig too much into it, though, as Angular greatly simplifies the application programming with an easy-to-use interface featuring a small number of high-level methods.

From the **Solution Explorer**, add a new **TypeScript File** in the /Scripts/app/ folder, call it item.service.ts, and fill it with the following code:

```typescript
import {Injectable} from "@angular/core";
import {Http, Response} from "@angular/http";
import {Observable} from "rxjs/Observable";
import {Item} from "./item";

@Injectable()
export class ItemService {
    constructor(private http: Http) { }

    private baseUrl = "api/items/";   // web api URL

    // calls the [GET] /api/items/GetLatest/{n} Web API method to retrieve
the latest items.
    getLatest(num?: number) {
        var url = this.baseUrl + "GetLatest/";
        if (num != null) { url += num; }
        return this.http.get(url)
            .map(response => response.json())
            .catch(this.handleError);
    }

    // calls the [GET] /api/items/GetMostViewed/{n} Web API method to
retrieve the most viewed items.
    getMostViewed(num?: number) {
        var url = this.baseUrl + "GetMostViewed/";
        if (num != null) { url += num; }
        return this.http.get(url)
            .map(response => response.json())
            .catch(this.handleError);
    }

    // calls the [GET] /api/items/GetRandom/{n} Web API method to retrieve
n random items.
    getRandom(num?: number) {
        var url = this.baseUrl + "GetRandom/";
        if (num != null) { url += num; }
        return this.http.get(url)
            .map(response => response.json())
```

```
            .catch(this.handleError);
    }

    // calls the [GET] /api/items/{id} Web API method to retrieve the item
with the given id.
    get(id: number) {
        if (id == null) { throw new Error("id is required."); }
        var url = this.baseUrl + id;
        return this.http.get(url)
            .map(res => <Item>res.json())
            .catch(this.handleError);
    }

    private handleError(error: Response) {
        // output errors to the console.
        console.error(error);
        return Observable.throw(error.json().error || "Server error");
    }
}
```

You will notice some major similarities between the preceding code and the `ItemsController.cs` source code. It's rather obvious since this is the class that our client will use to fetch the data from that Web API controller itself.

Let's see what these lines of code will actually do:

- In lines 1-4, we're importing the modules we need to perform our tasks. Notice that, in line 4, we're importing the `Item` class we created in the previous chapter, as we're going to use it here.
- In line 6, we make use of the `Injectable` decorator, declaring that ours is an `Injectable` class. Doing this will attach a set of metadata to our class that will be consumed by the DI system upon instantiation. Basically, what we're doing here is telling the DI injector that the constructor parameter(s) should be instantiated using their declared type(s). The TypeScript code allows a very fluent syntax to achieve this result at constructor level, as can be seen in line 8.
- In line 10, we define a variable containing our Web API-based URL, so we won't have to write it multiple times. Avoiding repetition is always a good thing and is one of the main rules to follow in order to write decent code.

- In the subsequent lines, we create our `getLatest()`, `getMostViewed()`, `getRandom()`, and `Get()` client-side methods that will call their Web API counterpart. Notice that the method names differ in the naming conventions, as we're respecting Javascript's `camelCase` here, while the `ItemsController` follows the `PascalCase` (also known as `UpperCamelCase`) .NET standard. We should also note how the retrieved `ItemViewModel` array of data is mapped to an equal number of `Item` objects by making use of the Angular native mapping module.
- Finally, there's a rudimental implementation of an exception handling method that will be triggered by the preceding two data-fetching methods, in the case of an error. For now, we'll just output the errors to the browser console.

Now that we've got an `Item` and an `ItemService`, we should have everything we need to display our listing of items except one thing: the Angular-based component that will dynamically build the list in plain HTML code. Let's close this gap.

 If you get the odd TypeScript compilation error after implementing this class, you might need to replace the `typescriptServices.js` file, as mentioned in `Chapter 1`, *Getting Ready*.

The ItemListComponent class

What we're going to do here is to create a dedicated component to handle the "display a list of items task." We could also do that in our already-present `AppComponent` class, but our app is growing fast. Sooner or later we will have to split it into multiple, reusable assets. That being the case, there's no reason to do it right from the start. To be more specific, we're aiming to have the following file structure:

- `app.component.ts`: Our **Welcome View**, with a number of references to sub-components enclosed by a lightweight HTML skeleton
- `item-list.component.ts`: A flexible, reusable item listing component that can be easily included by any view, one or multiple times

We'll stick to this pattern from now on, create a separate `xyz.component.ts` file for any component we'll require. Let's start with building the first one.

Again, from the **Solution Explorer**, add a new **TypeScript File** in the /Scripts/app/ folder, call it item-list.component.ts, and fill it with the following code:

```
import {Component, OnInit} from "@angular/core";
import {Item} from "./item";
import {ItemService} from "./item.service";

@Component({
    selector: "item-list",
    template: `
        <h2>Latest Items:</h2>
            <ul class="items">
            <li *ngFor="let item of items"
                [class.selected]="item === selectedItem"
                (click)="onSelect(item)">
                <span>{{item.Title}}</span>
            </li>
        </ul>
    `,
    styles: [`
        ul.items li {
            cursor: pointer;
        }
        ul.items li.selected {
            background-color: #cccccc;
        }
    `]
})

export class ItemListComponent implements OnInit {
    selectedItem: Item;
    items: Item[];
    errorMessage: string;

    constructor(private itemService: ItemService) { }

    ngOnInit() {
        this.getLatest();
    }

    getLatest() {
        this.itemService.getLatest()
            .subscribe(
            latestItems => this.items = latestItems,
            error => this.errorMessage = <any>error
            );
    }
```

```
    onSelect(item: Item) {
        this.selectedItem = item;
        console.log("item with Id " + this.selectedItem.Id + " has been
selected.");
    }
}
```

That's quite an amount of non-trivial source code. Let's see what we just did in detail:

- In line 1, we imported the Angular classes that we require. Since we're creating a component, we require the `Component` base class and need to implement the `OnInit` interface because our component will need to execute something upon its initialization.
- In lines 2-3, we import our previously created `Item` and `ItemService` classes. No surprises here, since we're obviously using them here.
- In lines 5-25, we set up the component UI aspect and settings. In particular, we'll perform the following tasks:
    - **Line 6**: We're defining the selector, which is the custom HTML element that will be replaced by the component itself.
    - **Lines 7-16**: We're creating the HTML structure of what will be rendered on screen. Note that we used a bit of Angular 2 Template Syntax there in order to get the job done. Specifically, we used a master template, a `ngFor` directive, a property binding, and an event binding. Notice how each command relies on some local properties and/or methods: `item`, `items`, `selectedItem`, and `onSelect()`. We will explain them soon enough, as they are declared further down.
    - **Lines 17-24**: We're adding some minimalistic CSS styles in order to have some visual feedback about what we're going to do, which is to change the background color of the currently selected item. We'll do something way better later on.

- In lines 27-51, we can find the core `ItemListComponent` class declaration, together with all its properties, constructor and methods:
  - **Lines 28-30**: Here, we define our class `Properties`, the same that we used in our template (see lines 7-16).
  - **Line 32**: The class constructor. Notice how we make use of the Angular 2 native dependency injection features. We're not instantiating the `ItemService` object, we let the framework do that instead. This means that our `ItemsComponent` class won't be creating an `ItemService`, it will just *consume* it right on the spot. While we're there we also made good use of the flexible constructor syntax provided by TypeScript, allowing us to declare the parameter and the property in a single shot.
  - **Lines 34-36**: The `ngOnInit` implementation, which is pretty much straightforward. The `getLatest()` internal method will be executed upon initialization and that's it.
  - **Lines 38-50**: these are the two methods that will be used, respectively, to retrieve the items (`getLatest`), and to handle the only user interaction we need our class to be aware of – the left-button mouse click (`onSelect`).

 If you feel curious about the aforementioned Angular 2 Template Syntax, don't worry! We're going to talk way more about that in a while. Nonetheless, if you just can't wait to get a hold on that, you can take a look at the official documentation available on the Angular 2 website: `https://angular.io/docs/ts/latest/guide/template-syntax.html`.

A quick implementation test

We just added three major things to our client-side app: a class (`Item`), a JSON-consuming service (`ItemService`), and a UI component specifically designed to use them both (`ItemListComponent`). Before going further, it may be a good call to see the results of our work up to this point to ensure that everything is working as expected.

The first thing we need to do is to add these new features to our application's root module. Open the `/Scripts/app/app.module.ts` file and add the following (new lines are highlighted):

```
///<reference path="../../typings/index.d.ts"/>
import {NgModule} from "@angular/core";
import {BrowserModule} from "@angular/platform-browser";
import {HttpModule} from "@angular/http";
import "rxjs/Rx";

import {AppComponent} from "./app.component";
import {ItemListComponent} from "./item-list.component";
import {ItemService} from "./item.service";

@NgModule({
    // directives, components, and pipes
    declarations: [
        AppComponent,
        ItemListComponent
    ],
    // modules
    imports: [
        BrowserModule,
        HttpModule
    ],
    // providers
    providers: [
        ItemService
    ],
    bootstrap: [
        AppComponent
    ]
})
export class AppModule { }
```

Let's now get back to our `/Scripts/app/app.component.ts` file, which is supposed to draw our **Welcome View**, and thus is the starting point of our whole app. We left it out near the end of Chapter 1, *Getting Ready*, when we used a minimalistic template, featuring a "… the best is yet to come!" catchphrase as its main content. Do you remember?

It's time to deliver something better. Replace it with the following code:

```
import {Component} from "@angular/core";

@Component({
    selector: "opengamelist",
    template: `
        <h1>{{title}}</h1>
        <item-list></item-list>
    `
})
export class AppComponent {
    title = "OpenGameList";
}
```

Let's say a few words about what we're doing here:

- In the template, we replaced our previous `hello-worldish` catchphrase with the `<item-list>` custom element, which is the defined selector of the `ItemListComponent` template. This basically means that an `ItemListComponent` will be instantiated there.
- While we were there, we added a title variable within the `AppComponent` class and used it in the template as well.

As soon as we perform these changes, we can launch our application in the debug mode by selecting **Debug | Start Debugging** from the main menu or by hitting *F5* and see if everything is working correctly. If that's the case, we should be able to see something like this:

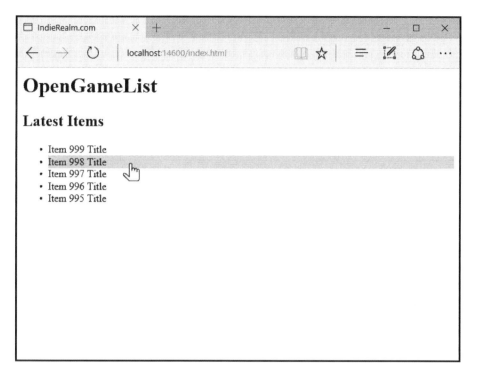

You should also be able to select any item with a left mouse click. The currently selected item will change its background color accordingly.

 Remember to activate the **Gulp** (or **Grunt**) default task, otherwise, your code changes won't be copied to the /wwwroot/ folder. If you'd forgotten to do that, you can do it now. Right-click on the gulpfile.js (or gruntfile.js) file and select the **Task Runner Explorer**. Once there, right-click on the **default** task, and activate it by clicking on **Run**.

This is more than enough to tell us that everything is going well. Now that we're sure about it, we can go back to work and add the component that will handle the item's detail view.

The ItemDetailComponent class

Once again, from the **Solution Explorer**, add a new **TypeScript File** in the /Scripts/app/ folder, call it item-detail.component.ts, and fill it with the following code:

```
import {Component, Input} from "@angular/core";
import {Item} from "./item";

@Component({
    selector: "item-detail",
    template: `
        <div *ngIf="item" class="item-details">
            <h2>{{item.Title}} - Detail View</h2>
            <ul>
                <li>
                    <label>Title:</label>
                    <input [(ngModel)]="item.Title" placeholder="Insert the
title..."/>
                </li>
                <li>
                    <label>Description:</label>
                    <textarea [(ngModel)]="item.Description"
placeholder="Insert a suitable description..."></textarea>
                </li>
            </ul>
        </div>
        `,
    styles: [`
        .item-details {
            margin: 5px;
            padding: 5px 10px;
            border: 1px solid black;
            background-color: #dddddd;
            width: 300px;
        }
        .item-details * {
            vertical-align: middle;
        }
        .item-details ul li {
            padding: 5px 0;
        }
        `]
})

export class ItemDetailComponent {
    @Input("item") item: Item;
}
```

Here we go. Let's take a quick look at what we're doing here:

- In lines 1-2, we're importing what we need. Notice that we're importing the `Input` module from Angular 2 Core, which we need to create a data-bound input property (see *line 39*). Needless to say, we also need to reference our `Item` class, as this component will display our item's details.

- In line 5, we define the `selector`, the custom HTML element that will be replaced by the component itself.

- In lines 6-22, we're creating the template UI, a simple HTML snippet to present our item details on screen. It's worth noting that the input elements of our simple form feature a strange `ngModel` attribute between parentheses and brackets. We'll dig into that in a while, but for now, let's just say that it's the directive that will enable the two-way data binding feature of Angular 2.

- In lines 23-37, we're adding another minimalistic set of CSS rules. This will still lead to a rather ugly outcome, but there's nothing to worry about. We're not in the styling phase yet, that will come later on. For now, let's just put something up in order to distinguish this component's HTML from the rest.

- Finally, in lines 40-42, we're declaring our `ItemDetailComponent` class. Note that it only has a single `item` property. We have also defined it as using a `@Input()` decorator function (see line 1), that will add the required metadata to make this property available for property binding. We need to do this because we expect this property to be populated from a binding expression within a parent component. We're going to do that in the next paragraph.

The `@Input()` decorator function deserves a couple more words. Note that it accepts an optional alias parameter, which we explicitly added (`"item"`) to demonstrate how it works under the hood. When we add our `ItemDetailComponent` in a parent component, we will also need to pass the item object to show. We'll do that using a custom attribute in the following way:

```
<item-detail *ngIf="selectedItem" [item]="selectedItem"></item-detail>
```

The alias parameter will be used to determine the attribute hosting the property binding. Its value will be dynamically bound to our target input property.

That being the case, you might be wondering why we called it optional. That's because it can be skipped as long as the attribute name matches the target input property name. In our case, they share the same name, so we could safely remove it.

More information regarding the input property is available through the following Angular 2 official documentation page: `https://angular.io/docs/ts/latest/guide/attribute-directives.html#!#why-input`.

Adding the @angular/forms library

Although the `ItemDetailComponent` component doesn't yet contain a proper `<form>` element, it has some input elements that can greatly benefit from the Angular 2 two-way data binding feature. To implement it, though, we need to add the `@angular/forms` library to our NPM package list.

To do that, open the `package.json` file and add the following highlighted line to the `dependencies` section, right below the other `@angular` packages:

```
"@angular/common": "2.0.0-rc.5",
"@angular/compiler": "2.0.0-rc.5",
"@angular/core": "2.0.0-rc.5",
"@angular/http": "2.0.0-rc.5",
"@angular/platform-browser": "2.0.0-rc.5",
"@angular/platform-browser-dynamic": "2.0.0-rc.5",
"@angular/upgrade": "2.0.0-rc.5",
"@angular/forms": "0.3.0",
```

Subsequently, open the `/wwwroot/systemjs.config.js` file and append the following highlighted line to the `ngPackageNames` array:

```
// configure @angular packages
var ngPackageNames = [
  'common',
  'compiler',
  'core',
  'http',
  'platform-browser',
  'platform-browser-dynamic',
  'upgrade',
  'forms'
];
```

This will allow us to import the `FormsModule` within our application's root module in the following paragraph, thereby enabling the two-way data binding feature.

Updating the root module

Every time we add an Angular 2 component we also need to import and declare it to our root module (or a nested module, which we don't have). The `ItemDetailComponent` won't be an exception, so we have to add it just like we did with the `ItemListComponent` a short while ago. On top of that, since the same rule also applies to modules and providers, we need to do that for the `FormsModule` as well.

Open the `/Scripts/app/app.module.ts` file and update its contents accordingly (new lines are highlighted):

```
///<reference path="../../typings/index.d.ts"/>
import {NgModule} from "@angular/core";
import {BrowserModule} from "@angular/platform-browser";
import {HttpModule} from "@angular/http";
import {FormsModule} from "@angular/forms";
import "rxjs/Rx";

import {AppComponent} from "./app.component";
import {ItemListComponent} from "./item-list.component";
import {ItemDetailComponent} from "./item-detail.component";
import {ItemService} from "./item.service";

@NgModule({
    // directives, components, and pipes
    declarations: [
        AppComponent,
        ItemListComponent,
        ItemDetailComponent
    ],
    // modules
    imports: [
        BrowserModule,
        HttpModule,
        FormsModule
    ],
    // providers
    providers: [
        ItemService
    ],
    bootstrap: [
        AppComponent
```

```
})
export class AppModule { }
```

Connecting the dots

Now that we have a component to display our item's details, we need to connect it to the item listing one we created previously. Doing that is as easy as adding a couple of lines to our ItemListComponent class.

From the **Solution Explorer**, open the /Scripts/app/item-list.component.ts file and change it as we have in the following code (added lines are highlighted):

```
import {Component, OnInit} from '@angular/core';
import {Item} from "./item";
import {ItemService} from "./item.service";

@Component({
    selector: "item-list",
    template: `
        <h2>Latest Items:</h2>
        <ul class="items">
            <li *ngFor="let item of items"
                [class.selected]="item === selectedItem"
                (click)="onSelect(item)">
                <span>{{item.Title}}</span>
            </li>
        </ul>
        <item-detail *ngIf="selectedItem" [item]="selectedItem"></item-
detail>
        `,
    styles: [`
        ul.items li {
            cursor: pointer;
        }
        ul.items li.selected {
            background-color: #dddddd;
        }
    `]
})

export class ItemListComponent implements OnInit {
    selectedItem: Item;
    items: Item[];
    errorMessage: string;

    constructor(private itemService: ItemService) { }
```

```
ngOnInit() {
    this.getLatest();
}

getLatest() {
    this.itemService.getLatest()
        .subscribe(
        latestItems => this.items = latestItems,
        error => this.errorMessage = <any>error
        );
}

onSelect(item: Item) {
    this.selectedItem = item;
    console.log("item with Id " + this.selectedItem.Id + " has been
selected.");
    }
}
```

All we did here was to add an `<item-detail>` element with an `item` property, which is the target of a property binding. This is the reason why it is in square brackets, to the left of the equal sign. We already knew about it from the previous paragraph, when we were referring to the `@Input()` decorator attribute and its optional alias parameter.

 It's worth noting that we don't need to import the `ItemDetailComponent` to use the `<item-detail>` element, as the compiler will automatically fetch that from the `AppModule`. That's precisely what our root module is for. Before Angular 2 RC5, we had to manually handle the required import throughout all the component files, resulting in major (and also error-prone) code repetition.

Testing it up

It's time to perform a full test of what we've built up to this point.

Click on **Debug | Start Debugging** (or hit *F5*) to display the same view from Image03.02 again, then browse through the items by clicking the left mouse button. You should be presented with something like the following:

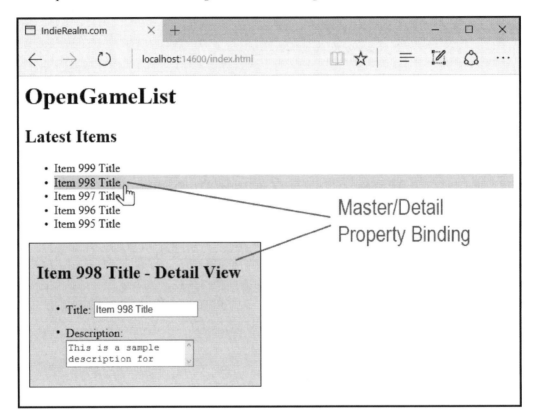

If everything is working as it should, as we change the selectedItem the **Detail View** panel should be updated as well, showing that item's details.

Adding additional lists

Our welcome page isn't done yet. Two out of three item lists are yet to be done, at least on the client side. We're talking about the most viewed items and the randomly picked ones, so let's add them to the loop. We basically have two ways to do this:

1. Adding two more Angular components that are very similar to the `ItemListComponent` one.
2. Extending our `ItemListComponent` and making it configurable, thereby making it able to handle all the three item listings.

Adding two more components would be rather easy. We could clone the `item-list.component.ts` file a couple of times, change the inner method of the two new files to make it fetch the relevant data from the other Web API method (respectively, `GetMostViewed()` and `GetRandom()`), define a different selector, add it to the `AppComponent` template code and we would be done.

Yet, it would also be a horrible approach. Let's restrain us from cloning any part of our code, unless there's really no other way to get the things done. We're using Angular 2 because we want to build versatile and reusable components, and we're going to stick to this path as much as we can. We also don't want to spawn unnecessary components, as it would be a pain to keep them in sync each and every time we have to apply a definition update, a member rename, an interface change, or any other source code modification that will affect either of them.

For the previous reasons, we'll definitely choose the second option. Not to mention the fact that it will be just as easy, once we know how to do it properly.

Regarding that choice, it's easy to see that we've already started off on the right foot. We called it `ItemListComponent`, instead of `LatestItemsComponent` because we never really wanted to have it showing the last inserted items only.

We could say that we already knew that we would be choosing the second option right from the start. It's hardly a surprise, though, since we're fully committed to building reusable components.

Multiple component instances

The first thing we need to do is to configure the AppComponent HTML template to make it render a couple more <item-list> component tags. While doing that, we also need to find a way to uniquely identify them in order to issue a different behavior for each instance: latest items, most viewed items, and random items.

Open the app.component.ts file and update our previous code in the following way (added/modified lines are highlighted):

```
import {Component} from '@angular/core';

@Component({
    selector: "opengamelist",
    template: `
        <h1>{{title}}</h1>
        <item-list class="latest"></item-list>
        <item-list class="most-viewed"></item-list>
        <item-list class="random"></item-list>
    `,
    styles: [`
        item-list {
            min-width: 332px;
            border: 1px solid #aaaaaa;
            display: inline-block;
            margin: 0 10px;
            padding: 10px;
        }
        item-list.latest {
            background-color: #f9f9f9;
        }
        item-list.most-viewed {
            background-color: #f0f0f0;
        }
        item-list.random {
            background-color: #e9e9e9;
        }
    `]
})
export class AppComponent {
    title = 'OpenGameList';
}
```

Let's take a closer look at what we did here:

- We added two more `<item-list>` elements.
- We defined a standard `class` attribute with a different value for each instance. This is what we will use to uniquely identify each one of them. Notice that we could've used the `id` attribute, or any other standard or custom attribute. Using `class` seems to be a rather elegant choice, as it can also be used to apply different styles.
- We took the chance to implement some minimalistic CSS styles to arrange the three elements horizontally and add some space between them. Since they have different `class` attribute values now, we also gave a unique background color to each element.

We're halfway through. Now we need to change the `ItemListComponent` class accordingly, so it can follow a different behavior depending on the type of attribute value.

Here's how we can do that (added/modified lines are highlighted):

```
import {Component, Input, OnInit} from "@angular/core";
import {Item} from './item';
import {ItemService} from './item.service';

@Component({
    selector: "item-list",
    template: `
        <h2>{{title}}</h2>
        <ul class="items">
            <li *ngFor="let item of items"
                [class.selected]="item === selectedItem"
                (click)="onSelect(item)">
                <span>{{item.Title}}</span>
            </li>
        </ul>
        <item-detail *ngIf="selectedItem" [item]="selectedItem"></item-detail>
        `,
    styles: [`
        ul.items li {
            cursor: pointer;
        }
        ul.items li.selected {
            background-color: #dddddd;
        }
    `]
})
```

```
export class ItemListComponent implements OnInit {
    @Input() class: string;
    title: string;
    selectedItem: Item;
    items: Item[];
    errorMessage: string;

    constructor(private itemService: ItemService) { }

    ngOnInit() {
        console.log("ItemListComponent instantiated with the following
type: "+this.class);
        var s = null;
        switch (this.class) {
            case "latest":
            default:
                this.title = "Latest Items";
                s = this.itemService.getLatest();
                break;
            case "most-viewed":
                this.title = "Most Viewed Items";
                s = this.itemService.getMostViewed();
                break;
            case "random":
                this.title = "Random Items";
                s = this.itemService.getRandom();
                break;
        }
        s.subscribe(
            items => this.items = items,
            error => this.errorMessage = <any>error
            );
    }

    onSelect(item: Item) {
        this.selectedItem = item;
        console.log("item with Id " + this.selectedItem.Id + " has been
selected.");
    }
}
```

We have a fair amount of changes here. Let's see what we did:

- In line 1, we added a reference to an old friend, the `Input` module from Angular 2 Core. We need it here so our class will be able to issue a data binding between the `class` input property (see line 39) and the attribute with the same name we defined in `AppComponent` within the previous code sample.

- In line 8, we replaced our static title string with a local `title` variable, thereby making it dynamic. From now on, this component's title will have to change accordingly with the `class` attribute value of the current instance.

- In line 29, we defined the `class` input property we mentioned previously. We'll be using it to determine how to initialize the current instance (see lines 37-59).

- In the subsequent lines, we implemented a brand new whole initialization logic based upon the preceding defined `class` input property. To be more specific, we switch through the three supported types and set the `title` and the `service` method accordingly.

You might have noticed that the `getLatest()` method is gone. We removed it because we transferred all the `service` method calls within the `ngOnInit()` method, so there's no need to keep it. That's a relief, as its name would also be rather obsolete now anyway.

It's time to see the results of what we just did. As usual, doing that is just as easy as hitting *F5* and waiting for our default browser to load:

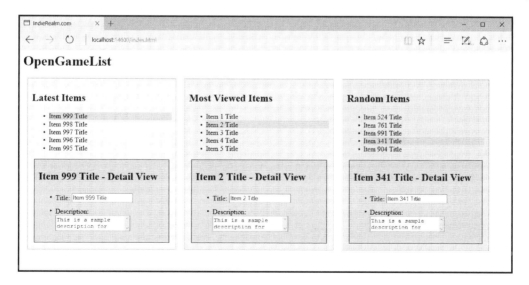

Our application is growing fast. We've got the Web API together with a small, yet versatile set of working Angular 2 components able to fetch and display our sample data.

We're still missing a fair amount of features, though, such as the following:

- Two-way binding
- Client-side routing

It's time to add both of them.

Two-way data binding

We already mentioned it a number of times, as it is one of the most convenient and widely known features of Angular 2, as well as many other reactive frameworks out there. Nonetheless, before going further, let's make sure we know what we're talking about.

Two-way data binding, also known as two-way binding, means that whenever the data model changes, the UI changes accordingly and vice versa. To be more specific:

- Whenever the model is updated, the changes are immediately reflected to the views implementing it.
- Whenever the view is updated, the changes are immediately reflected in the underlying model.

From a practical development perspective, two-way data binding will help us a lot because we won't have to manually synchronize the UI components with the data model.

The good news is, since we're using Angular 2, we're already set, and thanks to the `ngModel` we implemented earlier, our application is already equipped with a fully functional two-way data binding between the `Item` model and the two component classes implementing it: `ItemListComponents` and `ItemDetailComponent`.

We can easily check this out: hit *F5* again to run the application in the **Debug** mode, then select an item and change its `Title` property using the input textbox provided by the `ItemDetailComponent`. You will notice that any change will be immediately reflected to the `ItemListComponent` accordingly:

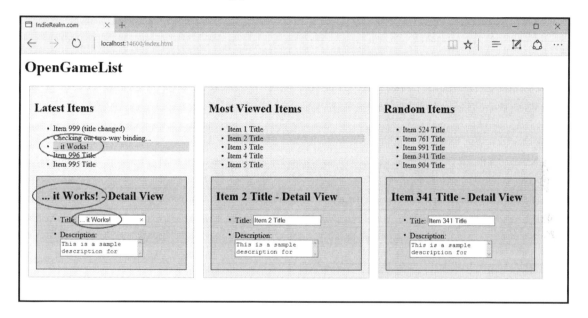

As we've already said, all of these things happen on the client side only. To persist them through the server model, we would need to implement a fully featured data source, which is something we're going to do in the next chapter.

Disabling two-way data binding

Wherever we don't want to have a two-way binding relationship, we can easily turn it off removing the parentheses around the `ngModel` directive, leaving only the brackets:

```
<input [ngModel]="item.Title" placeholder="Insert the title..." />
```

The parentheses within brackets that enable two-way binding `[()]` are widely known as banana brackets. This funny name has its roots in the **Adventure in Angular** podcast episode 078, featuring Brad Green, Misko Hevery, and Igor Minar, in which they referred to that syntax by calling it a *box of bananas*". Other than being an impressive visualization, the banana-box concept greatly helps to avoid common mistakes such as placing the brackets inside the parentheses.

Client-side routing

Our master-detail relationship is indeed working, yet it has some major flaws. The current in-page navigation approach, for example, is completely different from the original plan. We wanted our users to switch back and forth between the **Welcome View** and a dedicated **Item Detail View**, but instead we're opening a detail panel under the first one. No, not just one. Three different panels, one for each item list. That doesn't make any sense! We need to fix that as soon as possible.

While doing that, we also have another severe issue to solve. You might have noticed that regardless of what we do within our app, the URL in the browser's address bar is always the same. This means that we won't be able to share, say, a URL that will directly lead to a specific item detail view, we'll be forced to share the starting URL because it is the only supported one.

Wait a minute! Isn't it our native web application's most expected behavior? This is what the single-page approach is all about after all, isn't it?

The answer is no. The single-page application approach has nothing to do with keeping an immutable URL in the browser's address bar. URLs are not pages. As the name suggests, they are unique identifiers for accessing resources.

standard web applications are usually built upon a rather small number of pages that answer to multiple URLs and serve specific contents based upon query string parameter values and/or URL rewriting techniques. single-page applications make no exceptions, as they can adapt their inner state accordingly to the request URL and also track the user navigation by updating the browser's address bar accordingly.

This technique is called client-side routing, which has the same meaning as navigation. In order to add this much-needed feature, we're going to equip our application with a router, which is the mechanism that will handle the navigation from view to view.

Adding the @angular/router library

Luckily, we won't have to implement the router from scratch as there is already an excellent routing service, known as Angular 2 Component Router that seamlessly does all the hard work. We just need to install it, since it's not part of the Angular 2 core modules. We can still get it through NPM and then import it in our application just like we did with the `@angular/forms`.

Open the `package.json` file and append the following line to the `dependencies` section, right below the `@angular/forms` package:

```
"@angular/router": "3.0.0-rc.1",
```

Right after that, open the `/Scripts/app/app.module.ts` file and add the following highlighted lines:

```
///<reference path="../../typings/index.d.ts"/>
import {NgModule} from "@angular/core";
import {BrowserModule} from "@angular/platform-browser";
import {HttpModule} from "@angular/http";
import {FormsModule} from "@angular/forms";
import {RouterModule}  from "@angular/router";
import "rxjs/Rx";

import {AppComponent} from "./app.component";
import {ItemListComponent} from "./item-list.component";
import {ItemDetailComponent} from "./item-detail.component";
import {ItemService} from "./item.service";

@NgModule({
    // directives, components, and pipes
    declarations: [
        AppComponent,
        ItemListComponent,
        ItemDetailComponent
    ],
    // modules
    imports: [
        BrowserModule,
        HttpModule,
        FormsModule,
        RouterModule
    ],
    // providers
    providers: [
        ItemService
    ],
    bootstrap: [
        AppComponent
    ]
})
export class AppModule { }
```

Last but not least, open the `/wwwroot/systemjs.config.js` file and update the `ngPackageNames` array accordingly:

```
var ngPackageNames = [
    'common',
    'compiler',
    'core',
    'http',
    'platform-browser',
    'platform-browser-dynamic',
    'upgrade',
    'forms',
    'router'
];
```

Now that we made the component router available, we need to properly implement and configure it within our Angular 2 application to provide it with a decent navigation pattern. While doing this we'll also take the chance to refactor our app to make it more similar to our original plan.

PathLocationStrategy versus HashLocationStrategy

Before doing that, we need to understand how the router can help us to achieve what we want, which is changing the browser's location and history whenever the user navigates within the app, without triggering a new page request to the server.

We can configure the router to follow one of two different patterns: `PathLocationStrategy` or `HashLocationStrategy`. The former is based upon the HTML5 `history.pushState` technique, which is by far the preferable one, however, such a technique won't work well on older browsers because they will automatically send a page request every time the current `location.href` value changes, ruining the whole SPA approach, i.e., unless the change is limited to the part of the URL after the hash character (#).

The `HashLocationStrategy` pattern is mostly a workaround that exploits such behavior, as it will instruct the router to compose all the navigation URLs prepending them with a hash character (#) in the following way:

```
http://localhost:14600/app/#/item-detail/2
```

The Angular 2 routing library uses `PathLocationStrategy` by default, hence our app will do the same. Should we prefer to take the other route, we can switch to `HashLocationStrategy` with an override during the bootstrap phase and we will see how to do that in a short while.

Refactoring our app

The other step is a bit more complex, as it involves not only changing some of our application files in order to make the router service available but also changing the component file structure to make it routing-friendly. We should start with the latter, since it will necessarily involve some minor refactoring.

Let's try to get a visual picture of what we need to do before proceeding. It's time to get rid of this working, yet rather inconsistent, cascading structure:

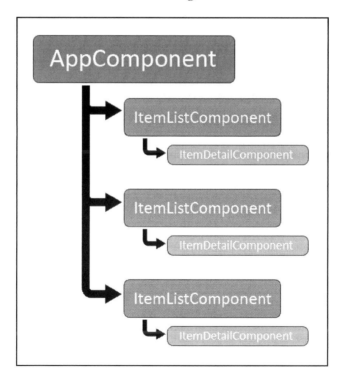

And switch to this truly navigable one:

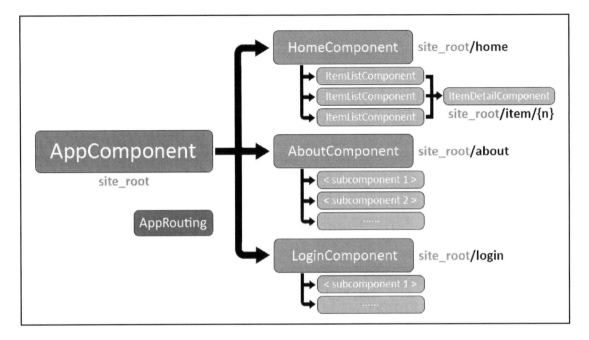

In order to achieve such a result, we need to take care of the following stuff:

- **Add an AppRouting scheme**: This is nothing more than a configuration object containing an array of routing rules called routes. Each one of them connects a URL path to a component, thus telling the client how to navigate.
- **Add a new HomeComponent**: This will behave just like the AppComponent does, so the latter can become a container of many different components, and configure it into the aforementioned AppRouting scheme.
- **Add more sample components**: This tests the routing behavior with a number of different requests and configures them into the AppRouting scheme as well.

Let's do it.

Adding the AppRouting scheme

From the **Solution Explorer**, right-click on the /Scripts/app/ folder and add a new app.routing.ts TypeScript file. Once done, fill it with the following code:

```
import {ModuleWithProviders} from "@angular/core";
import {Routes, RouterModule} from "@angular/router";

import {HomeComponent} from "./home.component";
import {AboutComponent} from "./about.component";
import {LoginComponent} from "./login.component";
import {PageNotFoundComponent} from "./page-not-found.component";

const appRoutes: Routes = [
    {
        path: "",
        component: HomeComponent
    },
    {
        path: "home",
        redirectTo: ""
    },
    {
        path: "about",
        component: AboutComponent
    },
    {
        path: "login",
        component: LoginComponent
    },
    {
        path: '**',
        component: PageNotFoundComponent
    }
];

export const AppRoutingProviders: any[] = [
];

export const AppRouting: ModuleWithProviders =
RouterModule.forRoot(appRoutes);
```

The content is quite self-explanatory. As we can see, it's merely a list of routing rules (we'll call them routes from now on) connecting a given path with a corresponding component of our choice. Just by looking at them we can easily infer the underlying logic:

1. All requests to / (the site root) will be routed to the HomeComponent.
2. All request to /home will be redirected to / (the site root).
3. All request to /about will be routed to the AboutComponent.
4. All request to /login will be routed to the LoginComponent.
5. All other requests will be routed to the PageNotFoundComponent.

As we can see there are two routes that behave quite differently from the other ones:

- Route #2 features a `redirect` instead of a `rewrite`. This means that it will tell the browser to go somewhere else instead of directly handling the request.
- Route #5 is basically a `catch-all` rule that will take care of any unmanned scenario, that is all the requests not directly handled by other routes.

Adding the HomeComponent

The next thing we need to do is to create a brand new `HomeComponent` that will basically behave just like the `AppComponent` actually does. The simplest way to achieve such a result is to copy our current `app.component.ts` file contents into a new `home.component.ts` file. Needless to say, since we're creating a new component, we also need to change the `selector`, `class`, and the `title` variable accordingly.

Here's how the new `home.component.ts` file should appear after our copy and replace work (relevant changes are highlighted):

```
import {Component} from "@angular/core";

@Component({
    selector: "home",
    template: `
        <h2>{{title}}</h2>
        <item-list class="latest"></item-list>
        <item-list class="most-viewed"></item-list>
        <item-list class="random"></item-list>
    `,
    styles: [`
        item-list {
            min-width: 332px;
            border: 1px solid #aaaaaa;
            display: inline-block;
            margin: 0 10px;
            padding: 10px;
        }
        item-list.latest {
            background-color: #f9f9f9;
        }
        item-list.most-viewed {
            background-color: #f0f0f0;
        }
        item-list.random {
            background-color: #e9e9e9;
        }
```

```
    `]
})
export class HomeComponent {
    title = "Welcome View";
}
```

As soon as we do that we can update the `AppComponent` file to act like a container of the currently active Component, as defined by the `AppRouting` scheme.

Open the `app.component.ts` file and entirely replace its now-replicated content with the following (relevant lines highlighted):

```
import {Component} from "@angular/core";

@Component({
    selector: "opengamelist",
    template: `
        <h1>{{title}}</h1>
            <div class="menu">
                <a class="home" [routerLink]="['']">Home</a>
                | <a class="about" [routerLink]="['about']">About</a>
                | <a class="login" [routerLink]="['login']">Login</a>
            </div>
        <router-outlet></router-outlet>

})

export class AppComponent {
    title = "OpenGameList";
}
```

What we did here is pretty simple: we created a simple minimalistic HTML menu that we can use to test our routing engine. The `[routerLink]` attribute directive will tell the component router to populate the `<router-outlet>` element below with the component corresponding to the given path.

That's more or less how the component router works to its simplest extent. While being only a fraction of its many available features, this is already a good portion of what we need to make our application work like we want it to.

Adding new components

It's definitely time to create the missing components we defined earlier within the `app.routing.ts` file, otherwise we would be unable to run our app. These are the following components:

- `AboutComponent`
- `LoginComponent`
- `PageNotFoundComponent`

They won't be much more than a placeholder, at least for now. We will properly implement each one of them as soon as we need to.

AboutComponent

From the **Solution Explorer**, add a new `about.component.ts` file in the `Scripts/app` folder and fill it with the following code:

```
import {Component} from "@angular/core";

@Component({
    selector: "about",
    template: `
        <h2>{{title}}</h2>
        <div>
            OpenGameList: a production-ready, fully-featured SPA sample
powered by ASP.NET Core Web API and Angular 2.
        </div>
        `
})

export class AboutComponent {
    title = "About";
}
```

To be honest, we ought to say that our app is neither production-ready nor fully featured yet, but that's what we're aiming for, so a little encouragement won't hurt. It won't be a lie forever, after all!

LoginComponent

Going back to the **Solution Explorer**, add another file in that same folder, name it `login.component.ts`, and fill it with following code:

```
import {Component} from "@angular/core";

@Component({
    selector: "login",
    template: `
        <h2>{{title}}</h2>
        <div>
            TODO: Not implemented yet.
        </div>
        `
})

export class LoginComponent {
    title = "Login";
}
```

As we have already said, this is just a placeholder. There's no way we can implement the login now, as we're still missing a real, persistent data source. Rest assured, though we could arrange another dummy data provider, there's no need to do that since we'll start implementing the real deal in the following chapter.

PageNotFoundComponent

Last but not least, add a new `/Scripts/app/login.component.ts` file with the following code:

```
import {Component} from "@angular/core";

@Component({
    selector: "page-not-found",
    template: `
        <h2>{{title}}</h2>
        <div>
            Oops.. This page does not exist (yet!).
        </div>
        `
})

export class PageNotFoundComponent {
    title = "Page not Found";
}
```

Doing this will put our Angular 2 application back on track, meaning that we should be able to compile it again. However, if we try to run it, we'll hit some run-time errors due to the fact that the AppModule is still completely unaware of what we did. This is an expected behavior. Now that we're done adding new stuff, we need to bring our root module up to speed.

Updating the root module

Open the /Scripts/app/app.module.ts file and add the new content accordingly (new lines highlighted):

```
///<reference path="../../typings/index.d.ts"/>
import {NgModule} from "@angular/core";
import {BrowserModule} from "@angular/platform-browser";
import {HttpModule} from "@angular/http";
import {FormsModule} from "@angular/forms";
import {RouterModule}  from "@angular/router";
import "rxjs/Rx";

import {AboutComponent} from "./about.component";
import {AppComponent} from "./app.component";
import {HomeComponent} from "./home.component";
import {ItemDetailComponent} from "./item-detail.component";
import {ItemListComponent} from "./item-list.component";
import {LoginComponent} from "./login.component";import
{PageNotFoundComponent} from "./page-not-found.component";import
{AppRouting} from "./app.routing";
import {ItemService} from "./item.service";

@NgModule({
    // directives, components, and pipes
    declarations: [
        AboutComponent,
        AppComponent,
        HomeComponent,
        ItemListComponent,
        ItemDetailComponent,
        LoginComponent,
        PageNotFoundComponent
    ],
    // modules
    imports: [
        BrowserModule,
        HttpModule,
        FormsModule,
        RouterModule,
```

```
        AppRouting
    ],
    // providers
    providers: [
        ItemService
    ],
    bootstrap: [
        AppComponent
    ]
})
export class AppModule { }
```

As we can see, to ensure that our routing rules are applied we have to add the `AppRouting` constant defined within the `app.routing.ts` file to the AppModule's `import` section.

Doing all that will put our Angular 2 application back on track, meaning that we should be able to compile it again.

 While we were there, we took the chance to separate the import references by type and sort them into alphabetical order. This will help us to manage them, as their number will further increase throughout the book.

Revising the master-detail strategy

We're not done yet. Our current implementation features a fully functional master-slave binding relationship between the `ItemListComponent` and the corresponding `ItemDetailComponent`. While it has been very useful to demonstrate how two-way binding works, it's time to replace it with a more reasonable, route-based navigation mechanism.

In order to do that, we need to do the following:

1. Add another route to the `AppComponent` class for the `ItemDetailComponent`.
2. Change the `ItemListComponent` behavior so it will issue a routing action towards the `ItemDetailComponent` instead of showing a built-in instance of it.
3. Modify the `ItemDetailComponent` initialization pattern to make it fetch the `item` data from the `Id` contained within the routing rule instead of relying upon an item object instantiated by the parent `ItemListComponent`.

Adding the ItemDetail route

Open the `/Scripts/app/app.routing.ts` file and add the following route to the `appRoutes` array, right below the one pointing to the `LoginComponent`:

```
{
    path: "item/:id",
    component: ItemDetailComponent
},
```

Consequently, add the relevant reference to the `import` statements on top:

```
import {ItemDetailComponent} from "./item-detail.component";
```

Changing the ItemListComponent

Right after that, open the `item-list.component.ts` file and update its code as follows (changed lines are highlighted):

```
import {Component, Input, OnInit} from "@angular/core";
import {Router} from "@angular/router";
import {Item} from "./item";
import {ItemService} from "./item.service";

@Component({
    selector: "item-list",
    template: `
        <h2>{{title}}</h2>
        <ul class="items">
            <li *ngFor="let item of items"
                [class.selected]="item === selectedItem"
                (click)="onSelect(item)">
                <span>{{item.Title}}</span>
            </li>
        </ul>
    `,
    styles: [`
        ul.items li {
            cursor: pointer;
        }
        ul.items li.selected {
            background-color: #dddddd;
        }
    `]
})

export class ItemListComponent implements OnInit {
```

```
    selectedItem: Item;
    @Input() class: string;
    title: string;
    items: Item[];
    errorMessage: string;

    constructor(private itemService: ItemService, private router: Router) {
}

    ngOnInit() {
        console.log("ItemListComponent instantiated with the following
class: " + this.class);
        var s = null;
        switch (this.class) {
            case "latest":
            default:
                this.title = "Latest Items";
                s = this.itemService.getLatest();
                break;
            case "most-viewed":
                this.title = "Most Viewed Items";
                s = this.itemService.getMostViewed();
                break;
            case "random":
                this.title = "Random Items";
                s = this.itemService.getRandom();
                break;
        }
        s.subscribe(
            items => this.items = items,
            error => this.errorMessage = <any>error
        );
    }

    onSelect(item: Item) {
        this.selectedItem = item;
        console.log("Item " + this.selectedItem.Id + " has been clicked:
loading ItemDetailComponent...");
        this.router.navigate(["item", this.selectedItem.Id]);
    }
}
```

We have a small number of important changes here:

- Within the class constructor, we defined a new DI for an object of the type `Router` to consume within our class. In order to use that, we also added the required `import` reference at the beginning of the file.
- Near the end of the file, we changed the implementation of the `OnSelect` event delegate to tell the router to trigger the `ItemDetail` route instead of loading a local `ItemDetailComponent` as we were doing before.
- Consequently, we removed the `<item-detail>` tag from the template HTML code accordingly.

Updating the ItemDetailComponent

The last thing we need to change is the `ItemDetailComponent` behavior, as it won't be able to get its required `item` data from a parent `ItemListComponent` anymore. We need to make it be able to fetch the data by itself using the only parameter it will receive from its routing entry, the unique `Id` of the `item` to display.

In order to do that, we need to add a couple of references at the beginning of the file:

```
import {Router, ActivatedRoute} from "@angular/router";
```

This way we'll be able to get the `Id` from the request URL and issue a call to the `itemService.get(id)` method to retrieve the item accordingly. That's why we also need to add a reference to the `ItemService` itself:

```
import {ItemService} from "./item.service";
```

What else do we need to do? Since we're removing the parent property binding, we can safely remove the reference to the `Input` interface module as well as the `@Input` decorator from our local `item` variable. We're not using them here anymore.

Yet we will need to retrieve the item data, which is something that's normally done during the initialization phase. That's why we need to add a reference to the `OnInit` interface we used before:

```
import {Component, OnInit} from "@angular/core";
```

We will also need a local variable to host the retrieved item, an improved constructor to instantiate an `ActivatedRoute` object instance through DI and an `OnInit` method to consume it when the class is initialized:

```
export class ItemDetailComponent {
```

```
    item: Item;

    constructor(private itemService: ItemService,
        private activatedRoute: ActivatedRoute) {
    }

    ngOnInit() {
        var id = +this.activatedRoute.params['id'];
        if (id) {
            this.itemService.get(id).subscribe(item => this.item = item);
            console.log(this.item);
        }
    }
}
```

Here's the full, updated `ItemDetailComponent` code with the relevant new/updated lines highlighted:

```
import {Component, OnInit} from "@angular/core";
import {Router, ActivatedRoute} from "@angular/router";
import {Item} from "./item";
import {ItemService} from "./item.service";

@Component({
    selector: "item-detail",
    template: `
        <div *ngIf="item" class="item-details">
          <h2>{{item.Title}} - Detail View</h2>
          <ul>
            <li>
                <label>Title:</label>
                <input [(ngModel)]="item.Title" placeholder="Insert the
title..."/>
            </li>
            <li>
                <label>Description:</label>
                <textarea [(ngModel)]="item.Description"
placeholder="Insert a suitable description..."></textarea>
            </li>
          </ul>
        </div>
    `,
    styles: [`
        .item-details {
            margin: 5px;
            padding: 5px 10px;
            border: 1px solid black;
            background-color: #dddddd;
```

```
                width: 300px;
            }
            .item-details * {
                vertical-align: middle;
            }
            .item-details ul li {
                padding: 5px 0;
            }
        `]
    })

export class ItemDetailComponent {
    item: Item;
    constructor(private itemService: ItemService,
        private router: Router,
        private activatedRoute: ActivatedRoute) {
    }
    ngOnInit() {
        var id = +this.activatedRoute.snapshot.params["id"];
        if (id) {
            this.itemService.get(id).subscribe(
                item => this.item = item
            );
        }
        else {
            console.log("Invalid id: routing back to home...");
            this.router.navigate([""]);
        }
    }
}
```

The use of the injected `ActivatedRoute` object instance here is a bit cryptic, so it deserves a brief explanation.

As we can easily see, it is an object containing information about route parameters, query parameters and URL fragments for the currently active route. In order to access the `id` query parameter, we need to look into the `params` property, which happens to be an `Observable` object. This basically means that we would normally need to `subscribe` to it in the following way:

```
this.activatedRoute.params.subscribe(
    params => {
        let id = +params['id'];
        // do something with id
    });
```

This would indeed work, however, we were able to retrieve the `id` parameter using less code and avoiding the `Observable` entirely thanks to the `snapshot` property, which returns a flattened representation of the currently active route. As a general rule of thumb, we can and should use the `snapshot` whenever we don't need to actively monitor the `Observable` changes.

 Observables are one of the most interesting features introduced by Angular 2. We'll talk more about them in `Chapter 5`, *Persisting Changes*.

This `ItemDetailComponent` update was the last thing we needed to do to finalize our refactoring task. The revamp of our app's client-side navigation is now complete. Before going further, let's perform a full routing and navigation test to see if everything is looking good up to this point.

Full routing test

It's time to hit *F5* and see if our refactoring worked out well. If we did everything correctly, we should be greeted with something like this:

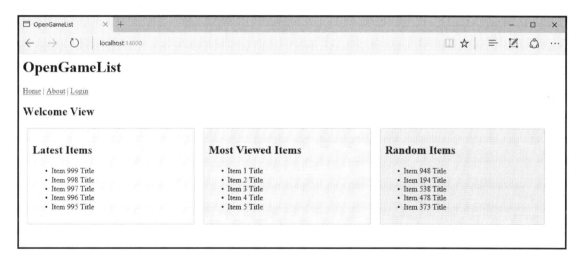

That's definitely the **Welcome View** we wanted. Let's see if the improved master-detail navigation pattern is working as well by left-clicking on one of the items. The view should change, displaying the item detail data.

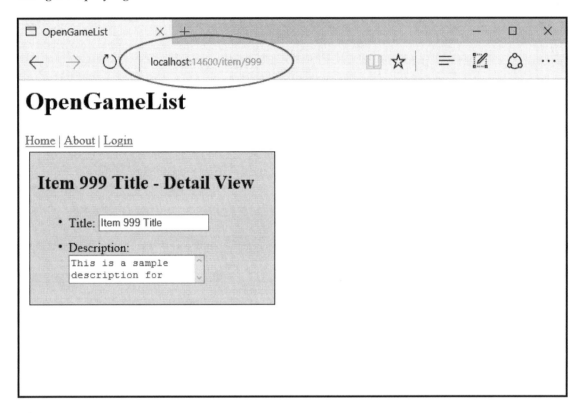

Notice how the URL in the address bar properly switches from `localhost` to `localhost/item/{n}`, reflecting the user navigation up to this point.

Since the master-detail route is working well, let's test our new navigation menu. Clicking on the **About** link element should update our page in the following way:

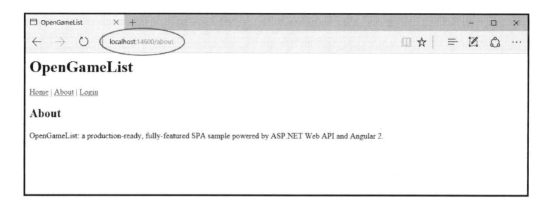

If this all works, there's no reason why the **Login** link shouldn't be working as well:

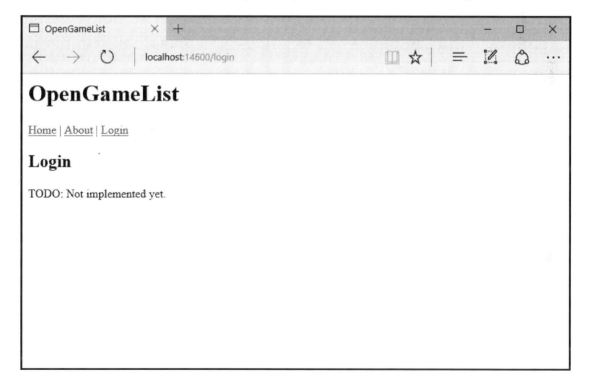

Finally, we can go back to the Home view and bring back the initial layout:

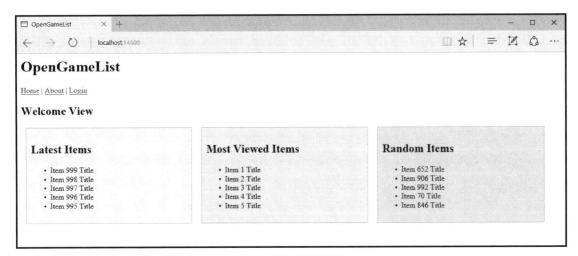

If we look closely at this welcome page we'll be able to see a small difference with the former one. The **Random Items** listing is showing different items. This is working as indented since we want our app to always refresh that content by issuing a new API call each time. Neither Angular 2 nor the Web API will serve cached content unless we instruct them to do so.

 Conversely, the web server and/or the browser could definitely do that due to their default behavior for static files, that's why we explicitly disabled file caching in Chapter 1, *Getting Ready*.

Handling rewrites in ASP.NET Core

In for a penny, in for a pound, there's still an issue we need to address before going further. We address that within our final test as it's something that can be better demonstrated here.

Showing the issue

We might notice that, if we issue a browser refresh by hitting *F5* on any page, we'll end up with an **HTTP 404 error** (page not found). This is what happens when we try this from the **About** view:

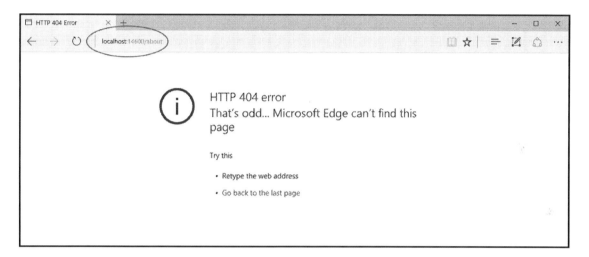

The same problem will occur whenever we try to refresh any of our app's URL including the **Item Detail View**, the **Login View**, and even the **Welcome View**. This is unacceptable for a production-ready app because our users won't be able to properly bookmark or share anything from our app, the sole exception being the `localhost/index.html` default starting URL.

Understanding the causes

The reasons for this are very simple. We have never told our web application how to properly handle these URLs; hence, it follows the default behavior: it looks for a matching `HttpModule` and checks the filesystem for a file or folder having the same name, then it gives up by returning an **HTTP 404 error** (page not found).

You might wonder why the issue is not affecting the **Welcome View**. If we navigate back there, then manually remove the `index.html` part and hit *F5* right after that, it will still work like a charm.

The reason for that is simple. Remember that `app.UseDefaultFiles()` line of code we added in the `Setup.cs` file back in Chapter 1, *Getting Ready*? That's it! Our `index.html` is clearly a default file, meaning that the web application will look for it even if it's not part of the requesting URL. Unfortunately, this behavior won't be able to solve the issue on any internal page. In order to fix that, we need to find a way to implement a custom set of URL rewriting rules.

Implementing the fix

In for a penny, in for a pound. We can tell our web server to rewrite all routing URLs, including the root one, to the `index.html` file by adding the following lines to the `<system.webServer>` section of our app's root `web.config` file:

```
<rewrite>
  <rules>
    <rule name="Angular 2 pushState routing" stopProcessing="true">
      <match url=".*" />
      <conditions logicalGrouping="MatchAll">
        <add input="{REQUEST_FILENAME}" matchType="IsFile" negate="true" />
        <add input="{REQUEST_FILENAME}" matchType="IsDirectory"
negate="true" />
        <add input="{REQUEST_FILENAME}" pattern=".*\.[\d\w]+$"
negate="true" />
        <add input="{REQUEST_URI}" pattern="^/(api)" negate="true" />
      </conditions>
      <action type="Rewrite" url="/index.html" />
    </rule>
  </rules>
</rewrite>
```

By implementing these rules we're basically asking our web server (IIS or IIS Express) to readdress any incoming request to the `/index.html` file, with the sole exception of those pointing to:

- Any existing file, to preserve references to actual `.js`, `.css`, `.pdf`, image files, and more.
- Any existing folder, to preserve references to actual, potentially browsable and/or Angular-unrelated subfolders.
- Any URL starting with `/api`, to preserve any call to our Web API Controllers.

It's worth mentioning that this implementation will only work under IIS if the URL Rewrite Module is properly installed. Conversely, IIS Express won't have this issue since that module is bundled as a built-in feature with all the latest versions.

We won't be digging into the URL Rewrite Module or URL Rewriting anytime soon. If you want to retrieve additional info regarding how it works and/or have a better grip of its `rule`/`match`/`conditions` syntax, we suggest reading the following official MSDN documentation page: `http://www.iis.net/learn/extensions/url-rewrite-module/creatin g-rewrite-rules-for-the-url-rewrite-module`.

Here's how the `web.config` file will look after these changes (new lines are highlighted):

```xml
<?xml version="1.0" encoding="utf-8"?>
<configuration>
  <!--
    Configure your application settings in appsettings.json. Learn more at
http://go.microsoft.com/fwlink/?LinkId=786380
  -->
  <system.webServer>
    <handlers>
      <add name="aspNetCore" path="*" verb="*" modules="AspNetCoreModule"
resourceType="Unspecified"/>
    </handlers>
    <aspNetCore processPath="%LAUNCHER_PATH%" arguments="%LAUNCHER_ARGS%"
stdoutLogEnabled="true" stdoutLogFile=".\logs\stdout"
forwardWindowsAuthToken="false" />
    <rewrite>
      <rules>
        <rule name="Angular 2 pushState routing" stopProcessing="true">
          <match url=".*" />
          <conditions logicalGrouping="MatchAll">
            <add input="{REQUEST_FILENAME}" matchType="IsFile"
negate="true" />
            <add input="{REQUEST_FILENAME}" matchType="IsDirectory"
negate="true" />
            <add input="{REQUEST_FILENAME}" pattern=".*\.[\d\w]+$"
negate="true" />
            <add input="{REQUEST_URI}" pattern="^/(api)" negate="true" />
          </conditions>
          <action type="Rewrite" url="/index.html" />
        </rule>
      </rules>
    </rewrite>
  </system.webServer>
</configuration>
```

Validating the outcome

Time to check out if the preceding implementation solves our 404 problems or not. Run the app again in debug mode (by hitting *F5* from Visual Studio IDE), wait for the browser to load the **Welcome View**, then refresh it by hitting *F5*. This time, instead of an **HTTP 404 error** (page not found), you should be able to see an actual page reload with the same contents as before (except for **Random Items**, as they will be reshuffled as always). Move to the **About View** and do the same, then follow-up with the **Login View** and the **Item Detail View** as well.

Suggested topics

XHR, two-way data binding, master-detail navigation patterns, `PathLocationStrategy`, `HashLocationStrategy`, `location.pushState`, URL Rewrite Module, URL Rewriting, `JavaScriptServices`.

Summary

A lot of things have happened here. We turned our attention to the client-side components of our app, switching the focus from the Web API to Angular 2; we chose to implement a **Welcome View** featuring multiple listings of clickable items, giving our users the chance to navigate to their detail page through a classic master-detail relationship.

To achieve such a result we created a bunch of Angular components: the `Item` class for the model, the `ItemService` class to retrieve the required data from the Web API and the `ItemListComponent` class to show them; then we connected them all using our already-existing `AppComponent`, updating it accordingly; we also added multiple lists to the **Welcome View**, improving our `ItemListComponent` and turning it into a versatile, reusable class.

Everything we did was indeed working, but it didn't match our expectations in terms of seamless navigation between views; we chose to address this issue with the help of the Angular 2 routing library; implementing the library triggered a major refactor of our components, which helped us to greatly improve our previous master-detail approach.

As soon as we had built our improved, navigation-based pattern we performed a final test to see if everything was working as expected. It turned out that our web server couldn't handle our new client-side routes, so we added a set of URL Rewrite rules to the `web.config` file to fix the issue.

Within the previous chapter we implemented a minimalistic, dummy-based, yet functional Web API; in this chapter, we built an unpolished, ugly-looking yet working Angular 2 client-side app. In the following chapters, we'll address these flaws by adding a data model, an improved set of controller methods and also some styling to improve the UI appearance.

4
The Data Model

Our app is growing fine, yet it's starting to show its limits. There's no way we can add, update or delete our items, or properly implement our **Login View**, since it would require handling some sort of user authentication in terms of credential storage and session persistence, to say the least. Truth be told, we can't even say we're actually showing something close to our original plan. Our items don't resemble open-source game entries at all, they're more like a generic container put together in a rather random fashion by a sample, method acting as a Dummy Data Provider.

It's time to get rid of that provisional demo and start working on the real thing. We won't use Angular for that, as what we need to implement has little or nothing to do with the *client-side* portion of our app. Nonetheless, we're fully aware of the fact that most *entities* of the **Data Model** we're about to build will have their correspondence in an Angular model class, just like we did with the C# **ItemViewModel** and the TypeScript **Item** classes, as long as we don't forget we're doing this to feed Angular, we'll be good.

Getting ready

We need to do a lot of things here, so it's better to avoid wasting our time by introducing the whole data model concept, as well as the various meanings of these two words. The experienced reader, as well as the seasoned developer, will be most likely aware of all the relevant stuff. We'll just say that, when we're talking about data model, we don't mean anything more or anything less than a lightweight, definitely-typed set of entity classes representing persistent, code-driven data structures that we can use as resources within our Web API code.

We used the term *persistent* here for a reason: we want our data structure to be stored in a database. That's rather obvious for any application based upon data. `OpenGameList`, won't be an exception since we want it to act as a directory of open source games, which is more than just requiring a database, our app is basically a database by itself.

Installing the EntityFramework Core

We're going to create ours with the help of the **EntityFramework Core** (**EF Core**), the well-known open-source **object-relational mapper** (**ORM**) for ADO.NET developed by Microsoft. The reasons for such a choice are many:

- Seamless integration with the Visual Studio IDE
- A conceptual model based upon entity classes (**Entity Data Model** (**EDM**)) that will enable us to work with data using domain-specific objects without the need to write data-access code, which is precisely what we're looking for
- Easy to deploy, use and maintain in development and production phases
- Compatible with all the major open-source and commercial SQL-based engines, including MSSQL, MySQL, PostgreSQL, Oracle, and more, thanks to the official and/or third-party EF-compatible connectors available via NuGet

 It's worth mentioning that the EF Core was previously known as EntityFramework 7 until its latest RC release. The name change follows the ASP.NET 5/ASP.NET Core perspective switch we've already talked about, as it also emphasizes the EF Core major rewrite/redesign.

You might be wondering why we're choosing to adopt a SQL-based approach instead of going for a NoSQL alternative. There are many good NoSQL products such as MongoDB, RavenDB, and CouchDB that happen to have a C# connector library. What about using one of them instead?

The answer is rather simple: they are not supported yet by the EF Core 1.0.0, which, at the time of writing, happens to be the latest stable release. If we look at the EF Core team backlog we can see that non-relational database providers, such as Azure Table Storage, Redis, and others, are indeed mentioned for upcoming support, but it's unlikely that we'll be able to see any of them implemented within the EF Core's future releases as well.

If you want to know more about the upcoming release, and/or if you feel bold enough to use it anyway maybe with a NoSQL DB as well, we suggest reading more about the EF Core project status by visiting the following links:

- **Project roadmap**:
  `https://github.com/aspnet/EntityFramework/wiki/Roadmap`
- **Source code on GitHub**:
  `https://github.com/aspnet/EntityFramework`
- **Official documentation**:
  `https://docs.efproject.net/en/latest/`

In order to install the EF Core, we need to add the relevant packages to the `dependencies` section of our `project.json` file. We can easily do that using the visual GUI like we did for the `Newtonsoft.json` package in the following way:

1. Right-click on the `OpenGameListWebApp` project.
2. Select **Manage NuGet Packages**.
3. Ensure that the **Package source** drop-down list is set to **All** and also that the **Include prerelease** switch is checked.
4. Go to the **Browse** tab and search for the packages containing the `EntityFrameworkCore` keyword.

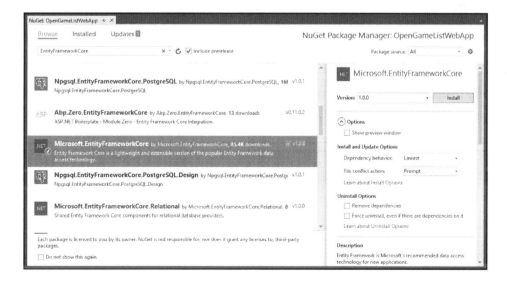

Next, install the following packages:

- `Microsoft.AspNetCore.Diagnostics.EntityFrameworkCore`
- `Microsoft.AspNetCore.Identity.EntityFrameworkCore`
- `Microsoft.EntityFrameworkCore`
- `Microsoft.EntityFrameworkCore.SqlServer`
- `Microsoft.EntityFrameworkCore.Design`

Alternatively, we could add the relevant packages manually within the `project.json` file as follows (new lines highlighted):

```
"dependencies": {
  "Microsoft.AspNetCore.Mvc": "1.0.0",
  "Microsoft.AspNetCore.Server.IISIntegration": "1.0.0",
  "Microsoft.AspNetCore.Server.Kestrel": "1.0.0",
  "Microsoft.Extensions.Configuration.EnvironmentVariables": "1.0.0",
  "Microsoft.Extensions.Configuration.FileExtensions": "1.0.0",
  "Microsoft.Extensions.Configuration.Json": "1.0.0",
  "Microsoft.Extensions.Logging": "1.0.0",
  "Microsoft.Extensions.Logging.Console": "1.0.0",
  "Microsoft.Extensions.Logging.Debug": "1.0.0",
  "Microsoft.Extensions.Options.ConfigurationExtensions": "1.0.0",

  "Microsoft.AspNetCore.Diagnostics": "1.0.0",
  "Microsoft.AspNetCore.Routing": "1.0.0",
  "Microsoft.AspNetCore.Authentication.JwtBearer": "1.0.0",
  "Microsoft.AspNetCore.StaticFiles": "1.0.0",
  "Microsoft.VisualStudio.Web.BrowserLink.Loader": "14.0.0",
  "Newtonsoft.Json": "9.0.1",

  "Microsoft.AspNetCore.Diagnostics.EntityFrameworkCore": "1.0.0",
  "Microsoft.AspNetCore.Identity.EntityFrameworkCore": "1.0.0",
  "Microsoft.EntityFrameworkCore": "1.0.0",
  "Microsoft.EntityFrameworkCore.SqlServer": "1.0.0",
  "Microsoft.EntityFrameworkCore.Design": "1.0.0-preview2-final",
}
```

 At the time of writing, the latest released version of EF Core was 1.0.0, with the sole exception of `Microsoft.EntityFrameworkCore.Design`, which is still in `1.0.0-preview2`. We're going to use these builds in our project.

As usual, the advantage of doing it manually is that we can keep the packages more organized by separating them into commented blocks.

Among the installed namespaces we can easily see the presence of the `EntityFrameworkCore.SqlServer`, a highly versatile connector providing an interface with the whole MSSQL server database family: SQL Server 2008-2014, as well as the Express and Compact editions for personal and development usage.

We're free to choose between using one of them and picking another DBMS engine such as MySQL, PostgreSQL, or any other EF-compatible product. Should we take this decision now? It entirely depends on the data modeling approach we want to adopt. For the time being and for the sake of simplicity, we'll be sticking to it.

Data modeling approaches

Now that we have EF installed, we have to choose between one of the three available approaches to model the data structure: model-first, database-first and code-first. Each one of them comes with its fair amount of advantages and disadvantages, as the experienced readers and seasoned .NET developers will most certainly know. While we won't dig too much into these, it could be useful to briefly summarize each one of them before making the choice.

The model-first approach

If you're not familiar with the Visual Studio IDE design tools such as the XML-based **DataSet Schema** (**XSD**) and the **Entity Designer Model XML** (**EDMX**) visual interface, the model-first approach can be rather confusing. The key to understanding it is to acknowledge the fact that the word model here is meant to define a visual diagram built with the design tools. This diagram will then be used by the framework to autogenerate the database SQL script and the data model source code files.

To summarize, we can say that choosing the model-first option means working on a visual EDMX diagram and letting EF create/update the rest accordingly.

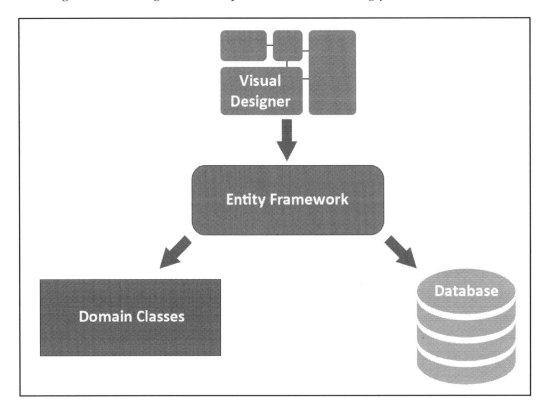

The model-first approach

Pros

- We will be able to create the database scheme and the class diagram as a whole using a visual design tool, which could be great when the data structure is quite big.
- Whenever the database changes, the model can be updated accordingly without data loss.

Cons

- The diagram-driven, autogenerated SQL scripts could lead to data loss in case of updates. An easy workaround for that would be generating the scripts on disk and manually modifying them, which would require decent SQL knowledge.
- Dealing with the diagram can be tricky, especially if we want to have precise control over our model classes. We wouldn't always be able to get what we want, as the actual source code would be auto-generated by a tool.

The database-first approach

Given the disadvantages of the model-first approach, we might think that the database-first approach might be the way to go. This could be true if we either have a database already or don't mind building it beforehand. That being the case, the database-first approach is similar to the model-first one, except it goes the other way around. Instead of designing EDMX manually and generating the SQL script to create the database, we build the latter and then generate the former using the ED Designer tool.

We can summarize it by saying that choosing the Database-first approach means building the database and letting EF create/update the rest accordingly.

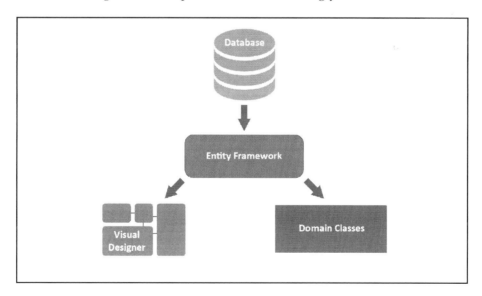

The database-first approach

Pros

- If we have an already-existing database in place, this will most likely be the way as it will spare us the need to re-create it.
- The risk of data-loss will be kept to a minimum because any change or update will be always performed on the database.

Cons

- Manually updating the database can be tricky if we're dealing with clusters, multiple instances or a number of development/testing/production environments, as we will have to manually keep them in sync instead of relying upon code-driven updates/migrations or autogenerated SQL scripts.
- We would have even less control over the autogenerated model classes (and their source code) than if we were using the model-first approach. It would require an extensive knowledge of EF conventions and standards, otherwise, we'll often struggle to get what we want.

The code-first approach

Last but not least comes the EF flagship approach since EF4, which enables an elegant, highly efficient data model development workflow. The appeal of this approach can easily be found in its premise: the code-first approach allows the developer to define model objects using only standard classes, without the need for any design tool, XML mapping files or cumbersome piles of autogenerated code.

To summarize, we could say that choosing the code-first approach means writing the **Data Model** entity classes we'll be using within our project and letting EF generate the database accordingly.

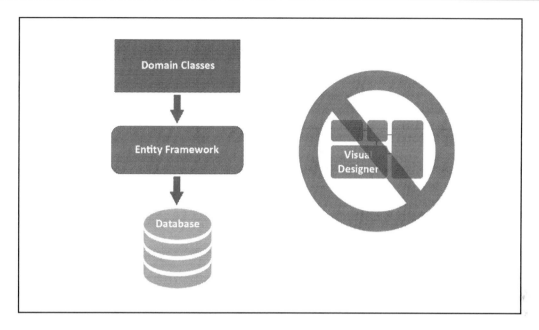

The code-first approach

Pros

- No need for diagrams and visual tools whatsoever, which could be great for small-to-medium size projects as it would save us a lot of time.
- A fluent code API that allows the developer to follow a convention over configuration approach, and to handle the most common scenarios, while also giving him the chance to switch to custom, attribute-based implementation overrides whenever he needs to customize the database mapping.

Cons

- A good knowledge of C# and updated EF conventions is required.
- Maintaining the database could be tricky sometimes, as well as handling updates without suffering data loss. The migrations support, added in 4.3 to overcome the issue which has been continuously updated since then, greatly mitigates the problem, although it has also affected the learning curve in a negative way.

Making a choice

As we can easily see by judging the advantage and disadvantage listings, there is no such thing as an overall better or best approach. Conversely, we could say that each project scenario will likely have a most suitable approach.

Regarding our project, considering the fact we don't have a database yet and we're aiming for a flexible, mutable small-scale data structure, adopting the code-first approach would probably be a good choice. That's what we're going to do, starting from the following paragraph.

Creating entities

We're definitely going to use one of the big advantages of the Code-First approach and start writing our entity classes immediately, without worrying too much about the database engine we're going to use.

Truth be told, we already know something about what we're eventually going to use. We won't be adopting a NoSQL solution, as they are not supported by EF yet; we also don't want to commit ourselves into purchasing expensive license plans, so Oracle and the commercial editions of SQL Server are most likely out of the picture as well.

This leaves us with relatively few choices: SQL Server Compact Edition, SQL Server Express, MySQL, or other less-known solutions such as PostgreSql. That being said, adopting the code-first approach will give us the chance to postpone the call until our data model is ready.

Items

Select the `OpenGameListWebApp` project from the **Solution Explorer**, then do the following tasks:

1. Create a `/Data/` folder: this will be where all our EF-related classes will reside.
2. Create a `/Data/Items/` folder.
3. Right-click on that folder and select **Add...** | **New Item**.

4. From the **Visual C#** items | **Code** | **Class**.
5. Name the new class `Item.cs` and create it.

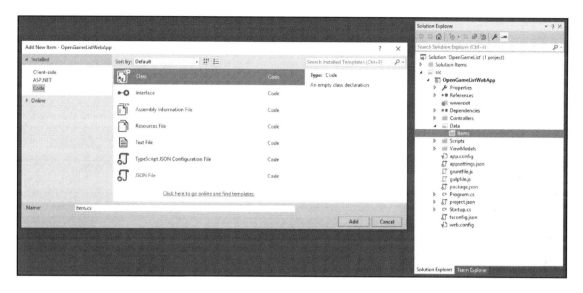

As for the source code, we could start with something like the following:

```csharp
using System;
using System.Collections.Generic;
using System.ComponentModel.DataAnnotations;
using System.ComponentModel.DataAnnotations.Schema;

namespace OpenGameListWebApp.Data.Items
{
    public class Item
    {
        #region Constructor
        public Item()
        {

        }
        #endregion Constructor

        #region Properties
        [Key]
        [Required]
        public int Id { get; set; }
        [Required]
        public string Title { get; set; }
        public string Description { get; set; }
```

```
            public string Text { get; set; }
            public string Notes { get; set; }
            [Required]
            public int Type { get; set; }
            [Required]
            public int Flags { get; set; }
            [Required]
            public string UserId { get; set; }
            [Required]
            public int ViewCount { get; set; }
            [Required]
            public DateTime CreatedDate { get; set; }
            [Required]
            public DateTime LastModifiedDate { get; set; }
            #endregion Properties
        }
    }
```

Note the presence of the `UserId` foreign key. We'll get to them soon.

It's also worth noting that we used a lot of `Data Annotations` attributes, those being the most convenient way to override the default the code-first conventions.

If you want to know more about `Data Annotations` in the EF Core, we strongly suggest reading the official documentation at the following URL: `https://docs.efproject.net/en/latest/modeling/index.html`.

As we can easily see, this entity class is very similar to the `ItemViewModel` class we created in `Chapter 2`, *ASP.NET Controllers and Server-Side Routes*. That's perfectly fine because that class was originally meant to resemble the public properties of the Web API underlying model, which is precisely what we're defining now.

The following diagram can help to better understand this:

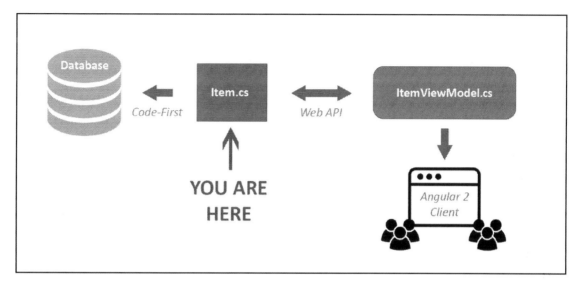

As we can see, we're creating the entity that will be used by EF to generate the database (using the code-first approach) and also translate (using property mapping) into the ItemViewModel we'll be using to serve our content to our Angular client.

As we might guess, the Item entity alone will hardly be enough. In order to complete our initial requirements we need to define a couple more entity classes:

- Comments, where we can store the comments related to each Item (if any).
- Users, which will serve as the main reference for all items and comments and also handle the authentication/login phase.

Comments

Let's start with the first one by doing the following:

1. Create a /Data/Comments/ folder.
2. Right-click to that folder and select **Add...** | **New Item**.
3. From the **Visual C#** items | **Code** | **Class**.
4. Name the new class Comment.cs and create it.

As for the code itself, here's a good start:

```
using System;
using System.Collections.Generic;
using System.ComponentModel.DataAnnotations;
using System.ComponentModel.DataAnnotations.Schema;

namespace OpenGameListWebApp.Data.Comments
{
    public class Comment
    {
        #region Constructor
        public Comment()
        {

        }
        #endregion Constructor

        #region Properties
        [Key]
        [Required]
        public int Id { get; set; }
        [Required]
        public int ItemId { get; set; }
        [Required]
        public string Text { get; set; }
        [Required]
        public int Type { get; set; }
        [Required]
        public int Flags { get; set; }
        [Required]
        public string UserId { get; set; }
        public int? ParentId { get; set; }
        [Required]
        public DateTime CreatedDate { get; set; }
        [Required]
        public DateTime LastModifiedDate { get; set; }
        #endregion Properties
    }
}
```

That's it. Notice that we have three foreign keys here:

- `ItemId`, pointing to the specific item a comment is about. This is a required field, since there won't be any comment without a related item.
- `UserId`, pointing to the comment's author, which is something we'll arguably set when we'll define the `User` entity later on. This is also a required field, as we're not planning to support any comment without an author.
- `ParentId`, pointing to the master comment this entry is replying to, or null if the comment is not a reply. This is a classic implementation of the standard recursive foreign key pattern (also known as the root-leaf or parent-child), which is one of the most common ways to handle threading.

To better understand how `ParentId` will work, consider the following image:

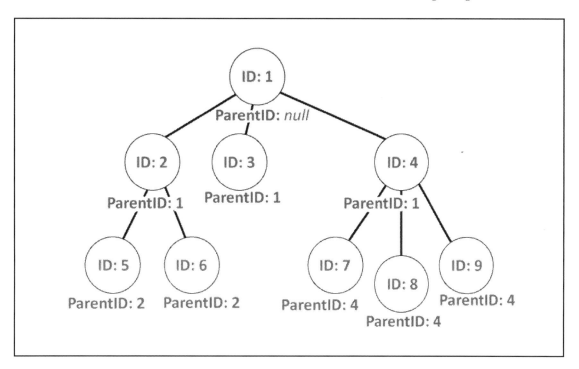

Users

It's time to add the `ApplicationUser` entity. Create a new `/Data/Users/` folder, add an `ApplicationUser.cs` class and fill it up with the following code:

```csharp
using System;
using System.Collections.Generic;
using System.ComponentModel.DataAnnotations;
using System.ComponentModel.DataAnnotations.Schema;
using System.Linq;
using System.Text;
using System.Threading.Tasks;

namespace OpenGameListWebApp.Data.Users
{
    public class ApplicationUser
    {
        #region Constructor
        public ApplicationUser()
        {

        }
        #endregion Constructor

        #region Properties
        [Key]
        [Required]
        public string Id { get; set; }
        [Required]
        [MaxLength(128)]
        public string UserName { get; set; }
        [Required]
        public string Email { get; set; }
        public string DisplayName { get; set; }
        public string Notes { get; set; }
        [Required]
        public int Type { get; set; }
        [Required]
        public int Flags { get; set; }
        [Required]
        public DateTime CreatedDate { get; set; }
        [Required]
        public DateTime LastModifiedDate { get; set; }
        #endregion Properties
    }
}
```

Here we go. Note that there are no foreign keys here, since the one-to-many relations with items and comments will be handled on the other side.

 We could ask ourselves why we used the `ApplicationUser` class name instead of `User`. The answer is pretty simple: `ApplicationUser` is the conventional name given to the class of the custom implementation of the `IdentityUser` base class used by the ASP.NET Identity module. We're using it in compliance with that convention, as we plan to implement this module later on.

Defining relationships

Now that we have built our main entity skeleton we need to create some relationships between them. We want to be able to do stuff like retrieving an `Item`, browsing to their related `Comments`, then getting the `ApplicationUser` for each one of them, and also the other way around. We can easily do that by implementing a set of related entity properties: EF will load them on demand using its default lazy-load retrieval feature.

The first thing we'll do is to add a new region to our `Item` class, containing two new properties:

```
#region Related Properties
/// <summary>
/// Current Item's Author: this property will be loaded on first use using
EF's Lazy-Loading feature.
/// </summary>
[ForeignKey("UserId")]
public virtual ApplicationUser Author { get; set; }

/// <summary>
/// Current Item's Comment list: this property will be loaded on first use
using EF's Lazy-Loading feature.
/// </summary>
public virtual List<Comment> Comments { get; set; }
#endregion Related Properties
```

To do this, we also have to add a reference to the following namespaces at the beginning of the file:

```
using OpenGameListWebApp.Data.Users;
using OpenGameListWebApp.Data.Comments;
```

Anyone who has some experience of EF won't miss the `ForeignKey` data annotation. This is one of the many code-first configuration overrides we'll need to use to have our data model properly built. There's nothing complex here, we're just telling EF that this property should be loaded using the `UserId` field. Needless to say, this will also create a one-to-many binding relationship (also known as a **constraint**), so long as our database supports it.

 In order to use the `ForeignKey` attribute (and all the other EF data annotation), remember to add the `System.ComponentModel.DataAnnotations.Schema` within the using section of the `Item` class.

Let's do the same with the `Comments` class:

```
#region Related Properties
/// <summary>
/// Current Comment's Item: this property will be loaded on first use using
EF's Lazy-Loading feature.
/// </summary>
[ForeignKey("ItemId")]
public virtual Item Item { get; set; }

/// <summary>
/// Current Comment's Author: this property will be loaded on first use
using EF's Lazy-Loading feature.
/// </summary>
[ForeignKey("UserId")]
public virtual ApplicationUser Author { get; set; }

/// <summary>
/// Parent comment, or NULL if this is a root comment: this property will
be loaded on first use using EF's Lazy-Loading feature.
/// </summary>
[ForeignKey("ParentId")]
public virtual Comment Parent { get; set; }

/// <summary>
/// Children comments (if present).
/// </summary>
public virtual List<Comment> Children { get; set; }
#endregion Related Properties
```

Again, remember to also add a reference to the following namespaces:

```
using OpenGameListWebApp.Data.Items;
using OpenGameListWebApp.Data.Users;
```

The `Related Properties` region is slightly more crowded here, as we have three foreign keys, but the beef is the same. For each `Comment`, we want to retrieve the related item, the user who wrote it, and also the parent comment it's replying to (if any): therefore, we define four properties and decorate them with the `ForeignKey` data annotation attribute; we also add a fourth property to keep track of the child comments (if present).

Last but not least, let's move on to the `ApplicationUser` entity class and add the following code to it:

```
#region Related Properties
/// <summary>
/// A list of items wrote by this user: this property will be loaded on
first use using EF's Lazy-Loading feature.
/// </summary>
public virtual List<Item> Items { get; set; }

/// <summary>
/// A list of comments wrote by this user: this property will be loaded on
first use using EF's Lazy-Loading feature.
/// </summary>
public virtual List<Comment> Comments { get; set; }
#endregion Related Properties
```

And the required namespace references as well:

```
using OpenGameListWebApp.Data.Items;
using OpenGameListWebApp.Data.Comments;
```

There's nothing fancy here, just a couple of lists we can use to track down all the contents posted by each user.

You will easily notice that each foreign key spawned the following:

- A single object entity property with the same type of the entity we're referring to in the class containing the foreign key
- A type-defined listing property in the related class

This pattern won't change as long as we're defining one-to-many relationships only, an object to the left, leading to a list of related objects to the right.

Are we done with our entities? Yes.

Are we ready to deploy our code-first database? Hardly. Before doing that, we need to do two things:

1. Set up an appropriate database context.
2. Enable the code-first migrations support to our project.

Let's do that right away.

Setting up DbContext

To interact with data as objects/entity classes, EF uses the `Microsoft.EntityFrameworkCore.DbContext` class also called `DbContext` or simply `Context`. This class is in charge of all the entity objects during execution, including populating them with data from the database, keeping track of changes, and persisting them to the database during CRUD operations.

We can easily create our very own `DbContext` class for our project, which we will call `ApplicationDbContext`, by performing the following tasks:

Right-click on the `/OpenGameList/Data` folder and add a new `ApplicationDbContext.cs` class. Fill it up with the following code:

```
using Microsoft.AspNetCore.Identity.EntityFrameworkCore;
using Microsoft.EntityFrameworkCore;
using Microsoft.EntityFrameworkCore.Metadata;
using OpenGameListWebApp.Data.Items;
using OpenGameListWebApp.Data.Users;
using OpenGameListWebApp.Data.Comments;

namespace OpenGameListWebApp.Data
{
    public class ApplicationDbContext : DbContext
    {
        #region Constructor
        public ApplicationDbContext(DbContextOptions options) :
base(options)
        {
        }
        #endregion Constructor

        #region Methods
        protected override void OnModelCreating(ModelBuilder modelBuilder)
        {
            base.OnModelCreating(modelBuilder);
```

```
modelBuilder.Entity<ApplicationUser>().ToTable("Users");
        modelBuilder.Entity<ApplicationUser>().HasMany(u =>
u.Items).WithOne(i => i.Author);
        modelBuilder.Entity<ApplicationUser>().HasMany(u =>
u.Comments).WithOne(c => c.Author).HasPrincipalKey(u => u.Id);

        modelBuilder.Entity<Item>().ToTable("Items");
        modelBuilder.Entity<Item>().Property(i =>
i.Id).ValueGeneratedOnAdd();
        modelBuilder.Entity<Item>().HasOne(i => i.Author).WithMany(u =>
u.Items);
        modelBuilder.Entity<Item>().HasMany(i => i.Comments).WithOne(c
=> c.Item);

        modelBuilder.Entity<Comment>().ToTable("Comments");
        modelBuilder.Entity<Comment>().HasOne(c => c.Author).WithMany(u
=> u.Comments).HasForeignKey(c =>
c.UserId).OnDelete(DeleteBehavior.Restrict);
        modelBuilder.Entity<Comment>().HasOne(c => c.Item).WithMany(i
=> i.Comments);
        modelBuilder.Entity<Comment>().HasOne(c => c.Parent).WithMany(c
=> c.Children);
        modelBuilder.Entity<Comment>().HasMany(c =>
c.Children).WithOne(c => c.Parent);
    }
    #endregion Methods

    #region Properties
    public DbSet<Item> Items { get; set; }
    public DbSet<Comment> Comments { get; set; }
    public DbSet<ApplicationUser> Users { get; set; }
    #endregion Properties
  }
}
```

There are a number of things worth noting here:

- In the second constructor method's implementation, we set the `DbInitializer`, which is the class that will handle the database initialization strategy. If you're used to EF6 you know why we need to do this, otherwise don't worry as we'll get there in the following paragraph.
- We overrode the `OnModelCreating` method to manually define our data model relationships for our `ApplicationUser`, `Item`, and `Comment` entity classes. Notice that we manually configured the table names for each entity using the `modelBuilder.Entity<TEntityType>().ToTable` method. We did that with the sole purpose of showing how easy it is to customize the code-first generated database.
- Finally, we added a `DbSet` property for each of our entities, so we can easily access them later on.

Database initialization strategies

Creating the database for the first time isn't the only thing we need to worry about, for example, how can we keep tracks of the changes that will definitely occur to our data model?

In EF's previous versions, we could choose between one of the database management patterns (known as database initializers or DbInitializers) offered by the code-first approach, that is picking the appropriate database initialization strategy for our specific needs: `CreateDatabaseIfNotExists`, `DropCreateDatabaseIfModelChanges`, `DropCreateDatabaseAlways`, and `MigrateDatabaseToLatestVersion`. Additionally, if we need to address specific requirements, we could also set up our own custom initializer by extending one of the preceding options and overriding their core methods.

The major flaw of DbInitializers was that they were not that immediate and streamlined for the average developer. They were viable, yet difficult to handle without an extensive knowledge of the whole EF logic.

In EF Core the pattern has been greatly simplified: there are no DbInitializers and automatic migrations have also been removed. The database initialization aspect is now entirely handled through PowerShell commands, with the sole exception of a small set of commands that can be placed directly on the `DbContext` implementation constructor to partially automatize the process:

- `Database.EnsureCreated()`
- `Database.EnsureDeleted()`
- `Database.Migrate()`

There's currently no way to create migrations programmatically, they must be added via PowerShell, as we're going to do shortly.

Choosing the database engine

Before doing that though, we need to choose which database engine we would like to use. We're going to take this as an opportunity to demonstrate the versatility of the code-first approach.

From the main menu, select **View | SQL Server Object Explorer** and look through the list of available development-ready databases:

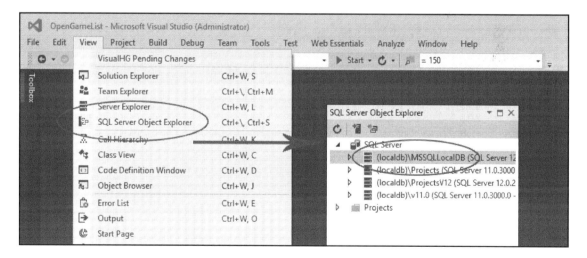

Open the SQL server node to show the `localdb` instances installed on your system. If you have one or more instances of SQL Server/SQL Express installed, you will also find a reference for each one of them.

If you have no entries there (no SQL server node), you are most likely missing the **SQL Server Data Tools** components from your Visual Studio 2015 installation. In order to fix that you need to close Visual Studio, go to **Control Panel | Programs and Features**, then select **Microsoft Visual Studio 2015** and choose **Change**: you'll be able to modify your existing installation by adding the **SQL Server Data Tools** components. Once you're done, restart Visual Studio: the default `localdb` instance should be ready and available.

For now, our pick will be the default`localdb` instance that comes with Visual Studio 2015, which goes by the name of `(localdb)\MSSQLLocalDB`. We need to keep track of that name, as we'll be using it in the `appsettings.json` file in a short while.

The default `localdb` instance we just chose might be viable enough for development, but it won't work in production. Don't worry, though, we will choose a whole different database engine when we get to deployment phase. As we said before, we're doing that on purpose in order to demonstrate the versatility of the code-first approach.

Updating appsettings.json

From the **Solution Explorer**, expand the `OpenGameListWebApp` project root node, open the `appsettings.json` file, and add the following (new lines highlighted):

```
{
  "Data": {
    "DefaultConnection": {
      "ConnectionString": "Data Source=(localdb)\\MSSQLLocalDB;Initial
Catalog=OpenGameList;Integrated Security=True;
MultipleActiveResultSets=True"
    }
  },
  "Logging": {
    "IncludeScopes": false,
    "LogLevel": {
      "Default": "Debug",
      "System": "Information",
      "Microsoft": "Information"
    }
```

```
    },
    "StaticFiles": {
      "Headers": {
        "Cache-Control": "no-cache, no-store",
        "Pragma": "no-cache",
        "Expires": "-1"
      }
    }
  }
}
```

This is the connection string we'll be referencing to in the `Startup.cs` file later on.

Creating the database

Now that we have our own `DbContext` and a valid `Connection String`, we can easily add the initial migration and create our database.

Updating Startup.cs

The first thing we have to do is add the EF support and our `ApplicationDbContext` implementation to our application startup class. Open the `Startup.cs` file and update the `ConfigureServices` method in the following way (new lines are highlighted):

```
public void ConfigureServices(IServiceCollection services)
{
    // Add framework services.
    services.AddMvc();

    // Add EntityFramework's Identity support.
    services.AddEntityFramework();
    // Add ApplicationDbContext.
    services.AddDbContext<ApplicationDbContext>(options =>
options.UseSqlServer(Configuration["Data:DefaultConnection:ConnectionString
"])         );
}
```

These new code lines will also require the following namespace references:

```
using Microsoft.EntityFrameworkCore;
using Microsoft.EntityFrameworkCore.Infrastructure;
using OpenGameListWebApp.Data;
```

Configuring the EF tools

Before we can use the required *PowerShell* commands we need to properly configure the EF Core tools. To do that, open the `project.json` file, locate the tools section, and add the following (new lines are highlighted):

```
"tools": {
    "Microsoft.AspNetCore.Server.IISIntegration.Tools": "1.0.0-preview2-
final",
    "Microsoft.EntityFrameworkCore.Tools": "1.0.0-preview2-final"
}
```

Right after that, it may be wise to issue a full rebuild to make sure there are no build errors in our updated code.

Adding the initial migration

Right after that, open a PowerShell command prompt and navigate through the project's root folder, which in our example is as follows:

`C:\Projects\OpenGameList\src\OpenGameListWebApp\`

Once there, type the following command to add the first migration:

`dotnet ef migrations add "Initial" -o "Data\Migrations"`

The optional `-o` parameter can be used to change the location where the migration code-generated files will be created. If we don't specify it, a root-level `/Migrations/` folder will be created and used as the default. Since we put all the EF Core classes into the `/Data/` folder, it's advisable to store migrations there as well.

Wait for the migration to be created, then type the following to execute it:

`dotnet ef database update`

Once done, open the **Server Object Explorer** and check that the `OpenGameList` database has been created, together with all their relevant tables:

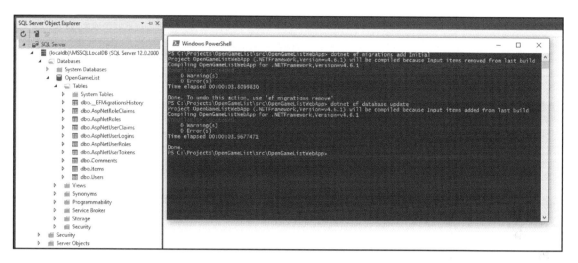

 Those who have used migrations before might be asking why we didn't use the Visual Studio's Package Manager Console to execute these commands, just like it used to be done in the past. The reason is simple: Unfortunately doing this won't work because the commands need to be executed within the project root folder, which is not where the Package Manager Console commands get executed. It is also unknown if that behavior will change in the near future, even though it would definitely make sense.

If we go back to Visual Studio, we can see that there's a new `/Data/Migrations/` folder containing the EF Core code-generated files.

Understanding migrations

Before going further it may be useful to spend a short while explaining what code-first migrations actually are and the advantages we gain by using them.

Whenever we're developing an application and defining a data model, we can be sure that it will change a number of times for many good reasons: new requirements from the product owner, optimization processes, consolidation phases and so on. A bunch of properties will be added, deleted, or have their type changed. Chances are that sooner or later we'll be adding new entities as well, and/or changing their relation pattern according to our ever-changing needs.

Each time we do something like that, we'll also put our data model out of sync with its underlying, code-first generated database. This usually won't be a problem when we're debugging our app within a development environment because that scenario usually allows us to recreate the database from scratch whenever the project changes.

Upon deploying the application into production we'll be facing a whole different story. As long as we're handling real data, dropping and recreating our database won't be an option anymore, which is precisely what the code-first migrations feature is meant to address, giving the developer a chance to alter the database schema without having to drop/recreate the whole thing.

 We won't dig more into this topic: EF Core is a world on its own and talking too much about it would undoubtedly bring us far from the scope of this book.
If you want to go further, we can suggest starting with the official documentation hosted by the EF Core documentation website at the following URL: `https://ef.readthedocs.io/en/latest/`.

Implementing a data seed strategy

We have created the database, yet it's still completely empty. In order to test it against our existing application, it could be useful to find an easy way to add some sample data programmatically.

In the most recent EF versions, up to and including EF6, it was possible to do that using the `DbMigrationsConfiguration.Seed()` method. Unfortunately though, a migrations configuration doesn't exist in EF Core: this seems to be more an implementation choice than a lack of features since the seeding tasks can now be handled directly within the `Startup.cs` file.

 Although this is definitely true, there is still a controversy going on between the EF Core developers community regarding that specific aspect. The absence of a high-level API and/or a consolidated pattern to run seeding after applying migrations is indeed something that should be addressed somehow, as executing such a delicate task during application running creates a number of issues, and it doesn't seem to be a viable solution in most scenarios.

Creating a DbSeeder class

Let's start with adding a `DbSeeder.cs` class in the `/Data/` folder. This class will be using the `ApplicationDbContext` to create sample data, so we'll have to find a way to have it available there without creating an additional instance. We can do that using the ASP.NET Core DI pattern in the following way:

```
using Microsoft.EntityFrameworkCore;
using Microsoft.EntityFrameworkCore.ChangeTracking;
using OpenGameListWebApp.Data;
using OpenGameListWebApp.Data.Comments;
using OpenGameListWebApp.Data.Items;
using OpenGameListWebApp.Data.Users;
using System;
using System.Linq;
using System.Threading.Tasks;

public class DbSeeder
{
    #region Private Members
    private ApplicationDbContext DbContext;
    #endregion Private Members

    #region Constructor
    public DbSeeder(ApplicationDbContext dbContext)
    {
        DbContext = dbContext;
    }
    #endregion Constructor

    #region Public Methods
    public async Task SeedAsync()
    {
        // Create the Db if it doesn't exist
        DbContext.Database.EnsureCreated();
        // Create default Users
        if (await DbContext.Users.CountAsync() == 0) CreateUsers();
        // Create default Items (if there are none) and Comments
        if (await DbContext.Items.CountAsync() == 0) CreateItems();
    }
    #endregion Public Methods

        #region Seed Methods
private void CreateUsers()
    {
        // local variables
        DateTime createdDate = new DateTime(2016, 03, 01, 12, 30, 00);
```

```
        DateTime lastModifiedDate = DateTime.Now;

        // Create the "Admin" ApplicationUser account (if it doesn't exist
already)
        var user_Admin = new ApplicationUser() { Id =
Guid.NewGuid().ToString(), UserName = "Admin", Email =
"admin@opengamelist.com", CreatedDate = createdDate, LastModifiedDate =
lastModifiedDate };

        // Insert "Admin" into the Database
         DbContext.Users.Add(user_Admin);

#if DEBUG
        // Create some sample registered user accounts (if they don't exist
already)
        var user_Ryan = new ApplicationUser() { Id =
Guid.NewGuid().ToString(), UserName = "Ryan", Email =
"ryan@opengamelist.com", CreatedDate = createdDate, LastModifiedDate =
lastModifiedDate };
        var user_Solice = new ApplicationUser() { Id =
Guid.NewGuid().ToString(), UserName = "Solice", Email =
"solice@opengamelist.com", CreatedDate = createdDate, LastModifiedDate =
lastModifiedDate };
        var user_Vodan = new ApplicationUser() { Id =
Guid.NewGuid().ToString(), UserName = "Vodan", Email =
"vodan@opengamelist.com", CreatedDate = createdDate, LastModifiedDate =
lastModifiedDate };

        // Insert sample registered users into the Database
        DbContext.Users.AddRange(user_Ryan, user_Solice, user_Vodan);
#endif
        DbContext.SaveChanges();
    }

    private void CreateItems()
    {
        // local variables
        DateTime createdDate = new DateTime(2016, 03, 01, 12, 30, 00);
        DateTime lastModifiedDate = DateTime.Now;

        var authorId = DbContext.Users.Where(u => u.UserName ==
"Admin").FirstOrDefault().Id;

#if DEBUG
        var num = 1000;  // create 1000 sample items
        for (int id = 1; id <= num; id++)
        {
            DbContext.Items.Add(GetSampleItem(id, authorId, num - id, new
```

```
DateTime(2015, 12, 31).AddDays(-num)));
        }
#endif

        EntityEntry<Item> e1 = DbContext.Items.Add(new Item()
        {
            UserId = authorId,
            Title = "Magarena",
            Description = "Single-player fantasy card game similar to
Magic: The Gathering",
            Text = @"Loosely based on Magic: The Gathering, the game lets
you play against a computer opponent or another human being.
                                The game features a well-developed AI, an
intuitive and clear interface and an enticing level of gameplay.",
            Notes = "This is a sample record created by the Code-First
Configuration class",
            ViewCount = 2343,
            CreatedDate = createdDate,
            LastModifiedDate = lastModifiedDate
        });

        EntityEntry<Item> e2 = DbContext.Items.Add(new Item()
        {
            UserId = authorId,
            Title = "Minetest",
            Description = "Open-Source alternative to Minecraft",
            Text = @"The Minetest gameplay is very similar to Minecraft's:
you are playing in a 3D open world, where you can create and/or remove
various types of blocks.
                        Minetest feature both single-player and multi-
player game modes.
                        It also has support for custom mods, additional
texture packs and other custom/personalization options.
                        Minetest has been released in 2015 under GNU Lesser
General Public License.",
            Notes = "This is a sample record created by the Code-First
Configuration class",
            ViewCount = 4180,
            CreatedDate = createdDate,
            LastModifiedDate = lastModifiedDate
        });

        EntityEntry<Item> e3 = DbContext.Items.Add(new Item()
        {
            UserId = authorId,
            Title = "Relic Hunters Zero",
            Description = "A free game about shooting evil space ducks with
tiny, cute guns.",
```

```
                Text = @"Relic Hunters Zero is fast, tactical and also very
smooth to play.
                        It also enables the users to look at the source
code, so they can can get creative and keep this game alive, fun and free
for years to come.
                        The game is also available on Steam.",
            Notes = "This is a sample record created by the Code-First
Configuration class",
            ViewCount = 5203,
            CreatedDate = createdDate,
            LastModifiedDate = lastModifiedDate
        });

        EntityEntry<Item> e4 = DbContext.Items.Add(new Item()
        {
            UserId = authorId,
            Title = "SuperTux",
            Description = "A classic 2D jump and run, side-scrolling game
similar to the Super Mario series.",
            Text = @"The game is currently under Milestone 3. The Milestone
2, which is currently out, features the following:
                        - a nearly completely rewritten game engine based
on OpenGL, OpenAL, SDL2, ...
                        - support for translations
                        - in-game manager for downloadable add-ons and
translations
                        - Bonus Island III, a for now unfinished Forest
Island and the development levels in Incubator Island
                        - a final boss in Icy Island
                        - new and improved soundtracks and sound effects
                        ... and much more!
                        The game has been released under the GNU GPL
license.",
            Notes = "This is a sample record created by the Code-First
Configuration class",
            ViewCount = 9602,
            CreatedDate = createdDate,
            LastModifiedDate = lastModifiedDate
        });

        EntityEntry<Item> e5 = DbContext.Items.Add(new Item()
        {
            UserId = authorId,
            Title = "Scrabble3D",
            Description = "A 3D-based revamp to the classic Scrabble
game.",
            Text = @"Scrabble3D extends the gameplay of the classic game
Scrabble by adding a new whole third dimension.
```

```
                    Other than playing left to right or top to bottom,
you'll be able to place your tiles above or beyond other tiles.
                    Since the game features more fields, it also uses a
larger letter set.
                    You can either play against the computer, players
from your LAN or from the Internet.
                    The game also features a set of game servers where
you can challenge players from all over the world and get ranked into an
official, ELO-based rating/ladder system.
                    ",
        Notes = "This is a sample record created by the Code-First
Configuration class",
        ViewCount = 6754,
        CreatedDate = createdDate,
        LastModifiedDate = lastModifiedDate
    });

    // Create default Comments (if there are none)
    if (DbContext.Comments.Count() == 0)
    {
        int numComments = 10;   // comments per item
        for (int i = 1; i <= numComments; i++)
DbContext.Comments.Add(GetSampleComment(i, e1.Entity.Id, authorId,
createdDate.AddDays(i)));
        for (int i = 1; i <= numComments; i++)
DbContext.Comments.Add(GetSampleComment(i, e2.Entity.Id, authorId,
createdDate.AddDays(i)));
        for (int i = 1; i <= numComments; i++)
DbContext.Comments.Add(GetSampleComment(i, e3.Entity.Id, authorId,
createdDate.AddDays(i)));
        for (int i = 1; i <= numComments; i++)
DbContext.Comments.Add(GetSampleComment(i, e4.Entity.Id, authorId,
createdDate.AddDays(i)));
        for (int i = 1; i <= numComments; i++)
DbContext.Comments.Add(GetSampleComment(i, e5.Entity.Id, authorId,
createdDate.AddDays(i)));
    }
    DbContext.SaveChanges();
}
#endregion Seed Methods

#region Utility Methods
/// <summary>
/// Generate a sample item to populate the DB.
/// </summary>
/// <param name="userId">the author ID</param>
/// <param name="id">the item ID</param>
/// <param name="createdDate">the item CreatedDate</param>
```

```
    /// <returns></returns>
    private Item GetSampleItem(int id, string authorId, int viewCount,
DateTime createdDate)
    {
        return new Item()
        {
            UserId = authorId,
            Title = String.Format("Item {0} Title", id),
            Description = String.Format("This is a sample description for
item {0}: Lorem ipsum dolor sit amet.", id),
            Notes = "This is a sample record created by the Code-First
Configuration class",
            ViewCount = viewCount,
            CreatedDate = createdDate,
            LastModifiedDate = createdDate
        };
    }

    /// <summary>
    /// Generate a sample array of Comments (for testing purposes only).
    /// </summary>
    /// <param name="n"></param>
    /// <param name="item"></param>
    /// <param name="authorID"></param>
    /// <returns></returns>
    private Comment GetSampleComment(int n, int itemId, string authorId,
DateTime createdDate)
    {
        return new Comment()
        {
            ItemId = itemId,
            UserId = authorId,
            ParentId = null,
            Text = String.Format("Sample comment #{0} for the item #{1}",
n, itemId),
            CreatedDate = createdDate,
            LastModifiedDate = createdDate
        };
    }
    #endregion Utility Methods
}
```

That's an impressive amount of code, yet there's nothing to worry about since it's full of repeating tasks. To properly understand what we're doing here let's split it into six parts, each one corresponding to a #region section we defined within the source code:

- The Private Members, where we define the DbContext object that we'll be using a lot in the methods in the following sections.
- The Constructor region, containing the aforementioned DbContext using DI.
- The Seed region, containing the only public method of this class: SeedAsync, which is in charge of the seeding task by making use of the other private methods defined in the following section.
- The Create Entities region, containing a couple of methods that will create the Admin user (plus a set of sample users) plus a grand total of 105 generic Item entities.
- The Utility Methods region, containing some internal functions used to create sample Item and Comment entities with bulk strategies.

Private members

Here we can find the reference for the ApplicationDbContext instance that we'll be using throughout all the classes.

Constructor

Within this region, we can find a classic class constructor implementing the standard DI pattern provided by the ASP.NET Core. An ApplicationDbContext will be requested of the DI container using the instantiation mode configured within the Startup.cs file and assigned to the DbContext private variable defined earlier for further reference.

Public methods

This region contains the SeedAsync method, the only one that can be called from outside to initiate or update the seeding task. It has been set to call the CreateUsers and/or CreateItems methods only if there are no users/items in the database already, to ensure that they won't get executed multiple times. There's not much else to say here, other than this being an async method to comply with the used EF Core async methods.

Seed methods

This region contains all the internal methods that actually insert one or more entities in our database: `CreateUsers` and `CreateItems`.

- `CreateUsers`: This method will add one or more `ApplicationUsers` to the database that will be used as authors for the `Items` and `Comments` that will be added soon after. It's worth mentioning that we used a C# pre-processor directive here (also known as conditional compilation directive), so we can use two different behaviors for our testing environment and for production. We don't want to create the sample users in our production environment, so we've put that part of code inside a conditional compilation block that gets executed only if the application is running in **Debug** mode.

- `CreateItems`: This method will add a number of `Items` to the Database that will populate the item listings of our web application. It will also conditionally create some sample `Comments` for each one of them by using the same compilation directives used within the `CreateUsers` method described previously. In our production environment, we'll have only five sample items and no comments.

Utility methods

We have two methods here: `GetSampleItem` and `GetSampleComment`. Both of them come with a self-explanatory name, as they will return a sample `Item` or `Comment` with some minimal, parameter-dependent logic to show small differences between them.

Notice that these methods don't write anything into the database, they only return sample entities that will be persisted by the caller methods mentioned previously.

> Notice how we implemented our `Seed()` method to be as conservative as possible, as it will be executed each and every time our data model changes. We don't want any user, item, or comment to be added twice, not to mention repeating role assignments. In order to avoid this, we make sure that all entities are not already present in the database right before adding them.

Adding the DbSeeder to Startup.cs

Our next task will be adding the `DbSeeder` to our `Startup` class. Since we've used DI, we need to do that using DI as well, adding it to the list of available services handled by the DI container (new lines are highlighted):

```
public void ConfigureServices(IServiceCollection services)
{
    // Add framework services.
    services.AddMvc();

    // Add EntityFramework's Identity support.
    services.AddEntityFramework();

    // Add ApplicationDbContext.
    services.AddDbContext<ApplicationDbContext>(options =>
options.UseSqlServer(Configuration["Data:DefaultConnection:ConnectionString
"])
        );

    // Add ApplicationDbContext's DbSeeder
    services.AddSingleton<DbSeeder>();
}
```

Notice how we used the `AddSingleton` operation mode, so that a single instance of it will be created for the whole application lifetime.

We can now use the `DbSeeder` in the `Startup.cs Configure` method, providing that we add the required parameter to have it injected there. Here's how it should be changed to reflect these changes (new/updated lines highlighted):

```
public void Configure(IApplicationBuilder app, IHostingEnvironment env,
ILoggerFactory loggerFactory, DbSeeder dbSeeder)
{
    loggerFactory.AddConsole(Configuration.GetSection("Logging"));
    loggerFactory.AddDebug();

    // Configure a rewrite rule to auto-lookup for standard default files
such as index.html.
    app.UseDefaultFiles();

    // Serve static files (html, css, js, images & more). See also the
following URL:
    // https://docs.asp.net/en/latest/fundamentals/static-files.html for
further reference.
    app.UseStaticFiles(new StaticFileOptions()
    {
```

```
        OnPrepareResponse = (context) =>
        {
            // Disable caching for all static files.
            context.Context.Response.Headers["Cache-Control"] =
Configuration["StaticFiles:Headers:Cache-Control"];
            context.Context.Response.Headers["Pragma"] =
Configuration["StaticFiles:Headers:Pragma"];
            context.Context.Response.Headers["Expires"] =
Configuration["StaticFiles:Headers:Expires"];
        }
    });

    // Add MVC to the pipeline
    app.UseMvc();

    // Seed the Database (if needed)
    try
    {
        dbSeeder.SeedAsync().Wait();
    }
    catch (AggregateException e)
    {
        throw new Exception(e.ToString());
    }
}
```

We won't talk about DI any further, as it would bring us far from the scope of this book.

For those who want to understand more about DI in ASP.NET we strongly suggest reading this awesome article by Steve Smith in the ASP.NET official documentation website: http://docs.asp.net/en/latest/funda mentals/dependency-injection.html.

Handling exceptions

Notice how we wrapped the dbSeeder.SeedAsync().Wait() call in a try-catch block to handle a specific type of Exception: the AggregateException, which is commonly used to group together multiple exceptions that might simultaneously occur during the execution of parallel processes. Needless to say, these are extensively used by EF Core.

The only real downside of `AggregateException` lies in the fact that we have to navigate through the `InnerExceptions` container property to figure out what really happened, which can be quite annoying. That's why it might be useful to catch and display them in a human-readable fashion. Luckily, the `AggregateException.ToString()` method implementation does exactly that, as it conveniently formats the inner exception messages for readability, with separators between them.

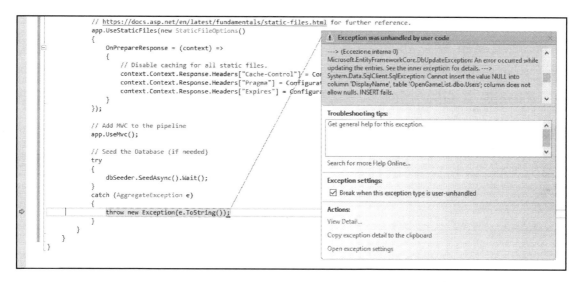

If we need further data about one or more `InnerExceptions`, we can still do that by placing a breakpoint inside the `catch` statement and analyzing them using the **Watch** panel.

Seeding the database

We're now ready to seed our database. Since we hooked the `DbSeeder.SeedAsync` to the `Startup` class, it'll be as easy as hitting *F5* and letting the application work its magic. If we have done everything correctly, our database should be populated in no time. In order to check that, we can:

1. Open the **Server Object Explorer** panel.
2. Expand the nodes up to our `OpenGameList` database.
3. Right-click on the `dbo.Items` table and select **View Data**.

Upon doing that, we should see something like the following:

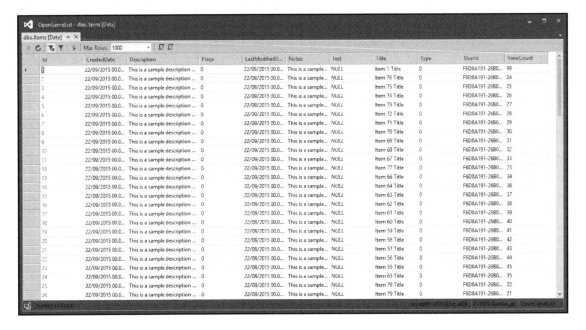

Updating the ItemsController

Last but not least, we need to modify our `ItemsController` to use the `ApplicationDbContext` to retrieve data, getting rid of our dummy data provider once and for all.

In order to do that, the first thing we need to do is find an efficient way to map each **Item** entity to a corresponding `ItemViewModel` object, as our new data provider won't generate them anymore. We can achieve such a result in a number of ways, including the following:

- Adding a `Helper` method, such as `GetItemViewModel(Item item)`, handling the mapping manually with a few lines of code
- Adding a `Constructor` method, such as `ItemViewModel(Item item)`, doing pretty much the same thing as the aforementioned helper method
- Adding one of the many object-to-object auto-mapping tools freely available via NuGet and configuring it to handle the mapping automatically whenever we need it

We'll definitely go for the latter.

Installing TinyMapper

ASP.NET features a lot of object-to-object mapping tools, AutoMapper being the most used and acknowledged one. You're free to use the one you like the most and/or are most used to. For the purpose of this book we're going to use TinyMapper because it's lightweight, simple to use, and often performs better than its big brothers.

From the **Solution Explorer**, right-click on the **OpenGameListWebApp** project and select **Manage NuGet Packages**. Make sure the **Browse** tab is selected, then type `TinyMapper` into the search box and press *Enter*. Select the appropriate result and hit the **Install** button to add it.

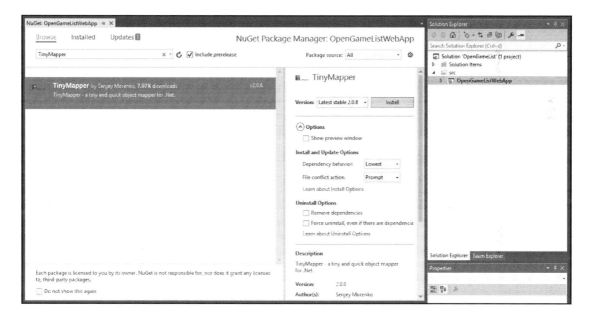

Alternatively, you can manually install it via the Package Manager Console by typing the following command:

```
Install-Package TinyMapper
```

The only real downside to TinyMapper is the lack of compatibility with the .NET Core CLR, meaning that we won't be able to use it unless we target the .NET Framework runtime. That's precisely what we did back in `Chapter 1`, *Getting Ready*, meaning that we're good to go. However, should we ever want to target the .NET Core runtime in the future, we will definitely have to replace it.

Implementing the mapping

Like most mappers, TinyMapper does its job using two main methods:

1. `TinyMapper.Bind`, to define/configure a binding between a source type and a target type.
2. `TinyMapper.Map`, to perform an actual map from the source object to target object.

We're going to register all the bindings on application start, so we'll be able to use the `Map` method only within our Web API controllers.

Open the `Startup.cs` file and add the following lines to the `Configure` method (new lines highlighted):

```
public void Configure(IApplicationBuilder app, IHostingEnvironment env,
ILoggerFactory loggerFactory, DbSeeder dbSeeder)
{
    loggerFactory.AddConsole(Configuration.GetSection("Logging"));
    loggerFactory.AddDebug();

    // Configure a rewrite rule to auto-lookup for standard default files
such as index.html.
    app.UseDefaultFiles();

    // Serve static files (html, css, js, images & more). See also the
following URL:
    // https://docs.asp.net/en/latest/fundamentals/static-files.html for
further reference.
    app.UseStaticFiles(new StaticFileOptions()
    {
        OnPrepareResponse = (context) =>
        {
            // Disable caching for all static files.
            context.Context.Response.Headers["Cache-Control"] =
Configuration["StaticFiles:Headers:Cache-Control"];
            context.Context.Response.Headers["Pragma"] =
Configuration["StaticFiles:Headers:Pragma"];
            context.Context.Response.Headers["Expires"] =
Configuration["StaticFiles:Headers:Expires"];
        }
    });

    // Add MVC to the pipeline
    app.UseMvc();

    // TinyMapper binding configuration       TinyMapper.Bind<Item,
```

```
ItemViewModel>();

    // Seed the Database (if needed)
    try
    {
        dbSeeder.SeedAsync().Wait();
    }
    catch (AggregateException e)
    {
        throw new Exception(e.ToString());
    }
}
```

On top of that, we also need to add the following references to the top of the file:

```
using Nelibur.ObjectMapper;
using OpenGameListWebApp.Data.Items;
using OpenGameListWebApp.ViewModels;
```

We're almost done. The last thing we need to do is open the `ItemsController.cs` file and do the following:

1. Add a `private` variable of the `ApplicationDbContext` type to host the `DbContext`.
2. Add a `Constructor` method to instantiate it via DI and set it to the private variable defined earlier.
3. Change the data-retrieval lines of code within the `Get`, `GetLatest`, `GetMostViewed`, and `GetRandom` methods to use the new `DbContext` instead of the old `GetSampleItems` method.
4. Update the last line of the aforementioned methods to return one or more `ItemViewModel` objects created via `TinyMapper`.
5. Remove the old `GetSampleItems` method entirely, as we don't need it anymore.

Here's the updated source code (new/modified lines are highlighted):

```
using System;
using System.Collections.Generic;
using System.Linq;
using System.Threading.Tasks;
using Microsoft.AspNet.Mvc;
using OpenGameListWebApp.ViewModels;
using Newtonsoft.Json;
using OpenGameListWebApp.Data;
using OpenGameListWebApp.Data.Items;
using Nelibur.ObjectMapper;
```

```
namespace OpenGameListWebApp.Controllers
{
    [Route("api/[controller]")]
    public class ItemsController : Controller
    {
        #region Private Fields
        private ApplicationDbContext DbContext;
        #endregion Private Fields
        #region Constructor
        public ItemsController(ApplicationDbContext context)
        {
            // Dependency Injetion
            DbContext = context;
        }
        #endregion Constructor

        #region RESTful Conventions
        /// <summary>
        /// GET: api/items
        /// </summary>
        /// <returns>Nothing: this method will raise a NotFound HTTP
exception, since we're not supporting this API call.</returns>
        [HttpGet()]
        public IActionResult Get()
        {
            return NotFound(new { Error = "not found" });
        }
        #endregion

        #region Attribute-based Routing
        /// <summary>
        /// GET: api/items/{id}
        /// ROUTING TYPE: attribute-based
        /// </summary>
        /// <returns>A Json-serialized object representing a single
item.</returns>
        [HttpGet("{id}")]
        public IActionResult Get(int id)
        {
            var item = DbContext.Items.Where(i => i.Id ==
id).FirstOrDefault();                return new
JsonResult(TinyMapper.Map<ItemViewModel>(item), DefaultJsonSettings);
        }

        /// <summary>
        /// GET: api/items/GetLatest
        /// ROUTING TYPE: attribute-based
        /// </summary>
```

```
/// <returns>An array of a default number of Json-serialized
objects representing the last inserted items.</returns>
[HttpGet("GetLatest")]
public IActionResult GetLatest()
{
    return GetLatest(DefaultNumberOfItems);
}

/// <summary>
/// GET: api/items/GetLatest/{n}
/// ROUTING TYPE: attribute-based
/// </summary>
/// <returns>An array of {n} Json-serialized objects representing
the last inserted items.</returns>
[HttpGet("GetLatest/{n}")]
public IActionResult GetLatest(int n)
{
    if (n > MaxNumberOfItems) n = MaxNumberOfItems;
    var items = DbContext.Items.OrderByDescending(i =>
i.CreatedDate).Take(n).ToArray();
    return new JsonResult(ToItemViewModelList(items),
DefaultJsonSettings);
}

/// <summary>
/// GET: api/items/GetMostViewed
/// ROUTING TYPE: attribute-based
/// </summary>
/// <returns>An array of a default number of Json-serialized
objects representing the items with most user views.</returns>
[HttpGet("GetMostViewed")]
public IActionResult GetMostViewed()
{
    return GetMostViewed(DefaultNumberOfItems);
}

/// <summary>
/// GET: api/items/GetMostViewed/{n}
/// ROUTING TYPE: attribute-based
/// </summary>
/// <returns>An array of {n} Json-serialized objects representing
the items with most user views.</returns>
[HttpGet("GetMostViewed/{n}")]
public IActionResult GetMostViewed(int n)
{
    if (n > MaxNumberOfItems) n = MaxNumberOfItems;
    var items = DbContext.Items.OrderByDescending(i =>
i.ViewCount).Take(n).ToArray();
```

```
            return new JsonResult(ToItemViewModelList(items),
DefaultJsonSettings);
        }

        /// <summary>
        /// GET: api/items/GetMostViewed
        /// ROUTING TYPE: attribute-based
        /// </summary>
        /// <returns>An array of a default number of Json-serialized
objects representing some randomly-picked items.</returns>
        [HttpGet("GetRandom")]
        public IActionResult GetRandom()
        {
            return GetRandom(DefaultNumberOfItems);
        }

        /// <summary>
        /// GET: api/items/GetRandom/{n}
        /// ROUTING TYPE: attribute-based
        /// </summary>
        /// <returns>An array of {n} Json-serialized objects representing
some randomly-picked items.</returns>
        [HttpGet("GetRandom/{n}")]
        public IActionResult GetRandom(int n)
        {
            if (n > MaxNumberOfItems) n = MaxNumberOfItems;
            var items = DbContext.Items.OrderBy(i =>
Guid.NewGuid()).Take(n).ToArray();
            return new JsonResult(ToItemViewModelList(items),
DefaultJsonSettings);
        }
        #endregion

        #region Private Members
        /// <summary>
        /// Maps a collection of Item entities into a list of ItemViewModel
objects.
        /// </summary>
        /// <param name="items">An IEnumerable collection of item
entities</param>
        /// <returns>a mapped list of ItemViewModel objects</returns>
        private List<ItemViewModel> ToItemViewModelList(IEnumerable<Item> items)
        {
            var lst = new List<ItemViewModel>();
            foreach (var i in items)
lst.Add(TinyMapper.Map<ItemViewModel>(i));
            return lst;
        }
```

```
/// <summary>
/// Returns a suitable JsonSerializerSettings object that can be
used to generate the JsonResult return value for this Controller's methods.
/// </summary>
private JsonSerializerSettings DefaultJsonSettings
{
    get
    {
        return new JsonSerializerSettings()
        {
            Formatting = Formatting.Indented
        };
    }
}

/// <summary>
/// Returns the default number of items to retrieve when using the
parameterless overloads of the API methods retrieving item lists.
/// </summary>
private int DefaultNumberOfItems
{
    get
    {
        return 5;
    }
}

/// <summary>
/// Returns the maximum number of items to retrieve when using the
API methods retrieving item lists.
/// </summary>
private int MaxNumberOfItems
{
    get
    {
        return 100;
    }
}
#endregion
    }
}
```

That's it. Notice that we also have added a private `ToItemViewModelList()` utility method to centralize the *Model-to-ViewModel* mapping task, avoiding code repetition and making it easier to update.

Testing the data provider

Before going further, it's time to perform a final test to see if our `ApplicationDbContext` is working as expected.

To do that, just launch the application in **Debug** mode by hitting the *F5* key. If everything has been implemented properly you should be presented with a **Welcome View** similar to the following one:

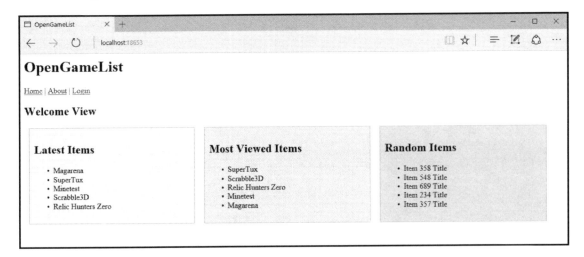

Although it doesn't seem too different from what we already had by the end of `Chapter 3`, *Angular 2 Components and Client-Side Routing*, we know that a lot of stuff has changed under the hood. Our application is now equipped with a persistent database built on top of a real data model handled by an EF-powered, migrations-aware `DbContext` available through DI upon a per-request scope.

Suggested topics

Data model, data provider, ADO.NET, object relational mapper, EF, `Entity` class, data annotations, NOSQL, MongoDB, RavenDB, `DbContext`, `AggregateException`, CRUD operations, DI, ORM mapping.

Summary

We started this chapter enumerating a number of things we couldn't implement due to our dummy data provider limitations. In order to overcome these, we chose to replace it with a real data provider built upon a persistent database.

ED Core seemed an obvious choice to get what we wanted, so we added its relevant packages to our project. We briefly enumerated the available data modeling approaches and we resorted to using code-first due to its flexibility.

Right after that, we proceeded to create our entity classes: `Item`, `Comment`, and `ApplicationUser`, together with a set of relationships taking advantage of the renowned EF's convention over configuration approach. Then we built our `ApplicationDbContext` class accordingly.

After completing our data model we chose the database engine, quickly resorting to the Visual Studio 2015 default `LocalDb` instance. We added the connection string to the `appsettings.json` file and passed it to the `ApplicationDbContext` through the `Setup` class. Doing this allowed us to add our first migration using PowerShell and, once done, use code-first to generate our database accordingly.

We didn't want to leave our database empty, so we implemented a `DbSeeder` class to seed it with some sample data by making good use of the ASP.NET Core DI approach. Doing that took some reasonable, yet well spent, amount of time.

Finally, we switched back to the `ItemsController` class and updated it to make it use the new data provider, replacing the outdated one. In order to do this in the best possible way, we also installed `TinyMapper`, a fast and easy to use ORM mapping tool that we used inside `ItemsController` to perform model-to-view model conversions with ease.

After completing all these tasks, we ran our application in Debug mode to test that everything was still working as intended. The **Welcome View** is very similar to the one we had at the end of `Chapter 3`, *Angular 2 Components and Client-Side Routing*, yet a lot of things have changed on the inside. Our application is now ready to grow the way we want it to.

5
Persisting Changes

In the previous chapter, we replaced our dummy data provider with a real data provider built upon EF Core using a code-first approach. Now that we have data persistence, we're ready to entrust our users with the ability to interact with our application; this means that we can implement some much needed features such as login view, access control, and server-side sessions, as well as specific views to create, edit, or delete our entities, whether they are Items, Comments, or Users, ensuring that all the changes will be reflected in the database.

In this chapter we will take care of the latter, leaving the authentication features out; we will address these later on, as they will have their own dedicated chapter.

Add, update, and delete items

The first thing we'll do is to implement the add, update, and delete methods for our Web API's ItemsController. We'll adhere to RESTful conventions and good practices, using the proper HTTP verb for each scenario: POST for create, PUT for update, and DELETE for delete.

 From now on, we won't explain how to select, open, add, rename, delete, or otherwise interact with your ASP.NET and/or Angular 2 files from **Solution Explorer**; we take for granted that you already know (or have figured out) how to navigate the GUI and what to do with the code samples.

Updating the Web API

Here are the new ItemsController.cs-relevant methods (new/updated lines are highlighted):

```
#region RESTful Conventions
/// <summary>
/// GET: api/items
/// </summary>
/// <returns>Nothing: this method will raise a NotFound HTTP
exception, since we're not supporting this API call.</returns>
[HttpGet()]
public IActionResult Get()
{
    return NotFound(new { Error = "not found" });
}


/// <summary>
/// GET: api/items/{id}
/// ROUTING TYPE: attribute-based
/// </summary>
/// <returns>A Json-serialized object representing a single
item.</returns>
[HttpGet("{id}")]
public IActionResult Get(int id)
{
    var item = DbContext.Items.Where(i => i.Id ==
id).FirstOrDefault();
    if (item != null) return new
JsonResult(TinyMapper.Map<ItemViewModel>(item), DefaultJsonSettings);
    else return NotFound(new { Error = String.Format("Item ID {0} has not been
found", id) });
}

/// <summary>
/// POST: api/items
/// </summary>
/// <returns>Creates a new Item and return it
accordingly.</returns>        [HttpPost()]
public IActionResult Add([FromBody]ItemViewModel ivm)
{
    if (ivm != null)
    {
        // create a new Item with the client-sent json data
        var item = TinyMapper.Map<Item>(ivm);
        // override any property that could be wise to set from
server-side only
        item.CreatedDate =
```

```
                    item.LastModifiedDate = DateTime.Now;
                    // TODO: replace the following with the current user's id
when authentication will be available.
                    item.UserId = DbContext.Users.Where(u => u.UserName ==
"Admin").FirstOrDefault().Id;
                    // add the new item
                    DbContext.Items.Add(item);
                    // persist the changes into the Database.
                    DbContext.SaveChanges();
                    // return the newly-created Item to the client.
                    return new JsonResult(TinyMapper.Map<ItemViewModel>(item),
DefaultJsonSettings);
                }
                // return a generic HTTP Status 500 (Not Found) if the client
payload is invalid.
                return new StatusCodeResult(500);
        }
        /// <summary>
        /// PUT: api/items/{id}
        /// </summary>
        /// <returns>Updates an existing Item and return it accordingly.
</returns>
        [HttpPut("{id}")]
        public IActionResult Update(int id, [FromBody]ItemViewModel ivm)
        {
            if (ivm != null)
            {
                var item = DbContext.Items.Where(i => i.Id ==
  id).FirstOrDefault();
                if (item != null)
                {
                    // handle the update (on per-property basis)
                    item.UserId = ivm.UserId;
                    item.Description = ivm.Description;
                    item.Flags = ivm.Flags;
                    item.Notes = ivm.Notes;
                    item.Text = ivm.Text;
                    item.Title = ivm.Title;
                    item.Type = ivm.Type;
                    // override any property that could be wise to set from
server-side only
                    item.LastModifiedDate = DateTime.Now;
                    // persist the changes into the Database.
                    DbContext.SaveChanges();
                    // return the updated Item to the client.
                    return new
JsonResult(TinyMapper.Map<ItemViewModel>(item), DefaultJsonSettings);
                }
```

```
                    }
                    // return a HTTP Status 404 (Not Found) if we couldn't find a
        suitable item.
                    return NotFound(new { Error = String.Format("Item ID {0} has
        not been found", id) });
            }
            /// <summary>
            /// DELETE: api/items/{id}
            /// </summary>
            /// <returns>Deletes an Item, returning a HTTP status 200 (ok) when
        done.</returns>
            [HttpDelete("{id}")]
            public IActionResult Delete(int id)
            {
                    var item = DbContext.Items.Where(i => i.Id ==
        id).FirstOrDefault();
                    if (item != null)
                    {
                        // remove the item to delete from the DbContext.
                        DbContext.Items.Remove(item);
                        // persist the changes into the Database.
                        DbContext.SaveChanges();
                        // return an HTTP Status 200 (OK).
                        return new OkResult();
                    }
                    // return a HTTP Status 404 (Not Found) if we couldn't find a
        suitable item.
                    return NotFound(new { Error = String.Format("Item ID {0} has
        not been found", id) });
            }
            #endregion
```

For the sake of simplicity, we haven't pasted the whole file; since we're following the RESTful conventions, we put all the new stuff into the region hosting these kinds of methods. Just remember to add a `using OpenGameListWebApp.Data.Items` line at the beginning of the file.

The code contains some comments that will help to focus on what we just did. Nonetheless, it would be useful to highlights some specific aspects of the new methods, such as the following:

- We didn't have to use the `Json.NET` library at all here, as the ASP.NET framework can automatically handle the conversion task between a JSON-type input and a `JsonSerializable` object; all we did was specify an object of type `ItemViewModel` as the main input parameter of the `Add` and `Update` methods and tell the framework to retrieve it from the request body.

- We used the `TinyMapper` mapping library at the end of the `Add` and `Update` methods to return a new `ItemViewModel` to the client built upon the created/modified `Item`. Notice how we didn't use it the other way around, that is, to populate the `Item` properties from the `ItemViewModel` instance built upon the JSON data sent by the client in the `Update` method, as we preferred to manually treat and check each of the properties separately.

We should also spend a few moments talking about *what we didn't do* here: no error-handling strategies, no specific controls on user input, and no authentication, just to name a few. This isn't a robust, production-ready code yet, and we need to be fully aware of that. There's nothing wrong with it; we're still in development phase, after all, and we'll refine these aspects once we get a good grip on the Web API features we need to know.

Adapting the client

Now that our Web API supports the four basic CRUD functions, we can modify our Angular 2 client to make use of them.

Improving the ItemService

Let's start with updating the code of our `ItemService` class. Open the `/Scripts/app/item.service.ts` file and change its contents with the following code:

```
import {Injectable} from "@angular2core";
import {Http, Response, Headers, RequestOptions} from "@angular/http";
import {Observable} from "rxjs/Observable";
import {Item} from "./item";

@Injectable()
export class ItemService {
    // private Data: { Latest: Item[], MostViewed: Item[], Random: Item[]
};
    private baseUrl = 'api/items/';  // URL to web api
    constructor(private http: Http) { }

    // calls the [GET] /api/items/GetLatest/{n} Web API method to retrieve
the latest items.
    getLatest(num?: number) {
        var url = this.baseUrl + "GetLatest/";
```

```
            if (num != null) url += num;
        return this.http.get(url)
            .map(response => response.json())
            .catch(this.handleError);
    }

    // calls the [GET] /api/items/GetMostViewed/{n} Web API method to
retrieve the most viewed items.
    getMostViewed(num?: number) {
        var url = this.baseUrl + "GetMostViewed/";
        if (num != null) url += num;
        return this.http.get(url)
            .map(response => response.json())
            .catch(this.handleError);
    }

    // calls the [GET] /api/items/GetRandom/{n} Web API method to retrieve
n random items.
    getRandom(num?: number) {
        var url = this.baseUrl + "GetRandom/";
        if (num != null) url += num;
        return this.http.get(url)
            .map(response => response.json())
            .catch(this.handleError);
    }

    // calls the [GET] /api/items/{id} Web API method to retrieve the item
with the given id.
    get(id: number) {
        if (id == null) throw new Error("id is required.");
        var url = this.baseUrl + id;
        return this.http.get(url)
            .map(res => <Item>res.json())
            .catch(this.handleError);
    }

    // calls the [POST] /api/items/ Web API method to add a new item.
    add(item: Item) {
        var url = this.baseUrl;
        return this.http.post(url, JSON.stringify(item),
        this.getRequestOptions())
            .map(response => response.json())
            .catch(this.handleError);
    }
    // calls the [PUT] /api/items/{id} Web API method to update an existing
item.
    update(item: Item) {
        var url = this.baseUrl + item.Id;
```

```
            return this.http.put(url, JSON.stringify(item),
    this.getRequestOptions())
                .map(response => response.json())
                .catch(this.handleError);
        }
        // calls the [DELETE] /api/items/{id} Web API method to delete the item
    with the given id.
        delete(id: number) {
            var url = this.baseUrl + id;
            return this.http.delete(url)
                .catch(this.handleError);
        }
        // returns a viable RequestOptions object to handle Json requests
        private getRequestOptions() {
            return new RequestOptions({
                headers: new Headers({
                    "Content-Type": "application/json"
                })
            });
        }

        private handleError(error: Response) {
            // output errors to the console.
            console.error(error);
            return Observable.throw(error.json().error || 'Server error');
        }
    }
}
```

Let's see what we did here:

- In line 2, we added a reference for the `Response` and `RequestOptions` classes from the Angular 2 built-in `http` service.
- We then implemented three public methods (`add`, `update`, and `delete`) to handle the corresponding Web API calls we added earlier.
- Since each of our new methods requires a `RequestOptions` object, we eventually created a `getRequestOptions` method to avoid repeating the same lines of codes multiple times. Since `add` and `update` are both sending JSON data, having a centralized factory method returning a `RequestOptions` object is definitely a good choice.

Updating the GUI

Now that we have these `insert`, `update`, and `delete` methods, we need to make the GUI aware of that by adding the relevant commands. The former should be put on our main menu, while the other two will be added to the item's detail view. The reason for that is simple: we want our users to be able to create a new item from any view, or `update`/`delete` only the specific item they clicked on.

Add new

Let's start with the `insert` command. Open the `\Scripts\app\app.component.ts` file and add the following element to our `@Component`'s `template` (new/updated lines are highlighted):

```
@Component({
    selector: "opengamelist",
    template: `
<h1>{{title}}</h1>
  <div class="menu">
    <a class="home" [routerLink]="['']">Home</a>
    | <a class="about" [routerLink]="['about']">About</a>
    | <a class="login" [routerLink]="['login']">Login</a>
    | <a class="add" [routerLink]="['item', 0]">Add New</a>
  </div>
  <router-outlet></router-outlet>
  `

})
```

Notice that we're deliberately exploiting the `item` route we already have in place, passing an `id` with a value of 0. This means that any item with an ID of 0, as per our internal convention, should be treated by our `ItemDetail` component as a new, not-yet-existing item.

Needless to say, in order to do that, we need to update our `item-detail.component.ts` file accordingly (new/modified lines are highlighted):

```
import {Component, OnInit} from "@angular/core";
import {Router, ActivatedRoute} from "@angular/router";
import {Item} from "./item";
import {ItemService} from "./item.service";

@Component({
    selector: "item-detail",
    template: `
        <div *ngIf="item" class="item-details">
```

```
            <h2>{{item.Title}} - Detail View</h2>
            <ul>
                <li>
                    <label>Title:</label>
                    <input [(ngModel)]="item.Title" placeholder="Insert the
title..."/>
                </li>
                <li>
                    <label>Description:</label>
                    <textarea [(ngModel)]="item.Description"
placeholder="Insert a suitable description..."></textarea>
                </li>
            </ul>
            <div *ngIf="item.Id == 0" class="commands insert">
                <input type="button" value="Save" (click)="onInsert(item)" />
                <input type="button" value="Cancel" (click)="onBack()" />
            </div>
        </div>
    `,
    styles: [`
        .item-details {
            margin: 5px;
            padding: 5px 10px;
            border: 1px solid black;
            background-color: #dddddd;
            width: 300px;
        }
        .item-details * {
            vertical-align: middle;
        }
        .item-details ul li {
            padding: 5px 0;
        }
    `]
})

export class ItemDetailComponent {
    item: Item;

    constructor(private itemService: ItemService,
        private router: Router,
        private activatedRoute: ActivatedRoute) {
    }

    ngOnInit() {
        var id = +this.activatedRoute.snapshot.params["id"];
        if (id) {
            this.itemService.get(id).subscribe(
```

```
                   item => this.item = item
            );
        }
        else if (id === 0) {
            console.log("id is 0: adding a new item...");
            this.item = new Item(0, "New Item", null);
        }
        else {
            console.log("Invalid id: routing back to home...");
            this.router.navigate([""]);
        }
    }

    onInsert(item: Item) {
        this.itemService.add(item).subscribe(
            (data) => {
                this.item = data;
                console.log("Item " + this.item.Id + " has been added.");
                this.router.navigate([""]);
            },
            (error) => console.log(error)
        );
    }
    onBack() {
        this.router.navigate([""]);
    }
}
```

Let's see what we did here:

- In the component's `template` section, we added a `<div>` element with an `*ngIf` condition bound to the `item.Id` being 0 so that it will only be added into the DOM if the user came here with the route designed for adding a new item.
- Within the aforementioned `<div>` element, we added a couple of `<input type="button">` fields, namely `Save` and `Cancel`, which we bound to the new `onInsert` and `onBack` methods (see later).
- We modified the `ngOnInit` method's behavior to support our internal convention that if the `id` is 0, it means that we're adding a new item.
- We implemented a new `onInsert` method, which will call the `add` method of our `ItemService` class we created earlier for adding the item through our Web API; we also added a subscription that will either return the user to the **Home** route (the **Welcome View**) in the case of success, or output an error to the console in the case of failure.

- We implemented a new `onBack` method, which will just trigger the **Home** route, returning the user back to the **Welcome View** without doing anything.

That's it for the `Add New` command; do not close the `item-detail.component.ts` file, though, as we'll need to update it further in order to implement the next ones.

Update and Delete

As we said earlier, the `Update` and `Delete` commands will take place within the `ItemDetail` component itself. This means that we'll need to keep working with the `item-detail.component.ts` file, adding a couple more buttons to the template and binding them to two new methods; that's basically the same thing we did in the previous section with the `Save/onInsert` and `Cancel/onBack` buttons/methods.

Here is the updated template (new/modified lines are highlighted):

```
template: `
    <div *ngIf="item" class="item-details">
      <h2>{{item.Title}} - Detail View</h2>
      <ul>
        <li>
            <label>Title:</label>
            <input [(ngModel)]="item.Title" placeholder="Insert the
title..."/>
        </li>
        <li>
            <label>Description:</label>
            <textarea [(ngModel)]="item.Description"
placeholder="Insert a suitable description..."></textarea>
        </li>
      </ul>
      <div *ngIf="item.Id == 0" class="commands insert">
          <input type="button" value="Save" (click)="onInsert(item)" />
          <input type="button" value="Cancel" (click)="onBack()" />
      </div>
      <div *ngIf="item.Id != 0" class="commands update">
          <input type="button" value="Update" (click)="onUpdate(item)"
/>
          <input type="button" value="Delete" (click)="onDelete(item)"
/>
          <input type="button" value="Back" (click)="onBack()" />
      </div>
    </div>
    `
```

And these are the new methods, to be placed just after the `onInsert` one:

```
onUpdate(item: Item) {
    this.itemService.update(item).subscribe(
        (data) => {
            this.item = data;
            console.log("Item " + this.item.Id + " has been updated.");
            this.router.navigate([""]);
        },
        (error) => console.log(error)
    );
}

onDelete(item: Item) {
    var id = item.Id;
    this.itemService.delete(id).subscribe(
        (data) => {
            console.log("Item " + id + " has been deleted.");
            this.router.navigate([""]);
        },
        (error) => console.log(error)
    );
}
```

What we did here is quite simple:

- We added another `<div>` element with an `*ngIf` condition that will handle the opposite case as before: `item.Id` is not 0, which means that we're dealing with an already existing item.
- The new `<div>` has three `<input type="button">` fields: `Update`, `Delete`, and `Back`, bound respectively to the `onUpdate`, `onDelete`, and `onBack` methods (see later).
- We implemented the new `onUpdate` and `onDelete` methods, which will call the `update` and `delete` method of our `ItemService` class, respectively; these will update or delete the currently selected item through our Web API. Again, we also added a subscription that will either return the user to the **Welcome View** or output an error to the console log.
- We didn't implement a new method for the **Back** button because we already have the `onBack` method, which does what we need, returning the user back to the **Welcome View** without doing anything.

With these additions, our GUI should be ready; before going further, let's perform a full surface test.

While we don't want to talk too much about Angular 2 and its `http` class, we should definitely spend a few words talking about its new abstraction pattern based upon observables.

One of the most relevant differences with the previous approach is that observables have a lazy behavior by design, meaning that they won't fire unless there is a valid subscription issued by a `.subscribe()` function call. This is a major perspective switch from the AngularJS Promises, which would execute right off the bat regardless of how the client code will use their result afterward.

Another important difference involves the `.subscribe()` function, which will be fired upon completion of the ItemService's `add` task. In Angular 2, subscriptions are designed to work just like a standard `.then()` or `.complete()` function featured in most async-based JavaScript libraries (AngularJS/Promises, JQuery/AJAX, and more), with the key difference that they are also bound to the `Observable` itself; this means that they won't just trigger once and resolve, but they will be executed each and every time the `Observable` completes its task(s) until it ceases to exist, unless they get cancelled by calling the `.unsubscribe()` function method on their `Observable`.

That said, we can easily notice that these HTTP requests are hardly a good example to demonstrate the advantages of this behavior, as these are observables that will fire only once; we'll see it better when we implement some reactive functionalities such as search with autocomplete and similar stuff.

Testing it out

Before hitting *F5* to launch the application in **Debug** mode, ensure that the `Gulp` (or `Grunt`) `default` task is properly running in the **Task Runner Explorer**, otherwise, the compiled scripts in the `www` folder won't be updated and you won't see the new stuff.

This is how our **Welcome View** should appear now:

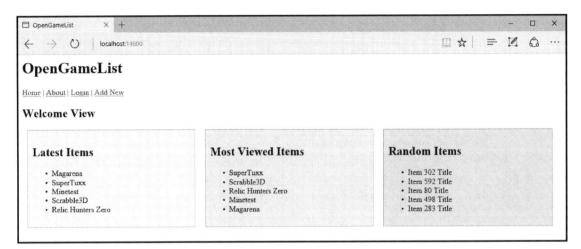

Notice the **Add New** menu command; by clicking on that, we will be brought to the updated **Item – Detail View**:

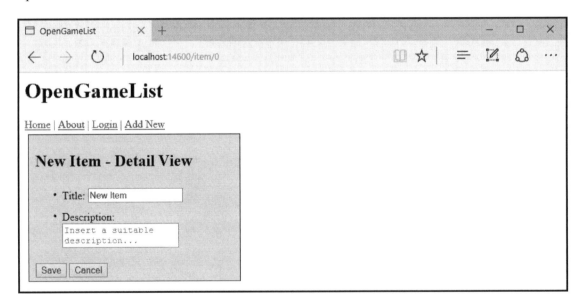

As we can see, the `ItemDetail` component is now aware of the fact that we're in the process of adding a new item; we can tell that by looking at the **Save** and **Cancel** buttons, which we know are only available when we're dealing with a new item, and also by examining the routed URL: `/item/0` matches our internal convention that an item with an `id` of 0 is a new, not-yet-existing item.

So far, so good; let's now click on the **Cancel** button. That should bring us back to the **Welcome View**. From there, click on one of the items contained in the **Last Inserted** listing panel, for example, **Magarena**. The **Item – Detail View** should be displayed again, this time in **Update** mode:

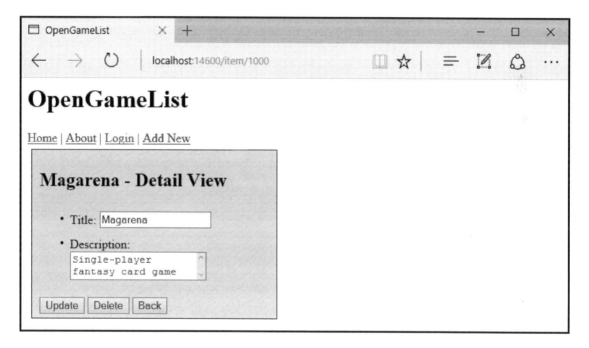

Again, we can confirm that by looking at the button set, **Update**, **Delete**, and **Back** are precisely what we're expecting to see when updating an item.

We're not done yet; now that we have tested the GUI, we need to see whether the `insert`, `update`, and `delete` methods are actually working. Ideally, the changes should be immediately seen by the user, meaning that:

- Whenever we add a new item, we want it to be shown in the **Welcome View** as the first entry of the **Last Inserted Items** panel as soon as we are sent back there

- Whenever we modify an item title, we want to see it updated in the **Welcome View** item listings (if present) as soon as we are sent back there
- Whenever we delete an item, we want it to disappear from the **Welcome View** as soon as we are sent back there

Adding a new test

From the **Welcome View**, click on the **Add New** menu item again to load the **Item – Detail View** in insert mode. Write `Sample Item` in the **Title** textbox and `Sample Description` in the **Description** text area; notice that, thanks to the Angular 2 two-way binding, the title shown within the view will be updated in *real time* as soon as we start typing, following our changes:

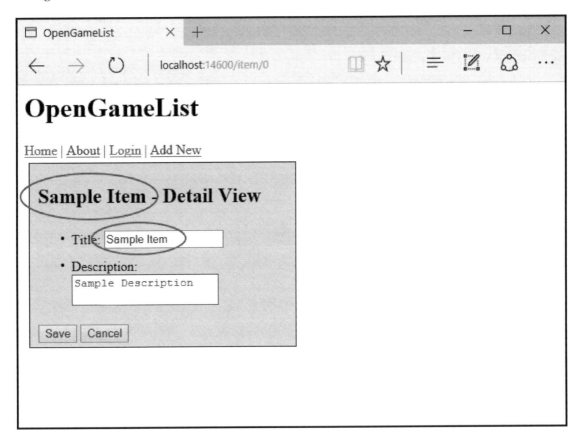

Now press the **Save** button to see whether the changes will be reflected in the **Welcome View**; if we did everything correctly, there's no reason why they shouldn't. We can also get a summary of the tasks performed by our application by looking at the developer**Console** log. In order to show it, press *F12* if we're using Microsoft Edge, or *CTRL + ALT + J* in case we're using Google Chrome or Mozilla Firefox:

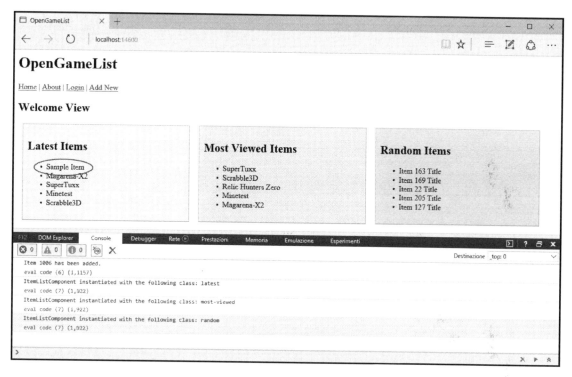

Everything is working as intended. Let's do a quick recap of what is happening under the hood:

- When the user clicks on the **Add New** menu item command, the application will show the **Item – Detail View** with an id of 0, which is our internal convention to trigger the insert mode.
- When the user fills up the **Title** and **Description** fields and confirms the insert operation by clicking on the **Save** button, the application will fire the onInsert function, which will use the ItemService to return an Observable object ready to issue an HTTP call to persist these changes to the database using the Web API Add method.

- The `Observable` object has a lazy behavior by design, meaning that it won't fire without a subscription. The `onInsert` method handles it fluently with a `.subscribe()` call which will trigger the `Observable` job and also set up a series of tasks to perform upon its completion:
  - In the case of success, update the local item object, output a message in the **Console** log, and re-route the user to the **Welcome View**
  - In the case of failure, output the error in the **Console** log
  - As soon as the user is sent back to the **Welcome View**, all the `ItemListComponents` will get re-instantiated again, so they will always load and display an updated set of lists containing the new item.

Update test

Let's try to modify the title of the new item and see whether our application behaves just as expected.

From the **Welcome View**, click on the **Sample Item** we just created; the **Item – Detail View** should be displayed in update mode, allowing us to change the item's field. Again thanks to the two-way binding, the title will be updated in real time as we type:

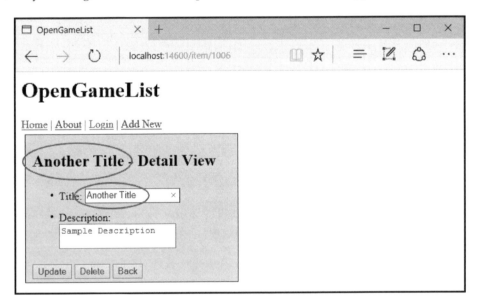

When we're done, we can click on the Update button to verify whether the changes are reflected in the **Welcome View**:

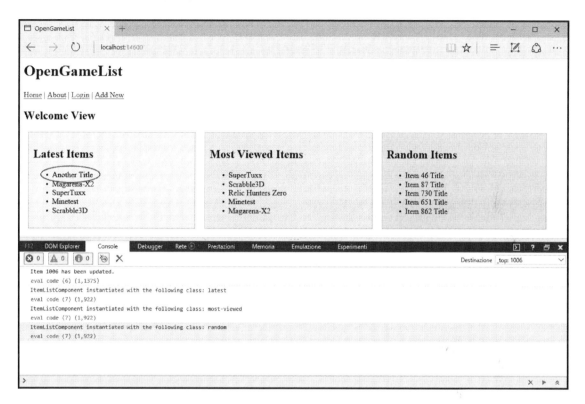

So far, so good. Again, let's see how it worked behind the scenes:

- Whenever the user selects an item from the **Welcome View**, the application will show the **Item – Detail View** in the update mode accordingly.
- Whenever the user performs a change to the item and confirms the operation by clicking on the **Update** button, the application will fire the onUpdate function. This will use the ItemService to return an Observable object ready to issue an HTTP call to persist these changes to the database using the Web API Update method.

- The `Observable` object will immediately fire thanks to the fluent `.subscribe()` call issued by the `onUpdate` function, which will also perform the following tasks:

  - In the case of success, update the local item object, output a message in the **Console** log, and re-route the user to the **Welcome View**
  - In the case of failure, output the error in the **Console** log
  - As soon as the user is sent back to the **Welcome View**, all the `ItemListComponents` will get re-instantiated again, so they will always load and display an updated set of item listings.

Delete test

Last but not least, we need to test the `delete` command.

From the **Welcome View**, click on the newly created (and updated) **Another Title** item to show the **Item – Detail View** in update mode. Immediately after clicking on the **Delete** button, we will be routed back to the **Welcome View**, where we can confirm that the item has actually gone:

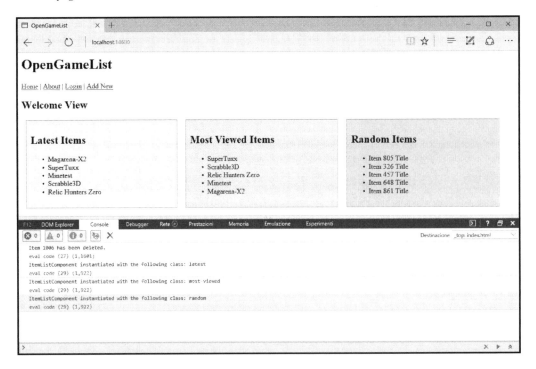

Everyone should have already figured it out by now, yet it's still useful to recap the workflow:

- When the user selects an Item from the **Welcome View**, the application will show the **Item – Detail View** in the update mode.
- When the user clicks on the **Delete** button, the application will fire the `onDelete` function, which will use the `ItemService` to return an **Observable** object ready to issue an HTTP call to delete the item from the database using the Web API `Delete` method.

- The `Observable` object will immediately fire thanks to the fluent `.subscribe()` call issued by the `onDelete` function, which will also perform the following tasks:
    - In the case of success, re-route the user to the **Welcome View**
    - In the case of failure, output the error in the Console log
    - As soon as the user is sent back to the **Welcome View**, all the `ItemListComponents` will get re-instantiated again, so they will always load and display an updated set of item listings (without the deleted item).

Splitting the ItemDetail component

Our application is going just fine, yet there are still some oddities that we should address as soon as we can. One of the most critical ones is that our `ItemDetail` component is acting like an editor way more than a viewer. Ideally, when the user clicks on an item, they should be presented with a view showing the item data in the display-only mode, with labels and text paragraphs instead of textboxes and text areas.

To better understand it, let's take a look at the following screenshot:

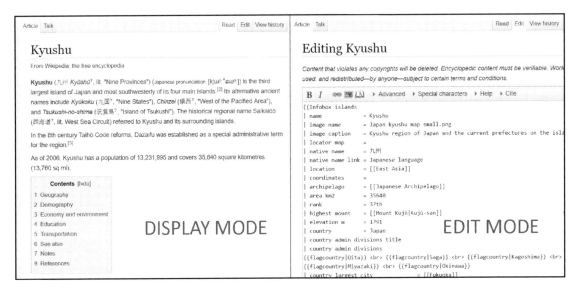

Source: Wikipedia

That's precisely what we're missing right now (and also the result we want to achieve). In order to do that, we need to split our current `ItemDetail` component into two different classes:

- `ItemDetailView`, to show the item just like the left side of the previous screenshot (**DISPLAY MODE**)
- `ItemDetailEdit`, to allow the user to insert or update items (**EDIT MODE**)

Most GUIs start with the former, allowing an authorized user to access the latter by clicking on an **Edit** button, link, or tab. Wikipedia/MediaWiki is no exception, as we can clearly see by looking at the tab menu near the top-right corner.

Notice that we put `Insert` and `Update` together; the reason for that is simple, they usually share the same fields, with very few exceptions, so it's usually fine to handle them within the same component class. As a matter of fact, we already did that within our current `ItemDetail` component, which is basically the `ItemEdit` we're talking about.

That said, here's a brief summary of what we're about to do:

1. Add a new `ItemDetailView` component.
2. Rename the existing `ItemDetail` to `ItemDetailEdit`, because that's what it is.
3. Update the application `Root` module according to these changes.
4. Replace the `ItemDetail` route with two new ones pointing to the new `ItemDetailView` and `ItemDetailEdit` components; the former one will be called upon clicking on an item from the **Welcome View**, while the latter will be activated within it.
5. Change all occurrences pointing to `ItemDetail` to `ItemDetailView` or `ItemDetailEdit` throughout the whole project.
6. Add a tab menu UI element to connect the `ItemDetailView` and `ItemDetailEdit` components, following the same Wikipedia/MediaWiki interface approach.

Let's get to work.

Adding the ItemDetailView component

We'll start by adding a new `item-detail-view.component.ts` TypeScript file into the `/Scripts/app/` folder. The code will be quite similar to the existing `ItemDetail` component, except for the following:

- We will have headers, labels, and paragraphs here, instead of textboxes and text areas.
- We won't have the `onInsert`, `onUpdate`, and `onDelete` functions, as they serve no purpose in a display-only component. We will have an `onEdit` function instead, which will be used to switch to the `ItemEdit` component upon user interaction.

Here's suitable source code for the new `ItemDetailViewComponent` class:

```
import {Component, OnInit} from "@angular/core";
import {Router, ActivatedRoute} from "@angular/router";
import {Item} from "./item";
import {ItemService} from "./item.service";

@Component({
    selector: "item-detail-view",
    template: `
      <div *ngIf="item" class="item-details">
```

```
                <h2>{{item.Title}}</h2>
                <p>{{item.Description}}</p>
            </div>
          `,
        styles: [`
            .item-details {
                margin: 5px;
                padding: 5px 10px;
                border: 1px solid black;
                background-color: #dddddd;
                width: 300px;
            }
            .item-details * {
                vertical-align: middle;
            }
            .item-details ul li {
                padding: 5px 0;
            }
        `]
    })

export class ItemDetailViewComponent {
    item: Item;

    constructor(private itemService: ItemService,
        private router: Router,
        private activatedRoute: ActivatedRoute) {
    }

    ngOnInit() {
        var id = +this.activatedRoute.snapshot.params["id"];
        if (id) {
            this.itemService.get(id).subscribe(
                item => this.item = item
            );
        }
        else if (id === 0) {
            console.log("id is 0: switching to edit mode...");
            this.router.navigate(["item/edit", 0]);
        }
        else {
            console.log("Invalid id: routing back to home...");
            this.router.navigate([""]);
        }
    }
}
```

Before going further, there are a couple things worthy of attention:

1. We added a reference to the `item/edit` route, which doesn't exist yet; we did that on purpose because we know that we'll soon implement it.
2. We added an `if` condition within the `ngOnInit()` method to ensure that, if this component is initialized with a non-existing or invalid `id`, we'll re-route the call to the `ItemDetailEdit` component instead of handling it. That's perfectly fine, assuming that this component will be unable to do its display-only job without a valid `id` being passed together with the route; if something like that happens, we could either display a "this item does not exist" error page, throw an exception, or assume that the caller wants to create a new item and route them there accordingly. Although displaying an error page is almost always the best choice in such scenarios, we went for the routing for demonstration purposes.

Refactoring ItemDetail into ItemDetailEdit

The next step is easy: we just have to rename `ItemDetail` to `ItemDetailEdit` within the filesystem and inside the source code.

To complete the first step, right-click on the `item-detail.component.ts` file and rename it to `item-detail-edit.component.ts`.

Right after that, we also need to open it and change a couple of references within the source code.

The first thing we have to do is to change the `selector` from `item-detail` to `item-detail-edit`:

```
selector: "item-detail-edit",
```

Then we need to change the class name from `ItemDetailComponent` to `ItemDetailEditComponent`:

```
export class ItemDetailEditComponent {
```

That's it. We don't need to change anything else within this file for now, yet we're far from being done; we still have to change all the references currently pointing to `ItemDetail` throughout all the other class/components/files, replacing them with `ItemDetailEdit` and/or `ItemDetailView` accordingly.

Updating the Root module

Let's start with the /Scripts/app/app.module.ts file. Open it and change the import line pointing to the old ItemDetailComponent in the following way:

```
import {ItemDetailEditComponent} from "./item-detail-edit.component";
import {ItemDetailViewComponent} from "./item-detail-view.component";
```

Then scroll down to the declarations section and do the same:

```
declarations: [
    AboutComponent,
    AppComponent,
    HomeComponent,
    ItemListComponent,
    ItemDetailEditComponent,
    ItemDetailViewComponent,
    LoginComponent,
    PageNotFoundComponent
],
```

Updating the Routes

The next thing we need to do is to update the /Scripts/app/app.routing.ts file. Open it and change its content accordingly (added/modified parts are highlighted):

```
import {ModuleWithProviders} from "@angular/core";
import {Routes, RouterModule} from "@angular/router";

import {AboutComponent} from "./about.component";
import {HomeComponent} from "./home.component";
import {ItemDetailEditComponent} from "./item-detail-edit.component";
import {ItemDetailViewComponent} from "./item-detail-view.component";
import {LoginComponent} from "./login.component";
import {PageNotFoundComponent} from "./page-not-found.component";

const appRoutes: Routes = [
    {
        path: "",
        component: HomeComponent
    },
    {
        path: "home",
        redirectTo: ""
    },
    {
```

```
            path: "about",
            component: AboutComponent
    },
    {
            path: "login",
            component: LoginComponent
    },
    {
            path: "item/edit/:id",
            component: ItemDetailEditComponent
    },
    {
            path: "item/view/:id",
            component: ItemDetailViewComponent
    },
    {
            path: '**',
            component: PageNotFoundComponent
    }
];

export const AppRoutingProviders: any[] = [
];

export const AppRouting: ModuleWithProviders =
RouterModule.forRoot(appRoutes);
```

As we can see, we performed two major changes here:

- Near the top of the file, within the import section, we did the same changes we made to the AppModule class a moment ago
- We replaced the now obsolete item route with two new routes, item/edit and item/view, respectively pointing to our brand new ItemDetailEdit and ItemDetailView component classes

Tracking the outdated references

Now we need to find all the references to the outdated `ItemDetail` component class within our application files and update them accordingly. Luckily enough we're using TypeScript, so we don't need to stoop to using find and replace or other loose techniques; we just have to look at our **Task Runner Explorer** window and see if there are compiler **Errors**:

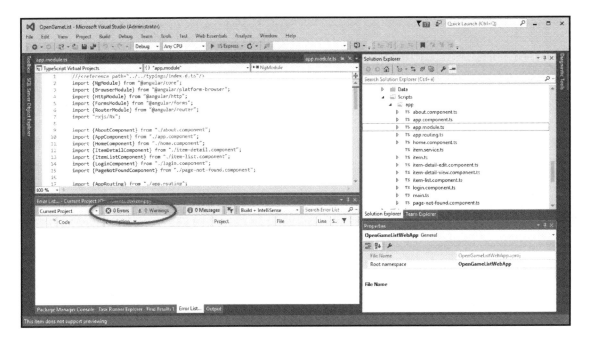

As we can see, we're quite lucky: there are no errors, meaning that there is no other class referencing the old `ItemDetail` class and/or the `item-detail.component.ts` filename.

The routes, however, are a whole different story; they work as literals, so there is no way the compiler will tell us anything. Luckily enough, there are only two components that were using the old `item` route: `AppComponent` and `ItemListComponent`.

To update the former, open the `/Scripts/app/app.component.ts` file and replace the value of the `routerLink` directive for adding a new item (updated lines are highlighted):

```
<h1>{{title}}</h1>
<div class="menu">
    <a class="home" [routerLink]="['']">Home</a>
    | <a class="about" [routerLink]="['about']">About</a>
    | <a class="login" [routerLink]="['login']">Login</a>
    | <a class="add" [routerLink]="['item/edit', 0]">Add New</a>
</div>
<router-outlet></router-outlet>
```

As for `ItemListComponent`, open the `/Scripts/app/item-list.component.ts` file, scroll down to the `onSelect` method, and change its contents accordingly (updated lines are highlighted):

```
onSelect(item: Item) {
    this.selectedItem = item;
    console.log("Item " + this.selectedItem.Id + " has been clicked:
loading item viewer...");
    this.router.navigate(["item/view", this.selectedItem.Id]);
}
```

Implementing the tab menu

We're still missing something very important: there's no way we can switch from `ItemDetailView` to `ItemDetailEdit` and vice versa, which is a required condition for our application to work; as a matter of fact, we can't even properly test what we've done up till now until we add something that would allow us to do that.

Without further ado, this means that it's time to implement the Wikipedia-style tab menu we were talking about a while ago. In order to do that, we need to update the following sections of the `item-detail-view.component.ts` and `item-detail-edit.component.ts` files:

- The `template`, because our tab menu will need an HTML structure
- The `class` implementation code, since we will definitely need to implement an event handler method to respond to user interaction (the actual tab click) and put it into action accordingly
- The `styles`, because we want our **tab menu** to blend with the components that will implement it in a nicely fashion

Template

Open the `item-detail-view.component.ts` file and replace the content of the `template` section with the following (new/updated lines are highlighted):

```
<div *ngIf="item" class="item-container">
    <div class="item-tab-menu">
        <span (click)="onItemDetailEdit(item)">Edit</span>
        <span class="selected">View</span>
    </div>
    <div class="item-details">
        <div class="mode">Display Mode</div>
        <h2>{{item.Title}}</h2>
        <p>{{item.Description}}</p>
    </div>
</div>
```

We changed quite a few things here, yet the template is simple enough to easily understand what happened:

- We wrapped everything within a `div` having an `item-container` CSS class. Notice that we also conveniently moved the `*ngIf` expression there, removing it from the `div.item-details` element as the latter isn't the main container anymore.
- We added a `div` with an `item-tab-menu` CSS class that is going to be our tab menu. It contains two `span` elements representing, respectively, the currently selected tab (**View**) and the tab we can switch to (**Edit**). Notice `onItemDetailEdit(item)` bound to the latter; we'll get to it soon enough.

Now open the `item-detail-edit.component.ts` file and again replace the `template` section content with the following (new/updated lines are highlighted):

```
<div *ngIf="item" class="item-container">
    <div class="item-tab-menu">
        <span class="selected">Edit</span>
        <span *ngIf="item.Id != 0"
(click)="onItemDetailView(item)">View</span>
    </div>
    <div class="item-details">
        <div class="mode">Edit Mode</div>
        <h2>{{item.Title}}</h2>
        <ul>
            <li>
                <label>Title:</label>
                <input [(ngModel)]="item.Title" placeholder="Insert the
title..." />
```

```
            </li>
            <li>
                <label>Description:</label>
                <textarea [(ngModel)]="item.Description"
    placeholder="Insert a suitable description..."></textarea>
            </li>
        </ul>
        <div *ngIf="item.Id == 0" class="commands insert">
            <input type="button" value="Save" (click)="onInsert(item)" />
            <input type="button" value="Cancel" (click)="onBack()" />
        </div>
        <div *ngIf="item.Id != 0" class="commands update">
            <input type="button" value="Update" (click)="onUpdate(item)" />
            <input type="button" value="Delete" (click)="onDelete(item)" />
            <input type="button" value="Cancel"
(click)="onItemDetailView(item)" />
        </div>
    </div>
</div>
```

As we can see, a lot of stuff happened here as well:

- Again, we wrapped everything into a div with an item-container CSS class, moving the *ngIf expression there.
- Again, we added the HTML structure of our tab menu; the two span elements are the same, yet they have obviously switched their respective roles: the **View** one has an onItemView(item) event attached, while **Edit** is now the selected one, so isn't expected to do anything. Notice that we added another *ngIf expression to the **View** tab menu item, meaning that it will show itself only if the id item is not 0; this will prevent the View tab from being displayed whenever this component is accessed for adding a new item. That's a good thing to do since we wouldn't be able to "view" an item that doesn't exist in the database yet.
- We renamed the **Back** button **Cancel** and changed its behavior accordingly; instead of going to the home/welcome view by using the onBack() method, it will now route to the current item's ItemDetailView using the onItemDetailView(item) method, which by the way is not implemented yet.

Class code

The next thing we have to do is to implement the missing methods that we already took for granted in the previous paragraph.

Go back to the `item-detail-view.component.ts` file and add a new
`onItemDetailEdit(item)` method right after the `ngOnInit` one:

```
onItemDetailEdit(item: Item) {
    this.router.navigate(["item/edit", item.Id]);
}
```

Right after that, switch to the `item-detail-edit.component.ts` file and add the
following code after the `onBack` method, which should be the last one:

```
onItemDetailView(item: Item) {
    this.router.navigate(["item/view", item.Id]);
}
```

That's it; both of these routes have already been set, so there is nothing else to do there.

Styles

It's time to pimp our components a little; we won't do anything fancy. We'll leave it to
`Chapter 6`, *Applying Styles*, yet we could use a slightly improved GUI to better acknowledge
what we're doing.

Let's start with the `item-detail-view.component.ts` file: open it up, then replace the
content of the `styles` section with the following:

```
.item-container {
    width: 600px;
}

.item-tab-menu {
    margin-right: 30px;
}

.item-tab-menu span {
    background-color: #dddddd;
    border: 1px solid #666666;
    border-bottom: 0;
    cursor: pointer;
    display: block;
    float: right;
    margin: 0 0 -1px 5px;
    padding: 5px 10px 4px 10px;
    text-align: center;
    width: 60px;
}
```

```
.item-tab-menu span.selected {
    background-color: #eeeeee;
    cursor: auto;
    font-weight: bold;
    padding-bottom: 5px;
}

.item-details {
    background-color: #eeeeee;
    border: 1px solid black;
    clear: both;
    margin: 0;
    padding: 5px 10px;
}

.item-details * {
    vertical-align: middle;
}

.item-details .mode {
    font-size: 0.8em;
    color: #777777;
}

.item-details ul li {
    padding: 5px 0;
}
```

Right after that, do the same with the styles section of the item-detail-
edit.component.ts file:

```
.item-container {
    width: 600px;
}

.item-tab-menu {
    margin-right: 30px;
}

.item-tab-menu span {
    background-color: #dddddd;
    border: 1px solid #666666;
    border-bottom: 0;
    cursor: pointer;
    display: block;
    float: right;
    margin: 0 0 -1px 5px;
    padding: 5px 10px 4px 10px;
```

```
        text-align: center;
        width: 60px;
}

.item-tab-menu span.selected {
        background-color: #eeeeee;
        cursor: auto;
        font-weight: bold;
        padding-bottom: 5px;
}

.item-details {
        background-color: #eeeeee;
        border: 1px solid black;
        clear: both;
        margin: 0;
        padding: 5px 10px;
}

.item-details * {
        vertical-align: middle;
}

.item-details .mode {
        font-size: 0.8em;
        color: #777777;
}

.item-details ul li {
        padding: 5px 0;
}

.item-details input[type="text"] {
        display: block;
        width: 100%;
}

.item-details textarea {
        display: block;
        width: 100%;
        height: 60px;
}

.commands {
        text-align: right;
        margin: 10px 20px 10px 10px;
}
```

Not much to explain here; we just changed the aspect of these two controls so the **tab menu** can fit into them in a decent-looking way for the upcoming test run.

Testing it out

Now that our splitting job is finally over, it's time to perform an extensive test on what we just did.

Launch the application by hitting *F5* and check that the **Home/welcome** page is still alive and well. We didn't change anything there, so we can go straight on to our brand new `ItemDetailView` component by left-clicking on one of the elements within the **Latest Items** listing, for example **Magarena-X2**.

If everything is working as it should, we should be greeted by something like the following:

We can easily see that we opened the **ItemDetailView** in **DISPLAY MODE** because:

- The **View** tab is clearly selected
- There's a **DISPLAY MODE** label in the top-left corner of the item containing box
- We don't see any input textboxes/text areas within the view

This is the first time we can see the Wikipedia-style tab menu we implemented in the previous paragraph; it seems to be working just like it should.

Let's now click on the **Edit** tab and see what happens:

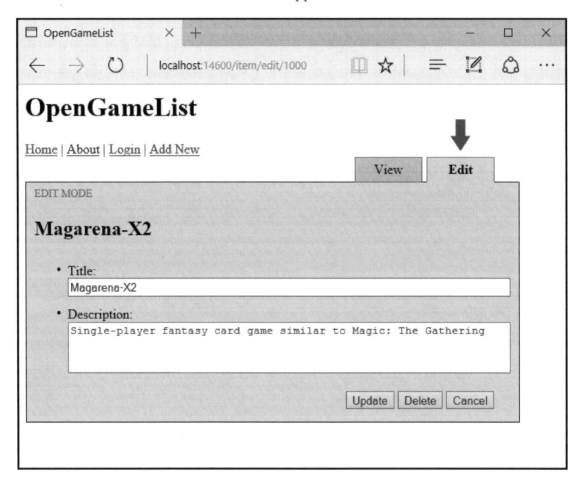

The **EDIT MODE** seems to be looking fine as well. The tab menu is also still working as expected, as the **Edit** tab is now clearly appearing as the one on top.

Let's try to append the following line to the description text area:

We can't call this a test without a sample update attempt.

Then, click on the **Update** button. As soon as we do that, we should see something like this:

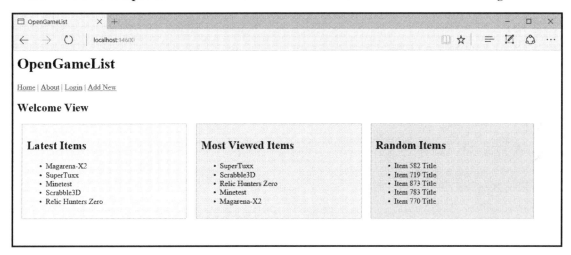

The **Update** button routed us back to the **Home/Welcome View;** we never changed its behavior, so it's still working like that. While this may have been viable when we only had a single `ItemDetail` controller, now it most certainly isn't; it should bring us back to `ItemDisplayView`, just like *Wikipedia/MediaWiki* works when we update an item there.

In order to fix that, open the `item-detail-edit.component.ts` file and perform the following changes to the `onUpdate` method (modified code is highlighted):

```
onUpdate(item: Item) {
    this.itemService.update(item).subscribe(
        (data) => {
            this.item = data;
            console.log("Item " + this.item.Id + " has been updated.");
            this.router.navigate(["item/view", this.item.Id]);
        },
        (error) => console.log(error)
    );
}
```

What we did here is quite obvious: We replaced the destination route from root one (bound to `HomeController`) to `item/view`, which is connected to `ItemDetailViewController`, also including the `id` parameter.

Let's test it out; hit *F5* to re-run the application in **Debug** mode, then left-click on the **Magarena-X2** item to launch the **ItemDetailView** controller again. Once there, click on the **Edit** tab and append another test line to the item's **Description** text area:

The previous attempt wasn't good enough; now it should work.

When we're done, click on the **Update** button and see what happens:

It seems like it worked! We managed to split the `ItemDetail` controller into two, reproducing a MediaWiki-like behavior when it comes to displaying and/or editing our items.

Suggested topics

RESTful conventions, HTTP verbs, HTTP status, Angular 2 observables, Angular 2 observers, Angular 2 subscriptions, MediaWiki, Cascading Style Sheets.

Summary

Before going further, let's do a quick recap of what we did throughout this chapter.

Having replaced the fake data provider with a real one, we made good use of it by implementing **Add**, **Update**, and **Delete** features for our **ItemDetail** controller. In order to do this, we improved our **ItemService**, implementing the corresponding add, update, and delete methods. Then we also updated the client GUI by creating new buttons, event handlers, and routes to properly handle them.

While implementing the process of creating a new item, instead of adding a new route, we chose to exploit the existing one already pointing to ItemDetail by passing an id with a value of 0, thus creating an internal convention for our own personal usage. Once done, we ran a full test of the updated UI to check that everything worked out well.

It most certainly was, yet we started noticing that our controller looked like an editor way more than a viewer. That didn't match the original plan, so we planned to split the ItemDetail controller into two separate classes: ItemDetailView to show the item in readable fashion (**DISPLAY MODE**) and ItemDetailEdit to handle add, update, and delete commands (**EDIT MODE**). We also thought about making the users able to toggle between them with the help of a dedicated tab menu just like to the one used by MediaWiki.

Splitting the ItemDetail controller implied a straightforward, yet rather long, series of tasks: we added a new TypeScript file for the ItemDetailView component, filling it with suitable code, then we put in place a full code and filesystem refactoring of the ItemDetail component, which we renamed to ItemDetailEdit everywhere; the TypeScript compiler saved us some valuable time here, identifying the outdated references and allowing us to promptly fix/update them.

Eventually we implemented the tab menu; in order to do that we had to perform some changes to the controller's templates and styles sections, as well as implementing the dedicated methods within the class code to handle the click event upon each tab.

After all these changes, we felt the urge to do another round of tests. It turned out it was a good call, as we found a minor issue within the ItemDetailEdit controller's onUpdate method, which was still calling the **Home** route upon completion instead of the more appropriate ItemDetailView one; we fixed it smoothly, making our application ready for the following chapters.

6
Applying Styles

Up to this point, we have done our best to keep the layout as simple as we could, so we could focus entirely on the server-side and client-side coding aspects of our app: ASP.NET Core Web API Controllers, Angular 2, C#, and TypeScript. Keeping the layout to a minimum is generally a wise approach when we're learning something new, it also has a few downsides, though, the biggest one being the blatant fact that our application is rather unattractive, to say the least: there is no user, client, or customer that wouldn't say that… or worse.

How bad is it, doc?

It almost entirely depends on what we're planning to do with the project we've been working on; as we just said, while we're working our way through tutorials, demos, or sample projects, it's not bad at all, for at least a couple of good reasons:

- We will greatly benefit from keeping our focus on .NET and Angular 2, leaving the rest for later; applying styles is something that w can easily do whenever we feel like it, even if we don't have a decent grip on stylesheet language already.
- It's generally a good idea to restrain ourselves from doing any relevant style implementation until we can fully understand where and how to do that conveniently; to put it in other words, we shouldn't do styles until we find a suitable approach for doing that within the given scenario and/or environment.

That's why we chose to take this path in the first place; we're definitely in the learning phase, after all. However, since we planned to build a production-ready native web application, we can't restrain ourselves from applying some styling any longer; there's no way that our imaginary product owner would be satisfied otherwise. It's time to dress our (mostly) naked doll and make it as pretty as we can.

Introducing LESS

If we've worked with style sheets within the last few years, there's no chance we won't have heard of **LESS**; however, for the sake of those who didn't, let's take a few words to talk about it. Before getting to that, though, we must briefly introduce the concepts of style sheet language and **Cascading Style Sheets** (**CSS**).

 This paragraph is mostly aimed at those who have never used LESS before. If you have some experience with LESS already or feel like you don't need to know anything else about why we're going to use it, you might as well skip it entirely and jump to the next paragraph: **Install and Configure LESS**.

Style sheet languages

A style sheet language, also known as style language, is a programming language used to define the presentation layer's UI design rules of a structured document. We can think of it as a skin or a theme that we can apply to a logical item (the structured document) to change its appearance. For example, we can make it look blue, red, or yellow; we can make the characters bigger or smaller, thinner or wider; we can change the text spacing, alignment, and flow; and so on.

Using dedicated style sheet languages gives developers the chance to separate the presentation layer's **code and structure** (respectively JavaScript and HTML) from the **UI design rules**, thus enforcing the **separation of concerns** (**SoC**) principle within the presentation layer itself.

When it comes to web pages, web applications, and anything else that mostly uses HTML, XHTML, XML, and other markup language-based documents, the most important style sheet language undoubtedly is CSS.

CSS

It was December 17, 1996, when the **World Wide Web Consortium** (**W3C**) released the official W3C CSS Recommendation for the style sheet language that would be known as CSS1. CSS2 came less than two years later (May 1998), while its revised version, CSS2.1, took considerably more time (June 2011).

Starting from CSS3, things started to become more complex, since the W3C ditched the single, monolithic specification approach by splitting it into separate documents called modules, each one of them following its very own publishing, acceptance, and recommendation history. Starting in 2012, with four of these (Media Queries, Namespaces, Selectors, and Color) being published as formal recommendations and full CSS2.1 backward-compatibility, CSS3 quickly became the most adopted style sheet language standard for the development of new websites.

CSS code sample

Regardless of their version, each adding new features while maintaining backward compatibility with the previous one(s), CSS stick to the following syntax:

```
.item-details {
    background-color: #dddddd;
    border: 1px solid black;
    margin: 0;
    padding: 5px 10px;
}
```

We've seen this code before; it's a class we added in our application's `item-detail-view.component.ts` file in a previous chapter. It says that any element with the `item-details` class will have a light-grey background color, a black, solid, and pixel-wide border, no margin against the surrounding elements, and a certain amount of padding between its borders and the content. Simple enough, isn't it?

What is LESS and why to use it

LESS is a cascading style sheet pre-processor; we can think of it as a server-side script for CSS files, enabling us to do a number of things that CSS doesn't support (yet), just like PHP and/or ASP can do for an HTML page. The following diagram should help us to better understand the concept:

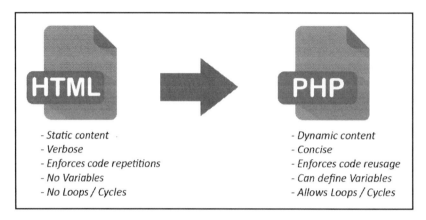

These are the main advantages of using a hypertext pre-processor instead of writing raw **HTML** pages; we're talking about **PHP**, but the same goes for ASP.NET Web Forms, Razor, and basically everything else.

The following are the advantages of using **LESS** instead of writing raw **CSS** files:

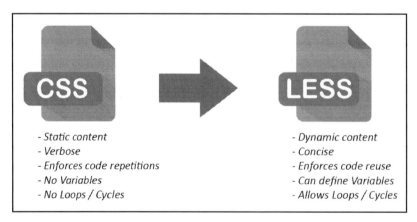

As we can see, they serve the exact same purpose in terms of assisting, improving, and enhancing the development effort.

Making the switch from static stylesheets to dynamic stylesheets is just as easy as switching from static HTML pages to PHP or ASP dynamic pages; they both feature a nested metalanguage that can extend the base static language in a pure backward-compatible fashion. This means that a valid CSS file is also a valid LESS file, just as a valid HTML file is also a valid PHP or ASP file.

There are also some key differences between hypertext pre-processors and stylesheet pre-processors, the most important being how web servers deal with them.

Hypertext pre-processors such as PHP and ASP are compiled by the Web Server upon each request; the Web Server compiles them on the fly and then serves the resulting HTML for each request-response flow. Conversely, Stylesheet pre-processor files are usually compiled into standard CSS files before being published; in other words, the web service doesn't know about the existence of these files, as it just serves the resulting CSS-compiled result.

This also means that using a stylesheet pre-processor will have no performance impact on the server, unless we choose to install some experimental and still highly inefficient handlers, extensions, modules, or client-side scripts that will compile the source files on the fly.

IMPORTANT NOTE

From now on, we'll take for granted that the reader has a decent knowledge of CSS files, syntax, selectors, and their common use within HTML pages.

If this is not the case, we strongly suggest to learn the core CSS concepts before going further, using the Learning CSS website, maintained and hosted by W3C, featuring a massive number of useful guides, tutorials, and articles: https://www.w3.org/Style/CSS/learning.

Variables

Among the most valuable LESS features, there is variable support. This is a brief example of what we can do with it:

```
// Variables can be declared as such:
@link-color: #red;
@link-color-hover: lightcoral;

// And then they can be referenced like this:
a, span. link {
    color: @link-color;
}

a:hover, span.link:hover {
```

```
    color: @link-color-hover;
}
```

As we might have noticed, double-slash style (//) inline comments are supported as well, while CSS only allows the slash-asterisk (/**/) syntax.

Import directives

Another LESS key feature is the capability of importing other CSS and LESS files. If we're familiar with the standard CSS @import, we know that it can only be used at the beginning of the file to issue the loading of an external CSS file. With LESS, we can do the following:

```
// look for a style.less file and process + import its contents.
@import "style";

// look for a style.less file and process + import its contents.
@import "style.less";

// look for a style.css file and import its contents (no processing).
@import "style.css";
```

Notice that the behavior depends on the imported file extension. These defaults can be overridden with the following options switches:

```
// link/use a Less file without including it in the output.
@import (reference) "something.less";

// include the file in the output without processing it.
@import (inline) "something.less";

// pretend this is a LESS file, regardless of the extension.
@import (less) "something.css";

// pretend this is a CSS file, regardless of the extension.
@import (css) "something.less";

// never include this file more than once (default behavior).
@import (once) "something.less";

// always include this file in the output, even multiple times.
@import (multiple) "something.less";

// do not break the compile operation if the file is not found.
@import (optional) "something.less";
```

If we need to specify multiple `options` within a single `@import` statement, we can do that by separating each one of them with a comma:

```
// take it as a LESS file, import once, skip if not found.
@import (less,once,optional) "something.css";
```

Nested selectors

We will be able to nest selectors within other selectors, thus making our code more succinct and readable. Just to use a quick example, we can shrink this:

```
item-list {
    border: 0;
    margin: 0;
    padding: 0;
    vertical-align: top;
    display: block;
}

item-list.latest {
        background-color: #f6f6f6;
}

item-list.latest h3 {
    background-image: url(/img/latest-icon.png);
}
```

Into something like the following:

```
item-list {
    border: 0;
    margin: 0;
    padding: 0;
    vertical-align: top;
    display: block;
    &.latest {
      // the & char represents the current selector parent.
      // in this scenario, it stands for: item-list.latest.
      background-color: #f6f6f6;
      h3 {
          background-color: @color-latest;
          background-image: url(/img/latest-icon.png);
      }
    }
}
```

It might not be such a big deal for small-scale CSS files, yet it's a great readability improvement for big ones.

Mixins

Being able to not repeat ourselves is a key principle of all computer programming languages; however, it's not easy to respect that within standard CSS files, because we would often be forced to write something like this:

```
.button-s {
    background-color: blue;
    border: 1px solid black;
    border-radius: 5px;
    font-family: Verdana;
    font-size: 0.8em;
    width: 100px;
}

.button-m {
    background-color: blue;
    border: 1px solid black;
    border-radius: 5px;
    font-family: Verdana;
    font-size: 1em;
    width: 200px;
}

.button-l {
    background-color: blue;
    border: 1px solid black;
    border-radius: 5px;
    font-family: Verdana;
    font-size: 1.2em;
    width: 300px;
}
```

With LESS, we can shrink it into this:

```
.button-s {
    background-color: blue;
    border: 1px solid black;
    border-radius: 5px;
    font-family: Verdana;
    font-size: 0.8em;
    width: 100px;
}
```

```
.button-m {
    .button-s;
    font-size: 1em;
    width: 200px;
}

.button-l {
    .button-s;
    font-size: 1.2em;
    width: 300px;
}
```

In other words, a mixin is a selector reference within another selector. That's another great feature that can save us a lot of time whenever we're dealing with large CSS files.

Extend pseudo-class

Another great feature is the LESS :extend pseudo-class, which can be used to apply all properties of a class to another class, optionally including, using the all keyword, all the child classes and pseudo-classes. To use a quick example, take the following CSS code:

```
.link {
    color: white;
    background-color: blue;
}

.link:before {
    content: ">";
}

.link-red {
    color: white;
    background-color: red;
}

.link-red:before {
    content: ">";
}
```

This could be conveniently written this way using LESS:

```
.link {
    color: white;
    background-color: blue;
```

```
    :before {
        content: ">";
    }
}

.link-red {
    &:extend(.link all);
    background-color: red;
}
```

Notice how, since we've used the `all` keyword, we don't have to repeat the `:before` pseudo-class of the base `.link` selector, as it will be applied to `.link-red` as well.

LESS docs and support

We won't go any further than that with LESS, as it would take us far from the scope of this book. From now on, we'll take for granted that everything that we're going to do with it will be acknowledged and understood.

For the sake of simplicity, we won't use anything different from what we briefly introduced in the previous chapters; however, we strongly suggest to take a look at the advanced features (parametric mixins, functions, loops, guards, and more) as soon as we have the chance; they can hardly fail to pay off. We can learn more about them from the LESS official webpage at the following URL: `http://lesscss.org/`

Systematically Awesome Style Sheets, Stylus, and other alternatives

As most readers probably know, or can easily imagine, LESS is not the only style sheet pre-processor language out there. As a matter of fact, it was released more than two years after **Systematically Awesome Style Sheets (Sass)**, also known as SCSS, which had served the exact same purpose since 2007. Sass can offer basically the same set of features as LESS and came out first, so why shouldn't it be used instead?

The answer is simple and strongly resembles what we have already said when we had to choose between `Gulp` and `Grunt` in `Chapter 1`, *Getting Ready,,* no one will ever get fired for picking Sass or other viable alternatives, such as Stylus and Switch CSS, instead of LESS. We're free to choose the style sheet pre-processor we like the most, as long as we can use it without issues, meaning that Visual Studio and/or the Task Runner we chose is able to support it. Luckily enough, all of them are now widely supported by many Visual Studio Extensions and `Gulp` plugins (or `Grunt` modules), so it won't make any significant difference. That said, we're going to set up and configure LESS because we find it more straightforward, easy to use, and slightly more suited for a Windows environment than its counterparts, at least for now.

Configuring LESS

LESS happens to be written in JavaScript, so installing it can be as easy as downloading its JavaScript library (`less.js`), linking it to our `index.html` page, and letting its magic work without having to set up anything else.

Should we do that, then? Not a chance. As we said earlier, delegating the compilation task on the client side would be highly inefficient, especially in a client-intensive Angular 2-based native web app. This is what we're going to do instead:

- Add a new `style.less` file to our project.
- Update our **Gulp** script to process and compile it, outputting the resulting `style.css` file into the `/wwwroot/` folder.
- Link the resulting `.css` file to the `/wwwroot/index.html` root application file.
- Make a quick test before starting our styling job.

Let's get to work.

Adding the LESS file

Considering how many files we've added so far, this is going to be a trivial task. Add a new `/less/` folder inside the `/Scripts/` root directory, then right-click on it, choose **Add | New Item**, and select **LESS Style Sheet** from the **client-side** set item tab: name the new file `style.less` and click on **OK**.

Once done, open the newly created file and add the following content:

```
item-list {
    min-width: 332px;
    border: 1px solid #aaaaaa;
    display: inline-block;
    margin: 0 10px;
    padding: 10px;
    &.latest {
        background-color: #f9f9f9;
    }
    &.most-viewed {
        background-color: #f0f0f0;
    }
    &.random {
        background-color: #e9e9e9;
    }
}
```

We might recognize the preceding lines, as these are the `styles` of our
`/Scripts/app/home.component.ts` Angular 2 component file, we just applied some
mixins as described previously to shrink the code a bit.

Updating Gulp script

The first thing we need to do is to add the LESS plugin for `Gulp`. Open the `package.json`
file, locate the `devDependencies` node and add the following line to the `gulp` section.
We'll be placing it right after the `gulp-concat` package to keep the alphabetical sorting:

```
"gulp": "^3.9.1",
"gulp-clean": "^0.3.2",
"gulp-concat": "^2.6.0",
"gulp-less": "^3.1.0",
"gulp-sourcemaps": "^1.6.0",
"gulp-typescript": "^2.13.6",
"gulp-uglify": "^2.0.0",
"typescript": "^1.8.10"
```

As soon as we save the file we'll issue a real-time refresh to the project's NPM
dependencies.

Now switch to the `gulpfile.js` file and get ready to add/modify a few lines of code (new/updated lines are highlighted):

```
var gulp = require('gulp'),
    gp_clean = require('gulp-clean'),
    gp_concat = require('gulp-concat'),
    gp_less = require('gulp-less'),
    gp_sourcemaps = require('gulp-sourcemaps'),
    gp_typescript = require('gulp-typescript'),
    gp_uglify = require('gulp-uglify');

/// Define paths
var srcPaths = {
    app: ['Scripts/app/main.ts', 'Scripts/app/**/*.ts'],
    js: [
        'Scripts/js/**/*.js',
        'node_modules/core-js/client/shim.min.js',
        'node_modules/zone.js/dist/zone.js',
        'node_modules/reflect-metadata/Reflect.js',
        'node_modules/systemjs/dist/system.src.js',
        'node_modules/typescript/lib/typescript.js'
    ],
    js_angular: [
        'node_modules/@angular/**'
    ],
    js_rxjs: [
        'node_modules/rxjs/**'
    ],
    less: [
        'Scripts/less/**/*.less'
    ]
};

var destPaths = {
    app: 'wwwroot/app/',
    css: 'wwwroot/css/',
    js: 'wwwroot/js/',
    js_angular: 'wwwroot/js/@angular/',
    js_rxjs: 'wwwroot/js/rxjs/'
};

// Compile, minify and create sourcemaps all TypeScript files and place
// them to wwwroot/app, together with their js.map files.
gulp.task('app', ['app_clean'], function () {
    return gulp.src(srcPaths.app)
        .pipe(gp_sourcemaps.init())
        .pipe(gp_typescript(require('./tsconfig.json').compilerOptions))
        .pipe(gp_uglify({ mangle: false }))
```

```
            .pipe(gp_sourcemaps.write('/'))
            .pipe(gulp.dest(destPaths.app));
});

// Delete wwwroot/app contents
gulp.task('app_clean', function () {
    return gulp.src(destPaths.app + "*.*", { read: false })
    .pipe(gp_clean({ force: true }));
});

// Copy all JS files from external libraries to wwwroot/js
gulp.task('js', function () {
    gulp.src(srcPaths.js_angular)
        .pipe(gulp.dest(destPaths.js_angular));
    gulp.src(srcPaths.js_rxjs)
        .pipe(gulp.dest(destPaths.js_rxjs));
    return gulp.src(srcPaths.js)
        .pipe(gulp.dest(destPaths.js));
});

// Delete wwwroot/js contents
gulp.task('js_clean', function () {
    return gulp.src(destPaths.js + "*.*", { read: false })
    .pipe(gp_clean({ force: true }));
});

// Process all LESS files and output the resulting CSS in wwwroot/css
gulp.task('less', ['less_clean'], function () {
    return gulp.src(srcPaths.less)
        .pipe(gp_less())
        .pipe(gulp.dest(destPaths.css));
});

// Delete wwwroot/css contents
gulp.task('less_clean', function () {
    return gulp.src(destPaths.css + "*.*", { read: false })
    .pipe(gp_clean({ force: true }));
});

// Watch specified files and define what to do upon file changes
gulp.task('watch', function () {
    gulp.watch([
        srcPaths.app,
        srcPaths.js,
        srcPaths.less],
        ['app', 'js', 'less']);
});
```

```
// Global cleanup task
gulp.task('cleanup', ['app_clean', 'js_clean', 'less_clean']);

// Define the default task so it will launch all other tasks
gulp.task('default', ['app', 'js', 'less', 'watch']);
```

What we did here was quite straightforward:

- At the beginning of the file, we added a reference to the gulp-less plugin, assigning it to the gp_less variable just like we did with the other plugins.
- We added the less key to the srcPaths variable; that key contains a listing of the locations of all the .less files we want to process: everything inside Scripts/less/, including subfolders, as long as it ends with the .less extension.
- We also added the css key to the destPaths variable, defining the folder where the resulting compiled .css files will be generated.
- Then we added two new tasks to instruct Gulp how to handle LESS files:
    - The less task to compile the .less files found inside the srcPaths.less folder(s) and then output the result to the wwwroot/css target folder.
    - The less_clean task to erase the contents of the target folder; since it does the same job as the other existing cleanup tasks, there's no need to explain how it works. We also added it as a dependent task to the previous one, just like we did with the app_clean and app tasks back in Chapter 1, *Getting Ready*.

As soon as we perform these changes and save the file, go to the **Task Runner Explorer** panel in Visual Studio 2015. Once there, stop the Gulpdefault task, then re-run it again: a new /wwwroot/css/ folder should be created shortly, together with a freshly-compiled style.css file inside. Open it and ensure it has the same content placed into the /Scripts/less/style.less file, then proceed to the next part.

Linking the stylesheet

Open the /wwwroot/index.html file and add the following line within the <head> block, right below the <meta> element:

```
<!-- Stylesheets -->
<link rel="stylesheet" type="text/css" href="/css/style.css" media="screen"
/>
```

Testing it up

Before going further, it's advisable to run a quick check in order to ensure that everything we made so far is working as it should.

Open the `/Scripts/app/home.component.ts` file and remove everything within the `styles` block so that it will look like the following:

```
styles: []
```

Alternatively, we could entirely remove it, as we're not going to use it anymore.

Once done, run the application in **Debug** mode by hitting *F5* and check if the `item-list` components still have their CSS styles applied to them:

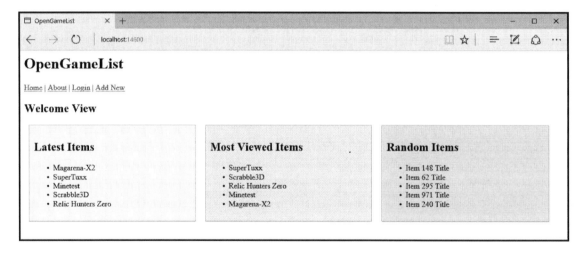

They definitely should, since we placed them on the `style.less` file that, in its `.css` compiled form, should now be linked to our application.

DIY versus framework-based styling

Now that we have added a fully-functional `style.less` stylesheet file, we could also move all our custom styles there, just like we did with the `home.component.ts` file; the question is, are they really worth that much? Hardly, considering that we put them together for demonstration purpose only, a *quick'n'dirty*, temporary solution until we could commit ourselves to the upcoming styling phase. Now that the time has come, we shouldn't bother too much about preserving these samples, we need to think about switching from a full *do-it-yourself* approach to a framework-based one.

Anyone who is into CSS design is well aware of such a debate, which we could summarize in the following single phrase:

> *Should we build our own grid-based responsive layout or use a responsive design framework instead?*

The answer is not that simple because either alternative has their set of advantages. Let's try to perform a quick recap of the most relevant arguments.

Do it yourself approach

The most classic approach: we build our very own grid-based layout, featuring a custom set of resizing raster and/or vector set of images and icon files, following the responsive design good practices and guidelines as issued by the famous Ethan Marcotte 2010 article published in the *A List Apart* blog:
`http://alistapart.com/article/responsive-web-design`

And also follow the subsequent, improved theories and patterns described in his following brief book (*Responsive Web Design*, *A Book Apart*, 2011).

Pros

- Faster loading times, as we will be able to only code, add, and/or include what we need.
- Unique design (all framework-based websites are supposed to look the same).

Cons

- Can be quite hard to handle, unless we're true CSS3/MediaQuery experts.
- **Slow development**, due to the massive amount of required tests for all the existing platforms (browsers, operating systems, mobile devices).
- **Hard to keep it updated** to the latest standards since there will be no one that will bother to test or improve that code other than us.

Framework-based approach

The common approach nowadays: we start from a consolidated, widely-accepted UI frontend framework such as Bootstrap, Foundation, Pure, or YUI and customize it to suit our needs. The word customizing can mean a number of things here, from picking a skin to completely changing the structural behavior of most classes, depending on how much we want to customize the results and/or how much time we are allowed to spend doing that.

Pros

- **Development speed**: These frameworks are a time-saver, as we will be able to use reliable, cross-browser compatible code blocks instead of coding everything from scratch.
- **Consistency**: One of the biggest frontend framework achievements is that they make designers and developers speak the same language, as they will both be able to acknowledge, understand, and apply their changes to the project in a consistent way.
- **Community support**: Each framework has a huge support community, meaning that we'll receive free code samples, support, and updates for as long as we need to. This can be huge, especially if we want to achieve good results without having to commit too much into cross-browser, responsive CSS design.

Cons

- **Limited knowledge**: We didn't write that code, so we won't always be able to understand what we're doing and *why* the stuff we're using behaves like that.
- **Performance heavy**: Even the most *lightweight* and modular framework will undoubtedly be packed with a lot of stuff we won't be using in our project: these contents will be sent by the web server and loaded by the client anyway.
- **Updating issues**: Whenever an improved build of the framework is out, we will have to choose between updating it, and taking the risk of breaking something, and not updating it, and risk losing the bug fixes and the added/improved support for the new CSS standards.

Conclusions

As we can see, both ways could be viable depending on our specific scenario; therefore, the decision between going with a custom grid and adopting a framework-based one should be made on a case-by-case basis.

That said, after our non-exhaustive analysis, we think that adopting a frontend framework might be a good call for our project; we'll also be picking Bootstrap for the task, since it happens to be one of the most suited ones for native web applications based on Angular 2, as we'll be able to see in the following paragraphs.

It's worth noting that by choosing Bootstrap we're ditching a great alternative that will surely pave its way in the upcoming months: we're talking about `material2`, a top-notch component library based upon material design.

The only reason we didn't pick it is that the project is still in alpha, yet there are already a couple of demos out that demonstrate its striking potential. If we're bold enough to try that, we can ditch this chapter entirely and learn our own way by looking at the official project page at the following URL: `https://material.angular.io/`

Or look at their source code repository on GitHub: `https://github.com/angular/material2`

Adding Bootstrap

Installing Bootstrap into our project is just as easy as adding the following line within the `<head>` block of our `wwwroot/index.html` file:

```
<link
href="https://maxcdn.bootstrapcdn.com/bootswatch/3.3.6/yeti/bootstrap.min.c
ss" rel="stylesheet" integrity="sha384-
yxFy3Tt84CcGRj9UI7RA25hoUMpUPoFzcdPtK3hBdNgEGnh9FdKgMVM+1bAZTKN2"
crossorigin="anonymous" />
```

It's advisable to place it right above the `style.css` link, so we'll be able to override the Bootstrap default rules with our own style sheet file.

As we can see, we'll be using the Bootstrap 3 Yeti Theme (actually the 3.3.6 build, the latest stable one at the time of writing), by linking a pre-built, minified `.css` file hosted by MaxCDN, which is the primary **content delivery network (CDN)** for Bootstrap and Bootswatch.

Using a CDN-hosted link for frontend frameworks is often a good practice and can be very advisable in most cases, as it will remove some weight from our web server for a relevant server-side performance benefit: however, it will also have some relevant downsides, such as preventing us from modifying the source CSS (or LESS) file(s).

If we feel like we'll be needing that, and/or if we don't want a CDN for other good reasons, we're also free to download the file locally and change the link so it will point to the project filesystem instead. The choice, as always, is entirely up to the developer.

We're choosing to stick with the v3 because Bootstrap 4, although almost ready, is currently still in a beta release. We want to adopt a stable, reliable, and widely-tested framework, we won't push things there, so we'll stick to the latest final instead.

We chose the Yeti theme because it features a minimalistic, yet suitable style that will nicely blend with our project; if you don't like it, you're free to choose another one from the Bootswatch project's page: `http://bootswatch.com/`
And here's a link to their primary CDN: `https://www.bootstrapcdn.com/bootswatch/`

Choosing a native directives module

If we've already worked with Bootstrap, we know that placing a link to the `.css` file isn't going to be enough: if we want to use transitions, modals, tabs, date/time pickers, and a lot of advanced yet very useful components, we'll also have to add a reference to the plugin's JavaScript code. In standard web projects, it's very common to do that by adding some `<script>` references to the HTML page. We could include each plugin individually, using their own Bootstrap `*.js` file, or all of them at once with a single reference to the pre-compiled `bootstrap.js` or `bootstrap.min.js` file, also available through various CDN repositories (including *MaxCDN*). In either case, we'll also need to add a reference to the *jQuery* JavaScript library, since all these plugins depend on jQuery.

However, since we're using Angular 2, we won't be following that route. We don't need to add jQuery, `bootstrap.js` or any plugin's individual `.js` file since we can install one of the available native directives modules specifically designed for implementing Bootstrap components.

Before going any further, we should spend a bit of time addressing a very reasonable question: why should we do that, instead of sticking to the good old `jquery.js` plus `bootstrap.js` path?

The reason is quite simple, although it might not be easy to understand for those with no Angular experience: we could say that it is strongly related to the unwritten yet very important rule of writing expressive code, preventing ourselves from doing any direct DOM manipulation unless it's unavoidable.

In Angular 2, there are few circumstances where directly manipulating the DOM is really necessary. The framework provides a native set of powerful, high-level APIs that can be used instead. Understanding, using, and leveraging these APIs is the best thing a developer can do to write successful applications because of the following distinctive advantages:

- **Unit testing**: Manipulating the DOM adds browser dependencies and also a level of complexity. Both of them will eventually lead to weaker and less consistent tests.
- **Decoupling**: Removing DOM dependencies will also allow our application to run outside of a browser, for example, in Node.js or any Node.js yet non-web-based environment, such as Electron.
- **Readability**: Using Angular 2's template syntax instead of relying on Bootstrap's attribute-based API or programmatic, JavaScript-based API will eventually lead to smaller, more readable code.
- **Maintainability**: Relying on Angular 2, jQuery, and the Bootstrap plugin script file(s) within the same project can be tricky and hard to maintain. The overhead will also be quite relevant in terms of both size and performance since there is an inevitable amount of repeated stuff in there.

Now that we've cleared our mind, we can choose the Angular 2 native directive modules we'll be using among the available ones. At the time of writing, the Angular 2 and Bootstrap communities seem to have put their hopes into these three very promising GitHub projects:

- `https://github.com/valor-software/ng2-bootstrap`
- `https://github.com/ng-bootstrap/core`
- `https://github.com/mlaval/angular2-bootstrap`

Among these, the first one, formerly `ng2-bootstrap`, seems to have the lead in terms of features and contributors. It's also the only one that comes with an extensive support of both Bootstrap 3 and 4, which is a very relevant thing for us since we'll be using Bootstrap 3.

Installing ng2-bootstrap

The easiest way to install `ng2-bootstrap` is using NPM. However, it also has a dependency on the `moment` JavaScript library, so we're going to install that as well. As usual, we can do that by adding the following lines to the `dependencies` section of our `package.json` file:

```
"moment": "^2.14.1",
"ng2-bootstrap": "^1.0.24",
```

As soon as we save the file, Visual Studio will fetch these NPM packages.

Right after that, we can add a reference to these new libraries to the srcPaths.js array variable declared in our gulpfile.js file, as we can see in the following excerpt (new lines have been highlighted):

```
var srcPaths = {
    app: ['Scripts/app/main.ts', 'Scripts/app/**/*.ts'],
    js: [
        'Scripts/js/**/*.js',
        'node_modules/core-js/client/shim.min.js',
        'node_modules/zone.js/dist/zone.js',
        'node_modules/reflect-metadata/Reflect.js',
        'node_modules/systemjs/dist/system.src.js',
        'node_modules/typescript/lib/typescript.js',
        'node_modules/ng2-bootstrap/bundles/ng2-bootstrap.min.js',
        'node_modules/moment/moment.js'
    ],
    js_angular: [
        'node_modules/@angular/**'
    ],
    js_rxjs: [
        'node_modules/rxjs/**'
    ],
    less: [
        'Scripts/less/**/*.less'
    ]
};
```

Last but not least, we need to add the <script> reference tags within our wwwroot/index.html page, right after the other Angular 2 library files:

```
<!-- Step 1. Load libraries -->
<!-- Polyfill(s) for older browsers -->
<script src="js/shim.min.js"></script>
<script src="js/zone.js"></script>
<script src="js/Reflect.js"></script>
<script src="js/system.src.js"></script>

<!-- Angular2 Native Directives -->
<script src="/js/moment.js"></script>
<script src="/js/ng2-bootstrap.min.js"></script>
```

That's about it.

Applying styles

We're ready to apply some styles to our project. Let's warm ourselves up with some plain Bootstrap class-based styling: while we're there, we'll also add some custom CSS classes and drop a couple of images here and there to make our native web app look a bit more distinctive.

Main navigation bar

Open the `Scripts/app.component.ts` file and, within the `@Component` section, replace the whole `template` with the following content:

```
<nav class="navbar navbar-default navbar-fixed-top">
    <div class="container-fluid">
        <input type="checkbox" id="navbar-toggle-cbox">
        <div class="navbar-header">
            <label for="navbar-toggle-cbox" class="navbar-toggle collapsed"
data-toggle="collapse" data-target="#navbar" aria-expanded="false" aria-
controls="navbar">
                <span class="sr-only">Toggle navigation</span>
                <span class="icon-bar"></span>
                <span class="icon-bar"></span>
                <span class="icon-bar"></span>
            </label>
            <a class="navbar-brand" href="#">
                <img alt="logo" src="/img/logo.svg" />
            </a>
        </div>
        <div class="collapse navbar-collapse" id="navbar">
            <ul class="nav navbar-nav">
                <li><a class="home" [routerLink]="['']">Home</a></li>
                <li><a class="about"
[routerLink]="['about']">About</a></li>
                <li><a class="login"
[routerLink]="['login']">Login</a></li>
                <li><a class="add" [routerLink]="['item/edit', 0]">Add
New</a></li>
            </ul>
        </div>
    </div>
</nav>
<h1 class="header">{{title}}</h1>
<div class="main-container">
    <router-outlet></router-outlet>
</div>
```

What we did here was nothing special. We added a couple of Bootstrap classes to our previous <ul> menu element and then wrapped it in a more accessible (and also Bootstrap-styled) <nav> element. We also introduced two custom CSS classes: header for the <h1> element and main-container for a brand new <div> element we used to wrap the <router-outlet> container. Finally, we added an image reference pointing to a logo.svg vector image file, so our navigation menu bar will have something distinctive. Needless to say, before being able to see how this restyling looks, we need to bring these custom items to life.

Let's start with the CSS classes: open the /Scripts/less/style.less file and append the following code:

```
h1.header {
    font-size: 40px;
    margin: 46px 0 0 0;
    padding: 20px 20px 20px 112px;
    background: url(/img/header-bg.png) no-repeat left top #efefef;
    text-align: left;
}

.navbar {
    margin-bottom: 0;
    img {
        width: 32px;
        height: 32px;
        margin: -4px 0 0 0;
        padding: 0;
    }

    #navbar-toggle-cbox {
        display:none;
        &:checked ~ .collapse {
            display: block;
        }
    }
}
```

We added another image reference here, a raster png that will serve as a background for our <h1 class="header"> file. That's another file we need to add to our project. In order to do that, create a new /img/ directory within the /wwwroot/ root folder and place the logo.svg and the header-bg.png file there.

This isn't a book about web image design, so we won't cover the image creation process. We'll just add some sample minimalistic images not too different from what we could be using in a real-case scenario. They can be found online at the following URL: `http://www.opengamelist.com/img/` Just add the file name to that base URL to view it online and/or download it; you can use this method for every image used within this chapter. If you need a sample favicon, you can find the one we're using here: `http://www.opengamelist.com/favicon.ico` Alternatively, you can design your own ones or get some from one of the royalty-free image and icon libraries available online.

Before going any further, it's time to run a quick test and see if everything is working properly. As usual, all we need to do is hit *F5* and take a look:

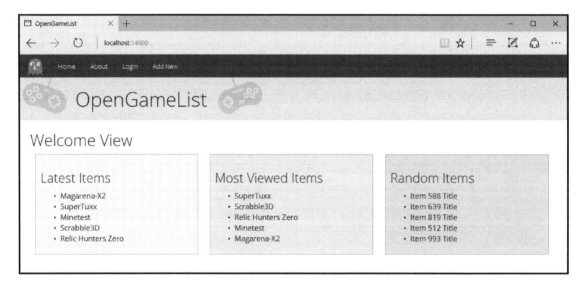

Not that bad, considering where we came from. Nonetheless, we can already see a minor flaw: the navigation bar doesn't tell us where we are, as the active route is not highlighted in any way.

If we inspect the Angular 2-generated HTML code with a DOM inspector, we can see that there actually is something that could help us to identify the active item: it's the `router-link-active` CSS class, which Angular 2 assigns automatically to the anchor who activated the route. Unfortunately, that class name cannot be changed and Bootstrap doesn't support it, as it's expecting the `active` class to be used instead, not to mention the fact that it also wants the class to be applied to the parent `<li>` element.

Taking these facts into account, we have the following options to achieve what we want:

- Completely ditch the Bootstrap standards, together with their .active class, and define our own .router-link-active class instead with full custom CSS code, logic and behavior.
- Use a CSS3 parent selector such as li < a.router-link-active and write our custom CSS code there. That rule will allow us to preserve some of the Bootstrap logic, as we would style the <li> element, but we would still be forced to write a lot of custom CSS code.
- Assign the Bootstrap class using JavaScript. We're joking, of course. There's no way we would do that, not after all we said regarding avoiding DOM manipulation earlier.
- Detect the active route and act accordingly using Angular 2 native components.

There's little doubt about which option we should choose.

Detecting the active route

A rather easy way to accomplish our task is using the Angular 2 **Router** class, which is part of the component router we introduced in Chapter 3, *Angular 2 Components and Client-Side Routing*. That class features a convenient isActive() method that seems to be perfect for our needs. If we look at the official Angular 2 API documentation at angular.io/docs/ we can read the following:

"Returns if the url is activated or not."

Source: https://angular.io/docs/ts/latest/api/router/index/Router-class.html#!#isActive-anchor.

The method accepts either a URL string or a UrlTree object, meaning that we need to generate one of them to use it. We can obtain the latter using the router.createUrlTree method, both provided by that same class.

To cut it short, we just need to add the Router class to our Angular 2 component's constructor, using dependency injection, just as we have done a number of times already, and use the aforementioned methods to understand the currently active route. Once we do that, we can easily add the active CSS class to the corresponding <li> element using the template syntax class bindings we've already used.

Let's put everything together. Open the `app.component.ts` file again and update it as follows (new/modified code has been highlighted):

```
import {Component} from "@angular/core";
import {Router} from "@angular/router";

@Component({
    selector: "opengamelist",
    template: `
<nav class="navbar navbar-default navbar-fixed-top">
    <div class="container-fluid">
        <input type="checkbox" id="navbar-toggle-cbox">
        <div class="navbar-header">
            <label for="navbar-toggle-cbox" class="navbar-toggle collapsed"
data-toggle="collapse" data-target="#navbar" aria-expanded="false" aria-
controls="navbar">
                <span class="sr-only">Toggle navigation</span>
                <span class="icon-bar"></span>
                <span class="icon-bar"></span>
                <span class="icon-bar"></span>
            </label>
            <a class="navbar-brand" href="#">
                <img alt="logo" src="/img/logo.svg" />
            </a>
        </div>
        <div class="collapse navbar-collapse" id="navbar">
            <ul class="nav navbar-nav">
                <li [class.active]="isActive([''])">
                    <a class="home" [routerLink]="['']">Home</a>
                </li>
                <li [class.active]="isActive(['about'])">
                    <a class="about" [routerLink]="['about']">About</a>
                </li>
                <li [class.active]="isActive(['login'])">
                    <a class="login" [routerLink]="['login']">Login</a>
                </li>
                <li [class.active]="isActive(['item/edit', 0])">
                    <a class="add" [routerLink]="['item/edit', 0]">Add
New</a>
                </li>
            </ul>
        </div>
    </div>
</nav>
<h1 class="header">{{title}}</h1>
<div class="main-container">
    <router-outlet></router-outlet>
</div>
```

```
})

export class AppComponent {
    title = "OpenGameList";

    constructor(public router: Router) { }
    isActive(data: any[]): boolean {
        return this.router.isActive(
            this.router.createUrlTree(data),
            true);
    }
}
```

Let's see what we did here:

- At the top of the file, we added the `Router` class from the `@angular2/router` package to the `import` list.
- At the bottom of the file, we added the constructor method with a router object instantiated through dependency injection. There's nothing new here, we already did that in Chapter 3, *Angular 2 Components and Client-Side Routing*.
- Right below the `constructor`, we added the `isActive()` internal helper method to avoid repeating some required lines of code more than once. The method accepts a required `data` variable that will be used to generate the required `UrlTree` object using the `router.createUrlTree` method and pass it to the `router.isActive` method. The latter will then return `true` if the given `UrlTree` matches the active route, and `false` otherwise.
- In the `@Componenttemplate` section, we use the `isActive()` internal method result to determine which `<li>` element should have the `active` CSS class bound to itself using template syntax.

Before testing it, we might find it useful to customize the background color of the `active` CSS class to make it more visible than the "black over dark grey" effect featured by our Yeti Bootstrap theme.

Open the `/Scripts/less/style.less` file and append the following:

```
.navbar-default .navbar-nav>.active>a,
.navbar-default .navbar-nav>.active>a:hover,
.navbar-default .navbar-nav>.active>a:focus {
    background-color: #863500;
}
```

Now we can run another quick test to see if the results match the expectations. Hit *F5* again and wait until we see the following:

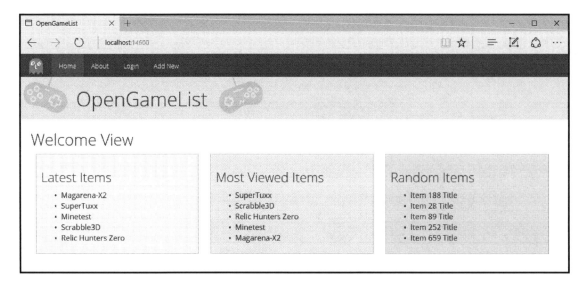

Click on the **About**, **Login**, and **Add New** navigation bar links to see the dark orange background following and highlighting the active route. From now on, our valued users will always know where they are.

Welcome View

It's time to give our **Welcome View** a new and (hopefully) better look.

The app.component.ts file is fine as it is, so we won't be touching it again for a while. We'll open the home.component.ts instead, and replace the existing template in the following way (new/updated code has been highlighted):

```
<h2>
    A non-comprehensive directory of open-source video games
    available on the web
</h2>
<div class="col-md-4">
    <item-list class="latest"></item-list>
</div>
<div class="col-md-4">
    <item-list class="most-viewed"></item-list>
</div>
<div class="col-md-4">
```

```
    <item-list class="random"></item-list>
</div>
```

What we did here was wrap our existing `<item-list>` elements in a Bootstrap grid system made of three `<div>` that will fill the viewport width. We also replaced the `<h2>` text content with a viable payoff for our **Welcome View**, replacing the previous working title.

 For more information about the Bootstrap grid system you can check the official documentation at the following URL:
`http://getbootstrap.com/css/#grid`

We already removed the `styles` within this file's `@Component` section, so we're done here.

Let's move to the `item-list.component.ts` file. Remove the `styles` section as well, then modify its `template` section in the following way (new/updated code has been highlighted):

```
<h3>{{title}}</h3>
<ul class="items">
    <li *ngFor="let item of items"
        [class.selected]="item === selectedItem"
        (click)="onSelect(item)">
        <div class="title">{{item.Title}}</div>
        <div class="description">{{item.Description}}</div>
    </li>
</ul>
```

Again, we did nothing special here, we just added the `item.Description` to the template right below the already existing `item.Title` and wrapped them both within some `<div>` elements so we can style them.

Now that we have set up the templates, we can open the `/Scripts/less/style.less` file and create some CSS classes. Here's how the revamped file will look:

```
// Some Variables that will be used below
@color-latest: #5a4d74;
@color-most-viewed: #4d6552;
@color-random: #703535;

// Header styling
h1.header {
    font-size: 40px;
    margin: 46px 0 0 0;
    padding: 20px 20px 20px 112px;
    background: url(/img/header-bg.png) no-repeat left top #efefef;
```

```scss
            text-align: left;
    }

    // Navbar styling
    .navbar {
        margin-bottom: 0;
        img {
            width: 32px;
            height: 32px;
            margin: -4px 0 0 0;
            padding: 0;
        }

        // Expand/collapse the navbar in mobile-friendly mode using pure CSS
    styling.
        // ref.: http://stackoverflow.com/a/31506685/1233379
        #navbar-toggle-cbox {
            display:none;
            &:checked ~ .collapse {
                display: block;
            }
        }
    }

    // Improve the visibility of the active navbar item (currently active
    route)
    .navbar-default .navbar-nav>.active>a,
    .navbar-default .navbar-nav>.active>a:hover,
    .navbar-default .navbar-nav>.active>a:focus {
        background-color: #863500;
    }

    h2 {
        margin: 20px;
        padding: 0;
        font-size: 1.4em;
        line-height: 1.4em;
        font-style: italic;
        color: #666666;
    }

    // item-list component(s) styling
    item-list {
        border: 0;
        margin: 0;
        padding: 0;
        vertical-align: top;
        display: block;
```

```less
&.latest {
    background-color: #f6f6f6;
    h3 {
        background-color: @color-latest;
        background-image: url(/img/latest-icon.png);
    }
}
&.most-viewed {
    background-color: #f0f0f0;
    h3 {
        background-color: @color-most-viewed;
        background-image: url(/img/most-viewed-icon.png);
    }
}
&.random {
    background-color: #e9e9e9;
    h3 {
        background-color: @color-random;
        background-image: url(/img/random-icon.png);
    }
}
h3 {
    color: #fefefe;
    margin: 0;
    padding: 10px 15px;
    background-repeat: no-repeat;
    background-position: 97% center;
}
ul {
    list-style-type: none;
    padding: 15px;
    li {
        cursor: pointer;
        margin-top: 20px;
        padding-top: 15px;
        border-top: 1px solid #c7c7c7;
        &:first-child {
            margin-top: 0;
            padding-top: 0;
            border-top-width: 0;
        }
        .title {
            font-size: 1.3em;
            font-weight: bold;
        }
        .description {
            margin-top: 3px;
            font-size: 15px;
```

```
                    line-height: 1.5em;
                    height: (15*1.5*2);
                    overflow: hidden;
                    display: -webkit-box;
                    -webkit-line-clamp: 2;
                    -webkit-box-orient: vertical;
                }
            }
        }
    }
```

As we can see, there's quite a lot of new stuff here. For the sake of readability, we also added some comments in order to explain the role of each CSS class. Let's focus on the most important things:

- We added a unique color and also an icon background image for each of our `<item-list>` component headers.
- We applied some styling to the `<item-list>` element and their children, up to the item's `Text` and `Description` containers.
- We improved the readability of the active `<nav>` element items and we also did what it takes to make the navigation menu work properly in its collapsed, mobile-friendly mode.

What we did was nothing more than a styling sample to give our **Welcome View** a fresh look: while we were there, we also took the chance to show some of the most useful LESS features and capabilities.

We can see the results of our hard work by hitting *F5*:

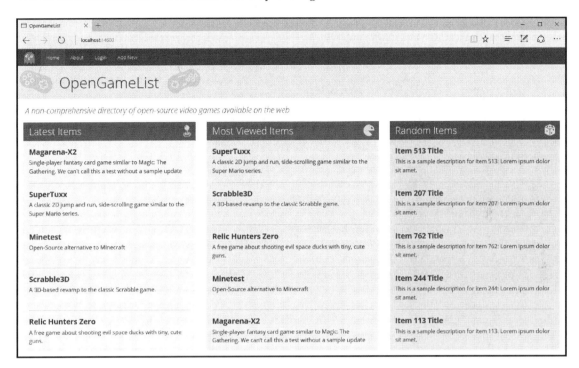

That's another significant improvement: our **Welcome View** is now looking quite good and, thanks to the Bootstrap grid system has gained some mobile-friendliness as well. Here's how it would look on an Apple iPhone 6:

Not bad at all, is it? Let's try to keep that pace.

Item Detail View

When we split our **Item Detail View** into two distinctive components (**View** mode and **Edit** mode), we also gave them a minimalistic, wiki-like tabbed interface. Now that we have Bootstrap we can further improve that approach by redesigning it into a more intuitive, visually engaging view-editor interface.

Display mode

Open the `/Scripts/app/item-detail-view.component.ts` and remove the `@Component`'s `styles` section entirely. We won't need it anymore, as we'll be using our `style.less` file from now on.

Right after that, replace the template section HTML content with the following code:

```
<div *ngIf="item">
    <h2>
        <a href="#" (click)="onBack()">&laquo; Back to Home</a>
    </h2>
    <div class="item-container">
        <ul class="nav nav-tabs">
            <li role="presentation">
                <a href="#" (click)="onItemDetailEdit(item)">Edit</a>
            </li>
            <li role="presentation" class="active">
                <a href="#">View</a>
            </li>
        </ul>
        <div class="panel panel-default">
            <div class="panel-body">
                <div class="item-image-panel">
                    <img src="/img/item-image-sample.png"
alt="{{item.Title}}" />
                    <div class="caption">Sample image with caption.</div>
                </div>
                <h3>{{item.Title}}</h3>
                <p>{{item.Description}}</p>
                <p>{{item.Text}}</p>
            </div>
        </div>
    </div>
</div>
```

There's a couple of things worth noting here:

- We added a second <p> element to display the item.Text property
- We don't support item image files yet, so we added a demo image to see how it might look
- We added a reference to an onBack() method to allow the user to navigate back to the **Welcome View** without having to resort to the navigation menu

The aforementioned onBack() method isn't there yet, so we need to implement it within the component class code section in the following way (added lines have been highlighted):

```
onItemDetailEdit(item: Item) {
    this.router.navigate(["item/edit", item.Id]);
    return false;
}

onBack() {
    this.router.navigate(['']);
}
```

Once we're done with that, we can get back to our styling task. Open the style.less file and add the following code:

```
// Item Detail View & Edit components styling
@color-panel: #f9f9f9;

.item-container {
    margin: 0 20px;
    .nav.nav-tabs {
        padding-right: 20px;
        li {
            &.active a {
                font-weight: bold;
                background-color: @color-panel;
            }
            float:right;
        }
    }
    .panel.panel-default {
        background-color: @color-panel;
        border-top-width: 0;
        .item-image-panel {
            width: 170px;
            min-height: 170px;
            float: right;
```

```
            padding: 10px;
            background-color: #f2f2f2;
            border: 1px solid #cccccc;
            img {
                width: 150px;
                height: 150px;
                border: 1px solid #e6e6e6;
            }
            .caption {
                margin-top: 5px;
                text-align: center;
                font-size: 0.8em;
            }
        }
    }
    h3 {
        margin: 10px 0 20px 0;
        font-weight: bold;
    }
}
```

Again, we're just applying some custom spacing, coloring, and aligning here and there, leaving all the rest to the standard Bootstrap `nav` and `panel` classes.

Here's our improved **Item Detail View** in **Display** mode:

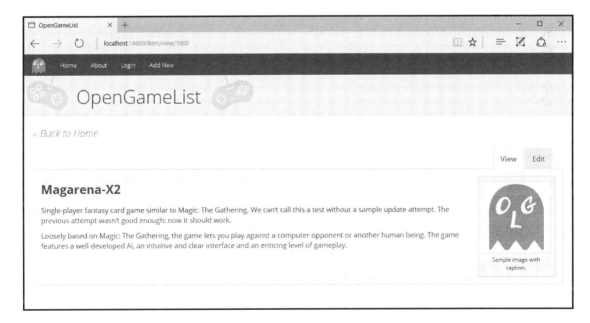

The mobile-friendly viewport mode is looking good as well:

At this point, we can say that the **Display** mode is looking fine. Let's move to the other tab.

Edit mode

When `<form>` elements are involved, UI styling usually gets tricky, as we need to handle things such as form validation, required inputs, and other similar issues that will most likely have some sort of impact on the styling job. However, thanks to Bootstrap and Angular 2, it won't be that hard.

Again, let's start with opening the `/Scripts/app/item-detail-edit.component.ts` and remove the `styles` section of `@Component`.

To make things clear, we don't have anything against in-component styling. It's just that we wouldn't be able to use LESS syntax sugar while being in there, not to mention the fact that restraining ourselves from using that will also reduce the chance of CSS code repetition between different components.

Right after that, move to the `template` section and replace its contents with the following:

```
<div *ngIf="item">
    <h2>
        <a href="#" (click)="onBack()">
            &laquo; Back to Home
        </a>
    </h2>
    <div class="item-container">
        <ul class="nav nav-tabs">
            <li role="presentation" class="active">
                <a href="#">Edit</a>
            </li>
            <li role="presentation" *ngIf="item.Id != 0">
                <a href="#" (click)="onItemDetailView(item)">View</a>
            </li>
        </ul>
        <div class="panel panel-default">
            <div class="panel-body">
                <form class="item-detail-edit">
                    <h3>{{item.Title}}</h3>
                    <div class="form-group">
                        <label for="input-title">Title</label>
                        <input id="input-title" name="input-title"
type="text" class="form-control" [(ngModel)]="item.Title"
placeholder="Insert the title..." />
                    </div>
                    <div class="form-group">
                        <label for="input-description">Description</label>
                        <textarea id="input-description" name="input-
description" class="form-control" [(ngModel)]="item.Description"
placeholder="Insert a suitable description..." required></textarea>
                    </div>
                    <div class="form-group">
                        <label for="input-text">Text</label>
                        <textarea id="input-text" name="input-text"
class="form-control" [(ngModel)]="item.Text" placeholder="Insert a suitable
description..."></textarea>
```

```
                      </div>
                      <div *ngIf="item.Id == 0" class="commands insert">
                          <input type="button" class="btn btn-primary"
 value="Save" (click)="onInsert(item)" />
                          <input type="button" class="btn btn-default"
 value="Cancel" (click)="onBack()" />
                      </div>
                      <div *ngIf="item.Id != 0" class="commands update">
                          <input type="button" class="btn btn-primary"
 value="Update" (click)="onUpdate(item)" />
                          <input type="button" class="btn btn-danger"
 value="Delete" (click)="onDelete(item)" />
                          <input type="button" class="btn btn-default"
 value="Cancel" (click)="onItemDetailView(item)" />
                      </div>
                  </form>
              </div>
          </div>
      </div>
  </div>
```

It seems like we've added a lot of new stuff here. Let's try to shed some light on what we did:

- The first lines of code are almost identical to the **Display** mode template: we have the same <h2> pointing back to the **Welcome View** route and also an identical <ul> element with the nav-tabs Bootstrap CSS class to render the tabs.

- Inside the panel we've declared the main <form> element and added a series of <div> elements with the form-group class replacing our previous list-based structure. This is the default CSS class used by Bootstrap to handle the various input fields within a form. Inside each one of them, we placed the same <input> and <textarea> we defined before for the Title item and Description, plus a new one for the Text.

- We added some <label> elements with proper Bootstrap CSS styling. Each one of them is linked to their respective input field by using the for HTML attribute.

- By looking at the <input> elements we can see that we're still using the same two-way data binding, ngModel-based implementation logic that we put in place when we created the template for this component for the first time. There's no need to change that, since everything was already working well on that part. However, we added an id attribute to have them linked to their respective labels (as stated previously) and the form-control Bootstrap CSS class to style them.

Here are the custom classes to add to our `style.less` file. Instead of just appending them at the end of the file, let's place them inside the existing `.item-container` selector since they are only relevant within that scope:

```less
// Form styling for item-detail-edit component
form.item-detail-edit {
    .empty-field {
        color: #f04124;
    }
    .form-group {
        label {
            font-size: 14px;
            font-weight: bold;
            display: block;
            background-color: #eaeaea;
            line-height: 1.4em;
            padding: 5px 10px;
        }
        textarea {
            &#input-description {
                height: 80px;
            }
            &#input-text {
                height: 150px;
            }
        }
    }
    .commands {
        text-align: right;
        input[type="button"] {
            margin-left: 5px;
        }
    }
}
```

Here's how the revamped **Edit** mode will look like after these changes:

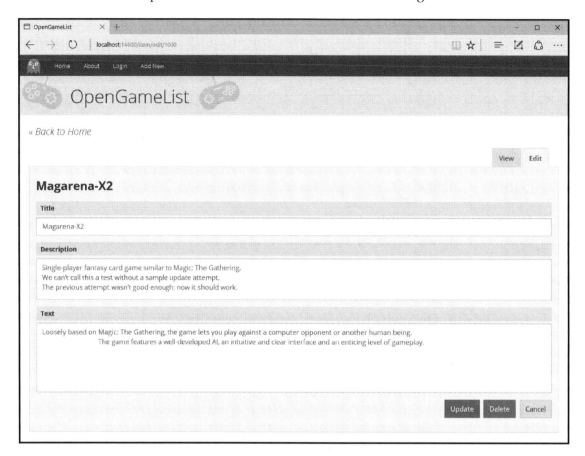

Not bad, but we can do better. We mentioned form validation and required items, yet we have done nothing about that yet. Let's see how we can do that with the item's `Title` property, which is definitely something that should never be empty or null in any given circumstance.

In order to do that, we need to go back to the `item-detail-edit.component.ts` file and apply the following changes.

In the `template` section, at the start of the existing `<form>` element, add the following code:

```
<h3>
    {{item.Title}}
    <span class="empty-field" [hidden]="dTitle.valid">
        Empty Title
    </span>
</h3>
```

Also in the `template` section, within the first `form-group` element, add the following code:

```
<div class="form-group has-feedback" [ngClass]="{'has-success':
dTitle.valid, 'has-error': !dTitle.valid}">
    <label for="input-title">Title</label>
    <input id="input-title" name="input-title" type="text" class="form-
control" [(ngModel)]="item.Title" placeholder="Insert the title..."
required #dTitle="ngModel" />
    <span class="glyphicon form-control-feedback" aria-hidden="true"
[ngClass]="{'glyphicon-ok': dTitle.valid, 'glyphicon-remove': !
dTitle.valid}"></span>
    <div [hidden]=" dTitle.valid" class="alert alert-danger">
        You need to enter a valid Title.
    </div>
</div>
```

This is a quite complex implementation, so we should take our time to fully understand it.

Let's start with the `<input id="input-title">` element, it being the center of everything. We can say that all the code we added here has the sole purpose of making the GUI react in real time whenever this input field enters in an invalid state. In order to achieve this outcome, we did the following:

- We added the `required` attribute to the input tag to ensure that it will become invalid whenever it's empty
- We assigned its `ngModel` to a template reference variable that we called `dTitle`, so we can track it in real time throughout our template
- We used the `dTitle` variable's `valid` property value to show/hide elements and/or assign CSS classes to impact the GUI, thus improving the user experience in a number of ways

Here's a detailed list of what we did with the dTitle variable:

- We added a `<span>` inside the top `<h3>` element, (only visible when the title control is not valid), featuring a short text whenever the item title is invalid.
- We added two new Bootstrap CSS classes to the title's `form-group` element. The first one (`has-feedback`) will always be present, while the second one will vary: `has-success` if the `dTitle.valid` property is `true`, `has-error` otherwise.
- Right after the `<input>` element we added a Bootstrap `glyphicon` component, which is basically a styled `<span>` that will render the icon bound to its given class. That class will be determined by an `[ngClass]` conditional directive based upon the `dTitle.Valid` property value: a green check if `true`, a red cross otherwise.
- We also added a standard alert panel that will be visible when the `dTitle` is not valid, just like the `<span>` within the `<h3>` mentioned before.

In order to implement form validation, we were forced to introduce some rather advanced Angular 2 concepts such as template reference variables (also known as `ref-vars`), the `ngControl` attribute, and its strictly related `ngControlName` directive.

To better understand these concepts, we strongly suggest reading the official Angular 2 API documentation at the following URLs:

- https://angular.io/docs/ts/latest/guide/template-syntax.html#!#ref-vars
- https://angular.io/docs/ts/latest/api/core/DirectiveMetadata-class.html#!#exportAs-anchor
- https://angular.io/docs/ts/latest/api/common/index/NgControlName-directive.html

It's time for us to open our `style.less` file again and add the new styling rules. This time we have used a lot of Bootstrap CSS default classes, so the update will be minimal:

```
.empty-field {
    color: #f04124;
    font-weight: normal;
    font-style: italic;
}
```

This selector should be kept inside the `form.item-detail-edit` block, as it's strictly related to that context and won't be used elsewhere.

Once we've done that, we're free to hit *F5* and see how all these efforts look on screen:

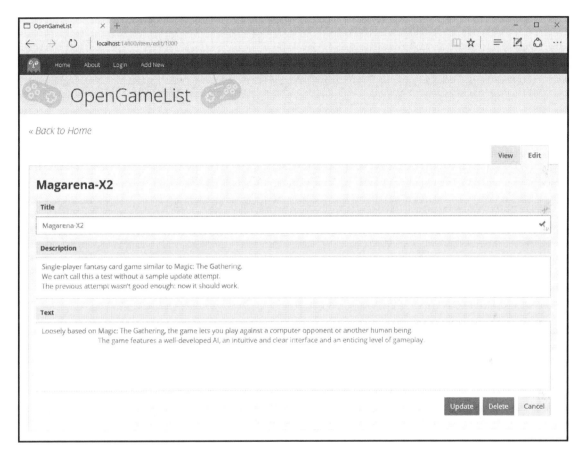

Form featuring a valid title

As we can see, as long as there's a valid `Title`, the input field will now feature a green border and also a green check to the right. Conversely, whenever the `Title` is invalid or becomes empty, a number of UI alerts will come to life: a red border on the input field, a red cross to the right, a red italic title, and also a white-on-red warning panel telling the user that there's a problem with the form:

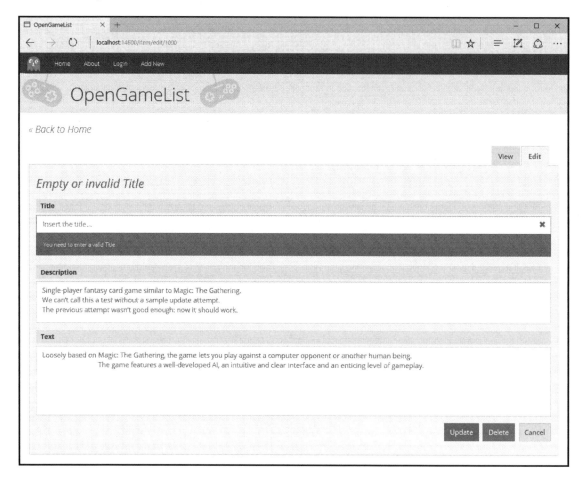

Form featuring an invalid title

It might even be too much for a missing title, yet it has been useful to demonstrate how much control we have upon the layout using Angular 2-plus-Bootstrap only: as a matter of fact, we didn't have to write a single line of JavaScript code.

Conclusions

That's it for now. We just added a simple yet very effective Angular 2 native form validation control. Of course, it has some downsides, such as being client-side only: no server-side feedback is handled in any way. Nonetheless, we can be greatly satisfied with such an outcome.

If we want to further improve what we've done, we can always take a look at the official Bootstrap form-styling documentation at the following URL:
`http://getbootstrap.com/css/#forms`

There are also a lot of examples that will most likely give we good suggestions about how to properly style `<input>` elements and present them to the user in an effective way.

Suggested topics

Style sheet language, SoC, CSS, CSS3, LESS, Sass , Stylus, Switch CSS, Material Design, Material2, Bootstrap, Bootswatch, CDN, expressive Code, unit testing, decoupling, Node.js, Electron, ng2-bootstrap, moment, CSS3 Parent Selector, grid system, Angular 2, NgModel, template reference variables, Angular 2 directives.

Summary

We started this chapter admitting that our ultra-minimalistic UI/UX approach wouldn't work for a potentially shippable product that our Native Web Application should eventually become. Having acknowledged that fact, we added a LESS-based custom stylesheet file to our project. Before doing that, for the benefit of those not familiar with the style sheet pre-processor approach, we spent some time enumerating some of the LESS main advantages.

Right after adding the `style.less` file to our project, we had to choose between adopting one of the popular CSS frameworks such as Bootstrap, YAML, or Foundation, or stick to a full do-it-yourself approach. We briefly enumerated some pros and cons of each alternative, then we opted for Bootstrap 3, mostly because of its great mobile-friendly grid system, saving us the need to write a huge set of layout rules. We chose a suitable theme, then imported it in the `<head>` section of our `index.html` file right before our custom LESS file, so that we could use the latter to apply some custom styling as well.

We then started to apply some Bootstrap and custom styling to the existing components. We started with the navigation menu, replacing our plain list of links with a Bootstrap `navbar` element. We also gave a brand new look and feel to the **Welcome View** and **Item Detail View** (**Display** and **Edit** modes) UI layouts, trying our best to make them prettier, more usable, and also mobile-friendly. While working in edit mode, we introduced some rather advanced Angular 2 concepts in order to implement a rudimental, client-only form validation pattern without writing a single line of JavaScript code.

7
Authentication and Authorization

Generally speaking, the term **authentication** refers to any process of verification that someone, be it a human being or an automated system, is who (or what) it claims to be. This is also true within the context of the **World Wide Web** (**WWW**), where that same word is mostly used to denote any technique used by a website or service to collect a set of login info from a user agent, typically a web browser, and authenticate them using a membership and/or **Identity** service.

Authentication should never be confused with **authorization**, as it is a different process and is in charge of a very different task: to give a quick definition, we could say that the purpose of authorization is to confirm that the requesting user is allowed to have access to the action they want to perform.

To better understand the distance between these two apparently similar concepts, we could think of two real-world scenarios:

- A free, yet registered account trying to gain access to a paid or premium only service or feature: this is a common example of *authenticated*, yet not *authorized* access.
- An anonymous user trying to gain access to a publicly available page or file: this is an example of *non-authenticated*, yet *authorized* access.

Do we really need these?

As a matter of fact, implementing **authentication** and/or **authorization** logic isn't mandatory for most web-based applications or services: there are a number of websites that still don't do that, mostly because they serve contents that can be accessed by anyone at any time. This used to be pretty common among most corporate, marketing, and informative websites until some years ago: that was before their owners learned how important it is to build a network of registered users and how much these *loyal* contacts are worth nowadays.

We don't need to be experienced developers to acknowledge how much the World Wide Web has changed in the last few years: each and every website, regardless of its purpose, nowadays has an increasing and more or less legitimate interest in tracking their users, giving them the chance to customize their navigation experience, interacting with their social networks, collecting e-mail addresses, and so on. None of the preceding could be done without an authentication mechanism of some sort.

There are billions of websites and services that require authentication to work properly, as most of their content and/or intents depend upon the actions of registered users: forums, blogs, shopping carts, subscription-based services, and even collaborative tools such as wikis (including ours).

Long story short, the answer is yes: as long as we aim to be a decent wiki, there is no doubt we should implement both an authentication and an authorization procedure. It is the only way to determine who will be able to view, add, update, or delete our valued items, not to mention perform administrative-level tasks, keep track of our users, and handle a lot of important tasks.

Authentication

Since the origin of the World Wide Web, the vast majority of authentication techniques rely upon **HTTP/HTTPS implementation standards**, and all of them work more or less in the following way:

1. A non-authenticated user-agent asks for a content that cannot be accessed without some kind of permissions.
2. The web application returns an authentication request, usually in form of an HTML page containing an empty web form to complete.
3. The user-agent fills up the web form with their credentials, usually a **username** and a **password**, and then sends it back with a POST command, which is most likely issued by a click on a **Submit** button.

4. The web application receives the POST data and calls the aforementioned server-side implementation that will try to **authenticate** the user with the given input and return an appropriate result.

5. If the result is successful, the web application will authenticate the user and store the relevant data somewhere, depending on the chosen authentication method: sessions/cookies, tokens, signatures, and so on (we'll talk about it later on). Conversely, the result will be presented to the user as a readable outcome inside an error page, possibly asking them to try again, contact an administrator, or something else.

This is still the most common approach nowadays. Almost all websites we can think of are using it, albeit with a number of big or small differences regarding security layers, state management, JWT, or other RESTful tokens, basic or digest access, single sign-on properties, and more.

Third-party authentication

Being forced to have a potentially different username and password for each website visit can be frustrating, other than requiring the users to develop custom *password storage techniques* that might lead to security risks. In order to overcome this issue, we can enhance, or even entirely replace, a standard HTTP-based authentication technique with an authentication protocol based upon third-party providers. The most notable of them is probably OpenID, available since 2005 and adopted early by some big players such as Google and StackOverflow, who based their authentication providers upon it. Here's how it works in few words:

- Whenever our application receives an OpenID authentication request, it opens a transparent connection interface through the requesting user and a trusted, third-party authentication provider (for example, the **Google Identity Provider**): the interface can be a popup, an AJAX, populated modal windows or an API call, depending on the implementation.

- The user sends his username and password to the aforementioned third-party provider, who performs the *authentication* accordingly and communicates the result to our application by redirecting the user back to where he came, together with a security token that can be used to retrieve the authentication result.

- Our application consumes the token to check the authentication result, authenticating the user in case of success or sending an error response in case of failure.

Authorization

In most standard implementations, including those featured by ASP.NET, the authorization phase kicks in right after the authentication, and it's mostly based on *permissions* or *roles*: any authenticated user might have their own set of permissions and/or belong to one or more roles, and thus be granted access to a specific set of resources. These *role-based* checks are usually set by the developer in a declarative fashion within the application source code and/or configuration files.

Authorization, like we said, shouldn't be confused with authentication, despite the fact it could be easily exploited to perform an implicit authentication as well, especially when it's delegated to a third-party actor.

Third-party authorization

The best known third-party authorization protocol nowadays is **OAuth**, developed by Blaine Cook and Chris Messina in 2006 and widely used by a lot of social networks, including Facebook and Twitter. It basically works like this:

- Whenever an existing user requests a set of permissions to our application via OAuth, we open a transparent connection interface between them and a third-party authorization provider that is trusted by our application (for example, *Facebook*).
- The provider acknowledges the user and, if they have the proper rights, responds entrusting them with a temporary, specific access key.
- The user presents the access key to our application and will be granted access.

> We can clearly see how easy it is to exploit this authorization logic for authentication purposes as well; after all, if Facebook says I can do something, shouldn't it also imply that I am who I claim to be? Isn't that enough?
>
> The short answer is no. It might be the case for Facebook, because their OAuth implementation implies that the subscriber receiving the authorization must have authenticated himself to Facebook first; however, this guarantee is not written anywhere, and even if Facebook won't ever change this, considering how many websites are using it for authentication purposes, there is no written guarantee about it. Theoretically speaking, they could split their authorization system from their authentication protocol at any time, thus leading our application's authentication logic to an unrecoverable state of inconsistency.

More generally, we can say that presuming something from something else is almost always a bad practice unless that assumption lies upon very solid, well-documented and (most importantly) highly guaranteed grounds.

Proprietary or third-party?

Theoretically speaking, it's possible to entirely delegate the authentication and/or authorization tasks to existing external, *third-party* providers such as those we mentioned before: there are a lot of web and mobile applications that proudly follow this route nowadays. There are a number of undeniable advantages in using such an approach, including the following:

- **No user-specific DB tables/data models**, just some provider-based identifiers to use here and there as reference keys.
- **Immediate registration**, since there's no need to fill in a registration form and wait for a confirmation e-mail: no username, no password. This will be appreciated by most users and probably increase our conversion rates as well.
- **Little or no privacy issues**, as there's no personal or sensitive data on the application server.
- **No need to handle usernames and passwords** and implement automatic recovery processes.
- **Fewer security-related issues** such as form-based hacking attempts or brute force login attempts.

Of course, there are also some downsides:

- **There won't be an actual user base** so it would be hard to get an overview of active users, get their e-mail address, do statistics, and so on.
- **The login phase might be resource-intensive**, since it will always require an external, back and forth secure connection with a third-party server.
- **All users will need to have (or open) an account with the chosen third-party provider(s)** in order to log in.
- **All users will need to trust our application** because the third-party provider will ask them to authorize it for accessing their data.
- **We will have to register our application with the provider** in order to be able to perform a number of required or optional tasks, such as receive our public and secret keys, authorize one or more URI initiators, and choose the information we want to collect.

Taking all these pros and cons into account, we could say that relying on third-party providers and avoid implementing a proprietary membership provider might be a great time-saving choice for small-scale apps, including ours.

However, we won't be taking that route, because we want the best of both worlds. That's why we'll create an **internal membership provider** that will handle authentication and provide its very own set of authorization rules. Nonetheless, our users will be also able to log in using their favorite *third-party* provider using the built-in OAuth2 providers support provided by the `AspNetCore.Identity` membership framework.

Choosing an authentication mode

The authentication alternatives made available by ASP.NET Core are basically the same supported by the previous versions of ASP.NET:

- **No authentication**: If we don't feel like implementing anything or if we want to use (or develop) something not relying upon the ASP.NET Identity system
- **Individual user accounts**: When we want to set up an internal database to store user data using the standard ASP.NET Identity interface
- **Azure Active Directory**: Using a token-based set of API calls handled by the **Azure AD Authentication Library** (**ADAL**)
- **Windows authentication**: Viable for local-scope applications only

In `Chapter 1`, *Getting Ready*, when we created our project, we made the choice to go with an empty project featuring **no authentication**. That was because we didn't want Visual Studio to add `AspNetCore.Identity` support right from the start. Now that we chose to use it, we need to manually add the proper packages.

Installing AspNetCore.Identity

In order to set up and configure the `AspNetCore.Identity` framework, we need to install the required **NuGet** package and perform a number of code changes in some of our project's entity classes.

Adding the package

The first thing we're going to do is to check for the existence of the `Microsoft.AspNetCore.Identity.EntityFrameworkCore`library package, which we should have already added in `Chapter 4`, *The Data Model*. If we missed it, we can fix the issue in a number of ways.

If we like to use the **Package Manager Console**, we can select the appropriate tab and write the following command:

```
> Install-Package Microsoft.AspNetCore.Identity.EntityFrameworkCore
```

If we prefer the **Package Manager GUI** interface, right-click in **Solution Explorer** to the **OpenGameListWebApp** project node, select **Manage NuGet Packages**, and act accordingly:

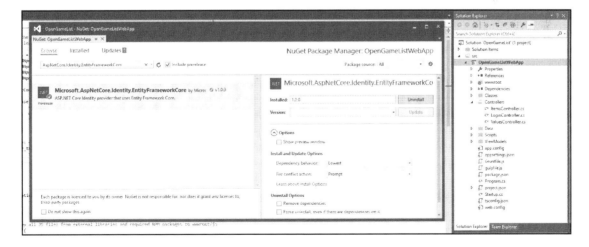

As usual, we can also manage everything directly from the `project.json` file by adding the following line to the `dependencies` section:

```
"Microsoft.AspNetCore.Identity.EntityFrameworkCore": "1.0.0"
```

Updating the project classes

Once done, we need to perform some changes to our project's classes to ensure a proper *Identity* support.

ApplicationDbContext.cs

Open the `Data/ApplicationDbContext.cs` class file and perform the following changes:

1. Add a `using` reference to `Microsoft.AspNetCore.Identity.EntityFrameworkCore`, as required by the new base class:

   ```
   using Microsoft.AspNetCore.Identity.EntityFrameworkCore;
   ```

2. Change the base class from `DbContext` to `IdentityDbContext<ApplicationUser>`:

   ```
   public class ApplicationDbContext :
   IdentityDbContext<ApplicationUser>
   ```

3. Remove the `DbSet<ApplicationUser> Users` property, as the `IdentityDbContext` base class already has it built in:

   ```
   #region Properties
   public DbSet<Item> Items { get; set; }
   public DbSet<Comment> Comments { get; set; }
   // public DbSet<ApplicationUser> Users { get; set; }
   #endregion Properties
   ```

ApplicationUser.cs

If we try to compile the project, this file will now produce an error, because our existing `ApplicationUser` class does not extend the `IdentityUser` type, which is a requirement for the `TUser`, generic type required by the `IdentityDbContext` class. To solve the error, switch to the `/ApplicationUsers/ApplicationUser.cs` class and add the `IdentityUser` base class in the following way:

```
namespace OpenGameListWebApp.Data.ApplicationUsers
{
    public class ApplicationUser : IdentityUser
    {
```

Needless to say, we'll have to add a reference to the `AspNetCore.Identity` namespace here as well:

```
using Microsoft.AspNetCore.Identity.EntityFrameworkCore;
```

As soon as we save the file, we'll get three green compilation notices for the `Id`, `Email`, and `UserName` properties, as they are all already present in the `IdentityUser` base class:

```
#region Properties
[Key]
[Required]
public string Id { get; set; }
[Required]
[MaxLength(128)]
public string UserName { get; set; }
[Required]
public string Email { get; set; }
[Required]
public int Type { get; set; }
[Required]
public int Flags { get; set; }
[Required]
public DateTime CreatedDate { get; set; }
[Required]
public DateTime LastModifiedDate { get; set; }
#endregion Properties
```

We don't need them anymore, so we can comment (or just remove) them as well:

```
//[Key]
//[Required]
//public string Id { get; set; }
//[Required]
//[MaxLength(128)]
//public string UserName { get; set; }
//[Required]
//public string Email { get; set; }
```

That's it! From now on, our `ApplicationUser` entity class is also an `IdentityUser` that can be used by `ASP.NET Identity` for authentication and authorization purposes.

Startup.cs

What we need to do now is to add the Identity-related services to our project's startup class. Open the `Startup.cs` file and add the following to the `ConfigureServices` method, right before the `DbContext` (new lines are highlighted):

```
public void ConfigureServices(IServiceCollection services)
{
    // Add framework services.
    services.AddMvc();

    // Add EntityFramework's Identity support.
    services.AddEntityFramework();

    // Add Identity Services & Stores
    services.AddIdentity<ApplicationUser, IdentityRole>(config => {
        config.User.RequireUniqueEmail = true;
        config.Password.RequireNonAlphanumeric = false;
        config.Cookies.ApplicationCookie.AutomaticChallenge = false;
    })
        .AddEntityFrameworkStores<ApplicationDbContext>()
        .AddDefaultTokenProviders();

    // Add ApplicationDbContext.
    services.AddDbContext<ApplicationDbContext>(options =>
options.UseSqlServer(Configuration["Data:DefaultConnection:ConnectionString
"])
        );

    // Add ApplicationDbContext's DbSeeder
    services.AddSingleton<DbSeeder>();
}
```

In order to make it work, we also need to add the following namespaces:

```
using OpenGameListWebApp.Data.Users;
using Microsoft.AspNetCore.Identity.EntityFrameworkCore;
```

DbSeeder.cs

Since we changed our `ApplicationUser` class to make it extend the `IdentityUser` base class, we most likely broke the seeding mechanism we set up back in `Chapter 4`, *The Data Model*. On top of that, we should also create some sample roles, since we now we can make good use of them. These are two good reasons to revise our current `DbSeeder` class.

Let's open our `/Data/DbSeeder.cs` file and update it accordingly. This is a fat class in terms of source code lines, so we'll just show the relevant changes.

The first thing we need to do is to add a **UserManager** and a **RoleManager**, as they are the required `Asp.NetCore.Identity` handler classes to properly work with users and roles. We can define a private variable for each one of them within the `#Private Members` region (new lines are highlighted):

```
#region Private Members
private ApplicationDbContext DbContext;
private RoleManager<IdentityRole> RoleManager;
private UserManager<ApplicationUser> UserManager;
#endregion Private Members
```

These references will require the following namespaces:

```
using Microsoft.AspNetCore.Identity;
using Microsoft.AspNetCore.Identity.EntityFrameworkCore;
```

We can then instantiate these new properties within the `Constructor` using the same dependency injection pattern we already used to instantiate our `ApplicationDbContext`:

```
#region Constructor
public DbSeeder(ApplicationDbContext dbContext, RoleManager<IdentityRole>
roleManager, UserManager<ApplicationUser> userManager)
    {
        DbContext = dbContext;
        RoleManager = roleManager;
        UserManager = userManager;
    }
#endregion Constructor
```

Right after that, we need to change our `CreateUsers` method to make use of these handlers. Since they all feature methods enforcing async/await programming pattern, we also need to make it `async` and change its return type from `void` to `Task`. Therefore, we will also conveniently rename it `CreateUsersAsync` as well. Here's the new method, rewritten from scratch:

```
private async Task CreateUsersAsync()
{
    // local variables
    DateTime createdDate = new DateTime(2016, 03, 01, 12, 30, 00);
    DateTime lastModifiedDate = DateTime.Now;
    string role_Administrators = "Administrators";
    string role_Registered = "Registered";

    //Create Roles (if they doesn't exist yet)
    if (!await RoleManager.RoleExistsAsync(role_Administrators)) await
RoleManager.CreateAsync(new IdentityRole(role_Administrators));
    if (!await RoleManager.RoleExistsAsync(role_Registered)) await
RoleManager.CreateAsync(new IdentityRole(role_Registered));

    // Create the "Admin" ApplicationUser account (if it doesn't exist
already)
    var user_Admin = new ApplicationUser() {
        UserName = "Admin",
        Email = "admin@opengamelist.com",
        CreatedDate = createdDate,
        LastModifiedDate = lastModifiedDate
    };

    // Insert "Admin" into the Database and also assign the "Administrator"
role to him.
    if (await UserManager.FindByIdAsync(user_Admin.Id) == null)
    {
        await UserManager.CreateAsync(user_Admin, "Pass4Admin");
        await UserManager.AddToRoleAsync(user_Admin, role_Administrators);
        // Remove Lockout and E-Mail confirmation.
        user_Admin.EmailConfirmed = true;
        user_Admin.LockoutEnabled = false;
    }

#if DEBUG
    // Create some sample registered user accounts (if they don't exist
already)
    var user_Ryan = new ApplicationUser() {
        UserName = "Ryan",
        Email = "ryan@opengamelist.com",
        CreatedDate = createdDate,
```

```
            LastModifiedDate = lastModifiedDate,
            EmailConfirmed = true,
            LockoutEnabled = false
        };
        var user_Solice = new ApplicationUser() {
            UserName = "Solice",
            Email = "solice@opengamelist.com",
            CreatedDate = createdDate,
            LastModifiedDate = lastModifiedDate,
            EmailConfirmed = true,
            LockoutEnabled = false
        };
        var user_Vodan = new ApplicationUser() {
            UserName = "Vodan",
            Email = "vodan@opengamelist.com",
            CreatedDate = createdDate,
            LastModifiedDate = lastModifiedDate,
            EmailConfirmed = true,
            LockoutEnabled = false
        };
        // Insert sample registered users into the Database and also assign the
"Registered" role to him.
        if (await UserManager.FindByIdAsync(user_Ryan.Id) == null)
        {
            await UserManager.CreateAsync(user_Ryan, "Pass4Ryan");
            await UserManager.AddToRoleAsync(user_Ryan, role_Registered);
            // Remove Lockout and E-Mail confirmation.
            user_Ryan.EmailConfirmed = true;
            user_Ryan.LockoutEnabled = false;
        }
        if (await UserManager.FindByIdAsync(user_Solice.Id) == null)
        {
            await UserManager.CreateAsync(user_Solice, "Pass4Solice");
            await UserManager.AddToRoleAsync(user_Solice, role_Registered);
            // Remove Lockout and E-Mail confirmation.
            user_Solice.EmailConfirmed = true;
            user_Solice.LockoutEnabled = false;
        }
        if (await UserManager.FindByIdAsync(user_Vodan.Id) == null)
        {
            await UserManager.CreateAsync(user_Vodan, "Pass4Vodan");
            await UserManager.AddToRoleAsync(user_Vodan, role_Registered);
            // Remove Lockout and E-Mail confirmation.
            user_Vodan.EmailConfirmed = true;
            user_Vodan.LockoutEnabled = false;
        }
#endif
        await DbContext.SaveChangesAsync();
```

```
}
```

As we can see, we made some relevant changes here:

- The `DbContext.Add` and `DbContext.AddRange` methods have been replaced by those provided by the `UserManager`. This allow us to specify a password that will be automatically hashed and also to avoid any explicit `Id` assignment, as they will be auto-generated.
- We used `RoleManager` to create two sample roles: administrators and registered.
- We modified our code to add the `admin` user to the administrators role and all the other sample users to the registered role.

Once done, we need to update the `SeedAsync` method to reflect the rename we just did on `CreateUsersAsync` and also handle the fact that the latter is now asynchronous as well:

```
#region Public Methods
public async Task SeedAsync()
{
    // Create default Users
    if (await DbContext.Users.CountAsync() == 0) await CreateUsersAsync();
    // Create default Items (if there are none) and Comments
    if (await DbContext.Items.CountAsync() == 0) CreateItems();
}
#endregion Public Methods
```

With this, we're done updating our project's classes.

Before going further, it might be wise to issue a whole project rebuild to make sure we're not getting build errors within our code.

Updating the database

It's time to create a new migration and reflect the code changes to the database by taking advantage of the code-first approach we chose in Chapter 4, *The Data Model*.

It's worth noting that if we were using *Entity Framework 6*, we could entirely skip this step by implementing the **auto-migration** feature it used to have. Unfortunately, there's no such thing in **EF core**, so we must add our migrations manually.

Let's open a Powershell command prompt and go to our project's root folder, then write the following:

```
> dotnet ef migrations add "Identity" –o "Data\Migrations"
```

A new migration will be added to the project. Right after that, we could choose to update our database...except it won't be a good idea. Applying the new migration will most likely cause some data loss or other consistency issues due to the fact that our ApplicationUser class experienced some major changes. Such a scenario is also clearly stated by the yellow message shown by the Powershell tool upon completing its given task:

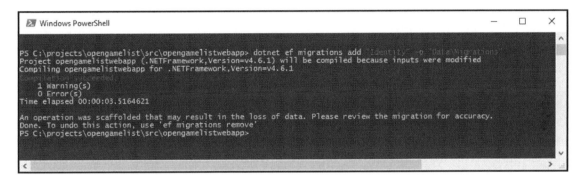

Since we updated our DbSeeder class to support the new changes, the best thing we can do would be letting it re-populate our database accordingly. Unfortunately, we know perfectly well that as long as there are some existing users and items in the database tables, it won't even run. This leaves us with nothing but one solution: drop and recreate the database, so the DbSeeder will kick in and re-populate everything on the first run.

 Although it might seem a horrible way to fix things, that's definitely not the case here, as we're still in development phase. We haven't touched our database contents yet, so we won't mind them being re-seeded from scratch into a new, Identity-aware form.

In order to do that, issue the following Powershell commands:

```
> dotnet ef database drop
> dotnet ef database update
```

We'll also have to hit *Y* to confirm the drop.

Once done, hit *F5* and wait for the `DbSeeder` to kick in. After that, it will do its magic. We'll have an updated database with full `AspNetCore.Identity` support.

Authentication methods

Now that we have updated our database to support the `AspNetCore.Identity` authentication workflow and patterns, we should choose which authentication method to implement.

As we most certainly know, the HTTP protocol is *stateless*, meaning that whatever we do during a request/response cycle will be lost before the subsequent request, including the authentication result. The only way we have to overcome this is to store that result somewhere, together with all its relevant data, such as user ID, login date/time, and last request time.

Sessions

Since few years ago, the most common and traditional method to do that was to store this data on the server by using either a memory-based, disk-based, or external session manager. Each session can be retrieved using a unique ID that the client receives with the authentication response, usually inside a *session cookie*, that will be transmitted to the server on each subsequent request.

Here's a brief diagram showing the **Session-Based Authentication Flow**:

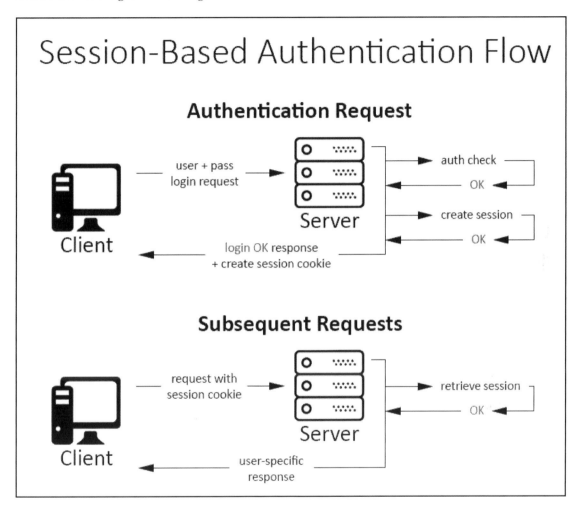

This is still a very common technique used by most web applications. There's nothing wrong with adopting this approach, as long as we are ok with its widely acknowledged downsides, such as the following:

- **Memory issues**: Whenever there are many authenticated users, the web server will consume more and more memory. Even if we use a file-based or external session provider, there will nonetheless be an intensive IO, TCP, or socket overhead.
- **Scalability issues**: Replicating a session provider in a scalable web farm might not be an easy task and will often lead to bottlenecks or wasted resources.
- **Cross-domain issues**: Session cookies behave just like standard cookies, so they cannot be easily shared among different origins/domains. These kinds of problem can be often solved with some workarounds, yet they will often lead to insecure scenarios to make things work.
- **Security issues**: There is a wide and detailed literature of security-related issues involving sessions and session cookies: XSS attacks, cross-site request forgery, and a number of other threats that won't be covered here for the sake of simplicity. Most of them can be mitigated by some countermeasures, yet they could be difficult to handle for first-hand developers.

As these issues arose over the years, there's no doubt that most analysts and developers put effort into figuring out different approaches.

Tokens

Token-based authentication has been increasingly adopted by single-page applications and mobile apps in the last few years for a number of undeniably good reasons that we'll try to briefly summarize here.

The most important difference between session-based authentication and token-based authentication is that the latter is *stateless*, meaning that we won't be storing any user-specific information on the server memory, database, session provider, or other data containers of any sort.

This single aspect solves most of the downsides that we pointed out earlier for session-based authentication. We won't have sessions, so there won't be an increasing overhead; we won't need a session provider, so scaling will be much easier; plus, for browsers supporting `LocalStorage`, we won't be even using cookies, so we won't get blocked by cross-origin restrictive policies and, hopefully, we'll get around most security issues.

Here's a typical **Token-Based Authentication Flow**:

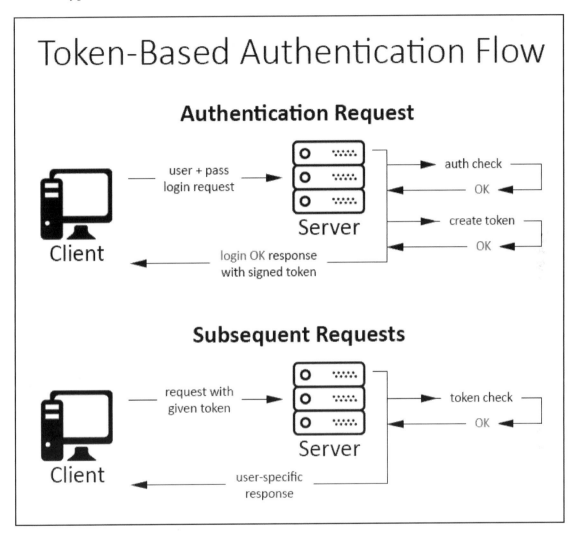

As we can see, the various steps seem very similar. The only big deal is the fact that we create/check tokens instead of creating/retrieving sessions from somewhere.

Signatures

This is a method used by most modern API-based cloud-computing and storage services, including **Amazon Web Services** (**AWS**). In contrast with session-based and token-based approaches, which rely upon a transport layer that can be theoretically accessed by/exposed to a third-party attacker, signature-based authentication performs a hash of the whole request using a previously shared `private` key. This ensures that no intruder or man-in-the-middle could ever act as the requesting user, as they won't be able to sign the request.

Two-factor

This is the standard authentication method used by most banking and financial accounts, being arguably the most secure one. The implementation may vary, but it always relies upon the following base workflow:

- The user performs a standard login with a username and password.
- The server identifies the user and prompts them with an additional, user-specific request that can be only satisfied by something obtained or obtainable through a different channel: an OTP password sent by SMS, a unique authentication card with a number of answer codes, a dynamic PIN generated by a proprietary device or a mobile app, and so on.
- If the user gives the correct answer, they get authenticated using a standard session-based or token-based method.

Conclusions

After reviewing all these authentication methods, we're going to use a token-based authentication approach featuring **JSON Web Tokens** (**JWT**), as it seems the most viable one for our specific scenario.

JWT is a JSON-based open standard explicitly designed for native web applications, available in multiple languages, such as .NET, Python, Java, PHP, Ruby, JavaScript/NodeJS, and PERL. We're choosing it because it's becoming a de facto standard for token authentication, as it's natively supported by most technologies.

For specific details about JWT, we recommend reading the following page:
`https://jwt.io/`

Implementing JSON web token authentication

In order to handle JWT-based token authentication, we need to implement the required middleware for doing these tasks:

- **Generating** the JWT tokens upon username/password `POST` requests coming from our client.
- **Validating** any JWT token coming with requests by looking at their `headers` and *cookies*

Although ASP.NET Core natively supports JWT tokens, the only available middleware is the one validating the request `headers` (`JwtBearerMiddleware`). This leaves us with two choices: manually implement what's missing or rely on a third-party library that does just that. We'll try the hand-made route throughout the rest of this chapter, leaving the other alternative to the following chapter.

The first thing to do is define the required steps we need to take care of:

1. Implement a custom **JWT provider** middleware to accept `POST` requests carrying a username and password, and generate JWT tokens accordingly.
2. Add it to the HTTP request pipeline, together with a properly configured `JwtBearerMiddleware` to validate incoming requests containing a JWT in their `headers` block.
3. Create an Angular 2 `Login` form to allow our users to perform the login.
4. Create an Angular 2 `Auth` service that will handle login/logout and store the JWT token so it can be reused.
5. Create an `AuthHttp` wrapper that will add the JWT (if present) to the `headers` block of each request.

Sounds like a plan…let's do this.

JWT provider

The first thing we need to do is to add the following packages to our project:

```
"Microsoft.IdentityModel.Tokens": "5.0.0",
"System.IdentityModel.Tokens.Jwt": "5.0.0"
```

As always, this can be done in a number of ways: **NuGet**, **GUI**, **project.json**, and others. We already know how to do that. The most recent version as we write is 5.0.0 for both packages, but we can expect it to change in the near future.

Once done, right-click to the **OpenGameListWebApp** project and create a /Classes/ folder. This is where we will put our custom implementations. We could also call it /AppCode/, /Infrastructure/, or anything else that we like.

Right-click on the new folder, choose the **Add | New Item** option, and add a new **ASP.NET | Middleware Class**, naming it JwtProvider.cs just like in the following screenshot:

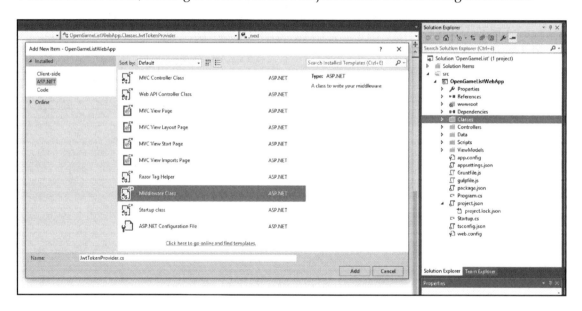

The new class will contain the default code for the ASP.NET core middleware class implementation pattern. We need to implement a lot of stuff here, so we'll split the content into several regions to make it more readable and understandable.

Private members

Let's add a **private members** region, wrapping the existing _next variable and adding the following (new lines highlighted):

```
#region private members
private readonly RequestDelegate _next;

// JWT-related members
private TimeSpan TokenExpiration;
private SigningCredentials SigningCredentials;
// EF and Identity members, available through DI
private ApplicationDbContext DbContext;
private UserManager<ApplicationUser> UserManager;
private SignInManager<ApplicationUser> SignInManager;
#endregion Private Members
```

Don't forget to add the required namespaces as well at the beginning of the file:

```
using Microsoft.IdentityModel.Tokens;
using Microsoft.AspNetCore.Identity;
using OpenGameListWebApp.Data.Users;
using OpenGameListWebApp.Data;
using System.Text;
```

As we can see, we're defining a number of variables here that we'll be using internally. Most of them will be instantiated in the constructor, either programmatically or by using the dependency injection pattern we've already used several times.

Static members

This region includes the minimum amount of info needed to sign in using a JWT token: a SecurityKey and an Issuer. We also define a TokenEndPoint here, which is the URL path that we will use to process the incoming authentication login requests. To put it in other words, it's the route that the JwtProvider will have to intercept (right before the standard MVC routing strategy) to properly handle the login requests:

```
#region Static Members
private static readonly string PrivateKey = "private_key_1234567890";
public static readonly SymmetricSecurityKey SecurityKey = new
SymmetricSecurityKey(Encoding.ASCII.GetBytes(PrivateKey));
public static readonly string Issuer = "OpenGameListWebApp";
public static string TokenEndPoint = "/api/connect/token";
#endregion Static Members
```

Notice that most of these static members have the `public` access modifier. That's because we'll be using them outside of this class when we'll have to configure the token verification middleware.

 Hardcoding these values in the provider source code is not ideal in production environments. We did it for the sake of simplicity, yet we should remember to adopt better and most secure approaches, such as storing them within an environment variable or a key management tool.

Constructor

Here's what the `Constructor` region looks like:

```
#region Constructor
public JwtProvider(
    RequestDelegate next,
    ApplicationDbContext dbContext,
    UserManager<ApplicationUser> userManager,
    SignInManager<ApplicationUser> signInManager)
{
    _next = next;

    // Instantiate JWT-related members
    TokenExpiration = TimeSpan.FromMinutes(10);
    SigningCredentials =  new SigningCredentials(SecurityKey,
SecurityAlgorithms.HmacSha256);

    // Instantiate through Dependency Injection
    DbContext = dbContext;
    UserManager = userManager;
    SignInManager = signInManager;
}
#endregion Constructor
```

Here, we define the JWT token expiration time and encrypt the symmetrical security key that will be used to validate JWTs using a standard `HmacSha256` encryption algorithm. We're also instantiating the EF/Identity members through DI, like we have done a number of times.

Public methods

Let's move to the `Invoke` method, which we conveniently wrapped inside the `public` methods region:

```
#region public methods
public Task Invoke(HttpContext httpContext)
{
    // Check if the request path matches our TokenEndPoint
    if (!httpContext.Request.Path.Equals(TokenEndPoint,
StringComparison.Ordinal)) return _next(httpContext);

    // Check if the current request is a valid POST with the appropriate
content type (application/x-www-form-urlencoded)
    if (httpContext.Request.Method.Equals("POST") &&
httpContext.Request.HasFormContentType)
    {
        // OK: generate token and send it via a json-formatted string
        return CreateToken(httpContext);
    }
    else
    {
        // Not OK: output a 400 - Bad request HTTP error.
        httpContext.Response.StatusCode = 400;
        return httpContext.Response.WriteAsync("Bad request.");
    }
}
#endregion public methods
```

Here, we need to check whether the request path matches the chosen login path. If it does, we continue execution, otherwise we entirely skip the request. Right after that, we need to check whether the current request is a valid *form-urlencoded* POST. If that's the case, we call the `CreateToken` internal method; otherwise, we return a `400` error response.

Private methods

The `CreateToken` method is where most of the magic takes place. We check the given username and password against our internal Identity database and, depending on the result, generate and return either a JWT token or an appropriate error response:

```
#region Private Methods
private async Task CreateToken(HttpContext httpContext)
{
    try
    {
        // retrieve the relevant FORM data
```

```
string username = httpContext.Request.Form["username"];
string password = httpContext.Request.Form["password"];

// check if there's an user with the given username
var user = await UserManager.FindByNameAsync(username);
// fallback to support e-mail address instead of username
if (user == null && username.Contains("@")) user = await
UserManager.FindByEmailAsync(username);

var success = user != null && await
UserManager.CheckPasswordAsync(user, password);
    if (success)
    {
        DateTime now = DateTime.UtcNow;

        // add the registered claims for JWT (RFC7519).
        // For more info, see https:
        //tools.ietf.org/html/rfc7519#section-4.1
        var claims = new[] {
        new Claim(JwtRegisteredClaimNames.Iss, Issuer),
        new Claim(JwtRegisteredClaimNames.Sub, user.Id),
        new Claim(JwtRegisteredClaimNames.Jti,
Guid.NewGuid().ToString()),
        new Claim(JwtRegisteredClaimNames.Iat, new
DateTimeOffset(now).ToUnixTimeSeconds().ToString(),
ClaimValueTypes.Integer64)
            // TODO: add additional claims here
        };

        // Create the JWT and write it to a string
        var token = new JwtSecurityToken(
        claims: claims,
        notBefore: now,
        expires: now.Add(TokenExpiration),
        signingCredentials: SigningCredentials);
        var encodedToken = new
JwtSecurityTokenHandler().WriteToken(token);

        // build the json response
        var jwt = new {
            access_token = encodedToken,
            expiration = (int)TokenExpiration.TotalSeconds
        };

        // return token
        httpContext.Response.ContentType = "application/json";
        await
httpContext.Response.WriteAsync(JsonConvert.SerializeObject(jwt));
```

```
        return;
      }
    }
  catch (Exception ex)
  {
      // TODO: handle errors
      throw ex;
  }

  httpContext.Response.StatusCode = 400;
  await httpContext.Response.WriteAsync("Invalid username or password.");
}
#endregion Private Methods
```

This will also require the following namespace references:

```
using System.IdentityModel.Tokens.Jwt;
using System.Security.Claims;
using Newtonsoft.Json;
```

The code is pretty much self-documented using some inline comments indicating what we're doing here and there. We can see how the username and password are retrieved from the `HttpContext` and checked using the `AspNetCore.Identity UserManager` class; if the user exists, we issue a JSON-formatted object containing a JWT token and its expiration time, otherwise we return a HTTP `400` error.

 It's also worth noting that, as an additional feature, we configured the method to allow clients to authenticate themselves using their *e-mail* address in place of the *username*; we did that to demonstrate how versatile this implementation actually is, since we do have full control over the whole authentication process.

Extension methods

The sample code provided for middleware classes includes a handy extension method that we can use to add our newborn provider to the request pipeline. We don't need to change it, so we'll just wrap it in an `extension methods` region:

```
#region Extension Methods
// Extension method used to add the middleware to the HTTP request
pipeline.
public static class JwtProviderExtensions
{
    public static IApplicationBuilder UseJwtProvider(this
IApplicationBuilder builder)
```

```
        {
            return builder.UseMiddleware<JwtProvider>();
        }
    }
    #endregion Extension Methods
```

Full source code

Here's how our `JwtProvider` class will look after all this hard work:

```
using System;
using System.Text;
using System.Threading.Tasks;
using Microsoft.AspNetCore.Builder;
using Microsoft.AspNetCore.Http;
using Microsoft.IdentityModel.Tokens;
using OpenGameListWebApp.Data;
using Microsoft.AspNetCore.Identity;
using OpenGameListWebApp.Data.Users;
using System.IdentityModel.Tokens.Jwt;
using System.Security.Claims;
using Newtonsoft.Json;

namespace OpenGameListWebApp.Classes
{
    public class JwtProvider
    {
        #region Private Members
        private readonly RequestDelegate _next;

        // JWT-related members
        private TimeSpan TokenExpiration;
        private SigningCredentials SigningCredentials;

        // EF and Identity members, available through DI
        private ApplicationDbContext DbContext;
        private UserManager<ApplicationUser> UserManager;
        private SignInManager<ApplicationUser> SignInManager;
        #endregion Private Members

        #region Static Members
        private static readonly string PrivateKey =
"private_key_1234567890";
        public static readonly SymmetricSecurityKey SecurityKey = new
SymmetricSecurityKey(Encoding.ASCII.GetBytes(PrivateKey));
        public static readonly string Issuer = "OpenGameListWebApp";
        public static string TokenEndPoint = "/api/connect/token";
```

```
        #endregion Static Members

        #region Constructor
        public JwtProvider(
            RequestDelegate next,
            ApplicationDbContext dbContext,
            UserManager<ApplicationUser> userManager,
            SignInManager<ApplicationUser> signInManager)
        {

            _next = next;

            // Instantiate JWT-related members
            TokenExpiration = TimeSpan.FromMinutes(10);
            SigningCredentials =  new SigningCredentials(SecurityKey,
SecurityAlgorithms.HmacSha256);

            // Instantiate through Dependency Injection
            DbContext = dbContext;
            UserManager = userManager;
            SignInManager = signInManager;
        }
        #endregion Constructor

        #region Public Methods
        public Task Invoke(HttpContext httpContext)
        {
            // Check if the request path matches our LoginPath
            if (!httpContext.Request.Path.Equals(TokenEndPoint,
StringComparison.Ordinal)) return _next(httpContext);

            // Check if the current request is a valid POST with the
appropriate content type (application/x-www-form-urlencoded)
            if (httpContext.Request.Method.Equals("POST") &&
httpContext.Request.HasFormContentType)
            {
                // OK: generate token and send it via a json-formatted
string
                return CreateToken(httpContext);
            }
            else
            {
                // Not OK: output a 400 - Bad request HTTP error.
                httpContext.Response.StatusCode = 400;
                return httpContext.Response.WriteAsync("Bad request.");
            }
        }
        #endregion Public Methods
```

```
#region Private Methods
private async Task CreateToken(HttpContext httpContext)
{
    try
    {
        // retrieve the relevant FORM data
        string username = httpContext.Request.Form["username"];
        string password = httpContext.Request.Form["password"];

        // check if there's an user with the given username
        var user = await UserManager.FindByNameAsync(username);
        // fallback to support e-mail address instead of username
        if (user == null && username.Contains("@")) user = await
UserManager.FindByEmailAsync(username);

        var success = user != null && await
UserManager.CheckPasswordAsync(user, password);
        if (success)
        {
            DateTime now = DateTime.UtcNow;

            // add the registered claims for JWT (RFC7519).
            // For more info, see
https://tools.ietf.org/html/rfc7519#section-4.1
            var claims = new[] {
                new Claim(JwtRegisteredClaimNames.Iss, Issuer),
                new Claim(JwtRegisteredClaimNames.Sub, username),
                new Claim(JwtRegisteredClaimNames.Jti,
Guid.NewGuid().ToString()),
                new Claim(JwtRegisteredClaimNames.Iat, new
DateTimeOffset(now).ToUnixTimeSeconds().ToString(),
ClaimValueTypes.Integer64)
                // TODO: add additional claims here
            };

            // Create the JWT and write it to a string
            var token = new JwtSecurityToken(
                claims: claims,
                notBefore: now,
                expires: now.Add(TokenExpiration),
                signingCredentials: SigningCredentials);
            var encodedToken = new
JwtSecurityTokenHandler().WriteToken(token);

            // build the json response
            var jwt = new {
                access_token = encodedToken,
                expiration = (int)TokenExpiration.TotalSeconds
```

```
                };

                // return token
                httpContext.Response.ContentType = "application/json";
                await
httpContext.Response.WriteAsync(JsonConvert.SerializeObject(jwt));
                return;
            }
        }
        catch (Exception ex)
        {
            // TODO: handle errors
        }

        httpContext.Response.StatusCode = 400;
        await httpContext.Response.WriteAsync("Invalid username or
password.");
    }
    #endregion Private Methods
}

#region Extension Methods
// Extension method used to add the middleware to the HTTP request
pipeline.
public static class JwtProviderExtensions
{
    public static IApplicationBuilder UseJwtProvider(this
IApplicationBuilder builder)
    {
        return builder.UseMiddleware<JwtProvider>();
    }
}
#endregion Extension Methods
}
```

Adding the middleware to the pipeline

Now that we have created our `JwtProvider` middleware, we can add it to the request pipeline together with the built-in `JwtBearerMiddleware`. In order to do that, open the `Startup.cs` file and add the following code to the `Configure` method (new lines highlighted):

```
public void Configure(IApplicationBuilder app, IHostingEnvironment env,
ILoggerFactory loggerFactory, DbSeeder dbSeeder)
{
    loggerFactory.AddConsole(Configuration.GetSection("Logging"));
```

```
    loggerFactory.AddDebug();

    // Configure a rewrite rule to auto-lookup for standard default files
such as index.html.
    app.UseDefaultFiles();

    // Serve static files (html, css, js, images & more). See also the
following URL:
    // https://docs.asp.net/en/latest/fundamentals/static-files.html for
further reference.
    app.UseStaticFiles(new StaticFileOptions()
    {
        OnPrepareResponse = (context) =>
        {
            // Disable caching for all static files.
            context.Context.Response.Headers["Cache-Control"] =
Configuration["StaticFiles:Headers:Cache-Control"];
            context.Context.Response.Headers["Pragma"] =
Configuration["StaticFiles:Headers:Pragma"];
            context.Context.Response.Headers["Expires"] =
Configuration["StaticFiles:Headers:Expires"];
        }
    });

    // Add a custom Jwt Provider to generate Tokens
    app.UseJwtProvider();
    // Add the Jwt Bearer Header Authentication to validate Tokens
    app.UseJwtBearerAuthentication(new JwtBearerOptions()
    {
        AutomaticAuthenticate = true,
        AutomaticChallenge = true,
        RequireHttpsMetadata = false,
        TokenValidationParameters = new TokenValidationParameters()
        {
            IssuerSigningKey = JwtProvider.SecurityKey,
            ValidateIssuerSigningKey = true,
            ValidIssuer = JwtProvider.Issuer,
            ValidateIssuer = false,
            ValidateAudience = false
        }
    });

    // Add MVC to the pipeline
    app.UseMvc();

    // TinyMapper binding configuration
    TinyMapper.Bind<Item, ItemViewModel>();
```

```
        // Seed the Database (if needed)
        try
        {
            dbSeeder.SeedAsync().Wait();
        }
        catch (AggregateException e)
        {
            throw new Exception(e.ToString());
        }
    }
```

To avoid compilation errors, be sure to declare the following namespaces to the beginning of the file:

```
using OpenGameListWebApp.Classes;
using Microsoft.IdentityModel.Tokens;
```

It's important to focus on two important things here:

- **Middleware order does indeed count**. Notice how MVC gets added after JwtProvider and JwtBearerAuthentication, so the MVC default routing strategies won't interfere with them.
- **There's no AspNetCore.Identity middleware in there**. We purposely avoided calling the app.UseIdentity() extension because it internally wraps app.UseCookieAuthentication(), which is something we don't need. We might want to add it if we want to support cookies over headers, or even use both of them.

> To know more about what's under the hood of app.UseIdentity(), it can be useful to take a look at the extension's source code, which is publicly available on **GitHub** at the following URL: https://github.com/aspnet/Identity/blob/dev/src/Microsoft.AspNetCore.Identity/BuilderExtensions.cs.

With this, we're done with the server-side part of our job. Let's switch to the client side.

Angular 2 login form

Remember that /Scripts/app/login.component.ts sample we created back in Chapter 3, *Angular 2 Components and Client-Side Routing*. The time has come to update it into a proper login form.

Open that file and modify the existing, almost empty `template` with the following code:

```
<div class="login-container">
    <h2 class="form-login-heading">Login</h2>
    <div class="alert alert-danger" role="alert" *ngIf="loginError">
        <strong>Warning:</strong> Username or Password mismatch
    </div>
    <form class="form-login" [formGroup]="loginForm"
(submit)="performLogin($event)">
        <input formControlName="username" type="text" class="form-control"
placeholder="Your username or e-mail address" required autofocus />
        <input formControlName="password" type="password" class="form-
control" placeholder="Your password" required />
        <div class="checkbox">
            <label>
                <input type="checkbox" value="remember-me">
                Remember me
            </label>
        </div>
        <button class="btn btn-lg btn-primary btn-block" type="submit">Sign
in</button>
    </form>
</div>
```

That's a simple login form with some Bootstrap and custom classes. Notice that we also defined an `ngFormModel` and an event handler method called `performLogin` that will trigger on each submit. Both should be added within the component's `class` implementation in the following way (new lines highlighted):

```
export class LoginComponent {
    title = "Login";
    loginForm = null;
    constructor(private fb: FormBuilder) {
        this.loginForm = fb.group({
            username: ["", Validators.required],
            password: ["", Validators.required]
        });
    }
    performLogin(e) {
        e.preventDefault();
        alert(JSON.stringify(this.loginForm.value));
    }
}
```

We're introducing two new classes here:

- **FormBuilder**: This is a factory class for creating instances of type `FormGroup`, which is how Angular 2 handles model-driven (or reactive) forms, we'll say more regarding this topic in a short while.
- **Validators**: Angular has three built-in form validations that can be applied using this class. These are `Validators.required`, `Validators.minLength(n)`, and `Validators.maxLength(n)`. The names are self-explanatory, so we'll just say that we're using the first one, at least for now.

In order to use these classes, we need to add the following `import` statement at the beginning of the file:

```
import {FormBuilder, Validators} from "@angular/forms";
```

As we can see, there's also a `performLogin` method that we didn't implement much. We're just opening a UI alert to ensure us that everything is working so far, then bring the user back to our welcome view.

While we're here, let's take the chance to also add the `Router` component, so we'll be able to send the user somewhere right after the login. We can easily do that using the same DI technique we've already used a number of times.

This is how the `login.component.ts` will look after these changes:

```
import {Component} from "@angular/core";
import {FormBuilder, Validators} from "@angular/forms";
import {Router} from "@angular/router";

@Component({
    selector: "login",
    template: `
    <div class="login-container">
      <h2 class="form-login-heading">Login</h2>
      <form class="form-login" [ngFormModel]="loginForm"
(submit)="performLogin($event)">
        <input ngControl="username" type="text" class="form-control"
placeholder="Your username or e-mail address" required autofocus />
        <input ngControl="password" type="password" class="form-control"
placeholder="Your password" required />
        <div class="checkbox">
          <label>
            <input type="checkbox" value="remember-me"> Remember me
          </label>
        </div>
        <button class="btn btn-lg btn-primary btn-block" type="submit">Sign
```

```
in</button>
        </form>
    </div>
    `
})

export class LoginComponent {
    title = "Login";
    loginForm = null;

    constructor(
        private fb: FormBuilder,
        private router: Router) {
        this.loginForm = fb.group({
            username: ["", Validators.required],
            password: ["", Validators.required]
        });
    }

    performLogin(e) {
        e.preventDefault();
        alert(JSON.stringify(this.loginForm.value));
    }
}
```

Adding styles

As for the custom CSS classes, we can add them to our `Scripts/less/style.less` file:

```
.login-container {
    max-width: 330px;
    padding: 15px;
    .form-login {
        margin: 0 0 10px 20px;
        .checkbox {
            margin-bottom: 10px;
        }
        input {
            margin-bottom: 10px;
        }
    }
}
```

Updating the root module file

Our renewed `LoginComponent` should compile just fine. However, if we try to run the app now, we would get a full-scale Angular 2 runtime error in the browser's console log:

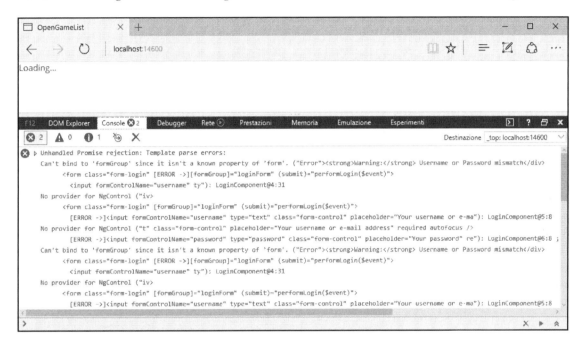

Pretty scary, isn't it?

When we see something like that in Angular 2, it usually means that we're missing a required module. That's exactly the case. In order to use reactive forms classes, we need to open our `/Scripts/app/app.module.ts` file and append `ReactiveFormsModule` to the following existing `import` statement, near the beginning of the file:

```
import {FormsModule, ReactiveFormsModule} from "@angular/forms";
```

And also add it to the `imports` array as follows:

```
imports: [
    BrowserModule,
    HttpModule,
    FormsModule,
    ReactiveFormsModule,
    RouterModule,
    AppRouting
],
```

Once done, our application will be able to run without errors.

Wait a minute...`FormsModule` has been there since `Chapter 3`, *Angular 2 Components and Client-Side Routing*! On top of that, we even used it to build the `ItemDetailEditComponent` form, which happens to work just fine! Why do we need `ReactiveFormsModule` now?

As a matter of fact, we don't; we could stick to the `FormsModule` and build another template-driven form just like the one we already did. As a matter of fact, since this is a tutorial application, we took the chance to use the alternative strategy provided by Angular 2 to build forms: the model-driven (or reactive) forms approach.

This clarification raises a predictable question: which one of them is better? The answer is not easy, as both techniques have their advantages. To keep it extremely simple, we can say that template-driven forms are generally simpler to pull off, but they're rather difficult to test and validate as they become complex; conversely, model-driven forms do have an harder learning curve but they usually perform better when dealing with large forms, as they allow us to unit test their whole validation logic.

 We won't explore these topics further, as they would take us way beyond the scope of this book. For more info regarding template-driven and model-driven forms, we strongly suggest reading the following article from the Angular 2 developers blog:
`http://blog.angular-university.io/introduction-to-angular-2-form` `s-template-driven-vs-model-driven/`
And also check out the official Angular 2 documentation regarding forms:
`https://angular.io/docs/ts/latest/guide/forms.html`

UI and validation test

Let's do a quick test right now. Hit *F5* and click on the **Login** top navigation bar. We should be welcomed by something like this:

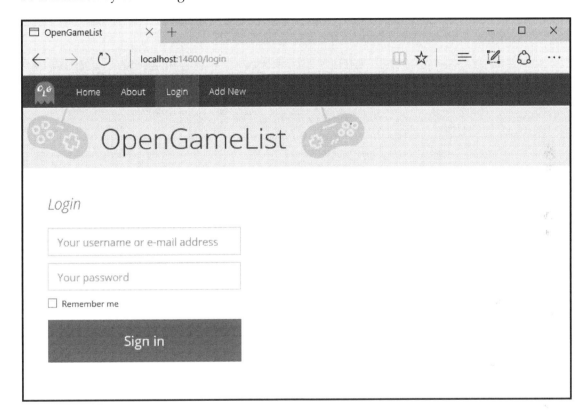

Let's now check the *validators* by hitting the **Sign in** button, leaving the input fields empty. We can see the two textboxes react accordingly, since they're both expecting a required value:

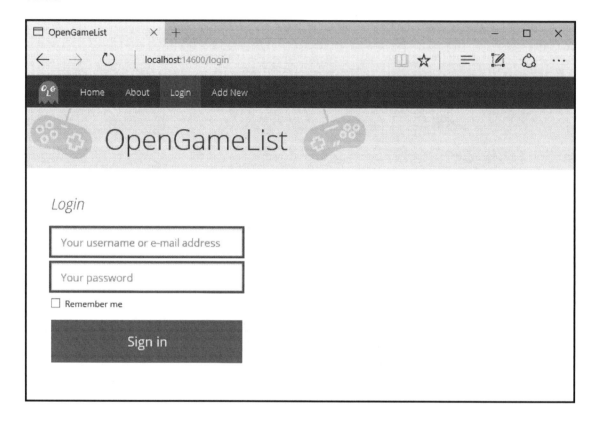

Finally, let's test the outcome JSON by filling up the input fields with some random values and pressing the **Sign in** button again:

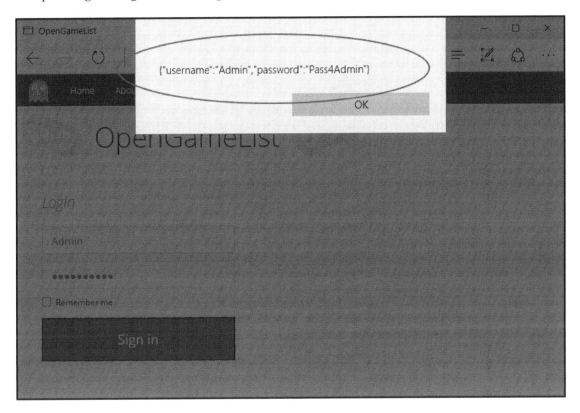

That's it. It seems that our login form is working fine.

AuthService component

Now we need to create a dedicated service to handle the login and logout operations.

Right-click on the /Scripts/app/ folder, select **Add** | **New Item** and add a new auth.service.ts file to the project, then fill it with the following code:

```
import {Injectable, EventEmitter} from "@angular/core";
import {Http, Headers, Response, RequestOptions} from "@angular/http";
import {Observable} from "rxjs/Observable";

@Injectable()
export class AuthService {
    authKey = "auth";

    constructor(private http: Http) {
    }

    login(username: string, password: string): any {
        var url = "api/connect/token";   // JwtProvider's LoginPath

        var data = {
            username: username,
            password: password,
            client_id: "OpenGameList",
            // required when signing up with username/password
            grant_type: "password",
            // space-separated list of scopes for which the token is issued
            scope: "offline_access profile email"
        };

        return this.http.post(
            url,
            this.toUrlEncodedString(data),
            new RequestOptions({
                headers: new Headers({
                    "Content-Type": "application/x-www-form-urlencoded"
                })
            }))
            .map(response => {
                var auth = response.json();
                console.log("The following auth JSON object has been
received:");
                console.log(auth);
                this.setAuth(auth);
                return auth;
            });
```

```
    }

    logout(): boolean {
        this.setAuth(null);
        return false;
    }

    // Converts a Json object to urlencoded format
    toUrlEncodedString(data: any) {
        var body = "";
        for (var key in data) {
            if (body.length) {
                body += "&";
            }
            body += key + "=";
            body += encodeURIComponent(data[key]);
        }
        return body;
    }

    // Persist auth into localStorage or removes it if a NULL argument is
given
    setAuth(auth: any): boolean {
        if (auth) {
            localStorage.setItem(this.authKey, JSON.stringify(auth));
        }
        else {
            localStorage.removeItem(this.authKey);
        }
        return true;
    }

    // Retrieves the auth JSON object (or NULL if none)
    getAuth(): any {
        var i = localStorage.getItem(this.authKey);
        if (i) {
            return JSON.parse(i);
        }
        else {
            return null;
        }
    }

    // Returns TRUE if the user is logged in, FALSE otherwise.
    isLoggedIn(): boolean {
        return localStorage.getItem(this.authKey) != null;
    }
}
```

This code has some resemblance to the one we used in the `item.service.ts` class. This can be expected, since both are Angular 2 service-type components used to instantiate service accessor objects, with the purpose of sending and receiving data to and from the web APIs. However, there are some key differences that might be worthy of attention:

- The content-type set for the `Login` method's `POST` request has been set to `application/x-www-form-urlencoded` instead of `application/json` to comply with the requirements set in the `JwtProvider` class.
- We store the result locally by making use of the `localStorage` object, which is part of HTML5's Web Storage API. This is a local caching object that keeps its content with no given expiration date. That's a great way to store our JWT-related JSON response, as we want to keep it even when the browser is closed. Before doing that, we choose to convert it into a `string` using `JSON.stringify`, since not all `localStorage` browser implementations can store JSON-type objects flawlessly.

 Alternatively, in case we were to delete the token whenever the user closes the specific browser tab, we could use the `sessionStorage` object, which stores data only until the currently active session ends.

It's worth noting that we defined three methods to handle `localStorage`: `setAuth()`, `getAuth()`, and `isLoggedIn()`. The first one is in charge of `insert`, `update`, and `delete` operations; the second will retrieve the `auth` JSON object (if any); and the last one can be used to check whether the current user is authenticated or not, without having to `JSON.parse` it.

Updating the AppModule

In order to test our new `AuthService` component, we need to hook it up to the `AppModule` and to the `LoginComponent` we created a short while ago.

Open the `/Scripts/app/app.module.ts` file and add the following `import` line between the `AppRouting` and `ItemService` lines:

```
import {AppRouting} from "./app.routing";
import {AuthService} from "./auth.service";
import {ItemService} from "./item.service";
```

Then scroll down to the providers array and add it there too:

```
providers: [
```

```
        AuthService,
        ItemService
    ],
```

Updating the LoginComponent

Once done, switch back to the `Scripts/app/login.component.ts` file and replace the content of the source code as follows (new/updated lines are highlighted):

```
import {Component} from "@angular/core";
import {FormBuilder, Validators} from "@angular/forms";
import {Router} from "@angular/router";
import {AuthService} from "./auth.service";

@Component({
    selector: "login",
    template: `
    <div class="login-container">
      <h2 class="form-login-heading">Login</h2>
      <div class="alert alert-danger" role="alert"
*ngIf="loginError"><strong>Warning:</strong> Username or Password
mismatch</div>
      <form class="form-login" [formGroup]="loginForm"
(submit)="performLogin($event)">
        <input formControlName="username" type="text" class="form-control"
placeholder="Your username or e-mail address" required autofocus />
        <input formControlName="password" type="password" class="form-
control" placeholder="Your password" required />
        <div class="checkbox">
          <label>
            <input type="checkbox" value="remember-me">
            Remember me
          </label>
        </div>
        <button class="btn btn-lg btn-primary btn-block" type="submit">Sign
in</button>
      </form>
    </div>
    `
})

export class LoginComponent {
    title = "Login";
    loginForm = null;
    loginError = false;

    constructor(
```

```
            private fb: FormBuilder,

    private router: Router,
      private authService: AuthService) {
            this.loginForm = fb.group({
                username: ["", Validators.required],
                password: ["", Validators.required]
            });
        }

        performLogin(e) {
            e.preventDefault();
            var username = this.loginForm.value.username;
            var password = this.loginForm.value.password;
            this.authService.login(username, password)
                .subscribe((data) => {
                    // login successful
                    this.loginError = false;
                    var auth = this.authService.getAuth();
                    alert("Our Token is: " + auth.access_token);
                    this.router.navigate([""]);
                },
                (err) => {
                    console.log(err);
                    // login failure
                    this.loginError = true;
                });
        }
    }
```

What we did here is pretty straightforward:

- We included the import reference for our `AuthService` component and added it to the constructor, so we can have it available using DI.
- We added a new `loginError` local variable that will reflect the outcome of the last login attempt.
- We added a `<div>` element acting as an alert, to be shown whenever the `loginError` becomes `true`.
- We modified the `performLogin` method to make it send the username and password values to the `AuthService` component's `login` method, so it can perform the following tasks:
    - Issue an HTTP request to the `JwtProvider` middleware
    - Receive a valid JWT accordingly and persist it into the `localStorage` object cache

- Return `true` in case of success or `false` in case of failure
- If everything goes as expected, we'll be shown a confirmation popup alert and route the user back to the welcome view; otherwise, we'll show the wrong username or password alert above the form

Login test

Let's run a quick test to see whether everything is working as expected. Hit *F5*, then navigate through the login view using the top navigation menu. Once there, fill in the login form with some incorrect data to test the **Wrong Username or Password** alert and left-click on the **Sign in** button:

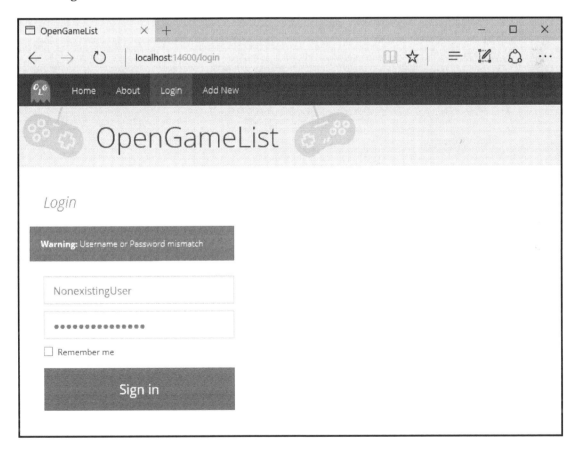

Now, let's test a successful login attempt by filling in the form again, this time using the actual Admin user credentials as defined within the `DbSeeder` class:

- E-mail: **Admin**
- Password: **Pass4Admin**

Then, left-click on the **Sign in** button.

If everything has been set up properly, we should receive the following response:

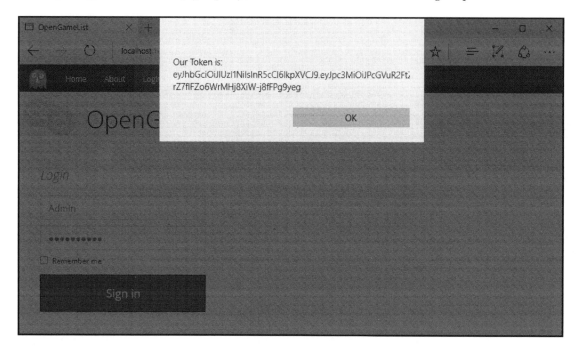

If we see something like this, it means that our `JwtProvider` works!

All we need to do now is to find a way to put that token inside the `headers` of all our subsequent requests, so we can check the token validation as well and complete our authentication cycle.

AuthHttp wrapper

A rather easy way to do that with Angular 2 is create a wrapper class that will internally use the standard `Http` component right after having it configured to suit our needs.

Right-click on the `/Scripts/app/` folder, then select **Add** | **New Item**. Add a new `auth.http.ts` file to the project and fill it with the following code:

```
import {Injectable} from '@angular/core';
import {Http, Headers} from '@angular/http';

@Injectable()
export class AuthHttp {
    http = null;
    authKey = "auth";

    constructor(http: Http) {
        this.http = http;
    }

    get(url, opts = {}) {
        this.configureAuth(opts);
        return this.http.get(url, opts);
    }

    post(url, data, opts = {}) {
        this.configureAuth(opts);
        return this.http.post(url, data, opts);
    }

    put(url, data, opts = {}) {
        this.configureAuth(opts);
        return this.http.put(url, data, opts);
    }

    delete(url, opts = {}) {
        this.configureAuth(opts);
        return this.http.delete(url, opts);
    }

    configureAuth(opts: any) {
        var i = localStorage.getItem(this.authKey);
        if (i != null) {
            var auth = JSON.parse(i);
            console.log(auth);
            if (auth.access_token != null) {
                if (opts.headers == null) {
```

```
                    opts.headers = new Headers();
                }
                opts.headers.set("Authorization", `Bearer
    ${auth.access_token}`);
            }
        }
    }
}
```

There's not much to say here, it's just a wrapper that calls the `configureAuth` method internally to add the JWT token stored in the browser's `localStorage`, if any, to each request's `headers`.

Since we'll be using the `AuthHttp` wrapper anywhere in our application, the first thing we need to do is add it to the application's `root` module, just like we did with the `AuthService` a short while ago. Open the `Scripts/app/app.module.ts` file and add the usual import line between `AppRouting` and `AuthService`:

```
import {AppRouting} from "./app.routing";
import {AuthHttp} from "./auth.http";
import {AuthService} from "./auth.service";
```

And also add it to the `providers` array as follows:

```
providers: [
    AuthHttp,
    AuthService,
    ItemService
],
```

Now we can update each and every `Http` reference included in our other Angular 2 files and replace them with `AuthHttp`. As we can easily guess, the affected components are the two service classes we're using to connect through the web API interface: `auth.service.ts` and `item.service.ts`.

For both of them, we need to add the following line at the beginning of the file:

```
import {AuthHttp} from "./auth.http";
```

And change the constructor parameters in the following way:

```
constructor(private http: AuthHttp) {
```

Adding authorization rules

It's time to see whether our manual JWT-based `auth` implementation is working as expected. Before doing that, though, we need to define some testable navigation patterns that will allow us to differentiate the logged-in user from the anonymous one. It's actually easy to do that, since we already have some content that should be made accessible to authenticated users only. We need to handle them on the client side and also on the server side.

Adapting the client

Let's start by updating the main menu navigation bar. Open the `Scripts/app/app.component.ts` file and add the following `import` reference near the top:

```
import {AuthService} from "./auth.service";
```

Right after that, change the `template` section in the following way (new/updated lines are highlighted):

```
<nav class="navbar navbar-default navbar-fixed-top">
    <div class="container-fluid">
        <input type="checkbox" id="navbar-toggle-cbox">
        <div class="navbar-header">
            <label for="navbar-toggle-cbox" class="navbar-toggle collapsed"
data-toggle="collapse" data-target="#navbar" aria-expanded="false" aria-
controls="navbar">
                <span class="sr-only">Toggle navigation</span>
                <span class="icon-bar"></span>
                <span class="icon-bar"></span>
                <span class="icon-bar"></span>
            </label>
            <a class="navbar-brand" href="javascript:void(0)">
                <img alt="logo" src="/img/logo.svg" />
            </a>
        </div>
        <div class="collapse navbar-collapse" id="navbar">
            <ul class="nav navbar-nav">
                <li [class.active]="isActive([''])">
                    <a class="home" [routerLink]="['']">Home</a>
                </li>
                <li [class.active]="isActive(['about'])">
                    <a class="about" [routerLink]="['about']">About</a>
                </li>
                <li *ngIf="!authService.isLoggedIn()"
```

```
                [class.active]="isActive(['login'])">
                    <a class="login" [routerLink]="['login']">Login</a>
                </li>
                 <li *ngIf="authService.isLoggedIn()">
                    <a class="logout" href="javascript:void(0)"
                    (click)="logout()">Logout</a>
                </li>
                <li *ngIf="authService.isLoggedIn()"
                [class.active]="isActive(['item/edit', 0])">
                    <a class="add" [routerLink]="['item/edit', 0]">Add
    New</a>
                </li>
            </ul>
        </div>
    </div>
</nav>
<h1 class="header">{{title}}</h1>
<div class="main-container">
    <router-outlet></router-outlet>
</div>
```

What we did here is pretty easy to understand:

- We added a `ngIf` built-in directive to the **Login** menu element, since we don't want it to appear if the user is already logged in.
- We also added another **Logout** menu element with similar yet opposing behavior, as we don't want it to be seen if the user is not logged in. Clicking on this element will trigger the `logout()` method, which we'll be adding shortly.
- We added another `ngIf` condition to the **New Item** menu element, as it should be seen by logged-in users only.

In order to use the `authService` object, we also need to instantiate it through *dependency injection* within the class constructor, which is another thing we have to change (new/updated lines highlighted):

```
constructor(public router: Router, public authService: AuthService) { }
```

Finally, we need to implement that `logout()` method we talked about earlier:

```
logout(): boolean {
    // logs out the user, then redirects him to Welcome View.
    if (this.authService.logout()) {
        this.router.navigate([""]);
    }
    return false;
}
```

Nothing odd here, just a standard logout and redirect behavior to adopt when the user chooses to perform a `logout`.

The changes we applied to the `AppComponent` template should also be performed in the `ItemDetailViewComponent` templates as well. Open `Scripts/app/item-detail-view.component.ts` and add the import line:

```
import {AuthService} from "./auth.service";
```

Then move to the constructor and add the `AuthService` reference there for DI (new code highlighted):

```
constructor(
    private authService: AuthService,
    private itemService: ItemService,
    private router: Router,
    private activatedRoute: ActivatedRoute) { }
```

And finally, update the `template` section accordingly, using the same `ngIf` built-in directive we used before to show/hide the **Edit** tab accordingly to the current user's logged in status:

```
<li *ngIf="authService.isLoggedIn()" role="presentation">
    <a href="javascript:void(0)" (click)="onItemDetailEdit(item)">Edit</a>
</li>
```

Testing the client

Let's hit *F5* and see whether everything is working as it should. We should start as anonymous users and see something like this:

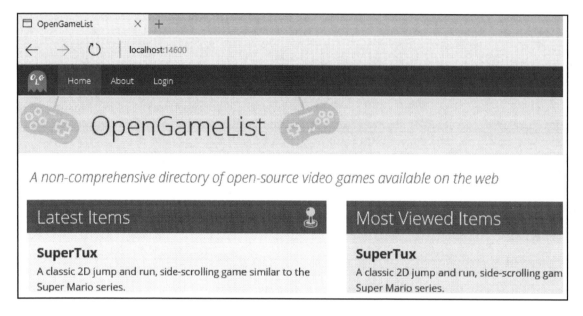

We can see that the **New Item** menu element is gone. That's expected; we're not logged in, so we shouldn't be able to add a new item.

From there, we can click the **Login** menu element and be brought to the login view, where we can input the admin credentials (`admin`/`pass4admin`, in case we forgot). As soon as we hit the **Sign In** button, we will be routed back to the welcome view, where we should be greeted by something like the following screenshot:

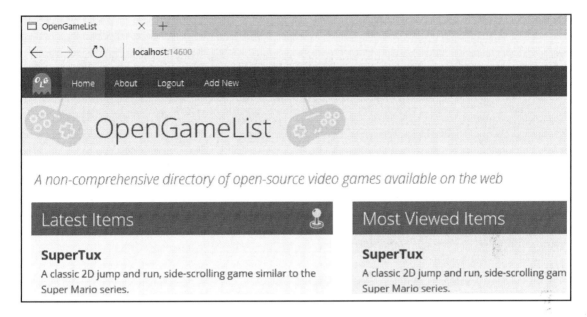

The **Login** menu element is gone, replaced by **Logout** and **Add New**. We can then click on **Logout** and see both of them replaced by the former again.

So far, so good. However, we're not done with the client yet. These modifications prevent the user from clicking some links they're not allowed to see, yet they are unable to stop the user from going to their given destinations. For example, the user could manually input the routes within the browser's navigation bar and go to the login view while being already logged in, or even worse access the add/edit item view despite being anonymous.

In order to avoid that, we can add a login status check within the `login.component.ts` constructor (new lines highlighted):

```
constructor(
    private fb: FormBuilder,
    private router: Router,
    private authService: AuthService) {
    if (this.authService.isLoggedIn()) {
        this.router.navigate([""]);
    }
    this.loginForm = fb.group({
        username: ["", Validators.required],
        password: ["", Validators.required]
    });
}
```

Also add it to the `ngOnInit` startup method within the `item-detail-edit.component.ts` file:

```
ngOnInit() {
    if (!this.authService.isLoggedIn()) {
        this.router.navigate([""]);
    }
    var id = +this.activatedRoute.snapshot.params["id"];
    if (id) {
        this.itemService.get(id).subscribe(
            item => this.item = item
        );
    }
    else if (id === 0) {
        console.log("id is 0: adding a new item...");
        this.item = new Item(0, "New Item", null);
    }
    else {
        console.log("Invalid id: routing back to home...");
        this.router.navigate([""]);
    }
}
```

Doing this will also require adding the corresponding `import` reference line near the topmost section of the `item-detail-edit.component.ts` file:

```
import {AuthService} from "./auth.service";
```

And the DI injection in the constructor method:

```
constructor(
    private authService: AuthService,
    private itemService: ItemService,
    private router: Router,
    private activatedRoute: ActivatedRoute) { }
```

That way, any unauthorized user will be bounced back whenever they try to manually hack our route mechanism by issuing a direct request to these views.

Protecting the server

Now that our client is more or less ready, it's time to shield our web API interface from unauthorized requests as well. We can easily do that using the `[Authorize]` attribute, which can be used to restrict access to any controller and/or controller method we don't want to open to unauthorized access.

To implement the required authorization behavior, it could be wise to use it on the Add, Update, and Delete methods of our ItemsController class (new lines are highlighted):

```
[HttpPost()]
[Authorize]
public IActionResult Add([FromBody]ItemViewModel ivm)
{
    [...]
}

[HttpPut("{id}")]
[Authorize]
public IActionResult Update(int id, [FromBody]ItemViewModel ivm)
{
    [...]
}

[HttpDelete("{id}")]
[Authorize]
public IActionResult Delete(int id)
{
    [...]
}
```

In order to use the [Authorize] attribute, we also need to declare the following namespace reference at the beginning of the file:

```
using Microsoft.AspNetCore.Authorization;
```

Now these methods are protected against unauthorized access, as they will accept only requests coming from logged-in users/clients with a valid JWT token. Those who don't have it will receive a 401 - Unauthorized HTTP error response.

Retrieving the user ID

Before closing the ItemsController class file, we should take the chance to remove the item.UserId value override we defined back in Chapter 5, *Persisting Changes*, when we had no authentication mechanism in place:

```
// TODO: replace the following with the current user's id when
authentication will be available.
item.UserId = DbContext.Users.Where(u => u.UserName ==
"Admin").FirstOrDefault().Id;
```

Now that we're working with real users, we definitely have to remove this ugly workaround and find a way to retrieve the actual user ID. Luckily enough, when we implemented our very own JWT provider earlier, we did actually put it in the claims JWT token (`JwtProvider` class, `CreateToken` method):

```
new Claim(JwtRegisteredClaimNames.Sub, user.Id),
```

This means that we can retrieve it in the following way (updated code is highlighted):

```
item.UserId = User.FindFirst(ClaimTypes.NameIdentifier).Value;>
```

Let's perform this change and move on.

 This minor update should be enough for now. However, it won't work when dealing with external OpenId and/or OAuth2 providers, as they will put their own data in these claims. Retrieving our local `UserId` in such scenarios will require some additional work, such as querying a dedicated lookup table. We'll see more about this during `Chapter 8`, *Third-Party Authentication and External Providers*.

Authorization test

Before going further, it's definitely time to perform a client/server interaction test to ensure that our authorization pattern is working as expected.

From the Visual Studio source code editing interface, we can put a breakpoint right below the `ItemsControllerAdd` method:

```
/// <summary>
/// POST: api/items
/// </summary>
/// <returns>Creates a new Item and return it accordingly.</returns>
[HttpPost()]
[Authorize]
public IActionResult Add([FromBody]ItemViewModel ivm)
{
    if (ivm != null)
    {
        // create a new Item with the client-sent json data
        var item = TinyMapper.Map<Item>(ivm);

        // override any property that could be wise to set from server-side only
        item.CreatedDate =
        item.LastModifiedDate = DateTime.Now;
```

Once done, we can hit *F5*, navigate from the welcome view to the login view, and authenticate ourselves. Right after that, we'll be able to click upon the **Add New** menu element.

From there, we can fill in the form with some random text and click on the **Save** button. The form will consequently call the Add method of ItemsController, hopefully triggering our breakpoint.

Open a **Watch** window (**Debug** | **Windows** | **Watch** | **Watch 1**) and check the HttpContext.User.Identity.IsAuthenticated property value:

```
/// <summary>
/// POST: api/items
/// </summary>
/// <returns>Creates a new Item and return it accordingly.</returns>
[HttpPost()]
[Authorize]
public IActionResult Add([FromBody]ItemViewModel ivm)
{
    if (ivm != null)
    {
        // create a new
        var item = Tiny

        // override any
        item.CreatedDate
        item.LastModifie

        // set a suitab
        // NOTE: we'll
        item.UserId = "

        // add the new item
        DbContext.Items.Add(item);
```

Watch 1	
Name	Value
HttpContext.User.Identity.IsAuthenticated	true

If it's true, it means that we've been successfully authenticated. That shouldn't be surprising, since our request already managed to get inside a method protected by an [Authorize] attribute.

Suggested topics

Authentication, authorization, HTTP protocol, Secure Socket Layer, Session State Management, Indirection, Single Sign-On, Azure AD Authentication Library (ADAL), AspNetCore Identity, OpenID, OAuth, Conversion Rate, Code-First Migrations, IdentityUser, Stateless, Cross-Site Scripting (XSS), Cross-Site Request Forgery (CSRF), LocalStorage, Web Storage API, Generic Types, JWT Tokens, Claims, Refresh Tokens, Sliding Sessions.

Summary

At the start of this chapter, we introduced the concepts of authentication and authorization, acknowledging the fact that most applications, including ours, do require a mechanism to properly handle authenticated and non-authenticated clients, as well as authorized and unauthorized requests.

We took some time to properly understand the similarities and differences between authentication and authorization, as well as the pros and cons of handling these tasks using our own internal provider or delegating them to third-party providers such as Google, Facebook, and Twitter. We also found out that, luckily enough, the `AspNetCore.Identity` framework can be configured to achieve the best of both worlds. To be able to use it we added the required packages to our project and did what was needed to properly configure them, such as performing some changes in our `ApplicationUser` and `ApplicationDbContext` classes and then adding a new `EntityFrameworkCore` migration to update our database accordingly.

We briefly enumerated the various web-based authentication methods available nowadays: sessions, tokens, signatures, and two-factor strategies of various sorts. After careful consideration, we chose to implement a token-based approach using Json Web Token (JWT), a solid and well-known standard for native web applications.

Implementing JWT within our application took us some time, as we had to take care of a number of steps: writing our own `JwtProvider` to generate the tokens; adding them to the HTTP request pipeline, together with the AspNetCore-native `JwtBearerMiddleware` needed to validate them; and finally, moving to our Angular 2 client app, creating a `login` form, an `AuthService`, and an `AuthHttp` wrapper class to handle everything on the client side.

Right after that, we implemented the required server-side and client-side authorization rules to protect some of our application views, routes, and APIs from unauthorized access.

8

Third-Party Authentication and External Providers

The hand-made authentication and authorization flow we put together in `Chapter 7`, *Authentication and Authorization*, is pretty much working. However, it lacks some very important features required for a production-ready environment, the most important ones being token expiration, token refresh, and sliding session support. Implementing them from scratch won't be easy and would take us far from the scope of this book. Luckily enough, there are a number of third-party packages that already went down that route with great results. Among them, the most promising one seems to be `OpenIddict`, an open-source project featuring an OAuth2/OpenID Connect provider based on **ASP.NET Core Identity** and **AspNet.Security.OpenIdConnect.Server** (also known as **ASOS**).

In this chapter, we'll learn how to properly install and configure it, as well as implement support for external authentication/authorization providers such as Google, Facebook, and Twitter.

Introducing OpenID connect servers

As the name suggests, `OpenIddict` is basically a (mostly) full-featured OAuth2/OpenID connect server that can be easily plugged into any ASP.NET Core application.

 In case we need a quick recap regarding OAuth2 and/or OpenID connect before going further, we can check a lot of useful info by visiting the following URLs:

- `https://tools.ietf.org/html/rfc6749`
- `http://openid.net/connect/faq/`

The main purpose of OAuth2/OpenID connect server interfaces such as `OpenIddict` is to support a wide amount of modern authentication standards, including, yet not limited to, JWT. As a matter of fact, they're not that different from the `JwtServer` we put together during the previous chapter, except that they come bundled with a lot of additional features we're still missing, such as the aforementioned token refresh and sliding expiration, thus releasing us from the need to manually implement them.

Choosing between replacing our custom `JwtProvider` with `OpenIddict` (or other similar third-party solutions) or not is mostly a matter of personal choice, depending on whether we feel more like coding our very own authentication layer or switching to a community-oriented approach. It won't even impact what we'll do in this chapter, as it will work with both.

 If you choose to keep using your own `JwtProvider`, you might want to skip the next paragraph entirely.

Installing OpenIddict

Let's start with the good news! Adding `OpenIddict` won't be hard, as we already did most of the required work. It's also worth noting that doing it is not a required step, as our hand-made alternative is working perfectly fine and will be fully compatible with the rest of the chapters.

The `OpenIddict` project is actively maintained by Kévin Chalet and licensed under the Apache License: `http://www.apache.org/licenses/LICENSE-2.0.html` This means that we are able to use, modify, and distribute it freely. For a better overview of the product, we strongly suggest taking a look at the official GitHub project page at the following URL: `https://github.com/openiddict/openiddict-core`

Adding MyGet to the package sources

The first thing we need to do is to add a new package source to the Visual Studio **NuGet package manager**:

At the time of writing, this is a required step, as `OpenIddict` has not been released to the official NuGet package archive. This will most likely change in the future, to the point that it could be useful to perform a quick search through the official packages before doing the following steps.

1. Right-click on the **OpenGameListWebApp** project node.
2. Select **Manage NuGet Packages** and open the pop-up window.
3. Locate the **Package Source** drop-down list to the upper-right corner and set it to **All**, then click on the cogwheel icon to its immediate right to access the **Options** modal window.
4. Left-click on the plus icon near the upper-right corner and add the following package source:

    Name: `myget.org`

    Source:
    `https://www.myget.org/F/aspnet-contrib/api/v3/index.json`

Once done, click the Update button. Right after doing that, we should be able to see something very similar to the following screenshot:

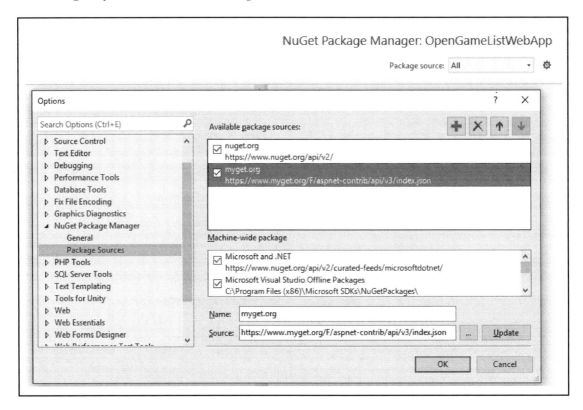

Ensure that the checkbox to the left of the new package source is checked, then click **Ok** to close the modal window.

Installing the OpenIddict package

Now we can issue a search for **OpenIddict** and be sure to actually find something relevant:

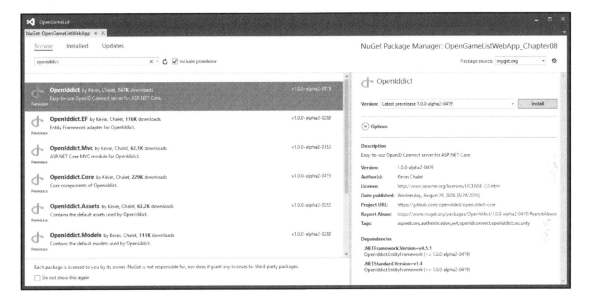

We're looking for the one called **OpenIddict**, which should be the first entry.

As always, ensure that the **Include prerelease** checkbox is checked to include the latest versions of the packages. We'll be using the **1.0.0-alpha2-0419** build, since it's the most recent one at the time of writing.

IMPORTANT

It's worth noting that, being still in alpha stage, the upcoming releases of **OpenIddict** might bring major changes to the interface, thus requiring some changes/updates to the source code we'll be using throughout this chapter.

Updating ApplicationUser and ApplicationDbContext

This step might look familiar, as we already did something very similar when we added `AspNetCore.Identity`. We basically need to change the base classes, replacing `IdentityUser` and `IdentityDbContext` with `OpenIddictUser` and `OpenIddictDbContext`.

These are the relevant code changes (new/updated code highlighted):

In the `/Data/Users/ApplicationUser.cs` file:

```
public class ApplicationUser: OpenIddictUser
```

In the `/Data/ApplicationDbContext.cs` file:

```
public class ApplicationDbContext : OpenIddictDbContext<ApplicationUser>
```

We also need to declare the following namespace in both of these files:

```
using OpenIddict;
```

This concludes the `OpenIddict` package implementation. However, we still need to update our database accordingly.

 We're about to venture again into migrations territory, so it might be wise to issue a full rebuild of our project to ensure that our code will compile without errors.

Adding a new migration

The `OpenIddict` module comes with a set of built-in entities that need to be added to our existing database. Luckily enough, since we're using code-first migrations, this is not a big deal.

Open a **PowerShell** command prompt and navigate through the project's root folder:

```
C:\Projects\OpenGameList\src\OpenGameListWebApp\
```

Once there, type the following command to add the new migration:

```
dotnet ef migrations add "OpenIddict" -o "Data\Migrations"
```

Wait for the migration to be created, then type the following to execute it:

```
dotnet ef database update
```

This will create the following new tables in our local database:

```
OpenIddictApplications
OpenIddictAuthorizations
OpenIddictScopes
OpenIddictTokens
```

 If the tables are not there or you run into some other issues, it could mean that EF Core is unable to handle a previously created migration. The best workaround to solve these kinds of problems is to delete the `Data\Migrations` folder and then run the preceding commands again. Alternatively, you can try the `database drop` and `database update` commands, just like we did in `Chapter 7`, *Authentication and Authorization*.

Updating the DbSeeder

One of the new tables, `OpenIddictApplications`, needs to be populated with a single row corresponding to our web application. The task can be easily performed by our `DbSeeder` class, which happens to do just that.

Open the `Data/DbSeeder.cs` file and add the following code to the constructor method (new lines are highlighted):

```
public async Task SeedAsync()
{
    // Create the Db if it doesn't exist
    DbContext.Database.EnsureCreated();
    // Create default Application
    if (!DbContext.Applications.Any()) CreateApplication();
    // Create default Users
    if (!DbContext.Users.Any()) await CreateUsersAsync();
    // Create default Items (if there are none) and Comments
    if (!DbContext.Items.Any()) CreateItems();
}
```

Right after that, locate the beginning of the `Seed` methods region and add the following method:

```
private void CreateApplication()
{
    DbContext.Applications.Add(new OpenIddictApplication
```

```
    {
        Id = "OpenGameList",
        DisplayName = "OpenGameList",
        RedirectUri = "/api/connect/token",
        LogoutRedirectUri = "/",
        ClientId = "OpenGameList",
        ClientSecret = Crypto.HashPassword("1234567890_my_client_secret"),
        Type = OpenIddictConstants.ClientTypes.Public
    });
    DbContext.SaveChanges();
}
```

Also, add the following required namespaces at the beginning of the file:

```
using OpenIddict;
using CryptoHelper;
```

Moving literal values to appsettings.json

As we can see, there are a lot of literal values here. Instead of having them hanging there, it could be wise to move them into the project's configuration file instead. Remember the `appsettings.json` file that we used back in Chapter 4, *The Data Model*, to add the database connection string? Open it, then add a new `Authentication` root key with the following content (new lines are highlighted):

```
{
  "Authentication": {
    "OpenIddict": {
      "ApplicationId": "OpenGameList",
      "DisplayName": "OpenGameList",
      "TokenEndPoint": "/api/connect/token",
      "ClientId": "OpenGameList",
      "ClientSecret": "1234567890_my_client_secret"
    }
  },
  "Data": {
    "DefaultConnection": {
      "ConnectionString": "Data Source=(localdb)\\MSSQLLocalDB;Initial
Catalog=OpenGameList;Integrated Security=True;
MultipleActiveResultSets=True"
    }
  },
  "Logging": {
    "IncludeScopes": false,
    "LogLevel": {
      "Default": "Debug",
```

```
      "System": "Information",
      "Microsoft": "Information"
    }
  },
  "StaticFiles": {
    "Headers": {
      "Cache-Control": "no-cache, no-store",
      "Pragma": "no-cache",
      "Expires": "-1"
    }
  }
}
```

We already know how to retrieve these values programmatically. As a matter of fact, we already did that a number of times, using the `Configuration` property defined within the `Startup` class. What we need to do now is to find a way to make it available through the `DbSeeder` class as well.

The best way to achieve that is via dependency injection (DI), just like we have already done a number of times. However, in order to make it work, we need to register a generic `IConfiguration` singleton object within the application's DI system beforehand.

To do that, open the `Startup.cs` file and add the following lines at the beginning of the `ConfigureServices` method:

```
public void ConfigureServices(IServiceCollection services)
{
    // Add a reference to the Configuration object for DI
    services.AddSingleton<IConfiguration>(
        c => { return Configuration; }
        );
```

This will allow us to retrieve that singleton instance anywhere we want using DI.

If we don't do that, we will get an `InvalidOperationException` error at runtime because the DI manager won't be able to find any suitable `IConfiguration` instances.

Let's make good use of what we just did. Open the `DbSeeder.cs` file and perform the following changes (new lines highlighted):

```
#region Private Members
private ApplicationDbContext DbContext;
private RoleManager<IdentityRole> RoleManager;
private UserManager<ApplicationUser> UserManager;
```

```
private IConfiguration Configuration;
#endregion Private Members

#region Constructor
public DbSeeder(
    ApplicationDbContext dbContext,
    RoleManager<IdentityRole> roleManager,
    UserManager<ApplicationUser> userManager,
    IConfiguration configuration)
{
    DbContext = dbContext;
    RoleManager = roleManager;
    UserManager = userManager;
    SignInManager = signInManager;
    Configuration = configuration;
}
#endregion Constructor
```

In order to use the IConfiguration interface, we also need to add the following namespace reference at the beginning of the file:

```
using Microsoft.Extensions.Configuration;
```

Now that we have a IConfiguration instance, we can easily use it to replace the literal values within the CreateApplication method:

```
private void CreateApplication()
{
    DbContext.Applications.Add(new OpenIddictApplication
    {
        Id = Configuration["Authentication:OpenIddict:ApplicationId"],
        DisplayName =
Configuration["Authentication:OpenIddict:DisplayName"],
        RedirectUri =
Configuration["Authentication:OpenIddict:TokenEndPoint"],
        LogoutRedirectUri = "/",
        ClientId = Configuration["Authentication:OpenIddict:ClientId"],
        ClientSecret =
Crypto.HashPassword(Configuration["Authentication:OpenIddict:ClientSecret"]
),
        Type = OpenIddictConstants.ClientTypes.Public
    });
    DbContext.SaveChanges();
}
```

That's it.

Configuring the Startup class

Last but not least, we need to add the `OpenIddict` service and middleware to our application's `Startup` class.

Open the `Startup.cs` file, locate the `ConfigureServices` method and add the following (new lines are highlighted):

```
public void ConfigureServices(IServiceCollection services)
{
    // Add a reference to the Configuration object for DI
    services.AddSingleton<IConfiguration>(
        c => { return Configuration; }
        );

    // Add framework services.
    services.AddMvc();

    // Add EntityFramework's Identity support.
    services.AddEntityFramework();

    // Add Identity Services & Stores
    services.AddIdentity<ApplicationUser, IdentityRole>(config => {
        config.User.RequireUniqueEmail = true;
        config.Password.RequireNonAlphanumeric = false;
        config.Cookies.ApplicationCookie.AutomaticChallenge = false;
    })
        .AddEntityFrameworkStores<ApplicationDbContext>()
        .AddDefaultTokenProviders();

    // Add ApplicationDbContext.
    services.AddDbContext<ApplicationDbContext>(options =>
options.UseSqlServer(Configuration["Data:DefaultConnection:ConnectionString
"])
        );

    // Register the OpenIddict services, including the default Entity
Framework stores.
    services.AddOpenIddict<ApplicationUser, ApplicationDbContext>()
        // Integrate with EFCore
        .AddEntityFramework<ApplicationDbContext>()
        // Use Json Web Tokens (JWT)
        .UseJsonWebTokens()
        // Set a custom token endpoint (default is /connect/token)
.EnableTokenEndpoint(Configuration["Authentication:OpenIddict:TokenEndPoint
"])
        // Set a custom auth endpoint (default is /connect/authorize)
```

```
.EnableAuthorizationEndpoint("/api/connect/authorize")
// Allow client applications to use the grant_type=password flow.
.AllowPasswordFlow()
// Enable support for both authorization & implicit flows
.AllowAuthorizationCodeFlow()
.AllowImplicitFlow()
// Allow the client to refresh tokens.
.AllowRefreshTokenFlow()
// Disable the HTTPS requirement (not recommended in production)
.DisableHttpsRequirement()
// Register a new ephemeral key for development.
// We will register a X.509 certificate in production.
.AddEphemeralSigningKey();

    // Add ApplicationDbContext's DbSeeder
    services.AddSingleton<DbSeeder>();
}
```

We can easily see how moving the `TokenEndPoint` value into the `appsettings.json` file was well worth the effort, as we can easily retrieve it from there. While we're here, we should take the chance to do the same with the `AuthorizationEndPoint` value as well.

Open the `appsettings.json` file and add the following line right above the `TokenEndPoint` key:

```
"AuthorizationEndPoint": "/api/connect/authorize",
```

Then go back to the `Startup.cs` file and reference it accordingly:

```
.EnableAuthorizationEndpoint(Configuration["Authentication:OpenIddict:Autho
rizationEndPoint"])
```

So far, so good. Let's now scroll the `Startup.cs` file down to the `Configure` method and change it like this (new/updated lines are highlighted):

```
public void Configure(IApplicationBuilder app, IHostingEnvironment env,
ILoggerFactory loggerFactory, DbSeeder dbSeeder)
{
    loggerFactory.AddConsole(Configuration.GetSection("Logging"));
    loggerFactory.AddDebug();

    // Configure a rewrite rule to auto-lookup for standard default files
such as index.html.
    app.UseDefaultFiles();

    // Serve static files (html, css, js, images & more). See also the
following URL:
    // https://docs.asp.net/en/latest/fundamentals/static-files.html for
```

```
further reference.
    app.UseStaticFiles(new StaticFileOptions()
    {
        OnPrepareResponse = (context) =>
        {
            // Disable caching for all static files.
            context.Context.Response.Headers["Cache-Control"] =
Configuration["StaticFiles:Headers:Cache-Control"];
            context.Context.Response.Headers["Pragma"] =
Configuration["StaticFiles:Headers:Pragma"];
            context.Context.Response.Headers["Expires"] =
Configuration["StaticFiles:Headers:Expires"];
        }
    });

    // Add a custom Jwt Provider to generate Tokens
    // app.UseJwtProvider();
    // Add OpenIddict middleware
    // Note: UseOpenIddict() must be registered after app.UseIdentity() and
the external social providers.
    app.UseOpenIddict();

    // Add the Jwt Bearer Header Authentication to validate Tokens
    app.UseJwtBearerAuthentication(new JwtBearerOptions()
    {
        AutomaticAuthenticate = true,
        AutomaticChallenge = true,
        RequireHttpsMetadata = false,
        Authority = "http://localhost:14600/",
        TokenValidationParameters = new TokenValidationParameters()
        {
            //IssuerSigningKey = JwtProvider.SecurityKey,
            //ValidateIssuerSigningKey = true,
            //ValidIssuer = JwtProvider.Issuer,
            ValidateIssuer = false,
            ValidateAudience = false
        }
    });

    // Add MVC to the pipeline
    app.UseMvc();

    // TinyMapper binding configuration
    TinyMapper.Bind<Item, ItemViewModel>();

    // Seed the Database (if needed)
    try
    {
```

```
        dbSeeder.SeedAsync().Wait();
    }
    catch (AggregateException e)
    {
        throw new Exception(e.ToString());
    }
}
```

Notice that we commented out the JwtProvider, together with some TokenValidationParameters within the JwtBearerAuthentication initialization; none of them are needed by the OpenIddict middleware. Conversely, we had to specify an explicit Authority property value to allow the JWT bearer middleware to download the signing key. Again, this is not something that should be kept in literal form, as we'll need to change that value when we push everything into production. The best thing to do is to move it into the configuration file, just like we did with the other OpenIddict-related values.

Open the appsettings.json file and add the following key to the Authentication:OpenIddict section:

```
"Authentication": {
  "OpenIddict": {
    "ApplicationId": "OpenGameList",
    "DisplayName": "OpenGameList",
    "TokenEndPoint": "/api/connect/token",
    "ClientId": "OpenGameList",
    "ClientSecret": "1234567890_my_client_secret",
    "Authority": "http://localhost:14600/"
  }
}
```

Right after that, replace the literal value in Setup.cs accordingly:

```
Authority = Configuration["Authentication:OpenIddict:Authority"],
```

Updating the Web.Config rewrite rules

It's time to update those rewrite rules that we pulled off back in Chapter 3, *Angular 2 Components and Client-Side Routing*. We need to do that to ensure that all the OpenIddict's endpoint URIs will be reachable by any internal and external actor involved in the authentication process.

To do that, open the web.config file and add the following lines to the system.webServer > Rewrite section (new lines highlighted):

```
<rewrite>
  <rules>
    <rule name="Angular 2 pushState routing" stopProcessing="true">
      <match url=".*" />
      <conditions logicalGrouping="MatchAll">
        <add input="{REQUEST_FILENAME}" matchType="IsFile" negate="true" />
        <add input="{REQUEST_FILENAME}" matchType="IsDirectory"
negate="true" />
        <add input="{REQUEST_FILENAME}" pattern=".*\.[\d\w]+$"
negate="true" />
        <add input="{REQUEST_URI}" pattern="^/(api)" negate="true" />
        <add input="{REQUEST_URI}" pattern="^/(.well-known)" negate="true"
/>
        <add input="{REQUEST_URI}" pattern="^/(signin)" negate="true" />
      </conditions>
      <action type="Rewrite" url="/index.html" />
    </rule>
  </rules>
</rewrite>
```

These lines will ensure that all the required OpenIddict endpoint URIs won't be rewritten to the index.html file, just like it is for the URLs starting with /api.

It's worth saying that we could also change all the endpoint URIs programmatically instead of updating the rewrite rule. However, it would imply changing a lot of default values, which is something that should be normally avoided when dealing with complex package libraries such as *EF Core*, *Identity Core*, and *OpenIddict*. Compared to that, the rewrite update we just made is definitely a simpler yet also more secure approach.

Seeding the database

We're ready to populate our database and test our new authentication provider. We can do that by hitting *F5*, let the `DbSeeder` middleware fill the database with the new required info, and checking out the resulting outcome.

If everything has been made correctly, we shouldn't be able to detect changes of any sort in our application's behavior, as the new provider is expected to hook on the same routes and use the same naming conventions as the previous one. This is hardly a coincidence; we purposely implemented both of them using the same criteria in order to make them interchangeable to the extent of our limited scenario.

External authentication providers

Now that we finally have a fully-featured, JWT-based internal authentication provider, we can start thinking about supporting other login alternatives. Hooking up some external authentication providers such as Google, Facebook, and Twitter will undoubtedly please our users and increase our application's overall appeal.

Luckily enough, AspNetCore.Identity comes bundled with a built-in set of middleware classes for the most used OAuth2 providers that will simplify each of these tasks.

OAuth2 authorization flow

Before we start, let's do a quick recap of how the OAuth2 authorization flow actually works:

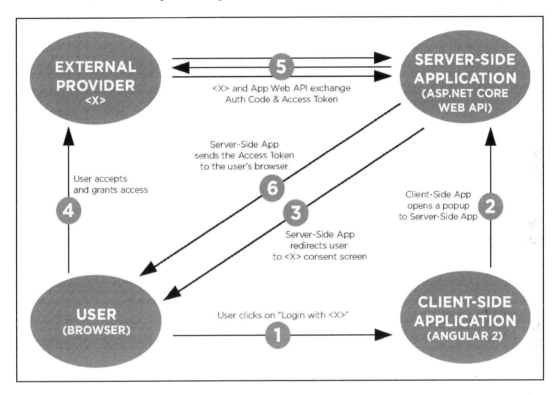

This, in short, is what will happen under the hood. Luckily enough, the AspNetCore middleware will do most of the job, as long as we provide a minimal amount of infrastructural logic to our Web API.

Facebook

Let's start with the big whale of the social networks.

The first thing we need to do is to obtain an `AppId` and an `AppSecret` that we can use to perform our first request against Facebook's OAuth2 authentication workflow.

To learn more about the OAuth2 authorization framework, we strongly suggest reading the following URLs:

- **Official Page**: `http://oauth.net/2/`
- **RFC 6749**: `https://tools.ietf.org/html/rfc6749`

Creating a Facebook App

Go to the Facebook Developer page at the following URL:
`https://developers.facebook.com/`.

In order to use it, we need to log in using a **Facebook Developer Account**. Once inside, click **Add a New App:,** select **Website**, fill in the required fields, and click **Create App ID**:

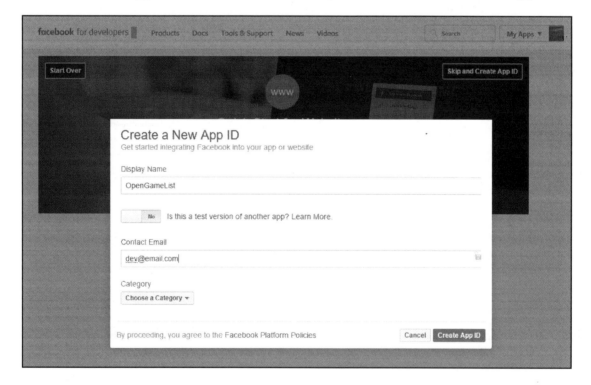

It's worth saying that external provider web platforms are subject to frequent and major changes. The actual Google, Facebook, and Twitter pages and forms might be different from those depicted by the screenshots made at the time of writing.

As soon as we get past the **CAPTCHA**, a new Facebook app will be added to our account and we'll be automatically brought to the **Add Products** selection screen. Once there, we should be able to add a new **Facebook Login** product by clicking on the **Get Started** button to the right:

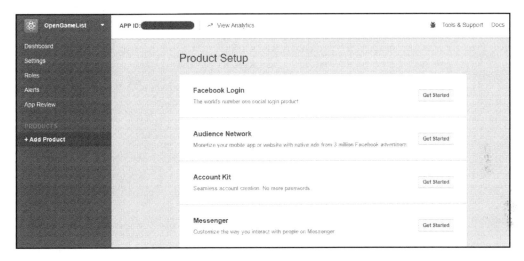

A modal window will open with a number of OAuth2-related options. The default values are OK, with the sole exception of the **Valid OAuth redirect URIs** textbox, which needs to be updated with our current URL endpoint. Since we're in development, we need to allow our local address and also the developer port we're using:

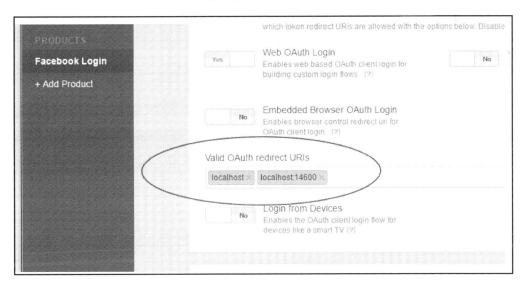

In the preceding example, we specified two valid URIs: `localhost` (which defaults to port 80) and `localhost:14600`, which is the one used by Visual Studio during our debug runs.

We don't need to configure anything else. Before leaving, we need to go to the **Dashboard** and retrieve the **App ID** and **App Secret** values, as we'll need them soon enough.

 If you want to apply further access restrictions to your Facebook App, you can go to **Settings** | **Advanced** and configure the **Server IP whitelist** on the **Security** panel. However, once you input something there, the whitelist logic will immediately kick in, blocking every other IP.

Storing the keys in App settings

Open the `appsettings.json` file, locate the `Authentication` root key we created earlier, and add a new `Facebook` key right below `OpenIddict`. Once done, use it to store the **App ID** and **App Secret** values of the previously-created Facebook app in the following way:

```
"Authentication": {
  "OpenIddict": {
    "ApplicationId": "OpenGameList",
    "DisplayName": "OpenGameList",
    "TokenEndPoint": "/api/connect/token",
    "ClientId": "OpenGameList",
    "ClientSecret": "1234567890_my_client_secret",
    "Authority": "http://localhost:14600/"
  },
  "Facebook": {
    "AppId": "__INSERT_APP_ID_HERE__",
    "AppSecret": "__INSERT_APP_SECRET_HERE__"
  }
}
```

Storing these values in plain text inside the `appsettings.json` file is not recommended, because they can be easily accessed by unauthorized people (network admins, server admins, and so on) or even checked into some public source control repositories by some developer's mistake. There are better alternatives nowadays, such as the **Secret Manager Tool**, granting a better level of security.

For more info about how to use it, it's highly advisable to carefully read the following guide from the official ASP.NET Core documentation website:

`https://docs.asp.net/en/latest/security/app-secrets.html.`

Adding the Facebook middleware

Now we need to add the Facebook middleware to the HTTP request pipeline.

Open the `project.json` file and add the following package:

```
"Microsoft.AspNetCore.Authentication.Facebook": "1.0.0"
```

Once done, open up the `Startup.cs` file, locate the `Configure` method, and add the following right above the **JwtProvider**/OpenIddict middleware, as follows (new lines are highlighted):

```
public void Configure(IApplicationBuilder app, IHostingEnvironment env,
ILoggerFactory loggerFactory, DbSeeder dbSeeder)
{
    loggerFactory.AddConsole(Configuration.GetSection("Logging"));
    loggerFactory.AddDebug();

    // Configure a rewrite rule to auto-lookup for standard default files
such as index.html.
    app.UseDefaultFiles();

    // Serve static files (html, css, js, images & more). See also the
following URL:
    // https://docs.asp.net/en/latest/fundamentals/static-files.html for
further reference.
    app.UseStaticFiles(new StaticFileOptions()
    {
        OnPrepareResponse = (context) =>
        {
            // Disable caching for all static files.
            context.Context.Response.Headers["Cache-Control"] =
Configuration["StaticFiles:Headers:Cache-Control"];
            context.Context.Response.Headers["Pragma"] =
```

```
Configuration["StaticFiles:Headers:Pragma"];
            context.Context.Response.Headers["Expires"] =
Configuration["StaticFiles:Headers:Expires"];
        }
    });
    // Add a custom Jwt Provider to generate Tokens
    // app.UseJwtProvider();

    // Add the AspNetCore.Identity middleware (required for external auth
providers)
    // IMPORTANT: This must be placed *BEFORE* OpenIddict and any external
provider's middleware
    app.UseIdentity();
    // Add external authentication middleware below.
     // To configure them please see
http://go.microsoft.com/fwlink/?LinkID=532715
    app.UseFacebookAuthentication(new FacebookOptions()
    {
        AutomaticAuthenticate = true,
        AutomaticChallenge = true,
        AppId = Configuration["Authentication:Facebook:AppId"],
        AppSecret = Configuration["Authentication:Facebook:AppSecret"],
        CallbackPath = "/signin-facebook",
        Scope = { "email" }
    });
    // Add OpenIddict middleware
    // NOTE: UseOpenIddict() must be registered after app.UseIdentity()
    // and all the external social provider middlewares (if any).
    app.UseOpenIddict();

    // Add the Jwt Bearer Header Authentication to validate Tokens
    app.UseJwtBearerAuthentication(new JwtBearerOptions()
    {
        AutomaticAuthenticate = true,
        AutomaticChallenge = true,
        RequireHttpsMetadata = false,
        Authority = Configuration["Authentication:OpenIddict:Authority"],
        TokenValidationParameters = new TokenValidationParameters()
        {
            //IssuerSigningKey = JwtProvider.SecurityKey,
            //ValidateIssuerSigningKey = true,
            //ValidIssuer = JwtProvider.Issuer,
            ValidateIssuer = false,
            ValidateAudience = false
        }
    });

    // Add MVC to the pipeline
```

```
        app.UseMvc();

        // TinyMapper binding configuration
        TinyMapper.Bind<Item, ItemViewModel>();

        // Seed the Database (if needed)
        try
        {
            dbSeeder.SeedAsync().Wait();
        }
        catch (AggregateException e)
        {
            throw new Exception(e.ToString());
        }
    }
```

As we already said, the middleware order is very important. Any internal, external, or third-party authentication middleware coming after `UseMvc` won't be able to hook up on any route.

Adding the AccountsController

Since this is our first external provider, we need to do some extra work here, adding a new controller to deal with a number of account-related tasks to use for this provider and also for those that will come next. We'll also extensively use it during Chapter 9, *User Registration and Account Edit*, when we'll be dealing with **User Registration** and **Edit Account** functions. Its name will be `AccountsController` and it will have a lot of features in common with the already existing `ItemsController`, such as an `AccountDbContext` DI instance to access the data provider, a `DefaultJsonSettings` property to format JSON data, the code required to fetch the authenticated user details, and so on.

Wait a minute… are we really going to duplicate all these code lines? We clearly shouldn't, unless we want to completely ditch the **DRY** principle, which is something that any developer should try to follow whenever they can.

 DRY stands for **Don't Repeat Yourself** and is a widely achieved principle of software development. Whenever we violate it we fall into a **WET** approach, which could mean *Write Everything Twice*, *We Enjoy Typing* or *Waste Everyone's Time*, depending on what you like the most.

As a matter of fact, we can avoid a lot of code repetition by adding a `BaseController` that will host these reusable objects, methods, and properties. This has always been a rather common DRY pattern for MVC and Web API and it's still very doable in ASP.NET Core.

BaseController

Let's do this. Right-click on the Controllers folder, select **Add | New Item** and add a new **Web API Controller** class. Name it `BaseController.cs` and click **OK** to add it to our project's tree:

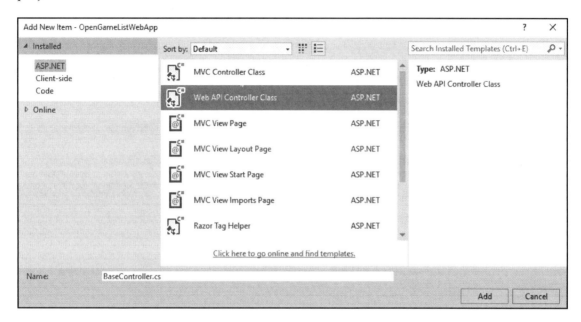

The `BaseController` will be the base class of our existing `ItemsController` and also of the new `AccountsController` we're about to create, so we have to put there everything that we reasonably expect both of them will use. With that in mind, this could be a good start:

```
using System;
using System.Security.Claims;
using System.Threading.Tasks;
using Microsoft.AspNetCore.Mvc;
using Microsoft.AspNetCore.Identity;
using OpenGameListWebApp.Data;
using OpenGameListWebApp.Data.Users;
using Newtonsoft.Json;

namespace OpenGameListWebApp.Controllers
{
    [Route("api/[controller]")]
    public class BaseController : Controller
    {
        #region Common Fields
```

```csharp
protected ApplicationDbContext DbContext;
protected SignInManager<ApplicationUser> SignInManager;
protected UserManager<ApplicationUser> UserManager;
#endregion Common Fields

#region Constructor
public BaseController(ApplicationDbContext context,
    SignInManager<ApplicationUser> signInManager,
    UserManager<ApplicationUser> userManager)
{

    // Dependency Injection
    DbContext = context;
    SignInManager = signInManager;
    UserManager = userManager;
}
#endregion Constructor

#region Common Methods
/// <summary>
/// Retrieves the .NET Core Identity User Id
/// for the current ClaimsPrincipal.
/// </summary>
/// <returns></returns>
public async Task<string> GetCurrentUserId()
{
    // if the user is not authenticated, throw an exception
    if (!User.Identity.IsAuthenticated)
        throw new NotSupportedException();

    var info = await SignInManager.GetExternalLoginInfoAsync();
    if (info == null)
        // internal provider
        return User.FindFirst(ClaimTypes.NameIdentifier).Value;
    else
    {
        // external provider
        var user = await UserManager.FindByLoginAsync(
            info.LoginProvider,
            info.ProviderKey);
        if (user == null) throw new NotSupportedException();
        return user.Id;
    }
}
#endregion Common Methods

#region Common Properties
/// <summary>
/// Returns a suitable JsonSerializerSettings object
```

```
/// that can be used to generate the JsonResult return value
/// for this Controller's methods.
/// </summary>
protected JsonSerializerSettings DefaultJsonSettings
{
    get
    {
        return new JsonSerializerSettings()
        {
            Formatting = Formatting.Indented
        };
    }
}
#endregion Common Properties
    }
}
```

Let's see what we put in there:

- Above the controller's `class` definition there's the `[Route]` attribute, which defines the default routing scheme. Nothing new there, just the standard api/[controller] attribute-based rule we've been using since Chapter 2, *ASP.NET Controllers and Server-Side Routes*. Since we want it for all Controllers, we chose to put it here so we won't have to type this single line of code more than once.

- Right before the constructor, we declared the local instances of the ASP.NET Identity handlers we'll be using throughout all our Controllers. Since we're going to need these everywhere, declaring them here is indeed the right thing to do to.

- The `GetCurrentUserId` method is something we've already seen before. It contains the *one-liner* we used back in Chapter 7, *Authentication and Authorization*, to retrieve the authenticated user's `Id`. That time, we said that we were going to change it in the near future and we actually did that: now it supports both internal and external providers, which is precisely what we need. We also took the chance to centralize it here, since we're going to use it more than once.

- The `DefaultJsonSettings` property is an old friend. We coded it back in Chapter 2, *ASP.NET Controllers and Server-Side Routes*. We put it there for obvious reasons, as this is something each Controller will most likely use.

AccountsController

Time to finally add the `AccountsController` to the loop. Once again, right-click on the **Controllers** folder, select **Add | New Item**, and add another **Web API Controller** class file. Name it `AccountsController.cs` and click **OK**.

Since we're going to write a good amount of code, we'll split it into multiple sections, wrapping them into regions as much as we can.

Namespaces

Let's start with the namespaces that we'll be using throughout the controller:

```
using System;
using System.Linq;
using System.Security.Claims;
using System.Threading.Tasks;
using Microsoft.AspNetCore.Authorization;
using Microsoft.AspNetCore.Identity;
using Microsoft.AspNetCore.Mvc;
using Newtonsoft.Json;
using OpenGameListWebApp.Classes;
using OpenGameListWebApp.Data;
using OpenGameListWebApp.Data.Users;
using OpenGameListWebApp.ViewModels;
```

As usual, we need to add them to the beginning of the file.

Class declaration

We don't need to define a default routing scheme since we already put that in the `BaseController` class. We just need to extend it within the class declaration, like the following:

```
public class AccountsController : BaseController
```

Constructor

We can use the constructor of the base class since we made it to suit our needs.

```
#region Constructor
public AccountsController(
    ApplicationDbContext context,
    SignInManager<ApplicationUser> signInManager,
    UserManager<ApplicationUser> userManager) : base(
    context,
    signInManager,
    userManager)
{ }
#endregion Constructor
```

Again, no big news here. This is the same DI pattern we've already used a number of times before. We'll be able to use these instances by accessing the `protected` local variables defined in the base class, which will be available here.

ExternalLogin

This is the method that our Angular 2 client will call whenever the user initiates an external login request:

```
#region External Authentication Providers
// GET: /api/Accounts/ExternalLogin
[HttpGet("ExternalLogin/{provider}")]
public IActionResult ExternalLogin(string provider, string returnUrl =
null)
{
    switch (provider.ToLower())
    {
        case "facebook":
        case "google":
        case "twitter":
            // Request a redirect to the external login provider.
            var redirectUrl = Url.Action("ExternalLoginCallback",
"Accounts", new { ReturnUrl = returnUrl });
            var properties =
SignInManager.ConfigureExternalAuthenticationProperties(provider,
redirectUrl);
            return Challenge(properties, provider);
        default:
            return BadRequest(new { Error = String.Format("Provider '{0}'
is not supported.", provider) });
    }
}
```

 Notice that we started a new region here: it will contain the whole set of methods required to properly handle the external authentication provider's authentication flow.

As we can see, it will configure the external request and initiates the authentication workflow against the given provider, assuming it's among the supported ones. If it's not, it will issue a `400 - Bad Request` HTTP error response instead.

ExternalLoginCallBack

This method will be executed at the end of the OAuth2 workflow to handle the authentication success or failure scenarios:

```
[HttpGet("ExternalLoginCallBack")]
public async Task<IActionResult> ExternalLoginCallback(string returnUrl =
null, string remoteError = null)
{
    try
    {
        // Check if the External Provider returned an error and act
accordingly
        if (remoteError != null)
        {
            throw new Exception(remoteError);
        }

        // Extract the login info obtained from the External Provider
        ExternalLoginInfo info = await
SignInManager.GetExternalLoginInfoAsync();
        if (info == null)
        {
            // if there's none, emit an error
            throw new Exception("ERROR: No login info available.");
        }

        // Check if this user already registered himself with this external
provider before
        var user = await UserManager.FindByLoginAsync(info.LoginProvider,
info.ProviderKey);
        if (user == null)
        {
            // If we reach this point, it means that this user never tried
to logged in
            // using this external provider. However, it could have used
other providers
            // and /or have a local account.
            // We can find out if that's the case by looking for his e-mail
address.

            // Retrieve the 'emailaddress' claim
            var emailKey =
"http://schemas.xmlsoap.org/ws/2005/05/identity/claims/emailaddress";
            var email = info.Principal.FindFirst(emailKey).Value;

            // Lookup if there's an username with this e-mail address in
the Db
```

```
            user = await UserManager.FindByEmailAsync(email);
            if (user == null)
            {
                // No user has been found: register a new user using the
info retrieved from the provider
                DateTime now = DateTime.Now;

                // Create a unique username using the 'nameidentifier'
claim
                var idKey =
"http://schemas.xmlsoap.org/ws/2005/05/identity/claims/nameidentifier";
                var username = String.Format("{0}{1}", info.LoginProvider,
info.Principal.FindFirst(idKey).Value);

                user = new ApplicationUser()
                {
                    UserName = username,
                    Email = email,
                    CreatedDate = now,
                    LastModifiedDate = now
                };

                // Add the user to the Db with a random password
                await UserManager.CreateAsync(user, "Pass4External");

                // Assign the user to the 'Registered' role.
                await UserManager.AddToRoleAsync(user, "Registered");

                // Remove Lockout and E-Mail confirmation
                user.EmailConfirmed = true;
                user.LockoutEnabled = false;
            }
            // Register this external provider to the user
            await UserManager.AddLoginAsync(user, info);

            // Persist everything into the Db
            await DbContext.SaveChangesAsync();
        }

        // create the auth JSON object
        var auth = new
        {
            type = "External",
            providerName = info.LoginProvider
        };

        // output a <SCRIPT> tag to call a JS function registered into the
parent window global scope
```

```
        return Content(
            "<script type="text/javascript">" +
            "window.opener.externalProviderLogin(" +
JsonConvert.SerializeObject(auth) + ");" +
            "window.close();" +
            "</script>",
            "text/html"
            );
    }
    catch (Exception ex)
    {
        // return a HTTP Status 400 (Bad Request) to the client
        return BadRequest(new { Error = ex.Message });
    }
}
```

This is where all the magic takes place, as we'll be checking for a number of things and take action accordingly:

1. Before anything else, we wrap all the method into a try/catch block, so any given Exception would result in a 400 - Bad Request HTTP error response.

2. We check the external provider error message (if any) by looking at the remoteError parameter value. If something went bad, we throw an Exception here, otherwise, we go ahead.

3. We extract the ExternalLoginInfo object using the SignInManager. This is a strongly-typed .NET object containing the response data sent by the external provider and decrypted by the *Facebook middleware*. In the unlikely case it happens to be null, we throw an Exception, otherwise, we go ahead.

4. We check whenever the user already authenticated himself with this external provider before using the UserManager.FindByLoginAsync method. If that's the case, we skip to step 8; otherwise, we need to do additional checks.

5. We need to check whether the user registered himself before using different providers. To do so, we retrieve the user e-mail from the ExternalLoginInfo object, so we can perform a database lookup to see whether we already have it. If that's the case, we skip to step 7; otherwise, we need to create it.

6. We create a new user using the data we can retrieve from the relevant ExternalLoginInfo claims, including a temporary (yet unique) username and a random password that they'll be able to change in the future. We also assign them the registered user role.

7. We associate the user with this external provider, so we'll be ready to handle further authentication attempts (skipping steps 5–7).

8. We create an `auth` JSON object with some useful data.

9. Finally, we output a `text/html` response containing a `<SCRIPT>` tag that will be executed by the client pop-up window to handle the external login on the client side.

The last step is very important and deserves some explanation. As we might already know, the OAuth2 authorization workflow is an interactive process where the user has to manually accept a consent form. In order to support that, we'll need to call these controller routes from a popup window. That's why we need to call a function registered within the parent window (`window.opener`) and also close the current one using `window.close()`.

Logout

Since the external provider implementation is based on cookies, we need to create a server-side method that will remove them (if present) when the user performs the logout. The `SignInManager.SignOutAsync` method automatically handles that:

```
[HttpPost("Logout")]
public IActionResult Logout()
{
    if (HttpContext.User.Identity.IsAuthenticated)
    {
        SignInManager.SignOutAsync().Wait();
    }
    return Ok();
}
#endregion External Authentication Providers
```

We're closing the external authentication providers region right after this method.

Updating the ItemsController

Before moving to Angular 2, we should really bring the `ItemsController` up to date with our recent changes. Open the `/Controllers/ItemsController.cs` file and append the following namespaces to the already existing `using` list:

```
using Microsoft.AspNetCore.Identity;
using OpenGameListWebApp.Data.Users;
```

Right after that, change the class declaration and the constructor to extend the `BaseController` in the following way:

```
public class ItemsController : BaseController
{
    #region Constructor
    public ItemsController(
        ApplicationDbContext context,
        SignInManager<ApplicationUser> signInManager,
        UserManager<ApplicationUser> userManager) : base(
        context,
        signInManager,
        userManager)
    { }
    #endregion Constructor
```

The `[Route]` attribute can be deleted, as well as the whole private fields `region` and the `DefaultJsonSettings` property near the end of the file. We'll get them all from the `BaseController`.

We still need to perform some changes to the `Add` method, as it still contains the outdated `UserId` retrieval method with no external provider support that we implemented in `Chapter 7`, *Authentication and Authorization*. We need to replace it with the updated version we implemented within the `BaseController` earlier:

```
item.UserId = await GetCurrentUserId();
```

However, since this is an `async` method, doing that will also require setting the `async` method:

```
public async Task<IActionResult> Add([FromBody]ItemViewModel ivm)
```

The server-side implementation tasks are finally done. Now we can switch back to Angular 2 and configure our client to properly handle what we just did.

 Before we continue, it might be wise to issue a full project **Rebuild** to ensure that there are no compile errors up to this point.

Configuring the client

Let's do a quick inventory of what we need to do within our Angular 2 client app to allow our users to log in with Facebook:

1. Add a **Login with Facebook** button to our login view, bound to a method that will fire the **OAuth2** initial request to our Web API. We also need to do that within a popup, since the user will be prompted by the Facebook consent form.

2. Change the `logout()` method within the `AuthService` class. We need it to issue a call to the new `Logout` web API to remove the authentication cookie placed by external providers (if any).

3. Update the `AppComponent` class with the new changes. Specifically, we need to do the following:

   - Change the internal `AppComponent.logout()` handler to match the new `AuthService.logout()` implementation.

   - Add an `externalProviderLogin` method to handle the external authentication outcome response. We also need to make it available in the global scope, as we know it will be called from a popup using the `window.opener` interface.

Challenge accepted. Let's do this.

Updating the LoginComponent

Open the `/Scripts/app/login.component.ts` file, locate the `template` section, and add the following (new lines are highlighted):

```
<div class="login-container">
    <h2 class="form-login-heading">Login</h2>
    <div class="alert alert-danger" role="alert" *ngIf="loginError">
        <strong>Warning:</strong> Username or Password mismatch
    </div>
    <form class="form-login" [formGroup]="loginForm"
(submit)="performLogin($event)">
        <input formControlName="username" type="text" class="form-control"
placeholder="Your username or e-mail address" required autofocus />
        <input formControlName="password" type="password" class="form-
control" placeholder="Your password" required />
        <div class="checkbox">
            <label>
                <input type="checkbox" value="remember-me">
                Remember me
            </label>
```

```
        </div>
        <button class="btn btn-lg btn-primary btn-block" type="submit">Sign
in</button>
    </form>
    <button class="btn btn-sm btn-default btn-block" type="submit"
(click)="callExternalLogin('Facebook')">
        Login with Facebook
    </button>
</div>
```

Once done, scroll down to the `class` section and add the following code (new lines are highlighted):

```
export class LoginComponent {
    title = "Login";
    loginForm = null;
    loginError = false;
    externalProviderWindow = null;

    constructor(
        private fb: FormBuilder,
        private router: Router,
        private authService: AuthService) {
        this.loginForm = fb.group({
            username: ["", Validators.required],
            password: ["", Validators.required]
        });
    }

    performLogin(e) {
        e.preventDefault();
        var username = this.loginForm.value.username;
        var password = this.loginForm.value.password;
        this.authService.login(username, password)
            .subscribe((data) => {
                // login successful
                this.loginError = false;
                var auth = this.authService.getAuth();
                alert("Our Token is: " + auth.access_token);
                this.router.navigate([""]);
            },
            (err) => {
                console.log(err);
                // login failure
                this.loginError = true;
            });
    }
```

```
callExternalLogin(providerName: string) {
    var url = "api/Accounts/ExternalLogin/" + providerName;
    // minimalistic mobile devices support
    var w = (screen.width >= 1050) ? 1050 : screen.width;
    var h = (screen.height >= 550) ? 550 : screen.height;
    var params = "toolbar=yes,scrollbars=yes,resizable=yes,width=" + w
+ ", height=" + h;
    // close previously opened windows (if any)
    if (this.externalProviderWindow) {
        this.externalProviderWindow.close();
    }
    this.externalProviderWindow = window.open(url, "ExternalProvider",
params, false);
    }
}
```

That's it.

Even if we added some logic to make things work on mobile devices, manually invoking `window.open` is not something we should be proud of. As a matter of fact, it's never a good practice for mobile-friendly web applications. There are a lot of existing client libraries, including Facebook and Google's OAuth2 JavaScript SDK, that can show, resize, and handle pop up and modal windows in a much better way than we can do in a bunch of JavaScript lines.

We're not using these to keep things as simple as possible, so we can focus on the core aspect of the process, which relieves us from adding external libraries and explaining how to properly use them. However, it's definitely advisable to migrate to a more robust solution before going live.

Updating the AuthService

When we built the `AuthService` class back in *Chapter 7, Authentication and Authorization,* we were thinking about supporting JWT tokens only. That's why we implemented a simple `logout()` method that basically just deletes the JWT tokens from `localStorage` and returns `true`. Now that we're adding the ASP.NET Core middleware for external providers, we need to delete their cookies as well. That's the reason why we added the `Logout()` Web API within our `AccountsController`, which now we need to call from Angular 2.

To do that, just open the `Scripts/app/auth.service.ts` file and change the existing `logout()` method in the following way:

```
logout(): any {
    return this.http.post(
```

```
        "api/Accounts/Logout",
        null)
        .map(response => {
            this.setAuth(null);
            return true;
        })
        .catch(err => {
            return Observable.throw(err);
        });
}
```

That's pretty straightforward. Instead of just removing the JSON web token from `localStorage`, we issue a call to the `api/Accounts/Logout` web API to delete the cookies. The `localStorage` cleansing will happen right after that. That way, we'll remove both the cookie-based external provider support and the JWT-based implementation that handles our internal accounts.

Updating the AppComponent

We're not done yet. The modifications we made must be also properly handled by the `AppComponent`, since it is our Angular 2 application's entry point. To be more specific, we need to change the internal `logout()` method to match the changes we made within the `AuthService` component and also implement the `externalProviderLogin` method.

Open the `/Scripts/app/app.component.ts` file and add change the following `import` line at the beginning of the file (new code is highlighted):

```
import {Component, NgZone} from "@angular/core";
```

Then change its `class` section just like the following (new/updated lines are highlighted):

```
export class AppComponent {
    title = "OpenGameList";

    constructor(
        public router: Router,
        public authService: AuthService,
        public zone: NgZone) {
        if (!(<any>window).externalProviderLogin) {
            var self = this;
            (<any>window).externalProviderLogin = function (auth) {
                self.zone.run(() => {
                    self.externalProviderLogin(auth);
                });
            }
        }
```

```
        }

        isActive(data: any[]): boolean {
            return this.router.isActive(
                this.router.createUrlTree(data),
                true);
        }

        logout(): boolean {
            // logs out the user, then redirects him to Welcome View.
            this.authService.logout().subscribe(result => {
                if (result) {
                    this.router.navigate([""]);
                }
            });
            return false;
        }

        externalProviderLogin(auth: any) {
            this.authService.setAuth(auth);
            console.log("External Login successful! Provider: "
                + this.authService.getAuth().providerName);
            this.router.navigate([""]);
        }
    }
```

The update within the `logout()` method is not a big deal. We just encapsulated its previous logic within a subscription to the updated `AuthService.logout()` return value, so we can be sure that the routing call won't be issued before the Web API call has been completed.

However, the new code we wrote to properly implement the `externalProviderLogin` method might be more difficult to understand, at least at first glance. Let's take a look at the new stuff, starting from the bottom.

The `externalProviderLogin` method itself is actually pretty straightforward: we receive the JSON `auth` object as input parameter and pass it to the `authService` that will store it in `localStorage`, then we redirect the (externally) logged-in user back to the welcome view.

Plain and simple, isn't it? If we could only call this method from outside our Angular 2 app, we would be done. That's precisely what we're doing within the `constructor` method, which now contains a short, yet quite obscure, piece of code. Let's try to understand what we're doing there.

Understanding zones

If we take another look at the `constructor` updated source code, we can see that we're injecting something new here: a `zone` instance of `NgZone` type. What are these zones and how do they work in Angular 2?

To get straight to the point, **zones** are execution contexts for encapsulating and intercepting JavaScript-based asynchronous activities. Each zone acts as a separate, persisting execution context that can be used to trace each asynchronous activity back to its originating source.

For a short yet enlightening definition of what zones are, we can use the words of Brian Ford of the Angular team during the presentation of the `Zone.js` library at Ng-Conf 2014:

> *"You can think of it as thread-local storage for JavaScript VMs."*

 The full talk is available at the following URL:
`https://www.youtube.com/watch?v=3IqtmUscE_U`.

As we already know, most modern JavaScript libraries execute a lot of asynchronous activities, such as DOM events, promises, and XHR calls. Being able to track these activities back to their issue would allow them to take action before and after each activity completes, thus providing great control over the whole execution flow.

This is most likely the reason that led Angular 2 developers to integrate the `Zone.js` within their framework. As a matter of fact, Angular 2 runs the application and all of its components in a specific zone, so it can listen to its own asynchronous events and react accordingly, checking for data changes, updating the information shown on screen via data binding, and so on.

We won't go further than that, as it would take us far from the scope of this book. The only thing we need to understand here is that whenever we need to call one of our application's methods from outside, we also need to run it within the Angular 2 zone; if we don't do that, Angular 2 won't be able to track the originating source, meaning that it won't react to model changes.

This is what would happen if we were to do that:

```
if (!(<any>window).externalProviderLogin) {
    (<any>window).externalProviderLogin = function (auth) {
        self.externalProviderLogin(auth);
    }
}
```

As we can see, there's no zone encapsulation anymore, so the method will be fired from a global context and Angular 2 event hooks will be cut out. This doesn't necessarily mean it won't work, but it would be a fire and forget way of exposing that method.

In our specific scenario, since routing is involved, it won't be the proper way to perform our task. We need to run our job within the same execution context used by our application.

This is precisely what we did within our `constructor` method (zone-encapsulation lines are highlighted):

```
if (!(<any>window).externalProviderLogin) {
    var self = this;
    (<any>window).externalProviderLogin = function (auth) {
        self.zone.run(() => {
            self.externalProviderLogin(auth);
        });
    }
}
```

Testing it out

It's time to run a full-surface test. Hit *F5* and wait for the welcome screen, then click the **Login** menu item to go to the updated `login` view:

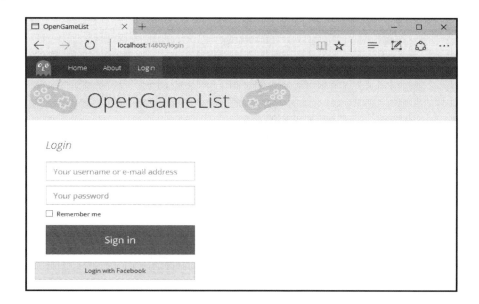

Click the **Login with Facebook** button. A pop-up window should appear shortly, containing the Facebook consent form:

 If we have never authenticated ourselves with Facebook using this browser, a login screen will be shown right before the consent form.

As soon as we click **Okay**, the OAuth2 authorization flow will continue. If we set everything up correctly, the pop-up screen should eventually close, bringing us back to the welcome view with an authenticated status. We can easily confirm our status by checking the presence of the **Logout** and **Add New** menu items since we previously set them to appear only if the user has been authenticated.

Google

As we said earlier, implementing additional providers will be much easier, as the external authentication infrastructure we built for Facebook will also take care of them.

Let's start with the big G. Again, the first thing we need to do is to configure our web application on Google servers to obtain the required credentials to configure the ASP.NET middleware.

Open the following URL:
`https://console.developers.google.com/projectselector/apis/credentials?pli=1`

Select **Create a new Project** from the drop-down list, then give it a suitable name and click the **Create** button:

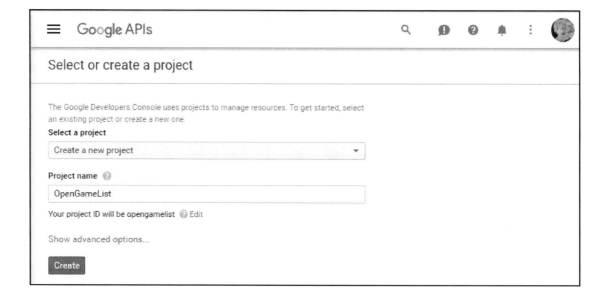

On the following screen, click the **Create credentials** button and select **OAuth client ID**:

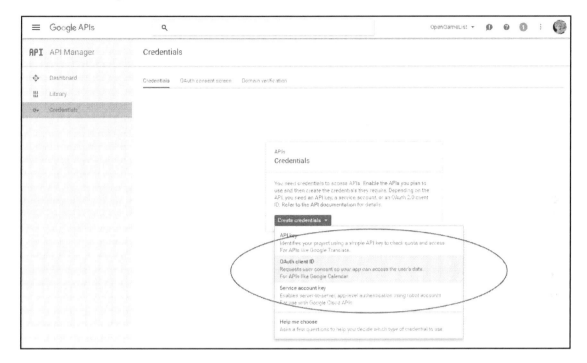

As soon as you confirm your choice, the Google platform will then warn you that you must create an **OAuth consent screen** for your application. We can do that by choosing an e-mail address and a product name shown to users (the remaining fields are optional).

Once done, we'll be allowed to add the **OAuth client ID**. Choose **Web Application** and fill in the form that will open with your application name and one (or more) JavaScript origins. It's pretty much the same thing we did with Facebook, with the only difference that we also have to specify the **Authorized redirect URIs** to match the format that will be internally used by ASP.NET Core, which defaults to the following: `http://<hostname>:<port>/signin-google`

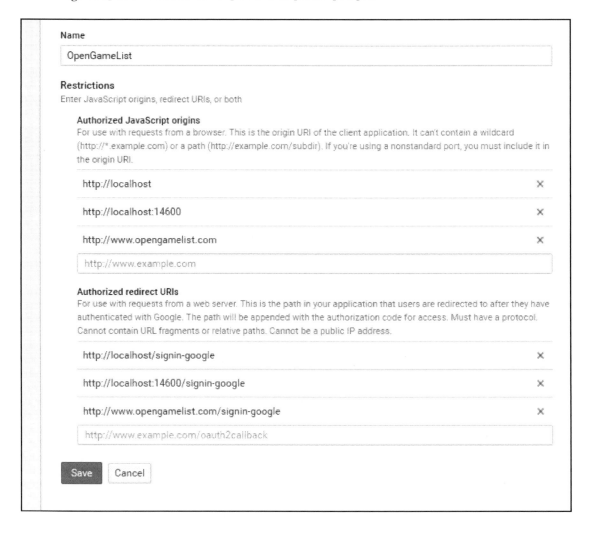

When we're ready, we can click on the Create button to get our new application's **ClientId** and **ClientSecret**. We can then put them in our project's `appsettings.json` file, right below the Facebook keys:

```
{
  "Authentication": {
    "Facebook": {
      "AppId": "___FB_APP_ID___",
      "AppSecret": "___FB_APP_SECRET___"
    },
    "Google": {
      "ClientId": "___GOOGLE_CLIENT_ID___",
      "ClientSecret": "___GOOGLE_CLIENT_SECRET___"
    }
  }
}
```

Before leaving the Google platform, we also need to add support for the **Google+ API**, otherwise, the OAuth2 login won't be able to work. To do that, go to **Library**, click the **Google APIs** tab, and look for **Google+ API** using the search textbox:

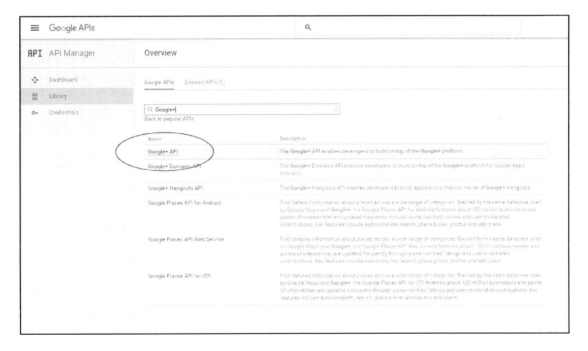

Select it, then click **Enable** to add the **Google OAuth2 authorization flow** support to our application.

Once done, we have to add the Google authentication package to our `project.json` file, right below the Facebook one:

```
"Microsoft.AspNetCore.Authentication.Google": "1.0.0"
```

Now we can open the `Startup.cs` file and add the Google Authentication middleware to the `Configure` method, right below the Facebook one:

```
app.UseGoogleAuthentication(new GoogleOptions()
{
    AutomaticAuthenticate = true,
    AutomaticChallenge = true,
    ClientId = Configuration["Authentication:Google:ClientId"],
    ClientSecret = Configuration["Authentication:Google:ClientSecret"],
    CallbackPath = "/signin-google",
    Scope = { "email" }
});
```

Last but not least, we need to add the Login with Google button within the HTML `template` of our Angular 2 application's `AppComponent` class. Open the `/Scripts/app/app.component.ts` file and add the following right below the existing Facebook button:

```
<button class="btn btn-sm btn-default btn-block" type="submit"
(click)="callExternalLogin('Google')">
    Login with Google
</button>
```

… and we're done.

Twitter

Adding Twitter to the loop is relatively easy, as the Twitter API is way simpler to use than Facebook's and Google's. However, it also has some pretty serious limitations when compared to their big brothers:

- It doesn't natively allow us to request the user's e-mail address, so we'll need to do an additional step.
- It requires a public facing URL to authenticate users. It won't work with `localhost` or unreachable hostnames.

To add it to our supported external providers list, go to https://apps.twitter.com/, sign in using your Twitter account, click on the **Add Application** button, then fill in the relevant data on the **Create an application** form that will appear:

Create an application

Application Details

Name *

OpenGameList

Your application name. This is used to attribute the source of a tweet and in user-facing authorization screens. 32 characters max.

Description *

A non-comprehensive directory of open-source video games available on the web

Your application description, which will be shown in user-facing authorization screens. Between 10 and 200 characters max.

Website *

http://www.opengamelist.com/

Your application's publicly accessible home page, where users can go to download, make use of, or find out more information about your application. This fully-qualified URL is used in the source attribution for tweets created by your application and will be shown in user-facing authorization screens.

(If you don't have a URL yet, just put a placeholder here but remember to change it later.)

Callback URL

Where should we return after successfully authenticating? OAuth 1.0a applications should explicitly specify their oauth_callback URL on the request token step, regardless of the value given here. To restrict your application from using callbacks, leave this field blank.

As soon as we accept the **Developer Agreement**, we'll be redirected to our new Twitter application's settings page. There we can retrieve the application's `ConsumerKey` and `ConsumerSecret` and paste them into our `appsettings.json` file, right below the Facebook and Google ones:

```
"Twitter": {
  "ConsumerKey": "___TWITTER_CONSUMER_KEY___",
  "ConsumerSecret": "___TWITTER_SECRET_KEY___"
}
```

Right after that, just like we did with Facebook and Google, we need to add the Twitter authentication package to our `project.json` file:

```
"Microsoft.AspNetCore.Authentication.Twitter": "1.0.0"
```

We also need to add the corresponding middleware to the `Startup.cs` file:

```
app.UseTwitterAuthentication(new TwitterOptions()
{
    AutomaticAuthenticate = true,
    AutomaticChallenge = true,
    ConsumerKey = Configuration["Authentication:Twitter:ConsumerKey"],
    ConsumerSecret =
Configuration["Authentication:Twitter:ConsumerSecret"],
    CallbackPath = "/signin-twitter"
});
```

And we also add the HTML button to the `/Scripts/app/app.component.ts` file:

```
<button class="btn btn-sm btn-default btn-block" type="submit"
(click)="callExternalLogin('Twitter')">
    Login with Twitter
</button>
```

Elevated permissions request

We're done coding, but we're not done yet because Twitter, just as we said at the beginning of this paragraph, won't natively send us the user's e-mail address.

To fix that, we need to manually fill in an elevated permissions request form where we ask Twitter to give to our application the chance to request e-mail addresses via OAuth2.

In order to do that, we need to perform the following steps:

1. Visit the following URL: `https://support.twitter.com/forms/platform`.
2. Locate the radio button list and select **I need access to special permissions**.
3. Enter the same **Application Name** we used when we registered our application with Twitter.
4. Enter the **Application ID**. This can be obtained by going to `https://apps.twitter.com/`, selecting our Twitter app, and then looking at the numeric parameter contained at the end of the URL itself.

5. Write the following within the **Authorization Request** text area: **E-Mail Address for OAuth2 sign-in**.

6. Click **Submit** button and wait for an e-mail response that will hopefully come in few hours. The e-mail will contain the instruction we need to follow to be able to request the user e-mail address. Until then the Twitter authentication won't work, as our `AccountsControllerExternalLoginCallback` method will throw an exception.

Troubleshooting

Learning how to properly handle external authentication providers is one of the most difficult aspects of this whole book. There are a lot of things that can go wrong, most of them not even under our control: `OpenIddict` behavior, Facebook/Google/Twitter configuration, permission handling, missing or incorrect endpoint URIs, security issues, and so on.

Understanding everything will require time and can be frustrating at times. That said, these are some useful suggestions that could save you a headache or two:

- We should always check our development browser's console log and network tabs, as these are an endless source of info regarding our web application's overall status: **HTTP 404** and/or **500** errors, missing resources, invalid JavaScript code, and so on, not to mention the console messages sent by our very own code.

- Every time we get an **Access Denied** exception, we should clean all browser cookies for our web application, especially the one called `Identity.External`, and also the relevant entry in our browser's `localStorage`. Both of them can be easily managed using the **Application** tab of the *Google Chrome* development tools, accessible by pressing *Shift + Ctrl + J*.

- Every time our .NET application crashes without satisfying browser output documenting the exception being thrown, we should check the **Output** tab of Visual Studio 2015. A lot of .NET Core libraries write their exceptions there.

- External OAuth2 providers will always give us the option to delete/deauthorize our web application from their web interface. Whenever we encounter problems with authentication, the best thing we can do to retrace our steps is to do precisely that and start over.

Conclusions

Here's how our application's login view should look after all this effort:

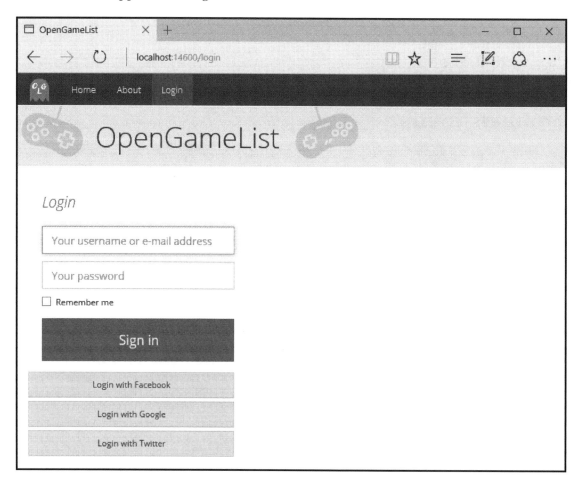

With this new authentication system, our application is now starting to become a potentially shippable product. However, we don't have a user profile view to handle user registrations, e-mail/password changes, and so on.

This feature, together with some other features, will be addressed in the following chapter.

Suggested topics

OpenID Connect, OpenIddict, OAuth2, OpenID Connect, RFC 6749, Secret Manager, DRY, WET, Zones, Zone.js, LocalStorage, Cookies.

Summary

Our `JwtProvider` was working fine, but it lacked some quite important features that had to be implemented as well in order to use it in a production-ready application such as the one we're aiming to build. To enable us to do that, we also identified **OpenIddict**, a viable open-source OAuth2/OpenID Connect provider that leverages ASP.NET Core Identity and ASOS, as a viable alternative, thus giving ourselves the choice between going for it and sticking with our handmade solution.

As soon as we chose our path, we implemented some external OAuth2 authentication providers such as Facebook, Google, and Twitter. The first was also the toughest one, as we needed to create our web API interface and understand how to properly handle the various scenarios for the first time. We definitely had an easier time with the other two, even if each one of them presented their own set of issues we had to address.

9

User Registration and Account Edit

In this chapter, we'll be adding a couple more account-related features that are still missing: user registration and edit user info.

User Registration

To implement a **User Registration** logic, we need to take care of the following tasks:

- Create a `UserViewModel` to send and receive data from and to the Web API, just like we did with items back in `Chapter 2`, *ASP.NET Controllers and Server-Side Routes*
- Add the `Get`, `Add`, `Update`, and `Delete` RESTful methods to the `AccountsController` Web API interface
- Handle all these methods in Angular 2 by updating the `AuthService` class
- Create a `UserEditComponent` class in our Angular 2 client to host the registration form, hooking it to the `AuthService` accordingly
- Update the other Angular 2 components, together with the existing client-side routing structure, in order to properly integrate it within the application workflow

Let's get it done.

UserViewModel

Right-click on the `/ViewModels/` folder and add a new C# class, naming it `UserViewModel.cs`. Replace the default content with the following code:

```
using System;
using System.ComponentModel;
using Newtonsoft.Json;

namespace OpenGameListWebApp.ViewModels
{
    [JsonObject(MemberSerialization.OptOut)]
    public class UserViewModel
    {
        #region Constructor
        public UserViewModel()
        {

        }
        #endregion Constructor

        #region Properties
        public string UserName { get; set; }
        public string Password { get; set; }
        public string PasswordNew { get; set; }
        public string Email { get; set; }
        public string DisplayName { get; set; }
        #endregion Properties
    }
}
```

We only declared the properties we're going to send to and/or receive from our Angular 2 client, just like we did with the `ItemViewModel`. The `PasswordNew` property is the only special case since it doesn't exist in the `ApplicationUser` class. We're going to use it by the end of this chapter, when we'll give our users some account-editing capabilities, such as being able to change their password.

AccountsController

Open the `/Controllers/AccountsController.cs` file we created in `Chapter 8`, *Third-Party Authentication and External Providers*, then add the following `region` between the existing constructor and external authentication providers regions:

```
#region RESTful Conventions
#endregion RESTful Conventions
```

This is where we're going to implement the `Get`, `Add`, `Update`, and `Delete` methods to properly handle all requests regarding user accounts.

Get

The `Get` request is commonly used any time the client wants to retrieve updated info regarding a given user.

To properly handle such requests, we need to define at least two implementations: a parameterless one, returning the currently active/logged in account (if any), and another one that will return the user corresponding to the requested ID.

The former is often used when the client needs to show the user their data, usually within a standard *view/edit account info* screen; the latter is required whenever we have a clickable user listing of any sort, or any other control that enables a visitor to see their fellow user's info:

```
/// <summary>
/// GET: api/accounts
/// </summary>
/// <returns>A Json-serialized object representing the current
account.</returns>
[HttpGet()]
public async Task<IActionResult> Get()
{
    var id = await GetCurrentUserId();
    var user = DbContext.Users.Where(i => i.Id == id).FirstOrDefault();
    if (user != null) return new JsonResult(new UserViewModel()
    {
UserName = user.UserName,
Email = user.Email,
DisplayName = user.DisplayName
    }, DefaultJsonSettings);
    else return NotFound(new { error = String.Format("User ID {0} has not
been found", id) });
}

/// <summary>
/// GET: api/accounts/{id}
/// ROUTING TYPE: attribute-based
/// </summary>
/// <returns>A Json-serialized object representing a single
account.</returns>
[httpget("{id}")]
public IActionResult Get(string id)
```

```
{
    return BadRequest(new { error = "not implemented (yet)." });
}
```

That's it. We don't have to implement the latter now, as we won't be using it by our application in this phase. We don't plan to add a clickable list of active and/or registered users, so we'll just emit a bad request HTTP error for now.

Add

This is a standard request to create a new user. We expect it to come right after the (new) user submitted a properly filled in registration form, so we restrict the method to POST requests only by using the HttpPost attribute:

```
/// <summary>
/// POST: api/accounts
/// </summary>
/// <returns>Creates a new User and return it accordingly.</returns>
[HttpPost()]
public async Task<IActionResult> Add([FromBody]UserViewModel uvm)
{
    if (uvm != null)
    {
        try
        {
            // check if the Username/Email already exists
            ApplicationUser user = await
UserManager.FindByNameAsync(uvm.UserName);
            if (user != null) throw new Exception("UserName already
exists.");
            user = await UserManager.FindByEmailAsync(uvm.Email);
            if (user != null) throw new Exception("E-Mail already
exists.");

            var now = DateTime.Now;

            // create a new Item with the client-sent json data
            user = new ApplicationUser()
            {
                UserName = uvm.UserName,
                Email = uvm.Email,
                CreatedDate = now,
                LastModifiedDate = now
            };

            // Add the user to the Db with a random password
```

```
        await UserManager.CreateAsync(user, uvm.Password);

        // Assign the user to the 'Registered' role.
        await UserManager.AddToRoleAsync(user, -Registered");

        // Remove Lockout and E-Mail confirmation
        user.EmailConfirmed = true;
        user.LockoutEnabled = false;

        // persist the changes into the Database.
        DbContext.SaveChanges();

        // return the newly-created User to the client.
        return new JsonResult(new UserViewModel()
        {
            UserName = user.UserName,
            Email = user.Email,
            DisplayName = user.DisplayName
        }, DefaultJsonSettings);
    }
    catch (Exception e)
    {
        // return the error.
        return new JsonResult(new { error = e.Message });
    }
}

// return a generic HTTP Status 500 (Not Found) if the client payload
is invalid.
    return new StatusCodeResult(500);
}
```

The implementation is quite long, but the code should be understandable enough. We check if the given username and/or e-mail address exist in our users archive. If they do, we emit an error message; otherwise, we create a new user account and return its relevant info in JSON format.

E-mail confirmation

We won't hide the fact that, for the sake of simplicity, we're purposely skipping the e-mail confirmation step, which has always been a distinctive feature of ASP.NET Identity as well as any existing web application since the dawn of time.

Luckily enough, implementing such a mechanism in ASP.NET Core isn't going to be hard at all. The task could be basically split into three relevant steps:

1. Instead of setting the user's `EmailConfirmed` property to `true` like we did, we should issue a call to the `GenerateEmailConfirmationTokenAsync()` method of `UserManager`.

2. The confirmation token should then be sent to the user's e-mail address so they can send it back to our web application as a URL parameter or inside an e-mail activation form.

3. Eventually, we should be able to validate it via a dedicated `AccountController` Web API using the `UserManager.ConfirmEmailAsync()` method.

Pretty straightforward, isn't it? Implementing it before going further is a great exercise to test our skills up to this point.

Update

The `Update` method is used to alter the data of an existing user. It's often called at the end of an edit profile info form of any sort, assuming that the currently active/logged in user is updating their own data. It can also be used by high-privileged users, such as administrators, to modify other user's data. However, we won't be supporting that within our application's first release, so we might as well skip that:

```
/// <summary>
/// PUT: api/accounts/{id}
/// </summary>
/// <returns>Updates current User and return it accordingly.</returns>
[HttpPut]
[Authorize]
public async Task<IActionResult> Update([FromBody]UserViewModel uvm)
{
    if (uvm != null)
    {
        try
        {
            // retrieve user
            var id = await GetCurrentUserId();
            ApplicationUser user = await UserManager.FindByIdAsync(id);
            if (user == null) throw new Exception("User not found");

            // check for current password
            if (await UserManager.CheckPasswordAsync(user, uvm.Password))
            {
                // current password ok, perform changes (if any)
```

```
                bool hadChanges = false;

                if (user.Email != uvm.Email)
                {
                    // check if the Email already exists
                    ApplicationUser user2 = await
UserManager.FindByEmailAsync(uvm.Email);
                    if (user2 != null && user.Id != user2.Id) throw new
Exception("E-Mail already exists.");
                    else await UserManager.SetEmailAsync(user, uvm.Email);
                    hadChanges = true;
                }

                if (!string.IsNullOrEmpty(uvm.PasswordNew))
                {
                    await UserManager.ChangePasswordAsync(user,
uvm.Password, uvm.PasswordNew);
                    hadChanges = true;
                }

                if (user.DisplayName != uvm.DisplayName)
                {
                    user.DisplayName = uvm.DisplayName;
                    hadChanges = true;
                }

                if (hadChanges)
                {
                    // if we had at least 1 change:
                    // update LastModifiedDate
                    user.LastModifiedDate = DateTime.Now;
                    // persist the changes into the Database.
                    DbContext.SaveChanges();
                }

                // return the updated User to the client.
                return new JsonResult(new UserViewModel()
                {
                    UserName = user.UserName,
                    Email = user.Email,
                    DisplayName = user.DisplayName
                }, DefaultJsonSettings);
            }
            else throw new Exception("Old password mismatch");
        }
        catch (Exception e)
        {
            // return the error.
```

```
            return new JsonResult(new { error = e.Message });
        }
    }
    // return a HTTP Status 404 (Not Found) if we couldn't find a suitable
item.
    return NotFound(new { error = String.Format("Current User has not been
found") });
}
```

Despite the fair amount of code, we should be able to understand everything. The first thing we do is check for the user's current password, which is required to perform any changes. If the password matches, we update the user fields accordingly with the new data. If the e-mail has been changed, we also check within our database to see if it already belongs to anyone else; if it does, we emit an error message. Otherwise, we go ahead.

If all checks pass, we update the `LastModifiedDate`, persist the new user info within our database, and return an updated set of data in JSON format; otherwise, we return a HTTP `Error 500`.

Delete

The `Delete` method is almost always a prerogative of administrators unless we want to allow our users to delete themselves. We're not planning to do that, neither are we building an administration panel in this phase, so we can safely skip both implementations for the time being:

```
/// <summary>
/// DELETE: api/accounts/
/// </summary>
/// <returns>Deletes current User, returning a HTTP status 200 (ok) when
done.</returns>
[HttpDelete()]
[Authorize]
public IActionResult Delete()
{
    return BadRequest(new { error = "not implemented (yet)." });
}

/// <summary>
/// DELETE: api/accounts/{id}
/// </summary>
/// <returns>Deletes an User, returning a HTTP status 200 (ok) when
done.</returns>
[HttpDelete("{id}")]
[Authorize]
```

```
public IActionResult Delete(string id)
{
    return BadRequest(new { error = "not implemented (yet)." });}
```

Now our Web API is ready to handle the most basic requests for adding and updating user accounts. We're going to call these new methods with our Angular 2 client in a short while.

User class

Time to switch to Angular 2. The first thing we need to do here is to add an Angular 2 `User` class. Right-click on `/Scripts/app/`, create a new `user.ts` TypeScript file, and fill it with the following code:

```
export class User {
    constructor(
        public UserName: string,
        public Password: string,
        public PasswordNew: string,
        public Email: string,
        public DisplayName: string) {}
}
```

This will be the client-side counterpart of the `UserViewModel` Web API class we just made.

AuthService

Open the `/Scripts/app/auth.service.ts` file and add the following import reference:

```
import {User} from "./user";
```

Then, implement the following methods:

```
get() {
    return this.http.get("api/Accounts")
        .map(response => response.json());
}

add(user: User) {
    return this.http.post(
        "api/Accounts",
        JSON.stringify(user),
        new RequestOptions({
            headers: new Headers({
                "Content-Type": "application/json"
```

```
            })
        }))
        .map(response => response.json());
    }

    update(user: User) {
        return this.http.put(
            "api/Accounts",
            JSON.stringify(user),
            new RequestOptions({
                headers: new Headers({
                    "Content-Type": "application/json"
                })
            }))
            .map(response => response.json());
    }
```

There's nothing special to explain here; we're just calling the Web APIs we added before, returning the resulting JSON objects.

UserEditComponent

Now we can create our **User Registration** form. Right-click on the `/Scripts/app/` folder and add a new `user-edit.component.ts` TypeScript file. Since the code is a bit complex, we'll split it up into parts.

Let's start with the `import` statements:

```
import {Component, OnInit} from "@angular/core";
import {FormBuilder, FormControl, FormGroup, Validators} from
"@angular/forms";
import {Router} from "@angular/router";
import {AuthService} from "./auth.service";
import {User} from "./user";
```

As we can see, we're referencing a lot of stuff here. By looking at the components we're pulling off from the `@angular2/forms` package, we can already guess that we're going to build a form using the model-driven pattern. We already used that when we built our minimalistic login form, yet we'll definitely see more about it here.

Here's the `@Component` section source code:

```
@Component({
    selector: "user-edit",
    template: `
```

```
<div class="user-container">
    <form class="form-user" [formGroup]="userForm" (submit)="onSubmit()">
        <h2 class="form-user-heading">{{title}}</h2>
        <div class="form-group">
            <input formControlName="username" type="text" class="form-
control" placeholder="Choose an Username" autofocus />
            <span class="validator-label valid"
*ngIf="this.userForm.controls.username.valid">
                <span class="glyphicon glyphicon-ok" aria-
hidden="true"></span>
                valid!
            </span>
            <span class="validator-label invalid"
*ngIf="!this.userForm.controls.username.valid &&
!this.userForm.controls.username.pristine">
                <span class="glyphicon glyphicon-remove" aria-
hidden="true"></span>
                invalid
            </span>
        </div>
        <div class="form-group">
            <input formControlName="email" type="text" class="form-control"
placeholder="Type your e-mail address" />
            <span class="validator-label valid"
*ngIf="this.userForm.controls.email.valid">
                <span class="glyphicon glyphicon-ok" aria-
hidden="true"></span>
                valid!
            </span>
            <span class="validator-label invalid"
*ngIf="!this.userForm.controls.email.valid &&
!this.userForm.controls.email.pristine">
                <span class="glyphicon glyphicon-remove" aria-
hidden="true"></span>
                invalid
            </span>
        </div>
        <div class="form-group">
            <input formControlName="password" type="password" class="form-
control" placeholder="Choose a Password" />
            <span class="validator-label valid"
*ngIf="this.userForm.controls.password.valid &&
!this.userForm.controls.password.pristine">
                <span class="glyphicon glyphicon-ok" aria-
hidden="true"></span>
                valid!
            </span>
            <span class="validator-label invalid"
```

```
*ngIf="!this.userForm.controls.password.valid &&
!this.userForm.controls.password.pristine">
                <span class="glyphicon glyphicon-remove" aria-
hidden="true"></span>
                invalid
            </span>
        </div>
        <div class="form-group">
            <input formControlName="passwordConfirm" type="password"
class="form-control" placeholder="Confirm your Password" />
            <span class="validator-label valid"
*ngIf="this.userForm.controls.passwordConfirm.valid &&
!this.userForm.controls.password.pristine &&
!this.userForm.hasError('compareFailed')">
                <span class="glyphicon glyphicon-ok" aria-
hidden="true"></span>
                valid!
            </span>
            <span class="validator-label invalid"
*ngIf="(!this.userForm.controls.passwordConfirm.valid &&
!this.userForm.controls.passwordConfirm.pristine) ||
this.userForm.hasError('compareFailed')">
                <span class="glyphicon glyphicon-remove" aria-
hidden="true"></span>
                invalid
            </span>
        </div>
        <div class="form-group">
            <input formControlName="displayName" type="text" class="form-
control" placeholder="Choose a Display Name" />
        </div>
        <div class="form-group">
            <input type="submit" class="btn btn-primary btn-block"
[disabled]="!userForm.valid" value="Register" />
        </div>
    </form>
</div>

})
```

As expected, there's a lot of new stuff here. We made extensive use of the `valid` property exposed by the `FormGroup` container and also by their inner `FormControl` input controls, as it's a convenient way to check the status of these items in real time.

We're using these values to change the GUI behavior in a number of ways, including disabling the **Register** button until the form is valid:

```
<input type="submit" class="btn btn-primary btn-block"
[disabled]="!userForm.valid" value="Register" />
```

Both the `Form` components and their `Validators` are set in the `class` source code, which we split into three parts for better reading. The first one features the `constructor`, which instantiates the services we'll be using via dependency injection:

```
export class UserEditComponent {
    title = "New User Registration";
    userForm: FormGroup = null;
    errorMessage = null;

    constructor(
        private fb: FormBuilder,
        private router: Router,
        private authService: AuthService) {
        if (this.authService.isLoggedIn()) {
            this.router.navigate([""]);
        }
    }
}
```

We know these objects already, so there's no need to explain them again. We can even recognize the highlighted part, as we already used it in our `LoginComponent` for the same purpose. If the user is already logged in, they shouldn't be allowed to fill in a registration form, so we're redirecting them to the **Welcome View**.

Here's the `ngOnInit` method, where we initialize the form using `FormBuilder`:

```
ngOnInit() {
    this.userForm = this.fb.group(
        {
            username: ["", [
                Validators.required,
                Validators.pattern("[a-zA-Z0-9]+")
                ]],
            email: ["", [
                Validators.required,
                Validators.pattern("[a-z0-9!#$%&'*+/=?^_`{|}~-]+(?:\.[a-
z0-9!#$%&'*+/=?^_`{|}~-]+)*@(?:[a-z0-9](?:[a-z0-9-]*[a-z0-9])?\.)+[a-
z0-9](?:[a-z0-9-]*[a-z0-9])?")
                ]],
            password: ["", [
                Validators.required,
                Validators.minLength(6)]],
```

```
            passwordConfirm: ["", [
                Validators.required,
                Validators.minLength(6)]],
            displayName: ["", null]
        },
        {
            validator: this.compareValidator('password', 'passwordConfirm')
        }
    );
}
```

As we can see, we're using a wide set of `Validators` here. Most of them are shipped with the `@angular2/forms` package:

- `Validators.required` is an old friend, as we already used it for our login form. Its behavior is quite self-explanatory: it will invalidate the control as long as its value is empty. We're using this on all our input controls except for `displayName`, since it's not a required field.
- `Validators.pattern` is basically a **regular expression (regex)** validator. It will check the control value against the given **regex** and invalidate it until it matches. We used it together with a very basic regex to allow only alphanumeric characters for the `username`, and then with a **RFC 2822** compliant regex to check for invalid e-mail addresses. Although it won't save us from scammers, it will do a decent job to save our real users from the most common typing errors.
- `Validators.minLength` does what its name suggests: it will invalidate the control until its value reaches the specified minimum character count.

The last validator we used, `this.compareValidator`, is a custom one: we made it to check if the `password` and `passwordConfirm` input values are the same or not and let the user know in real time, which is a common feature of modern registration forms. Technically, it's nothing more than a standard function that we can append right after the `ngOnInit` method:

```
compareValidator(fc1: string, fc2: string) {
    return (group: FormGroup): { [key: string]: any } => {
        let password = group.controls[fc1];
        let passwordConfirm = group.controls[fc2];
        if (password.value === passwordConfirm.value) {
            return null;
        }
        return { compareFailed: true }
    }
}
```

It's worth noting that form-level validators such as this are required to either return `null` if there are no errors, or a `{ [key: string]: any }` object in case of failure. The used `key` can be checked within the `template` by using the `FormControl.hasError(key)` method, just like we did in the preceding form.

Right after that, we can implement the `onSubmit` function, which will be executed when the **Submit** button is clicked:

```
onSubmit() {
    this.authService.add(this.userForm.value)
        .subscribe((data) => {
            if (data.error == null) {
                // registration successful
                this.errorMessage = null;
                this.authService.login(
                    this.userForm.value.username,
                    this.userForm.value.password)
                    .subscribe((data) => {
                        // login successful
                        this.errorMessage = null;
                        this.router.navigate([""]);
                    },
                    (err) => {
                        console.log(err);
                        // login failure
                        this.errorMessage =
                            "Warning: Username or Password mismatch";
                    });
            }
            else {
                // registration failure
                this.errorMessage = data.error;
            }
        },
        (err) => {
            // server/connection error
            this.errorMessage = err;
        });
}
```

As we can see, if the `onSubmit` method is completed without errors we will issue a call to `authService.login` to authenticate the user and, right after that, redirect them back to the **Welcome View**.

> Don't forget to add a closing parenthesis right after the `onSubmit` method to close the `class` block.

Connecting the dots

Now that we have set up our controller/service/component chain, we need to wrap everything up within the client application's loop.

Updating the root module

Let's start by adding the new-born class to the application's root module. Open the `/Scripts/app/app.module.ts` file, then add the following line to the `import` references right after the `PageNotFoundComponent`:

```
import {UserEditComponent} from "./user-edit.component";
```

Don't forget to update the declarations array accordingly:

```
declarations: [
    AboutComponent,
    AppComponent,
    HomeComponent,
    ItemListComponent,
    ItemDetailEditComponent,
    ItemDetailViewComponent,
    LoginComponent,
    PageNotFoundComponent,
    UserEditComponent
],
```

Implementing the route

The next step will be adding the `register` route to the routing class file. Open the `/Scripts/app/app.routing.ts` file and add this to the `import` references:

```
import {UserEditComponent} from "./user-edit.component";
```

Then scroll down to the routing rules and add the following, right after the `Login` one:

```
{
    path: "register",
    component: UserEditComponent
},
```

That's it. Now that we've defined the route, we need to make good use of it.

Adding the Register link

Open the `/Scripts/app/login.component.ts` file and add this to the `import` references:

```
import {UserEditComponent} from "./user-edit.component";
```

Then scroll down to the `template` section and add the following (new lines highlighted):

```html
<div class="login-container">
    <h2 class="form-login-heading">Login</h2>
    <div class="alert alert-danger" role="alert" *ngIf="loginError">
        <strong>Warning:</strong> Username or Password mismatch
    </div>
    <form class="form-login" [formGroup]="loginForm"
(submit)="performLogin($event)">
        <input formControlName="username" type="text" class="form-control"
placeholder="Your username or e-mail address" required autofocus />
        <input formControlName="password" type="password" class="form-
control" placeholder="Your password" required />
        <div class="checkbox">
            <label>
                <input type="checkbox" value="remember-me">
                Remember me
            </label>
        </div>
        <button class="btn btn-lg btn-primary btn-block" type="submit">Sign
in</button>
    </form>
    <div class="register-link">
        Don't have an account yet?
        <a (click)="onRegister()">Click here to register!</a>
    </div>
    <button class="btn btn-sm btn-default btn-block" type="submit"
(click)="callExternalLogin('Facebook')">
        Login with Facebook
    </button>
    <button class="btn btn-sm btn-default btn-block" type="submit"
```

```
(click)="callExternalLogin('Google')">
        Login with Google
    </button>
</div>
```

Keep scrolling down and implement the `onRegister()` method within the class structure, right after the `performLogin()` method:

```
onRegister() {
    this.router.navigate(["register"]);
}
```

With this, we're done here as well.

Defining the styles

Open the `/Scripts/less/style.less` file, then append the following to style up the `UserEditComponent` we just made:

```
.user-container {
    max-width: 500px;
    padding: 15px;
    .form-user {
        margin-left: 20px;
        input {              .
            margin-bottom: 10px;
            margin-right: 5px;
            max-width: 330px;
            display: inline;
        }
        .validator-label {
            &.valid {
                color: green;
            }
            &.invalid {
                color: red;
            }
        }
    }
    .register-link {
        cursor:pointer;
        font-size: 0.8em;
        margin: 10px 0;
    }
}
```

Right after that, add the CSS class we attached to the link panel that we put in the `UserLoginComponent` file:

```
.register-link {
    cursor:pointer;
    font-size: 0.8em;
    margin: 10px 0;
}
```

Updating the menu

Last but not least, we should find a way to let our users know that our **Login** view now also features a link to the brand new **User Registration** feature we just made. The best thing we can do is to bring the information up to the menu itself.

Switch back to the `/Scripts/app/app.component.ts` file and modify the navigation menu in the following way (updated code is highlighted):

```
<div class="collapse navbar-collapse" id="navbar">
    <ul class="nav navbar-nav">
        <li [class.active]="isActive([''])">
            <a class="home" [routerLink]="['']">Home</a>
        </li>
        <li [class.active]="isActive(['about'])">
            <a class="about" [routerLink]="['about']">About</a>
        </li>
        <li *ngIf="!authService.isLoggedIn()"
[class.active]="isActive(['login']) || isActive(['register'])">
            <a class="login" [routerLink]="['login']">Login / Register</a>
        </li>
        <li *ngIf="authService.isLoggedIn()">
            <a class="logout" href="javascript:void(0)"
(click)="logout()">Logout</a>
        </li>
        <li *ngIf="authService.isLoggedIn()"
[class.active]="isActive(['item/edit', 0])">
            <a class="add" [routerLink]="['item/edit', 0]">Add New</a>
        </li>
    </ul>
</div>
```

Testing it out

This is what our new user **Login** view will look like:

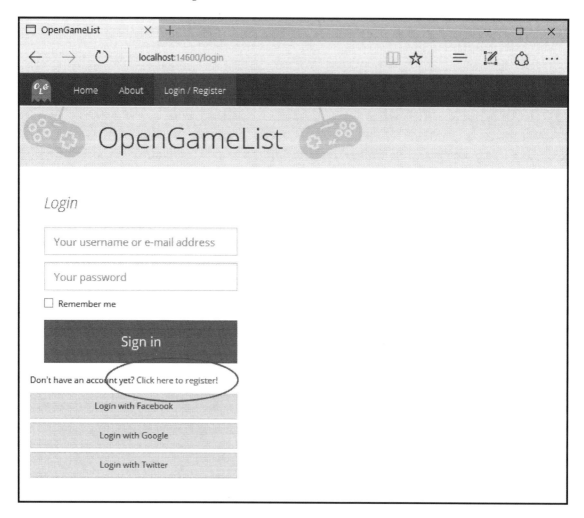

And here's the **User Registration** view, which is accessible by clicking on the **Click here to register!** link:

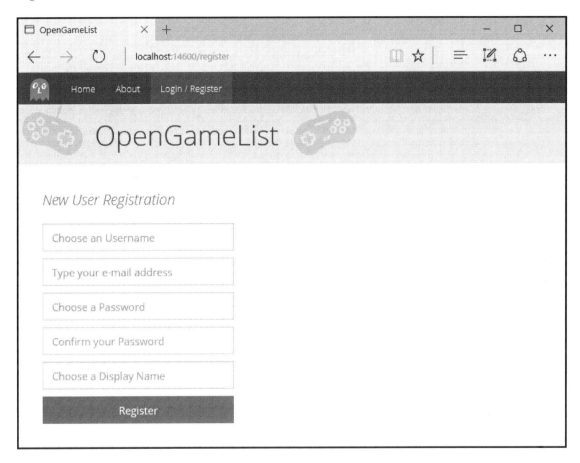

We can play a bit with the form to see how our module-driven approach actually works. As soon as we start typing something, we will get an instant feedback that will guide us to compile each field properly:

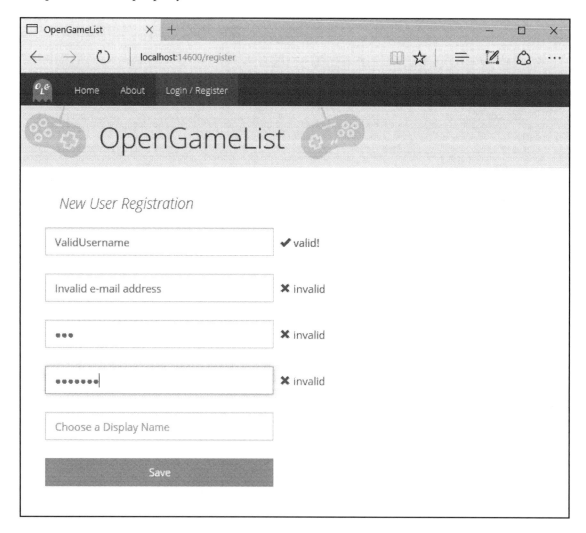

When we are ready to create our new account, we can click on the **Register** button and submit the form. A new user will be created and authenticated, then we will be redirected to the **Welcome View**.

Edit Account

Out of the three RESTful methods, we implemented in our Web API and `AuthService` interfaces, the whole **User Registration** view only took one. The `Get` and the `Update` methods are still there, waiting for us to make use of them.

The best thing we can do to test them both is to implement an **Edit Account** view to give our users the chance to change a limited set of their account info, such as e-mail address, password, and display name.

Luckily enough, we already did most of the job: the `UserEditComponent` already does most of what we need; we just have to tweak it a bit more so it can be used to update an existing account as well as register a new one.

Two routes, one component

In contrast with what we did for the `ItemDetailEditComponent`, we don't need to handle a `get` parameter because the account we want to update cannot be chosen: users will only be able to edit their own one. However, we still need to add an additional route, so we'll be able to distinguish between **User Registration** and an account update requests.

Open the `/Scripts/app/app.routing.ts` file and add the following route, right after the `register` one:

```
{
    path: "account",
    component: UserEditComponent
},
```

Adapting the UserEditComponent

The next thing we need to do is to fetch the currently active route within the
UserEditController and act accordingly. Go back to the /Scripts/app/user-
edit.component.ts file and add the ActivatedRoute class reference to the
@angular/routerimport line:

```
import {Router, ActivatedRoute} from "@angular/router";
```

This will allow us to define isRegister Boolean variable and set it accordingly to the
active route (new/updated lines are highlighted):

```
export class UserEditComponent {
    title = "New User Registration";
    userForm: FormGroup = null;
    errorMessage = null;
    isRegister: boolean;

    constructor(
        private fb: FormBuilder,
        private router: Router,
        private activatedRoute: ActivatedRoute,
        private authService: AuthService) {
        // determine behavior by fetching the active route
        this.isRegister = (activatedRoute.snapshot.url.toString() ===
"register");
        if ((this.isRegister && this.authService.isLoggedIn())
            || (!this.isRegister && !this.authService.isLoggedIn())) {
            this.router.navigate([""]);
        }
        if (!this.isRegister) {
            this.title = "Edit Account";
        }
    }
```

Once assigned, we immediately used the isRegister variable to improve our redirect
strategy: as we don't want registered users to play with our registration form, we also can't
allow unregistered users to edit their (non-existing) account. Right after that, we use it again
to conditionally change the title to a most suited one.

The next change we need to do is at the end of the ngOnInit method (new lines are
highlighted):

```
ngOnInit() {
    this.userForm = this.fb.group(
        {
```

```
        username: ["", [
            Validators.required,
            Validators.pattern("[a-zA-Z0-9]+")
        ]],
        email: ["", [
            Validators.required,
            Validators.pattern("[a-z0-9!#$%&'*+/=?^_`{|}~-]+(?:\.[a-
z0-9!#$%&'*+/=?^_`{|}~-]+)*@(?:[a-z0-9](?:[a-z0-9-]*[a-z0-9])?\.)+[a-
z0-9](?:[a-z0-9-]*[a-z0-9])?")
        ]],
        password: ["", [
            Validators.required,
            Validators.minLength(6)]],
        passwordConfirm: ["", [
            Validators.required,
            Validators.minLength(6)]],
        displayName: ["", null]
    },
    {
        validator: this.compareValidator('password', 'passwordConfirm')
    }
);

if (!this.isRegister) {
    this.userForm.addControl("passwordCurrent",
        new FormControl("", Validators.required));
    var password = this.userForm.find("password");
    password.clearValidators();
    password.setValidators(Validators.minLength(6));
    var passwordConfirm =
        this.userForm.find("passwordConfirm");
    passwordConfirm.clearValidators();
    passwordConfirm.setValidators(Validators.minLength(6));
    this.authService.get().subscribe(
        user => {
            this.userForm.find("username")
                .setValue(user.UserName);
            this.userForm.find("email")
                .setValue(user.Email);
            this.userForm.find("displayName")
                .setValue(user.DisplayName);
        }
    );
}
}
```

These few lines of code depict a number of tasks we need to perform whenever `this.isRegister` is `false`:

- Adding a new `passwordCurrent` control with a `required` validator as we'll use it to request the user's current password, which will be required to perform any change to their account.
- Removing the `required` validator from the `password` and `passwordConfirm` controls: the reason for this is pretty simple; when we're in **Edit Account** mode, these controls will be used to change the current password, which should never be a required operation. The only validator we're keeping for these controls is the `minLength(6)`. The user won't be forced to change it; however, if he chooses to do that, we won't accept anything less than the six-character length.
- Retrieving the current `UserName`, `Email`, and `DisplayName` values, so the user will be able to review them before performing any change. It's worth noting that they will be set asynchronously, as soon as the `authService` method `get` will fetch the data from the `AccountsController`.

Right after that, we need to perform the following changes to the `onSubmit` method (new/updated lines are highlighted):

```
onSubmit() {
    if (this.isRegister) {
        this.authService.add(this.userForm.value)
            .subscribe((data) => {
                if (data.error == null) {
                    // registration successful
                    this.errorMessage = null;
                    this.authService.login(
                        this.userForm.value.username,
                        this.userForm.value.password)
                        .subscribe((data) => {
                            // login successful
                            this.errorMessage = null;
                            this.router.navigate([""]);
                        },
                        (err) => {
                            console.log(err);
                            // login failure
                            this.errorMessage =
                                "Warning: Username or Password mismatch";
                        });
                }
                else {
                    // registration failure
                    this.errorMessage = data.error;
```

```
                }
            },
            (err) => {
                // server/connection error
                this.errorMessage = err;
            });
    }
    else {
        let user = new User(
            this.userForm.value.username,
            this.userForm.value.password,
            this.userForm.value.passwordNew,
            this.userForm.value.email,
            this.userForm.value.displayName);
        this.authService.update(user)
            .subscribe((data) => {
                if (data.error == null) {
                    // update successful
                    this.errorMessage = null;
                    this.router.navigate([""]);
                }
                else {
                    // update failure
                    this.errorMessage = data.error;
                }
            },
            (err) => {
                // server/connection error
                this.errorMessage = err;
            });
    }
}
```

There's nothing special here. We wrapped the `authService.add` method into an `if` condition to ensure that it will be executed only when the form is being used in **User Registration** mode; we then added a call to the `authService.update` method for the new **Edit Account** scenario.

We're not done yet. Before being able to test it, we need to make some changes to the `template` section too. Scroll up to it, look for the `<input>` HTML element that handles the username, and conditionally disable it in the following way (updated code is highlighted):

```
<input [disabled]="!this.isRegister" formControlName="username" type="text"
class="form-control" placeholder="Choose an Username" autofocus />
```

This is required to make the user aware of the fact that won't be able to change its username.

Once done, scroll down to the `<div class="form-group">` containing the `password` input control and place the following code right before it:

```
<div *ngIf="!this.isRegister" class="form-group">
    <input formControlName="passwordCurrent" type="password" class="form-
control" placeholder="Current Password" />
    <span class="validator-label invalid"
*ngIf="!this.userForm.controls.passwordCurrent.valid">
        <span class="glyphicon glyphicon-remove" aria-hidden="true"></span>
        required
    </span>
</div>
```

This is the HTML code for the `passwordCurrent` control we added programmatically in the `ngOnInit` method a short while ago. We already explained why we need this, so we can go ahead.

The last thing we need to do here is to apply a minor update to the submit button text value. We certainly don't want our users to click on **Register** when they are editing their account!

Scroll down to that HTML code and change it as follows (updated code is highlighted):

```
<div class="form-group">
    <input type="submit" class="btn btn-primary btn-block"
[disabled]="!userForm.valid" value="{{this.isRegister ? 'Register' :
'Save'}}" />
</div>
```

That's much better. On top of that, we're now aware of the fact that Angular 2 Template Syntax allows the usage of ternary operators. That's great to know!

Updating the navigation menu

We're almost done. We just need to connect the `account` route with our navigation menu so that our users will be able to access it.

Open the `/Scripts/app/app.component.ts` file and add the following `<li>` element to the `<ul>` container in the `template` section, right under the **Add New** one:

```
<li *ngIf="authService.isLoggedIn()" class="right"
[class.active]="isActive(['account'])">
    <a [routerLink]="['account']">Edit Account</a>
</li>
```

Adding styles

We added the `right` CSS class to our new `<li>` element for a reason: we want our **Edit Account** menu item to appear near the upper-right corner of the browser screen, just like the majority of websites actually do. Needless to say, in order to make it happen, we also need to define a `.class` selector and configure it with the appropriate style sheet rules.

Open the `/Scripts/less/style.less` file and append the following code:

```
@media (min-width: 768px) {
    .nav.navbar-nav {
        float: none;
        li.right {
            float: right;
        }
    }
}
```

That's it. As we can see, we added some floating rules to put the menu item to the rightmost part of the screen. These rules are conveniently wrapped into a Media Query that will ensure they will be applied only when we have enough width (`768px` or more). This means that our desired right-most effect will work on a desktop environment only, leaving the mobile browsers layout unaffected.

> Media Queries are a powerful CSS3 feature. UI designers can use them to tailor their presentations to a specific range of output devices without changing the content of the page itself. To know more about them, we strongly suggest reading the following URL:
> `https://www.w3.org/TR/css3-mediaqueries/`

Before going further, we should check that the **Task Runner** is actually running, so the compiled client code will be updated with our latest changes.

Final test

Now we can hit *F5* and see what our new **Edit Account** view looks like:

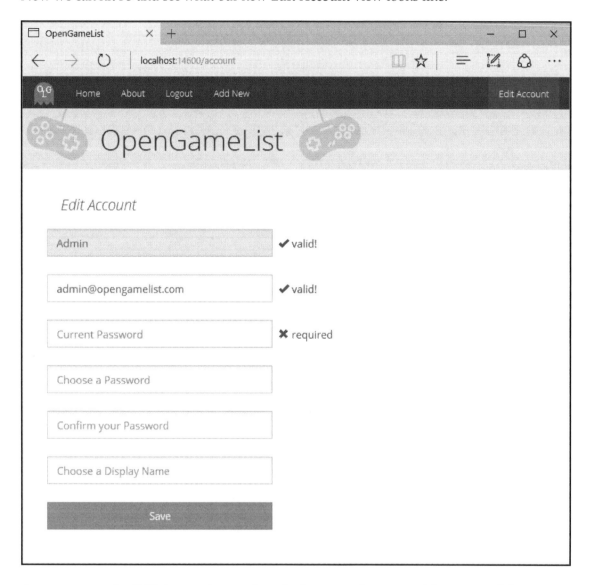

As we can see, the **Edit Account** menu item is shown on the *upper-right* corner of the screen. This is definitely a better place for all the options that controls the user account status, as they won't be confused with the *navigation* part of the main menu.

Wouldn't it be great if the **Login/Register** and **Logout** commands could be there too? Let's take this chance to do that.

Open the `/Scripts/app/app.component.ts` file and rearrange the navigation menu `<li>` elements in the following way:

```
<ul class="nav navbar-nav">

    <!-- Navigation commands for everyone -->
    <li [class.active]="isActive([''])">
        <a class="home" [routerLink]="['']">Home</a>
    </li>
    <li [class.active]="isActive(['about'])">
        <a class="about" [routerLink]="['about']">About</a>
    </li>

    <!-- Navigation commands for authenticated users -->
    <li *ngIf="authService.isLoggedIn()"
[class.active]="isActive(['item/edit', 0])">
        <a class="add" [routerLink]="['item/edit', 0]">Add New</a>
    </li>

    <!-- Account-related commands -->
    <li *ngIf="!authService.isLoggedIn()" class="right"
[class.active]="isActive(['login']) || isActive(['register'])">
        <a class="login" [routerLink]="['login']">Login / Register</a>
    </li>
    <li *ngIf="authService.isLoggedIn()" class="right">
        <a class="logout" href="javascript:void(0)"
(click)="logout()">Logout</a>
    </li>
    <li *ngIf="authService.isLoggedIn()" class="right"
[class.active]="isActive(['account'])">
        <a [routerLink]="['account']">Edit Account</a>
    </li>

</ul>
```

All we did here was reposition the content we already had add a couple HTML comments to split these elements into three groups: the navigation commands accessible to everyone, those restricted to authenticated users only, and the account/related ones. We also added the `right` CSS class to the **Login/Register** and **Logout** elements as we moved them into the latter group.

Before moving out, let's hit *F5* one last time to see what our improved menu looks like:

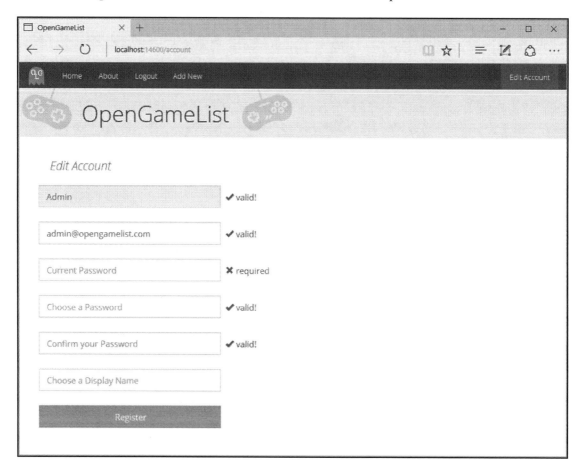

Conclusions

Our sample SPA application is mostly done. We are perfectly aware of the fact that a number of relevant features are still missing, such as the inability to refresh JWT Tokens, the lack of View Comments/Insert Comment components, the missing support for user-uploaded item image files, and so on. However, it is undoubtedly a potentially shippable product that will most likely meet our product owner's expectations.

All we have to do now is add some finishing touches and then publish it in a production environment, which is precisely what we're going to do in the next chapter.

Suggested topics

Template-driven forms, model-driven forms, FormBuilder, regex, Angular 2 Template Syntax, ternary operators, Media Queries.

Summary

Our native web application is slowly coming to an end, with most of its expected features ready and working. In this chapter, we implemented two of them that were still missing: a **User Registration** view, where new users can register themselves, and an **Edit Account** view they can use to change their e-mail address, password, and/or display name.

For each one of them, we added a Web API interface using standard RESTful methods, a set of Angular 2 `AuthService` methods, and a client-side routing strategy. While we were there, we also made some cosmetic changes to the navigation menu items and their corresponding style sheets to grant our visitors a better user experience.

10
Finalization and Deployment

Our valuable journey through ASP.NET Core Web API and Angular 2 development is coming to an end. The native web application we've been working on since Chapter 2, *ASP.NET Controllers and Server-Side Routes*, is now a potentially shippable product, ready to be published in a suitable environment for evaluation purposes.

However, in order to do that, we need to give our project some finishing touches.

Switching to SQL Server

Although localDB proved itself to be a great development choice, it's not a good idea to use it in production as well. That's why we'll replace it with **SQL Server**. As for the chosen edition, we can either go for Express, Web, Standard, or Enterprise depending on what we need and/or can afford.

For the sake of simplicity, we'll be using SQL Server 2016 Express Edition, which can be downloaded for free from the following Microsoft official URL: https://www.microsoft.com/en-US/server-cloud/products/sql-server-editions/sql-server-express.aspx

Needless to say, we need to install it on a machine that is reachable from our web server via a **Local Area Network (LAN)**.

Installing SQL Server 2016 Express

The installation process is pretty straightforward. Unless we don't need anything specific, we can just go for the basic type:

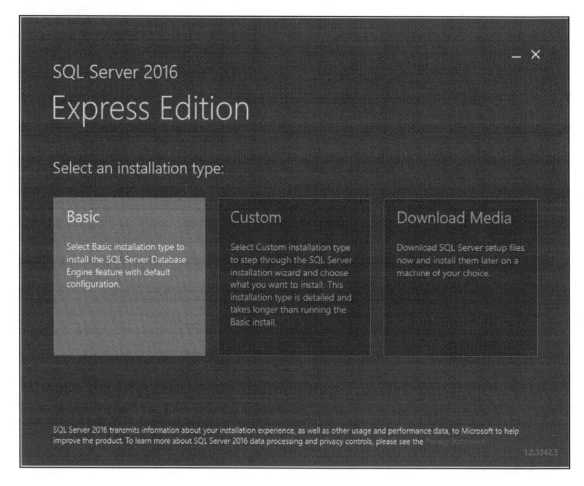

Eventually, we'll be prompted with an **Installation Complete** window, which will also give us some useful info, including the database instance name and a default connection string ready for a connection test:

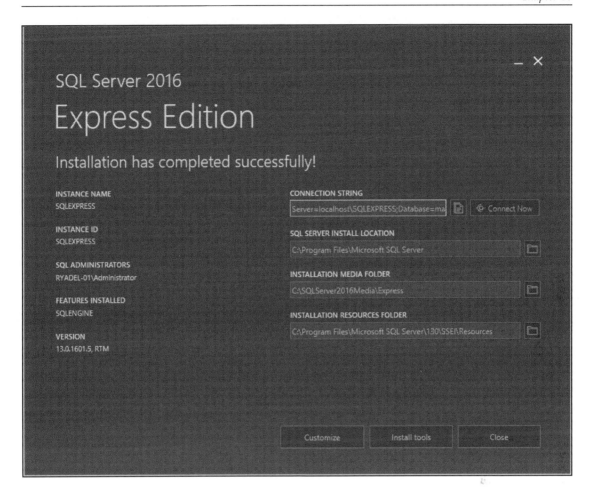

Installing SQL Server Management Studio

From here, we can click the **Install tools** button and download SQL Server Management Studio, a tool that we can use to create the OpenGameList database and also a dedicated user that can access it.

 SQL Server Management Studio is a separate product available for free download at the following URL:
https://msdn.microsoft.com/en-us/library/mt23829.aspx

Configuring the database

Once we've downloaded and installed it, launch the SQL Server Management Studio. We will be prompted by a **Connect to Server** modal window that will allow us to connect to our local SQL Server instance.

To do this, select the **Database Engine** server type and then, from the **Server name** combo box, choose **<Browse for more…>**. Another pop-up window will appear, from which we'll be able to select the database engine we just installed on our server:

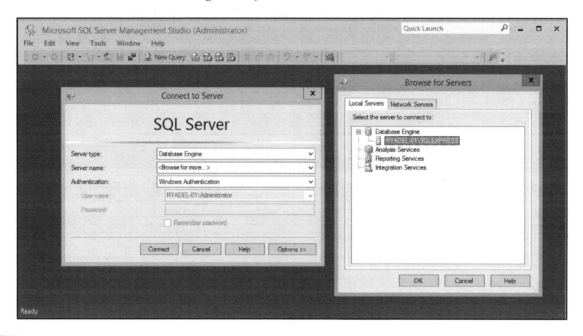

As for the **Authentication** part, we can leave **Windows Authentication**, the default SQL Server authentication mode.

When we're done, click on the **Connect** button and a **Server Explorer** window will appear, containing a tree view representing the structure of your SQL Server instance. This is the interface we'll use to create our database and also the user/password that our application will use to access it.

If you have a strong knowledge of SQL Server, you might want to skip the following steps and configure your instance as you prefer; otherwise, keep reading.

Changing the authentication mode

The first thing we need to do is to change the default SQL Server authentication mode, so we won't be forced to use an existing Windows account. To do so, right-click on the root tree view node, which represents our SQL Server instance, and select **Properties** from the contextual menu. From the modal window that appears, select the **Security** page, then switch from **Windows Authentication mode** to **SQL Server and Windows Authentication mode**:

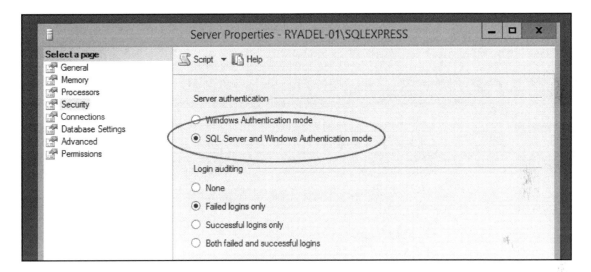

Adding the OpenGameList database

Now we can create the database that will host our application's tables. Right-click on the **Databases** folder and choose **Add Database** from the contextual menu. Give it the **OpenGameList** name and click on **OK**.

Adding the OpenGameList login

Go back to the root**Databases** folders, then expand the **Security** folder, which should be just below it. From there, right-click on the **Logins** subfolder and choose **New Login**. Again, give it the OpenGameList name. From the radio button list below, select **SQL Server Authentication** and set a suitable password (for example, SamplePassword123), then click on **OK**.

If you want a simpler password, such as OpenGameList, you might have to also disable the **enforce password policy** option.

Mapping the login to the database

The next thing we need to do is to properly map this login to the OpenGameList database we added earlier. From the navigation menu to the left, switch to the **User Mapping** tab. Click on the checkbox right to the OpenGameList database, then write OpenGameList in the **User** cell and assign the **db_owner** membership role:

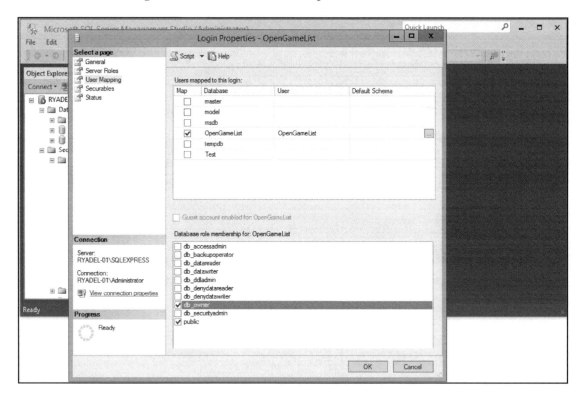

As soon as we click on the **OK** button, a new OpenGameList user will be added to the OpenGameList database with full administrative rights.

We can easily confirm that by going back to the root **Databases** folder and expanding it to **OpenGameList** | **Security** | **Users**:

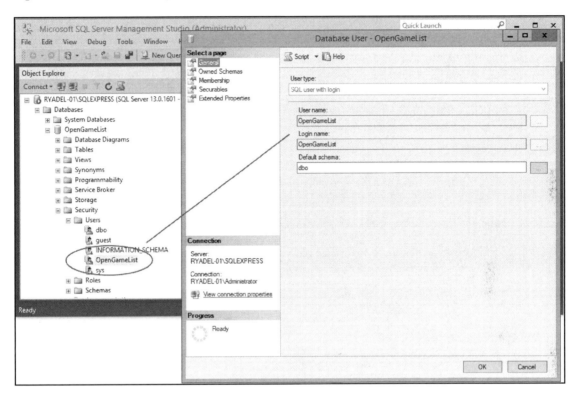

That's it! Now we'll be able to access our brand new `OpenGameList` database with a standard connection string using the credentials we just created.

Adding a SQL Server connection string

Now that the SQL Server database has been set up, we need to tell our application to use it instead of `localDb` while in production. We can easily do that by adopting the ASP.NET Core default pattern for configuring application behavior across multiple environments.

To implement it within our project, we need to perform the following steps:

1. Create an `appsettings.production.json` file to override the `localDb` connection string with the SQL Server one when the application runs in a production environment.
2. Configure the `publishOptions` within the `project.json` file to publish these kinds of file.
3. Check that our `Startup` class is properly configured to load the application settings files using a cascading logic that privileges the current running environment.
4. Update the `launchSettings.json` file to ensure that the production environment will be set whenever we publish our project.

Creating an application settings file for production

Right-click to the project's root and select **Add | New Item**. Choose **ASP.NET Configuration File**, name it `appsettings.production.json`, and click on **OK**.

An environment-specific version of the `appsettings.json` file will be created accordingly.

Visual Studio should also nest it below the main configuration file, as can be seen in the following screenshot:

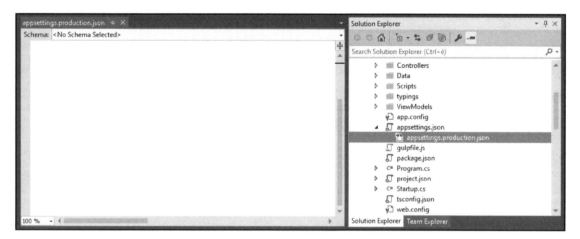

From now on, any key/value pair we'll include within the
`appsettings.production.json` file will override the corresponding key/value in the
main configuration file whenever the application will run within a production environment.
It means that we can use it to redefine a number of production-specific values there,
including (yet not limited to) the default connection string.

As a matter of fact, that's precisely what we need to do. Open the new
`appsettings.production.json` file and replace the sample contents with the following
code:

```
{
  "Data": {
    "DefaultConnection": {
      "ConnectionString":
"Server=localhost\\SQLEXPRESS;Database=OpenGameList;User
Id=OpenGameList;Password=SamplePassword123;Integrated
Security=False;MultipleActiveResultSets=True"
    }
  }
}
```

Updating AppSettings

Another important thing we definitely need to override within the
`appsettings.production.json` file is the `Authority` that will be used to issue (and
check) our JWT Tokens. To do that, add the following lines right before the `data` key we
just added:

```
"Authentication": {
  "OpenIddict": {
    "Authority": "http://www.your-website-url.com/"
  }
},
```

Be sure to check the other settings before closing the file, changing them accordingly to a
production environment. For example, we might want to switch to a less resource-intensive
debugging behavior:

```
"Logging": {
  "IncludeScopes": false,
  "LogLevel": {
    "Default": "Warning",
    "System": "Error",
    "Microsoft": "Error"
  }
},
```

We might also want to increase our caching policy for local files:

```
"StaticFiles": {
  "Headers": {
    "Cache-Control": "max-age=3600",
    "Pragma": "cache",
    "Expires": null
  }
}
```

This will tell the browser client (and/or a proxy) to keep all the static files for one hour.

Updating external providers

If we implemented one or more external providers (see `Chapter 8`, *Third-Party Authentication and External Providers*), we'll probably need to replace the redirect URIs we configured earlier and also add our public facing URL (`www.our-website-url.com`) to the allowed JavaScript origins URL list. For a detailed guide about how to do that, we can refer to `Chapter 8`, *Third-Party Authentication and External Providers.*

Although most providers will allow to set multiple values for the allowed origin URIs, it's strongly advisable to add a whole new app, such as `OpenGameList_Production`, to use for production purposes. If you do that you will also have to override the public and private keys, but you won't compromise your development environment.

Configuring the publishOptions

We now need to update the root `project.json` file to include these files whenever we publish our application. Within that file, look for the `publishOptions` key and change the `include` array values to the following (updated lines are highlighted):

```
"publishOptions": {
  "include": [
    "wwwroot",
    "Views",
    "Areas/**/Views",
    "appsettings*.json",
    "web.config"
  ]
},
```

This small change ensures that, whenever we publish our application, each and every `appsettings` file will be included as well.

Checking the Startup class

The application settings file(s) loading logic can be customized within the `Startup` method of the `Startup` class.

The `Startup.cs` file bundled with the default ASP.NET Core project template that we chose back in `Chapter 1`, *Getting Ready*, already features a cascading logic in place that perfectly suits our needs. All we need to do is to ensure that it's still there. We can easily check that by opening the `Startup.cs` file and having a look at the two `AddJsonFile` method calls within the constructor:

```
public Startup(IHostingEnvironment env)
{
    var builder = new ConfigurationBuilder()
        .SetBasePath(env.ContentRootPath)
        .AddJsonFile(
"appsettings.json",
            optional: true,
            reloadOnChange: true)
        .AddJsonFile(
$"appsettings.{env.EnvironmentName}.json",
            optional: true)
        .AddEnvironmentVariables();
    Configuration = builder.Build();
}
```

We can see how the first highlighted line will load the default `appsettings.json` file, while the second will look for an (optional) environment-specific version containing the relevant value overrides. If everything is still in place, we don't need to change anything, since the existing behavior perfectly fits what we want.

Updating the launchSettings.json

Last but not least, we need to set up our app so that it will run in a production environment whenever we publish it.

To do that, open the `/properties/launchSettings.json` file and change the `ASPNETCORE_ENVIRONMENT` variable within our application's profile from `Development` to `Production` in the following way:

```
"OpenGameListWebApp": {
  "commandName": "Project",
  "launchBrowser": true,
  "launchUrl": "http://localhost:5000/api/values",
  "environmentVariables": {
    "ASPNETCORE_ENVIRONMENT": "Production"
  }
}
```

This will ensure the proper loading of the `appsettings.production.json` file.

Publishing our native web application

Installing and/or configuring a production-ready web server, such as **Internet Information Services (IIS)** or Apache, can be a very complex task depending on a number of things that we can't address now, as they would easily bring us far beyond the scope of this book.

To keep things simple, we'll just assume that we already have access to an up and running, physical or virtualized Windows Server machine featuring a running IIS instance (we'll call it web server from now on) that we can configure to suit our needs. Ideally, we'll be able to do that via a dedicated management interface such as Remote Desktop, IIS Remote Configuration, Plesk, or any other remote administration mechanism made available by our web farm and/or service provider.

Windows 2008 R2 (or newer) and IIS 7.5 (or above) will be required to host a .NET Core web application, as stated by the official Microsoft publishing and deployment documentation available at the following URL: `https://docs.asp.net/en/latest/publishing/iis.html`

Last but not least, we'll also assume that our web server provides FTP-based access to the `/inetpub/` folder that we can use to publish our web projects.

If we're facing a different scenario, it could be advisable to skip this chapter entirely and follow the instructions given by our chosen web hosting provider instead.

Creating a Publish profile

The most convenient way to deploy a web-based project in Visual Studio is creating one or more **Publish** profiles. Each one of them is basically an XML configuration file with a `.pubxml` extension that contains a set of deployment-related information, most of which depends on the server/target we're deploying our application into, Azure, FTP, filesystem and more.

We can easily set up one or more **Publish** profile files using the **Publish** profile wizard. As soon as we have at least one ready, we'll be able to execute it with a single mouse click and have our application published.

To open the **Publish** profile wizard, right-click on the project's root node (`OpenGameListWebApp` in our case) and select the **Publish...** option from the contextual menu. A pop-up window should open showing the following welcome screen:

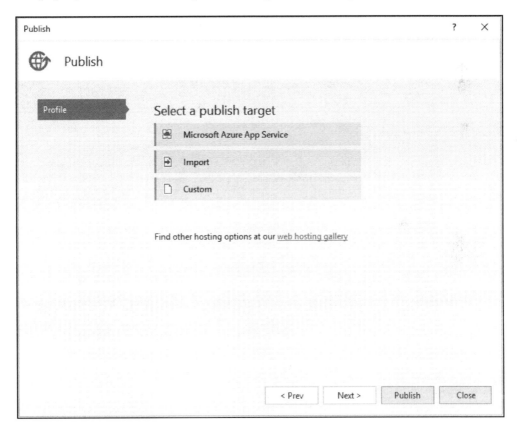

File System Publish profile

Among the various available profiles, the easiest to configure is the one that builds everything into a dedicated folder within our local File System. To create it, follow these steps:

1. Select the **Custom** publish target.
2. Give a suitable name to the profile, such as `Production-FileSystem`.
3. Select the **File System** publish method.
4. When prompted for a **Target Location**, specify the path of the folder that will contain the published application. Visual Studio will suggest a path located within the application's `/bin/Release/` subfolder. However, it's strongly advisable to change it and to choose an external directory instead.
5. Set **Configuration** to **Release**.
6. Set the **Target Framework** accordingly to what we used for our project (**.NET Framework 4.6.1** in our example).

We can then click on the **Publish** button to start the publishing process. Once done, we'll have to manually upload the generated contents to the web server.

FTP Publish profile

As a viable alternative we can also create a **Publish** profile that will automatically upload our web project to our web server using a properly configured FTP connection endpoint: we will then link the remote destination folder to a new website project using IIS.

> As we said earlier, we're doing all that assuming that we have a web server accessible through FTP, since it's one of the most common deployment scenarios. If that's not the case, we might as well skip this paragraph and configure a different **Publish** profile.

We already know how to launch the wizard. Right-click on the project's root node and select **Publish**. Wait for it to start, then do the following:

1. Select the **Custom** publish target.
2. Give a suitable name to the profile, such as `Production-FTP`.
3. Select the **FTP** publish method.
4. When prompted for a **Server**, specify the FTP server URL, such as `ftp.your-ftp-server.com`. In the **Site Path** option, insert the target folder from the FTP server root, such as `/OpenGameList/`.

5. Set the **Passive Mode**, **Username**, and **Password** according to our FTP server settings.
6. Set **Configuration** to **Release**.
7. Set the **Target Framework** accordingly to what we used for our project (**.NET Framework 4.6.1** in our example).

Right after that, the wizard's **Connection** tab should eventually look not too different from the following screenshot:

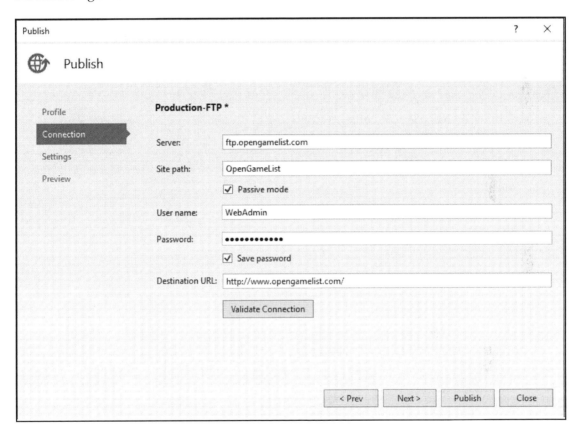

Configuring IIS

We should now connect to our web server and set up our web application within IIS.

 As we said earlier, configuring a web application can be either a very easy or an insanely complex task depending on a number of things, such as caching, load balancing, CPU optimization, database load, and security issues.

Although the most common issues will be briefly handled within this chapter, it's advisable to follow a dedicated guide to properly handle each one of them.

Installing the ASP.NET Core module for IIS

We might think that IIS is the ideal platform to host ASP.NET Core applications, as it always has been since the first release of ASP.NET. As a matter of fact, it's not. ASP.NET Core web applications run via the highly optimized Kestrel server. Whenever we choose to host one of them with IIS, we basically need it to act as a reverse proxy for the underlying Kestrel server.

The good news is that we don't need to configure anything by ourselves, because the ASP.NET Core template we used back in Chapter 1, *Getting Ready*, provided us with a root web.config file containing all the settings, to do just that.

The relevant configuration lines should be contained within the <system.webServer> element, which should resemble the following XML code:

```
<system.webServer>
  <handlers>
    <add name="aspNetCore" path="*" verb="*" modules="AspNetCoreModule"
resourceType="Unspecified"/>
  </handlers>
  <aspNetCore processPath="%LAUNCHER_PATH%" arguments="%LAUNCHER_ARGS%"
stdoutLogEnabled="false" stdoutLogFile=".\logs\stdout"
forwardWindowsAuthToken="false"/>
</system.webServer>
```

We can see that we have a dedicated aspNetCore handler and some related configuration placeholders that will be transformed into actual values upon publication.

As we said earlier, we don't need to change anything, as the handler will do everything by itself, assuming that it is installed on the Web Server. Since ASP.NET Core is a rather new technology, this might as well not be the case, so we could need to download and install it.

At the time of writing, we need to obtain the .NET Core Windows Server Hosting bundle, which conveniently includes all the required packages to host a .NET Core application on a IIS powered server machine: the .NET Core Runtime, the .NET Core Library, the ASP.NET Core module, and also the required reverse proxy between IIS and the Kestrel server.

The bundle can be downloaded from the following URL:
`https://go.microsoft.com/fwlink/?LinkId=817246`

For further references regarding ASP.NET Core IIS publishing settings, it's strongly advised to check out this official guide:
`https://docs.asp.net/en/latest/publishing/iis.html#iis-configuration`
A (mostly) complete list of all the available .NET Core related packages (SDK, IIS module, and more) is also available at the following URL:
`https://www.microsoft.com/net/download`

Adding the website

As soon as we install the .NET Core Windows Server Hosting bundle, we'll be able to configure our IIS instance to host our application.

As we said earlier in this chapter, to host ASP.NET Core web applications, we're going to need IIS 7.5 or above.

From the **IIS Manager** interface, right-click on **Sites** and choose the **Add New Website** option. Name it `OpenGameList`. By looking at the read-only textbox to the immediate right, we can see that a new **Application Pool** will also be created with that same name. Take a mental note of it, as we'll need to configure it soon enough.

Set the physical path of the **Content Directory** to the folder we targeted for FTP publishing.

In our previous example, it should be something like `C:\inetpub\OpenGameList\`, assuming that the FTP root for the web admin user points to `C:\inetpub\`.

Be sure to target the application's root folder, not the \wwwroot\ one.

> Needless to say, we need to grant read/write permissions for that folder to the IUSR and/or IIS_IUSRS accounts, or any other identity our Application Pool is using.

As for the bindings, either choose a specific IP address or leave the **All Unassigned** option and choose a **Host name** that is already configured to redirect to our web server via DNS:

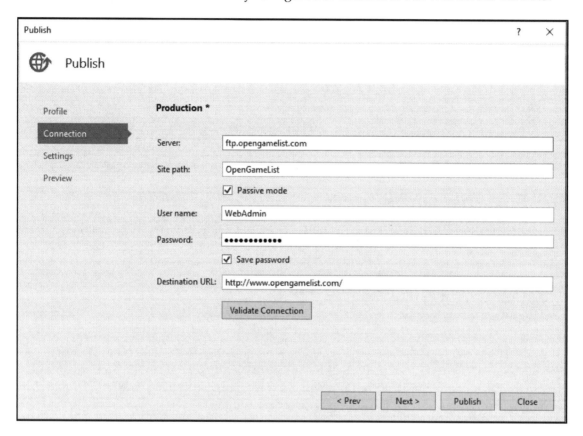

In our example, we already set up http://www.opengamelist.com, so we'll just use that.

Before clicking on the **OK** button, ensure that the **Start Website immediately** option is checked, so the website will be immediately available.

> We're assuming that the server comes with the .NET Framework installed, as it's a default package with all the latest Windows Server versions. In case it doesn't, we can manually install it either via Server Manager, Web Platform Installer, or Windows Update.

Configuring the Application Pool

We can now switch to the **Application Pools** node. Select the **OpenGameList** one, the same that we created a short while ago, and set the **.NET CLR version** to **No Managed Code**:

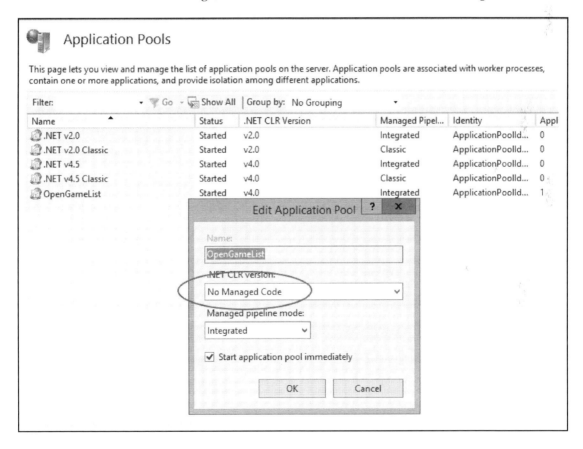

This might seem rather counterintuitive, as it looks like we're ruling out ASP.NET. As a matter of fact, that's the exact opposite: since we're publishing an ASP.NET Core application, we need to ensure that the soon-to-be-outdated .NET 4 CLR won't get in the way. Since the former is still (at the time of writing) in a pre-release state, it isn't available yet within the GUI, leaving us with the only option to remove any reference here. We already configured the .NET Core module for IIS to do the required job anyway.

 This is one of the many things that will surely change in the future. There is a good chance that, by the time you're reading this book, the new CLR will be integrated within the **Application Pool** GUI settings.

Firing up the engine

It's time to publish our native web application. Before doing that, ensure that the **Task Runner** `default` task is running, as we want to upload the latest version of our client files.

Right-click on the project's root node, then left-click on **Publish**. Select the **Production-FTP** profile and hit the **Publish** button to start the build and upload process.

The whole publishing process flow can be checked in real time within the Visual Studio **Output** window. As soon as the FTP connection will be attempted, we'll be asked for username and password, unless we gave our consent to store our login credentials within the `Production-FTP.pubxml` file.

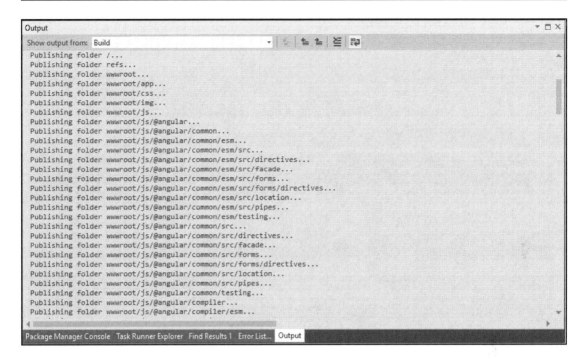

The publishing task will require a lot more time than it used to be for ASP.NET 4 applications, because the whole set of ASP.NET Core libraries will be published in the destination folder, together with all the required Angular 2 modules and dependencies.

 There's nothing to worry about, as this is another thing that will surely change once the ASP.NET Core framework reaches its final stage.

Once done, our default web browser will be automatically launched against the URL we specified within the **Publish** profile settings.

If everything has been set up properly, our native web application will show itself in all its splendor:

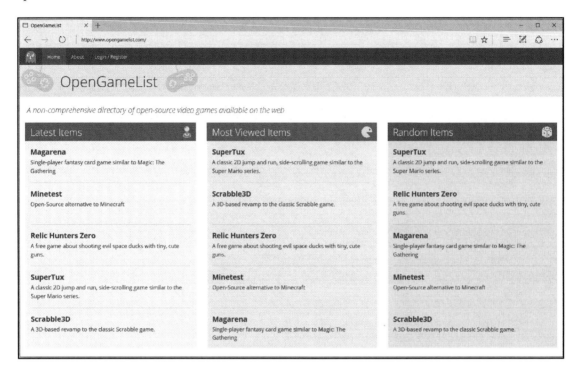

Troubleshooting

...Or maybe not. The deployment task isn't always easy, as there could be a number of issues (mostly depending on the server machine state) that can prevent it from going well. This statement is particularly true for ASP.NET Core application IIS-based deployments, as the reverse proxy mechanism undeniably adds an additional level of complexity.

These are the three best things we can do to diagnose the most common problems:

1. Read the browser's output messages.
2. Examine the Event Viewer's application log.
3. Enable the ASP.NET Core module `stdout` logging feature.

The first one is rather obvious: who doesn't look at the browser output? However, for ASP.NET Core applications, it's far less effective than it used to be since most errors are still unhandled and won't appear there.

The Event Viewer is often underestimated, yet it's very important for debugging ASP.NET Core application for the same reason as before: we will find most of the relevant stuff there.

The ASP.NET Core Module Log is a new feature brought by the new CLR. However, when it comes to troubleshooting issues, it happens to be the real deal. Activating it is just as easy as opening the root `web.config` file and change the `stdoutLogEnabled` attribute from `false` to `true`.

We also need to manually create a `/logs/` folder inside the root application folder on the web server, otherwise the logs won't be generated.

 The log folder, location, and filename prefix can be configured by changing the `stdoutLogFile` attribute value. Remember to manually create the chosen folder whenever you change it and also to grant read/write permissions to the identity used by the **Application Pool**.

The Kestrel test

A quick and effective way to check if the application is working properly is to entirely skip IIS and run it directly on Kestrel. Doing this is just as easy as opening the application folder on the Web Server, locating the `OpenGameList.exe` file, and executing it with (or without) administrative rights.

Doing this will open a command prompt where we'll be able to see the whole application bootstrap process. Once it completes, we should be able to test the application by opening a web browser and pointing it to `http://localhost:5000/`, 5000 being the default TCP listening port for Kestrel as defined in the `/settings/launchSettings.json` file:

If the application completes its boot phase and starts running, the issue is most likely related to the IIS configuration and/or the ASP.NET Core module; otherwise, there's a good chance that our problem lies within the application code itself.

If that's the case, checking the Event Viewer and the aforementioned `stdout` logs will be our best weapons to identify and overcome the issue.

Suggested topics

LAN, SQL Server 2016, SQL Server Management Studio, Windows Server, IIS, Apache, FTP server, **Publish** profile, ASP.NET Core module for IIS, ASP.NET 5, .NET CLR v4, Kestrel, `stdout` log.

Summary

Eventually, our journey through ASP.NET Core MVC/Web API and Angular 2 has come to an end. Our last effort was getting our native web application ready for being published into a production environment, where it can be checked by the product owner as the potentially shippable product it now definitely is.

The first thing we did was changing the underlying database from `localDb` to a real SQL Server instance. For the sake of simplicity, we chose to install SQL Server 2016 Express, which is freely available for download from the Microsoft Download Center. We briefly installed it, together with the SQL Server Management Studio tools, then we used the latter to properly configure the former: creating the database, adding the login credentials, and doing what it takes to make our application able to connect using a standard connection string. We also took advantage of the ASP.NET Core default pattern to handle multiple environments by defining an application settings file for production, which we used to override the `localDb` connection string with the SQL Server one.

The next step was creating a **Publish** profile for our Visual Studio project. We evaluated two alternatives, File System and FTP, each one of them being viable or not depending on our own deployment scenario.

Eventually, we switched to the **Web Server**, where we found out that configuring IIS was not as easy as it used to be for ASP.NET 4 and below because the new CLR isn't fully integrated within the GUI yet. We had to install the ASP.NET Core module for IIS which does all the required jobs, making IIS act like a reverse proxy for the underlying Kestrel server. Right after that, we were able to create our **website** entry together with its related **Application Pool**.

Once we did all that, we were able to actually publish our native web application and watch the result on the web browser. In the event that something didn't go as expected, we took some time to analyze the most common troubleshooting issues and give some useful advice to overcome them.

Index